A History of Colombian Economic Thought

Ever since the quest for independence between 1810 and 1819, economic thought in Colombia has been shaped by policy debates and characterized by a pragmatic and eclectic approach. Economic thought in Colombia can only be revealed through the exploration of economists' practices and the role of economic arguments within broader public debate. This history of Colombian economic thought provides a detailed account of major issues that have marked the constant feedback between economic ideas and economic practice in Colombia during the 19th and 20th centuries. This volume is thus a history of the interaction between ideas and policy. Those involved in these debates – politicians, public officials, journalists, and, latterly, professional economists – established direct contact with what can be identified as the centers of production of economic theory (both in Europe and the US) and entered regional and local networks in economics, but were not just importers of ideas or theories. The way in which they read, discussed, transformed and applied economic theories in Colombia makes for a rich environment for the production and implementation of economic policies that drew, diverged and transformed the way economics was understood and used as a source of knowledge for practical concerns. This is why the history of Colombian economic thought does not fit into traditional typologies of economic schools and why it must be understood as part of a political debate and within a political, social and cultural context that demanded specific solutions to urgent social demands. Through the study of what was taught, when and how, at the beginnings of the republican era, and why and how professional economists came to lead public debate and economic policy making in the 20th century, this book explores the foundations of this permanent interaction between theory and practice. This book will be of significant interest to readers of history of economic thought, economic history and the history of Colombian and Latin American economic, political and social life more broadly.

Andrés Álvarez, Universidad de los Andes, Colombia

Jimena Hurtado, Universidad de los Andes, Colombia

The Routledge History of Economic Thought

For more information about this series, please visit: www.routledge.com/The-Routledge-History-of-Economic-Thought/book-series/SE0124

A History of Colombian Economic Thought

The Economic Ideas that Built Modern Colombia

Edited by Andrés Álvarez and Jimena Hurtado

Routledge
Taylor & Francis Group

LONDON AND NEW YORK

First published 2024
by Routledge
4 Park Square, Milton Park, Abingdon, Oxon OX14 4RN

and by Routledge
605 Third Avenue, New York, NY 10158

Routledge is an imprint of the Taylor & Francis Group, an informa business

British Library Cataloguing-in-Publication Data
A catalogue record for this book is available from the British Library

ISBN: 978-1-032-26645-9 (hbk)
ISBN: 978-1-032-26650-3 (pbk)
ISBN: 978-1-003-28924-1 (ebk)

DOI: 10.4324/9781003289241

Typeset in Times New Roman
by SPi Technologies India Pvt Ltd (Straive)

Contents

Figures

Tables

Preface

Colombia has had, for better or worse, an exceptional, political and economic history during its republican existence. David Bushnell (1994) described it as "a nation despite itself" in the title of his comprehensive book about the making of modern Colombia. In the 19th century, exceptionality meant a segmented country, crossed by three mountain ranges, precarious inland routes, a capital city at 2,600 meters above sea level, and the most important seaport on the Caribbean 1,000 km away. Like the rest of Latin America, Colombia inherited debts from independence, a strong Catholic tradition, and a formally segregated population. During the 20th century, exceptionality took the form of macroeconomic stability, no foreign debt crisis nor stagflation, long-standing democratic institutions, except for the 1953–57 military government, and 60 years of civil conflict and increasing inequality. The part that economics and economists have played in this exceptionality is the subject of this book. How economics, as scholarly knowledge, found its place in public debate and was instrumental in the building of the nation is the question that leads this analysis.

We must go beyond the question of how economic theory arrived in Colombia. In this volume, we show that the study of the history of economics in countries traditionally considered peripheral must go beyond the question of how economic ideas arrive and surpass the usual categories of schools of economic thought. The relevant question is how economics is practiced rather than how economic knowledge is produced.

Economics has played a leading role in the way political elites, from the end of the Spanish colonial system until today, built their narratives about the characteristics and role of a modern state and the social project it should pursue to promote a peaceful and prosperous society open to the world. This volume presents a detailed analysis of different episodes where public debate and the design of economic and political institutions interacted with the economic education and practice of those who would do economics in decision-making and policy design. Throughout the 19th and 20th century, state credibility is directly linked to economic knowledge, making economics a key element in the construction of the nation.

Throughout the different chapters, the authors explore how economic knowledge has been used since independence to design institutions and policies to advance the modernization project that ruling elites have proposed since 1819. The science of freedom, as political economy was known in the first half of the 19th century, became the architectonic science. A modern republic was associated with free and enlightened citizens, who would pursue their self-interest through the market, producing a peaceful and prosperous society. Overcoming the colonial past and taking full advantage of the market required new political and economic institutions to be built. The challenge of development, in the 20th century, was also associated with the need to modernize a backward economy that needed an institutional framework for people to participate productively in the market economy. In the last century, the science of freedom became the technical analysis needed to produce appropriate development policies that would bring growth and political stability. The change in the role economics and economists play in policy making explain the structure of the book. The book is divided into two parts, the first devoted to the 19th and the second to the 20th century, acknowledging not only the chronological divide but especially the change in the goal of economic knowledge from building a new republic to development policy.

Writing a history of Colombian economic thought is a challenge in several dimensions. Even though Colombia is a relatively young country, its history is rich and complex. The period covered in this book includes the independence from the Spanish crown, the beginnings of the Republic and the attempts at building a new national identity with what at the time were considered, modern institutions, the multiple civil wars showing the fragility of those same institutions, and the country's several economic and political attempts at finding a path towards what in the 20th century would be called development. Political and economic crises marked the 19th century, which continued during the next century except for the noticeable fact that the Colombian economy became one of the most macroeconomically stable economies in the region during the second half of the 20th century. "The economy is doing well, and the country is doing poorly" became a common dictum to describe the Colombian situation.

During the first decades of the 19th century, the country's economy relied mostly on gold exports, combined with a low-technology agricultural sector, and an almost non-existent national market that meant low growth rates. Debt and low growth hindered the construction of a state capable of providing public goods, protecting civil and individual rights, or enforcing public policies. The second half of the 19th century brought the modernization of gold and silver mining and the production of tobacco, indigo, cinchona bark, and coffee.

Profound changes, periods of protectionism and market liberalization, and political violence marked the greater part of the 20th century. Macroeconomic stability allowed for modest but stable growth rates, improvement of social indicators, and a relatively more diversified economy with commodities still leading exports. Exports began to soar in the first 30 years of the 20th century, with increasing coffee production that enabled a boost in public infrastructure expenditure and led to higher national growth rates. By 1926 coffee exports accounted for almost 80% of total exports and coffee remained the main export product until the last decade of the 20th century. International coffee prices determined the Colombian economic cycle and made the coffee-growing industry the center of economic and political power. Industrialization and urbanization pushed the demographic transition and allowed for a constant but deeply unequal improvement of living conditions. The modernization dream has been accompanied by illegal and informal economies that place a large part of the population in vulnerability rather than in the middle class.

In this context, policy and policymaking are the places that have dominated the production of economic thought. Here lies another challenge authors face in this book. Until now, scholars have assessed the history of Colombian economic ideas against the background of traditional, "universal" schools of thought. Historians, economists, and historians of economics have been interested in retracing what people read, how they interpreted and transformed the ideas they received, and how they used them to formulate policy. This has led to Colombian economic thinkers being classified as physiocrats, mercantilists, followers of some classical political economists, utilitarians, or, more recently, neoliberals. Some historians have said there was no real economic thought in Colombia during the 19th century because David Ricardo was not widely read, or that it only seriously began in the mid-20th century when Karl Marx became a very influential thinker. However, with the possible major exception of Ezequiel Rojas in the 19th century, it is likely that none of the people who were reading, writing, and doing economics thought of themselves as part of a particular school of thought or, until the second half of the 20th century, considered themselves economists.

But even Ezequiel Rojas (1804–1873), one of the protagonists of the first chapter, was looking for ideas, tools, and instruments to enlighten people and make this a modern country. Rojas, a close collaborator of Francisco de Paula Santander (independence hero, Vice President, and President of the Republic) was a well-known public figure, senator, state minister, economics professor, diplomat, and founder of the Liberal Party, who through his courses, publications and legislative actions came to be known as the representative of utilitarianism in the country. Rojas was convinced that utilitarianism and its direct product, political economy, were the inspiration needed to build the foundations of a modern republic. A combination of Christian values and utilitarianism would necessarily produce an enlightened citizenship capable of understanding how the private initiative, self-interest, comprehension of social and economic interdependence, and the principles of modern science promoted the common good. Rojas produced a new version of utilitarianism, combining it with Christian values, that merged the two as the foundations of a prosperous political organization.

Rojas faced the ferocious opposition of Miguel Antonio Caro (1843–1909), almost 40 years younger than him, who came to be one of the main figures of the Conservative Party, Vice President and Acting President of Colombia, the artificer of the *Regeneración* and the Political Constitution of 1886 and man of letters. Caro, who defined himself as a defender of the Catholic Church rather than a conservative, participated in most of the debates around the use of utilitarian texts (i.e., Jeremy Bentham, Antoine-Louis-Claude Destutt de Tracy, and Jean-Baptiste Say) in higher education and wrote innumerable articles and speeches denouncing utilitarianism as a materialistic philosophy that promoted *laissez-faire* and corrupted good Colombian Catholics. Utilitarianism was contrary to the national Catholic tradition that should be the building block of the Republic. Reconstructing the history of the political economy course that was compulsory during most of the Republican 19th century in higher education, Andrés Álvarez, Jimena Hurtado, and Sofía Meléndez show, in Chapter 1, how economic education became a battlefield to control and produce the ideas that would shape the nation.

Even if both Rojas and Caro shared the aspiration of building a modern republic, their opposition shows the clash of ideas that would lead to very different institutional arrangements in the 19th century. Edna Carolina Sastoque, in Chapter 2, shows that the debate between liberals and conservatives was never really about the implementation of a free market economy, but rather about the timing of the project. The monetary issues and policies, James Torres discusses in Chapter 4, inherited from the last part of the colonial period, already show the complexity and richness of economic thought related to the debate about the right policies for modernization and their timing.

After 1819, free trade was not an issue. The right time to implement it was. The liberal governments and especially the Radicals who came to power in 1863, many of them Rojas's disciples, promoted free markets with policies that abolished trade barriers. The pushback came in 1885, with the conservatives taking over power after yet another civil war. A new constitution was proclaimed and the *Regeneración*, led by three-time President Rafael Núñez, a former member of the Liberal Party, and Caro, marked the beginning of half a century of conservative hegemony. Stability and progress required order and responsible freedom. A centralized nation with administrative and political unity under the direction of the state would ensure the flourishing of a Catholic nation. Censorship and political persecution against the liberals ensued. Protectionist policies were put in place to prepare the national industry for foreign competition. Free markets would have to wait.

Other policy measures, however, could not wait. The tension between the Catholic tradition and the search for modern ideas is traced in the next three chapters of the book. Conservatives trying to preserve and adapt the Catholic tradition opposed liberals trying to replace the tradition and its institutions with more liberal and republican ones. In Chapter 4, Edna Carolina Sastoque, Claudia Pico, and Luis Sandoval go beyond economic policy to show how economic ideas also permeated the debate and design of criminal law. The participants in the economic debate were also those who would model the justice administration system. The conservatives Caro and Núñez confronted the liberals Florentino González and José María Samper on all aspects of policy design. In the case of justice administration, their starting point was the ideas of Cesare Beccaria and Jeremy Bentham, showing how the debate on utilitarianism transcended the political economy course. But, as the chapter shows, the passage from ideas to practice made the philosophical influence almost unrecognizable.

In the next two chapters, Edwin López-Rivera (5) and Carlos Brando (6) focus on the fiscal capacity of the state and the design of financial institutions. López-Rivera explores the consequences for the fiscal autonomy of the state of the liberal experiment truncated by the centralized design of the conservative Catholicism of the *Regeneración*. According to this Catholic position, the modernizing path required specific development banking institutions capable of promoting peasant landownership and agriculture rather than industrialization and urbanization.

The first part of the book shows that a central question about institutional design, dating from the Bourbon reforms of the 1780s, nourishes the economic debates of the first half of the 19th century. James Torres (Chapter 2) explores the monetary debates of the end of the colonial period. He examines the technical and theoretical aspects of the colonial economic administration. His exploration of these dimensions reveals the depth of knowledge of Criollo intellectuals and businessmen. With independence and the failure of organizing larger federal nations like the United States, policy and institutional design faced the challenge of recovering an economy that had virtually disappeared from the international context and had to find its place in the world. The dream of the construction of an enlightened and free society clashed with the reality of a country incapable of building a state that could regulate and provide public goods. The fragility of the state explains the emergence of alternative welfare projects inspired by Catholic charity, as Brando shows in Chapter 6. Catholic ideas found their place in institution and policy design with the *Regeneración* and remained decisive up to the 1940s with the Caja Agraria, a financial institution created in 1931, as its most salient example.

The second part of the book shows how, as in the 19th century, the practice of economics was associated with institution and policy design. The state had a constant demand for economic knowledge. By the second half of the 20th century, this demand became a requirement for expert and technical economic analysis. In Chapter 8, Andrés Álvarez, Juanita Villaveces, Sofía Meléndez, and Ricardo Peña explore one specific instance in which this technical analysis led to the formulation of informality as a specific and structural feature of the Colombian economy. International expert knowledge pushed the demand for national professional economists.

However, with Guiot-Isaac's analysis in Chapter 7, it is possible to see that higher education institutions had no formal economic undergraduate or graduate programs until the 1940s when they began training entrepreneurs rather than professional economists. Before the 1960s, with the first formal programs, hands-on training in the state provided the people needed to design and implement economic policy. Economic academia remained incipient and research centers suffered from what came to be known as the revolving door between the state and academia. This explains the coexistence of a strong technocratic state with a weak economic academia. Economists were practitioners, and some of them spent some time in academia where they reflected upon their technocratic practice, especially in the formulation and design of macroeconomic policy.

The production of expert knowledge in economics was directly associated with expert practice in the state. Economic experts built international networks that they also used to strengthen academic economics. In a similar way to what had happened before the *Regeneración* in the 19th century, economists discussed and kept close contact with international scholars and economic ideas they considered useful for the Colombian context, noticeably some that were outside the mainstream. With the *Regeneración* and until the 1950s, the economic conversation turned in upon itself, and national and regional historicism projects emerged.

Economic history became the field for an alternative project to that of the elites. In the 20th century, economic history provided a narrative about Colombia's history and the reasons for its economic backwardness and failed attempts to become a modern nation. Contemporary academic economics in Colombia began with the search for an alternative to the official economic model. As Salomón Kalmanovitz shows in Chapter 11, it emerged in the 1940s and 1960s as a heterodox attempt built under Marxist influences to produce a historicist history of Colombia's failed economic development. Opposed to the international trends of economics under Paul Samuelson's influence, economics in Colombia at the time built a cultural narrative to disentangle the sources of the profound social crisis that led to *La Violencia*. Adolfo Meisel in Chapter 10 explores the works of Luis Eduardo Nieto Arteta (1913–1956) and Luis Ospina Vásquez (1905–1977) as examples of how economic history provided the evidence to show that development would not be possible in a country of regions under the centralized model that had existed since the *Regeneración*.

With no room in academia, neither in the social sciences nor in economics, the project for an alternative or heterodox economic theory inspired by structuralism and CEPAL failed. Juan Carlos Villamizar explores this episode of Colombian economic thought in Chapter 9. CEPAL participated in the expert missions that came to the country and was instrumental in the formulation of the ten-year development plan that allowed Colombia to seek financial resources from the partners of the US Alliance for Progress. But the plan was never put into practice. Carlos Lleras Restrepo, president between 1966 and 1970, answering to the demand for professional economists, created the first economic technocracy calling on young engineers and economists pursuing their graduate studies abroad to work for the central government. They became planning experts in their way with no specific ideological allegiance besides modernization and the shared belief that economics was a technical practice.

Economics could not find its place within the social sciences. Sociology and anthropology occupied the academic space where they developed quantitative and field methods to assess the same development issues that economics explored. Scholarly attempts in economics clashed with the modernizing projects of education institutions. The most influential universities, Nacional and Los Andes, invested their resources in training entrepreneurs, leaving no space for this historicist and alternative economics nor for a more technical formation. There was nothing in between the intellectuals who followed the historical approaches and the formation of entrepreneurs. There was no formal place to train economic policymakers. The modernizing attempts of the state suffered from a lack of trained economists. Engineers became economists through on-the-job training. They were the first technocrats. The state moved faster than academia in the technical formation of economists. The influence of economic experts, who came with international economic missions, like Lauchlin Currie and Albert O. Hirschman, materializes, as Andrés Mauricio Guiot-Isaac shows in Chapter 7, with the creation of graduate economic programs under the influence of the United States government and several philanthropic foundations, notably the Rockefeller and Ford Foundations.

The professionalization of economics and its institutionalization in academia came in the 1960s after reports from multilateral expert missions on the Colombian economy. While Chapter 7 shows how the demand for technical analysis and expert knowledge led, as in many other parts of the world, to the creation of formal academic programs to train professional economists, those same economists are traced by Ricardo Salas in Chapter 12 on the Governing Board of the Banco de la República. In the final chapter (13), Marta Juanita Villaveces-Niño, Ricardo José Salas-Díaz, and Pilar Torres-Alvarado trace the evolution of how women economists came to be appointed to positions of power and participated in the definition and implementation of public policies. This last chapter leads us to the current state of the professionalization of economics, leaving us with questions about its evolution in terms of its diversity and inclusion.

The history of economic thought in Colombia is a history of practical ideas. Ideas are put to the test in institutional and policy design in the pursuit of a modernizing national project.

Acknowledgements

This book would not have been possible without the support, patience, and collaboration of a host of people. The editors would like to start by thanking the authors who found the time to write, revise, discuss, and comment on their manuscripts. Anonymous referees helped us improve the overall project, participants at several academic conferences, and especially those at the 2022 meeting of the Asociación Latinoamericana de Historia del Pensamiento Económico (ALAHPE), and at a 2022 lunch workshop session at the Center for the History of Economic Thought (HOPE Center), allowed us to present and improve our ideas. Special thanks to Mary Morgan for her careful reading of the Introduction to the volume. Ari Vélez-Olivera and company provided help, support, and careful copy-editing and proofreading. The Centro de Estudios sobre Desarrollo Económico (CEDE) at the Economics Department, Universidad de los Andes, provided funding to support the editorial process, and the HOPE Center offered Jimena Hurtado the perfect environment to revise and edit the first final versions of the chapters that make up this volume. Finally, we would like to thank Routledge for approaching us to pursue this editorial project.

Contributors

Andrés Álvarez is Associate Professor of Economics at the Economics Department, Universidad de los Andes.

Carlos Andrés Brando has been visiting lecturer at Pompeu Fabra University, Dean of the Economics Faculty at Universidad Tadeo Lozano, and adjunct lecturer in economic history at the Colegio de Estudios Superiores en Administración.

Andrés M. Guiot-Isaac is an LSE Fellow in the Department of Economic History at the London School of Economics.

Jimena Hurtado is Professor of Economics at the Economics Department, Universidad de los Andes.

Salomón Kalmanovitz is Emeritus Professor of the Universidad Nacional, and former member of the Board of Directors of the Banco de la República.

Edwin López-Rivera is an associate professor at the School of Economics and Management, Universidad Jorge Tadeo Lozano, and editor of *Las cuentas del federalismo colombiano* with Salomón Kalmanovitz (2019).

Adolfo Meisel is the President of Universidad del Norte and a former member of the Board of Directors of the Banco de la República.

Sofía Meléndez is a historian and economist from Universidad de los Andes. She works at the National Planning Department (DNP) in Colombia.

Claudia Milena Pico is a professor of economics and at Universidad de la Costa (CUC).

Ricardo Peña is a consultant in health economics. At the time of writing the chapter for this book, Ricardo was an MA student and research assistant at the Economics Department, Universidad Nacional.

Ricardo José Salas-Díaz studied economics at the Universidad de los Andes and Universidad Nacional de Colombia. Ricardo is a Ph.D. student at the University of Massachusetts - Amherst.

Luis Eduardo Sandoval is a professor and researcher at the Faculty of Economics of the Universidad Militar Nueva Granada.

Edna Carolina Sastoque is a professor and researcher at the Faculty of Economics of the Externado de Colombia University.

James V. Torres is an assistant professor at Universidad de los Andes.

Pilar Torres-Alvarado is the coordinator of the data analysis group at the Directorate of Knowledge Management, Chamber of Commerce of Bogotá.

Juan Carlos Villamizar is a professor of history at Universidad Nacional de Colombia.

Marta Juanita Villaveces-Niño is an associate professor and Dean of the Faculty of Economic Science, Universidad Nacional de Colombia.

Part I
The Long First Century of a Nascent Republic

1 Teaching Political Economy in the Awakening of a Modern Republic

Colombia 1825–1885

Andrés Álvarez, Jimena Hurtado and Sofía Meléndez

1.1 Introduction[1]

Education was a significant concern in the new republics in Latin America after the independence revolutions that took place throughout the 19th century. The new governments, especially liberal governments, undertook several educational reforms, programs, and projects at the time (Ahern, 1991 [1947]; Cataño, 1995; Gaitán Bohórquez, 2010). Courses, textbooks, and syllabi were essential to transmit new cultural and moral principles, socialize future citizens, legitimize the state, and create popular support for government measures and programs (Cardona Zuluaga, 2007, p. 90). Higher education was part of this national purpose of preparing citizens to undertake the tasks required in a modern republic. Here, we aim to assess how the new Colombian Republic dealt with a specific aspect of higher education: the textbooks and professors in a compulsory political economy course for jurisprudence students.

Public education, including the textbooks used in formal, private, and public education, was highly regulated from the beginning of the republic. After creating several public commissions to evaluate and plan education, in 1826, under Francisco de Paula Santander's administration, a law was issued announcing the foundation of public universities, establishing a General Directorate of Education and various committees to determine the syllabus for all levels of education. This law included the textbooks assigned for each course. There were books by David Hume, Jean-Baptiste Say, Benjamin Constant, Antoine-Louis-Claude Destutt de Tracy, Étienne Bonnot de Condillac, and Jeremy Bentham, amongst others.[2] For the students in jurisprudence, a course in political economy was mandatory (Ministerio de Gobierno, 1924, Art. 32 Par.3). In this course, they read Say. Other educational plans and decrees followed, including specific syllabi and texts. The only exceptions to this flow of educational laws and regulations were between 1845 and 1847, and 1850. Tomás Cipriano de Mosquera's administration decreed absolute academic freedom, and José Hilario López's administration suppressed universities and academic titles (Burbano-López, 2008, pp. 179–180; Cataño, 1995). During those periods, several schools offered a political economy course, including

DOI: 10.4324/9781003289241-2

those institutions where future politicians and public officers pursued their studies (Cataño, 1995). Textbooks in the new republic were instrumental in introducing a new language to build a new public debate where it would be possible to reconcile the conflicting influences of the Catholic and scholastic tradition, perceived as opposed to the modern world, and the desire for "liberty and order" associated with the promises of the Enlightenment.

Tracing textbooks and their use, we follow a growing literature on institutionalizing and disseminating political economy through books and manuals primarily concentrated on Europe, the United States, and Japan. We aim to explore "how textbooks and manuals contributed to the creation of market economy agents" (Augello & Guidi, 2012, p. 3). We concentrate on official texts that determine the contents taught in secondary and higher education. We consider these texts as expressions of an explicit public policy aimed at educating modern citizens capable of participating fully in the world market economy and building a national market economy. Establishing compulsory classes in political economy in schools and universities shows that "[e]conomics was therefore socially constructed and at the same time it constructed the objective reality that it interpreted" (Augello & Guidi, 2012, p. 6).

This chapter presents political economy as a fundamental part of civic education. We focus on how public policy is planned and economic education used for political purposes. We use syllabi, textbooks, public announcements of graduation exams, and library catalogs to trace the emphasis, theoretical influences, and manuals used to teach political economy[3] to fill the gap in the analysis of economic education in Colombia two centuries ago. We complement Correa Restrepo's (2001) study and edition of Santiago Pérez's lectures at the University of El Rosario and the Universidad Nacional from his students' notes, dating from the 1880s, Hurtado's (2016) analysis of Ezequiel Rojas'[4] syllabi of his courses in political economy, Pico's (2016) description of the teaching of political economy during the 19th century, and Meléndez's (2019) study of the contents of the courses in political economy during the transition from the period of radical liberalism to the so-called *Regeneración* (1885–1905).[5] To our knowledge, this is the first attempt at systematizing this evidence to trace the changes in teaching political economy at the time, its impact on the formation of the political elites, and the implementation of economic policies and institutions.

In what follows, we provide evidence of how the contents of the courses evolved from mainly theoretical and moral philosophy discussions, part of the education of lawyers and lawmakers, towards more practical considerations concerning economic policies. We also show how the contents and structure of the courses became more original and eclectic, evolving from a standard design based on Say's *Treatise*[6] to original textbooks that Colombian authors wrote, adapting and drawing inspiration from the French liberal school. By the end of the century, Leroy-Beaulieu's *Cours d'Économie Politique* became a standard reference and the course's primary influence during the first decades of the 20th century.

This study allows an understanding of how political economy, particularly liberal economic ideas, were initially the common grounds where both conservatives and liberals converged with the primary purpose of modernizing the economic and political institutions of the postcolonial era. Free trade was initially a common purpose for the governing elite. However, the political factions became increasingly divided, and a more apparent contradiction of views in political economy appeared. During the 1850s and the 1860s, a young faction of the Liberal Party emerged and imposed their radical liberal views and reforms, including the disentailment of the Catholic Church lands and the adoption of a free banking monetary system. Radical liberals were often professors of political economy, and they created new universities to reinforce the influence of liberal economic ideas on the elite. In the 1880s, a nationalist faction of the Conservative Party took power. It overthrew the liberal reforms and criticized political economy as the source of anticlerical and immoral ideas against a Catholic social tradition. The course continued to be taught, although significant changes occurred regarding the content and the professors in charge.

The following three sections of this paper contain an analysis of Colombian elites' modernizing and civilizing role in teaching political economy. Section 1.3 describes the archival material and follows the nationwide spread and transformations of the courses and textbooks throughout the 19th century. We finally propose some concluding remarks.

1.2 Political Economy as Civic Education in Universities[7]

The plan to reform higher education in Colombia dates from before independence. Antonio Moreno y Escandón (1736–1792) produced a provisional plan that contained, among other things, the creation of a public university and a scholastic teaching method for practical, empirical, and applied knowledge with courses in science and mathematics (Gaitán, 2010, pp. 106–107).[8] The plan was never implemented, leaving national education in the hands of the Catholic Church.

With independence and under the influence of the Enlightenment, the new governments considered education the direct path to modernization. Building a modern republic required educated citizens, capable of reading and writing and knowledgeable in science and technology. Students should also have notions of political economy to understand interdependence and markets as the foundations of free and prosperous societies. Preparing citizens to participate in the market economy was also a way to create and consolidate a nationwide market (Augello & Guidi, 2012, p. 9). The practical component of political economy was privileged in the syllabi of courses, aiming to prepare future public officials to design and implement public policies and prepare young generations for "honorable lives in state service" (Uribe-Urán, 2000, p. 114). Liberal governments also considered political economy a form of civic and moral education that would balance the influence of what they considered a backward-looking premodern Catholic church. Rather than displace religious education, they were trying to promote an understanding of religious beliefs compatible with the modern world, associated with the true – deinstitutionalized – religion directly derived from the lessons of Jesus.

In 1820, Francisco de Paula Santander (1792–1840), vice-president of the Republic, promoted the construction of a new public education system (Ahern, 1991, p. 13). In 1826, following the mandates of the decree of March 18, the executive power issued a general education plan secularizing the Catholic Universidad del Rosario and creating several public universities: Universidad Central de Bogotá, Universidad de Boyacá, Universidad de Popayán, and Universidad del Magdalena e Istmo (Elías-Caro & Renán-Rodríguez, 2016). The plan included specific authors for each course. In English and French classes, students had to read David Hume, Jean-Baptiste Say, and Benjamin Constant; in philosophy and natural sciences classes, the authors were Antoine-Louis-Claude Destutt de Tracy and Étienne Bonnot de Condillac; for universal, civil, and criminal law courses, Jeremy Bentham was the reference; for lessons in political public and constitutional law and administrative science Benjamin Constant, Charles-Louis de Secondat Baron de la Brède et de Montesquieu, Gabriel Bonnot de Mably, Destutt de Tracy, and Albert Fritot; and Jean-Baptiste Say's *Treatise on Political Economy* was the reference for classes in political economy, part of the jurisprudence program (Hurtado, 2016, pp. 40–42). These classes dated from 1824, when political economy was part of the training of lawyers at the Colegio Mayor de San Bartolomé, one of the most, if not the most, influential institutions in higher education in the country at the time.

In 1842, the conservative government of Mariano Ospina Rodríguez (1805–1885) issued another official education plan without any mandatory textbooks or authors and eliminated Bentham's and Tracy's books. It aimed to reintroduce religious education and religious supervision over education in the country, keep courses in sciences, and introduce industrial and technical education (Soto, 2005, p. 114). The most significant changes touched legal education but kept political economy, as "authorities regarded [political economy] as uncontroversial and practical in nature" (Uribe-Urán, 2000, p. 112). It also tried to overcome the dangerous trend of *empleomanía* or the young students' aim of becoming public officials, which the government thought was a possible threat to political stability because public bureaucracy could not employ all young graduates (Uribe-Urán, 2000, p. 112).

Afterwards, depending on whether liberals or conservatives were in office, different public education plans were decreed, excluding or including religious education. In 1850, the government abolished universities, and people did not need a diploma to practice any profession except pharmacology. However, political economy teaching continued between 1850 and 1863, when a new constitution was adopted. The constitution presented education as part of civil rights under the state's responsibility, an instrument to educate citizens, and part of a national strategy to improve productivity. In 1867, the Universidad Nacional was created, offering traditional programs, engineering, natural sciences, and technical diplomas. The Universidad de Antioquia, also public, was founded in 1870 and offered a political economy course.

1.2.1 Public Debates on Bentham and Destutt de Tracy's Books

Besides the debates surrounding these laws, serious discussion appeared explicitly around the use of specific texts. In 1827, for example, the government established an official committee to study the consequences of having Bentham's *Introduction to the Principles of Morals and Legislation* in law studies. The committee concluded there was no need to eliminate the study of the book. Nevertheless, criticism continued spreading until, in 1828, President Bolívar banned its use for its materialistic and hedonistic bent, which made it a source of immorality. The decision showed that the Catholic Church had recovered its political influence (Ahern, 1991, p. 28). After the attempt on Bolívar's life in September 1828, the government considered that the pernicious influence of Bentham's texts had prompted the young law students to participate in the plot. The government suspended courses using his texts because the authorities claimed they contained, alongside brilliant doctrines, others contrary to "religion, morality, and the people's tranquility." Other texts that taught the doctrine of the Roman Catholic religion should replace them (Uribe-Urán 2000, p. 109).

In 1832 the ban was abolished. The government re-established the 1826 education plan and ratified it in 1835. With Bentham included, the debate was open again. In one of the most well-documented episodes in the history of education in Colombia (cf. López Domínguez, 1993), known as the Benthamite Controversy, there was an intense debate in the Senate, official reports, and the press. The controversy also covered Destutt de Tracy's *Idéologie*, presenting both authors either as representatives of modern science or as enemies of public morality. Accusations of materialism and sensationism were uttered against both, considered enemies of the Catholic tradition of the country; the arguments were countered, showing they separated the study of morals and religion, making the first the object of academic research through moral philosophy and the second the object of faith. As the educational process aims to educate rational individuals, it should be free from the influence of religion, and in no way should it impose or weaken the private individual's faith. The debate continued throughout the 19th century, alternating between the official endorsement of the books and their prohibition.

Caro's position anticipates the decline of political economy during the *Regeneración* when the conservatives, including Caro, were in office. Caro was one of the fiercest critics of utilitarianism, considering it ripped up the Catholic roots that should be the foundations of the republican social project. Caro and Ezequiel Rojas – a liberal political leader – engaged in a well-known debate over utilitarianism that reached the Académie des Sciences Morales et Politiques.[9] Whereas Rojas attempted to prove that utilitarianism was compatible with natural religion and the Christian lessons of charity, fraternity, and universal love, Caro underscored its materialistic tendency that founded human behavior on desire, pains, and pleasures. Seeking pleasure would go against social order, devaluing austerity and stability and promoting greed and ambition. Utilitarianism, the moral philosophy Caro associated with political economy, introduced foreign values contrary to the Colombian people's Catholic idiosyncrasy, which were precise characteristics Rojas associated with the premodern and archaic spirit that should be overcome to build a modern republic.

In 1870, Congress imposed Destutt de Tracy's *Idéologie* at Universidad Nacional. An academic debate followed. The university asked Miguel Ancízar, Miguel Antonio Caro, and Francisco Eustaquio Álvarez, all prominent public figures, for their advice (Universidad Nacional de los Estados Unidos de Colombia, 1870). The advice was contradictory: Ancízar considered political authorities could not make academic decisions; Caro stated that Destutt de Tracy's theory was outdated and false; and Álvarez defended *Idéologie*. Finally, the university asked the government to respect academic autonomy in selecting teaching material (Tovar González, 2002, pp. 39–40).

These debates about the contents and texts of public education, in general, and higher education in particular attest to the political issues at stake. Governments increasingly included teaching political economy even in programs for primary education. The formation of modern citizens and a governing elite – capable of guiding and designing the necessary institutions for the inclusion of the new republic in the world context – had to do, on the part of the liberals, with a concern of infusing an entrepreneurial spirit in young minds that could reconcile modernity – associated with reason (Augello & Guidi, 2012, p. 9), technology and progress – with a Catholic tradition that underscored solidarity, care for the most vulnerable and charity as opposed to ambition and self-interest. Archival evidence shows that political economy was taught even in primary schools in different regions, such as Colegio de Vélez, Colegio de Chiquinquirá, Colegio de Ibagué, and Colegio de Santa Marta.

This education also aimed at transforming economic institutions and, from early on, included practical concerns. In line with the strong influence of French liberalism, course syllabi underscored applying economic theory and doctrine to practical issues, especially in the creation, construction, and consolidation of private and public economic institutions, mainly financial and banking institutions. Teachers explained the theoretical arguments defending laissez-faire and the free market, connecting the theory of value and utility to the institutions needed in the real economy to guarantee currency flow and diminish transaction costs. Practical issues led to specific concerns about the education of civil servants capable of implementing the necessary reforms to create a favorable environment for modern prosperity. An education that would also be suitable to guide modern entrepreneurs to lead the transformation of the economy.

1.2.2 Public Consensus on Say's Books

The debate about the texts did not include Say's books. Even if Say was Bentham's declared disciple and a recognized member of the sensationist school, no public or private authority condemned his books. Say was Colombia's primary reference in economics during the 19th century (cf. Hurtado, 2017). In the debate over moral education and the values and beliefs of the new generations of citizens, Say was never considered a threat, unlike Bentham and Destutt de Tracy. Say's success echoes his reception in Spain, where he was also the primary reference in economics education between 1807 and 1835, and other countries in Latin America (López Castellano, 2009). Say was perceived as an advocate of liberal economic policies, underscoring the role of the entrepreneur, and laying down the path to prosperity through the promotion of a free market with a clear institutional framework. Say gave the new rulers, liberal or conservative, the theoretical and technical tools they needed to actively build a liberal social order based on free markets and private initiative without threatening religious beliefs (Hurtado, 2017).

Social economy, the new name Say gave to the discipline in 1821, helped this favorable reception. Social economy conveyed the idea that economics was beyond political debate and only responded to laws and principles beyond the reach of politics. The young republic welcomed this individualistic, apolitical view of economics with a solid pragmatic approach as part of a more ambitious social project. Economics showed how society worked as a living complex, the appropriate functions of each part, and how individuals and the state could strive to become wealthy, prosperous, and virtuous.

As explained in Say's texts, beyond any government intervention and with no need for permanent government supervision, the correct functioning of the economy guaranteed self-sustained growth and increasing wealth for all. This proper functioning included individual rules of behavior needed to preserve and comply with natural laws. Economic education explicitly aimed at reconciling private and public interest and teaching "that the market could only work if economic agents acknowledged its governmentality and adopted behaviors consistent with it" (Augello & Guidi, 2012, p. 29).

Policymakers found Say's work appealing because he "understood [political economy] as a science seeking to enlighten the citizens of industrial societies" (Steiner, 2012, p. 77) and as "a useful and necessary knowledge for the new society emerging from the revolutionary period" (Steiner, 2012, p. 77). Moreover, his educational work reflected his belief that the motor force of social life was industry rather than politics and daily individual actions and behaviors (Steiner, 2012, p. 77). This message of being able to overcome politics and political disputes deemed useless in this newly industrialized world appeared as a neutral and beneficial terrain to build the needed new mentality that would foster entrepreneurship.[10] The shared aim of liberals and conservatives to adopt market-friendly policies and promote industrialization seems to be the main reason for adopting Say's lessons, easily adapting them to both liberal and conservative policies (Steiner, 2012, p. 78).

In 1844 the General Directorate of Public Instruction approved a political economy course syllabus that made Say's influence even more salient. Rojas, considered the foremost representative and defender of the utilitarian-sensationist school, politician, public official, and one of the most influential professors of the Radical generation, designed this syllabus closely following Say's *Treatise* and his *Course*. The syllabus was 62 pages long, had 117 chapters with a section on "Preliminary Notions," covered 1105 questions, and was officially published, with minor changes, as a reference in 1866 (Hurtado, 2016). Rojas started with epistemological and methodological considerations about economics, dealing with its definition, scope, and method. He linked economics with individual needs and desires, leading directly to the relationship between utility and value. Hence, economics dealt with wealth production, distribution, consumption, and the direct relationship between individual behavior and national prosperity. The role of the entrepreneur and practical considerations about the organization of economic institutions and policies made up more than half of the rest of the syllabus.

Beyond Say's theory's significant and long-lasting influence, the French liberal school and his followers considerably affected Colombian political economy. Pierre-Paul Leroy-Beaulieu and Jean-Gustave Courcelle-Seneuil, two leading figures of the French school, became as popular as the master, especially after the end of the 1850s. Courcelle-Seneuil was much more influential and renowned in Latin America than in France. Courcelle-Seneuil's entrance door to South America was Chile, and his role as a money doctor interested Colombian liberals. Adopting a free banking system was one of the main legacies of French liberal ideas in Colombia.

1.3 Courses, Professors, and Institutions

Bogotá boasted the leading educational centers in the 19th century: elites attended El Rosario and San Bartolomé. Students from all over the country came to these institutions to pursue higher education. When they left Bogotá, if they did and became professors themselves, these students reproduced the canon they had learned. Only a few professors, like Florentino González, another prominent public official considered the first Colombian economist, wrote their manuals and textbooks. Some authors dedicated theirs to "young people" but found little to no room in classes. Most professors used foreign books, especially Destutt de Tracy's and Say's. Other foreign texts were popular in the national debate, and Colombian authors translated books like Frédéric Bastiat's *Economic Harmonies* (1850) to advance their arguments, but they were not used to teach.[11]

The abundant presence of books in French in private collections later added to the National Library suggests that the students and teachers read in French. Say's books appear in the early 19th-century library catalogs in French and in the well-known *Librería Colombiana Camacho Roldán y Tamayo* in 1887.[12] Two registers of book lists are available in the National Library from this bookstore. Destutt de Tracy's *Traité* in French appears in those inventories, and the Spanish translation was listed in the National Library in 1824. Those professors who had visited France or expressed their admiration for France used French texts from liberal thinkers in their classes. Articles and columns in national newspapers and magazines quote from French authors, which explains their higher relative circulation than other authors.

Prominent national figures taught the political economy compulsory course in the most renowned institutions. Francisco Soto was the first professor in charge of the course in 1825 at San Bartolomé, and also taught the course at the University la Gran Colombia.[13] Soto was a liberal political figure, a congressman and Senate President, representative of the province of Santander at the Ocaña convention between April and June 1828, and Secretary of the Treasury several times between 1835 and 1837. During the Ocaña Convention, Mariano Ospina Rodríguez, his former student, future President of the Republic between 1857 and 1861, and member of the Conservative Party, retained the compulsory course in his administration's education plans. The fact that liberals and conservatives agreed on keeping the course attests to the importance of political economy beyond partisan political frontiers and interests. The absence of controversy about the political economy courses and Say's books to teach the subject "confirms that the intra-elite disputes were not so much over economic doctrines and interests" (Uribe-Urán, 2000, pp. 112–113). All political parties and factions agreed on the benefits of free trade and "on economic doctrines and policies, first pragmatically protectionist and later liberal" (Uribe-Urán, 2000, p. 114). Ezequiel Rojas succeeded Soto in 1832[14] and Santiago Pérez succeeded him. Besides his affiliation with the utilitarian-sensationist school and outstanding career in the public sector, Rojas was the founder of the Liberal Party, President of San Bartolomé, and was named the first President of the Universidad Nacional but could not accept the appointment due to his advanced age.

Along with all the texts, program exams, and syllabi from El Rosario and San Bartolomé dating from 1834 to 1860, other archival evidence attests to the continuity of the political economy course (see Table 1.1 for some examples). Public announcements of examinations from Vélez, a city in Santander in the northeastern part of the country, to Medellín, in the central-western region of Antioquia, including others from Cartagena, in the Caribbean region, Panamá (still a Colombian province), Cauca, Chiquinquirá, Ibagué, Guanentá, Pamplona and Santa Marta include information about the professor in charge for each year and, for most of them, the books used. Like Soto, Rojas, and Pérez, many professors were public figures: Estanislao Vergara Sanz de Santamaría (1790–1855), President 1828–1830; Manuel Ancízar (1812–1882), Minister of Foreign Affairs 1861–1862, and first President of the Universidad Nacional; or Salvador Camacho Roldán (1827–1900), presidential candidate and considered the founder of sociology in Colombia, among others.

Table 1.1 Archival evidence

Title	Year	Institution	City	Professor	Material type	Archive
Certámenes del Colejio del Rosario, Año de 1833	1833	Colejio del Rosario	Bogotá	José María del Castillo y Rada	Exams	AHUR
Colección de asertos de las materias que defenderán en certámenes públicos en el Colejio de San Bartolomé, año de 1835	1835	Colejio de San Bartolomé	Bogotá	Ezequiel Rojas	Exams	AHUR
Certámenes literarios que presentarán la escuela de primeras letras i las clases del Colejio de la Ciudad de Vélez, año de 1836	1836	Colejio de la Ciudad de Vélez	Vélez	Rafael María Vasquez	Exams	AHUR
Colección de los asientos que contienen los principios sobre que se versaron los actos literarios del Colégio Mayor de Nuestra Señora del Rosario en el año escolar de 1837	1837	Colejio del Rosario	Bogotá	Juan Nepomuceno Gómez	Exams	AHUR
Asertos para los certámenes públicos del Colejio Mayor de Nuestra Señora del Rosario en 1839	1839	Colejio del Rosario	Bogotá	Manuel Cañarete	Exams	AHUR
Colección de programas para los certámenes públicos que las clases de la Universidad del Cauca presentan en el mes de julio de 1839	1839	Universidad del Cauca	Popayán	Domingo Medina	Exams	AHUR
Objetos sobre que deben versarse los exámenes públicos del Colejio de Jesús, María y José de Chiquinquirá en 1840	1840	Colejio de Jesús, María y José	Chiquinquirá	Francisco C. Fajardo	Exams	AHUR
Colección de los asertos formados por los catedráticos del Colejio de San Simón de Ibagué, 1840	1840	Colejio de San Simón de Ibagué	Ibagué	Manuel Camacho	Exams	AHUR

Document	Year	Institution	City	Author	Type	Source
Programa de los principios que los cursantes de la Universidad Central espondran en los certámenes públicos, 1840	1840	Universidad Central	Bogotá	Ezequiel Rojas	Exams	AHUR
Colección de programas para los certámenes literarios del Colejio de San José de Pamplona, año de 1840	1840	Colejio de San José de Pamplona	Pamplona	No se específica	Exams	AHUR
Colección de asertos en que se ofrecen sostener en certámen público los alumnos del Colejio de Guanentá, año de 1840	1840	Colejio de Guanentá	San Gil-Guanentá	No se específica	Exams	AHUR
Certámen de Economía Política, Universidad del Magdalena e Istmo	1841	Universidad del Magdalena e Istmo	Cartagena	Antonio del Real	Exams	AHUR
Carta de Manuel Cañarete al rector donde le presenta los textos para su cátedra de Jurisprudencia	1851	Colejio del Rosario	Bogotá	Manuel Cañarete	Correspondence	AHUR
Lecciones de estadística: Estractadas de Moreau de Jonnes	1851	Universidad Nacional	Bogotá	José Antonio de Plaza	Lessons	Biblioteca Nacional
Prospecto de estudios (1852)	1852	Colejio del Rosario	Bogotá	Juan Nepomuceno Gómez	Syllabus	AHUR
Certámenes del Colejio del Rosario, Año de 1865	1865	Colejio del Rosario	Bogotá	Manuel Ancízar	Exams	AHUR
Colejio de San Bartolomé. Cuadro de calificaciones de los alumnos de este colegio en los exámenes intermedios (agosto de 1867)	1867	Colejio de San Bartolomé	Bogotá	Colejio de San Bartolomé	Grade Report	AHUR
Certámenes públicos que presenta el Colejio Nuestra Señora del Rosario, 1869	1869	Colejio del Rosario	Bogotá	Francisco Eustaquio Alvarez	Exams	AHUR

(Continued)

Table 1.1 (Continued)

Title	Year	Institution	City	Professor	Material type	Archive
Programa de Economía Política	1873	Universidad Nacional	Bogotá	Manuel Ancízar	Lessons	Biblioteca Nacional
Acta de exámen de la clase de Economía Política y Estadística	1880	Universidad Nacional	Bogotá	Santiago Pérez	Exams	ACHUN
Carta al Secretario de Instrucción Pública solicitando 28 copias de la obra "Estudios Económicos y Fiscales" de Aníbal Galindo para los alumnos de Economía Política de la Universidad de Colombia	1881	Universidad Nacional	Bogotá	N/A	Correspondence	AGN
Registros de asistencia/conducta en la Escuela de Jurisprudencia	1883	Universidad Nacional	Bogotá	N/A	Attendance Records	ACHUN
Listas Facultad de Jurisprudencia 1889	1889	Universidad Nacional	Bogotá	Nicolás J. Casas	Attendance Records	ACHUN
Reglamento para la Facultad de Derecho y Ciencias Políticas de la Universidad Nacional	1890	Universidad Nacional	Bogotá	N/A	Documents	Biblioteca Nacional
Plan de estudios de la Facultad de Derecho	1890	Universidad Nacional	Bogotá	N/A	Syllabus	Biblioteca Nacional
Listas Facultad de Jurisprudencia 1892	1892	Universidad Nacional	Bogotá	Carlos Martínez Silva	Attendance Records	ACHUN
Catálogo de los libros de la Biblioteca de la Facultad de Derecho y Ciencias Políticas	1898	Universidad Nacional	Bogotá	N/A	Library Catalog	ACHUN

After Rojas' death, Pérez became the most influential political economy professor until the end of the 19th century. Pérez's public career took him to the Presidential Office of the United States of Colombia in 1874. He taught at El Rosario and Universidad Nacional, and spent his last years teaching at El Externado University. Correa Restrepo (2001) edited Pérez's lectures at El Rosario and the Universidad Nacional using his students' notes in 1880. The manuscript *Political Economy and Statistics* is divided into 17 chapters dealing with exchange, value, trade, currency, credit, banks, distribution, consumption, population, statistics, and the division of labor. The influence of Bentham, Say, Malthus, and Bastiat is visible. Their connection lies in their utilitarian views, as the roots of the free market that would overcome the Malthusian trap.

An exam program from Universidad Católica is a notable exception to the national standard using Say's books as the primary reference from 1836 to the 1870s. Spanish texts were not included in the official textbooks and were not part of the material for graduation exams. Universidad Católica's announcement shows that Manuel Colmeiro's *Treatise* was the primary reference. However, the French influence is still present as Colmeiro was one of the main representatives of French liberalism in Spain. Colmeiro's *Treatise* was often used in Spain, around 1856, as a substitute for Joseph Garnier's *Éléments d'économie politique* (Hernández & Tortorella Esposito, 2017, p. 22)

This widespread teaching of political economy among the elites fostered a general interest in the topic – prestigious figures delivered and published public lectures during the second half of the 19th century. Aníbal Galindo, finance minister and scholar, gave some of these lectures at El Externado and Republican University. Galindo wrote extensively on economic matters, primarily financial and monetary issues analyzing the determinants of capital accumulation and microeconomic savings decisions. In the published lectures, Galindo (1978) acknowledges in the title his debt to Say; he also includes empirical evidence from other sources, such as "an English Review from August 1887," to illustrate the amounts of capital accumulation and total savings in different British countries (p. 27). His lectures were used in 1881 as course material at Universidad Nacional.

There was little national production of books on the subject. Constancio Franco, with no known institutional affiliation, published in 1876 a *Tratado de economía política*. The book's structure is like Leroy-Beaulieu's *Traité Théorique et Pratique*. The book illustrates the changes in contents after 1860 with chapters dedicated to transport infrastructure (pp. 93–98) discussing the role of state financing in developing railways and other "mechanical means of transportation."

Political economy lessons transcended the classroom, especially during the second half of the 19th century. Governments implemented three main economic reforms in the 1850s: trade, disentailment of the Catholic Church, and the monetary system. Conservatives and liberals had shared an interest in implementing free trade policies since the 1820s. Liberal reforms went as far as eliminating all tariffs on commonly imported goods and colonial monopolies.

The disentailment of the Catholic Church aimed at creating a land market, redefining land property, and, in general, the distribution of wealth and economic powers (Jaramillo & Meisel, 2009). This reform also marked the rupture between conservatives and liberals on economic matters. The latter aimed at deepening the separation of state and Church, while the former denounced the use of political economy to implement anticlerical measures. Monetary issues also became a source of disagreement. After several attempts at stabilizing monetary circulation through different proposals to create a national bank, in 1865, private banks of issue became the rulers of the economic and financial architecture (Álvarez, 2016; Álvarez, 2017, pp. 213–214). During the 1860s and 1870s, merchants, bankers, and commodity exporters became the primary political support for the Radical Liberal Party against artisans, farmers, and traditional landowners who consolidated a nationalist faction of the Conservative Party. The nationalists came to power in 1880 and implemented protectionist and centralizing policies under the name of *Regeneración*. The conservative government changed the free banking system to a monetary system based on legal tender paper money under the monopoly of a national bank.

The increasing divide between liberals and conservatives was apparent in education policy. From 1878 onwards, the government began implementing different measures to centralize education and put it under the direct supervision of the executive (*Anales de Instrucción Pública de Colombia*). Through the creation of the Secretary of Public Instruction and the suppression of the Universidad Nacional´s Council, the government reversed the educational reforms of 1863 (Rodríguez, 2018, pp. 78–79).

1.4 The Conservative Repression

Censorship had become predominant in the intellectual environment since 1880 (Rodríguez, 2018, p. 233). Rafael Núñez, representing a coalition between liberal dissidents and the Conservative Party, was elected President that year for a two-year term. He was re-elected in 1884, and liberals were voted out of office in 1885. Radical leaders were forced into exile. The Catholic Church regained its control over education, and the government closed down newspapers, producing a hostile environment for liberal ideas.[15]

In 1886, the new political constitution proclaimed a centralized political organization with a single central executive power and common legislation for the country (Correa Restrepo, 2001). States disappeared, and the President, now with six instead of four years in office, appointed provincial governors. Moreover, the constitution granted the President the possibility of assuming extraordinary powers in the event of disturbances to public order. Rafael Núñez, as President, used his newly acquired powers to support an economic model based on agricultural exports and counter free trade policies because "spontaneous capitalism corroded the pillars of any type of progress: authority, religious tradition, and the central State" (Correa Restrepo, 2001, p. 17). The state should actively participate in economic activity to ensure social order. The Núñez administration implemented protectionist policies imposing tariffs on certain imported products and actively controlled the country's economic policy and banking system.

The 1886 Constitution also declared in article 38 that "The Catholic, Apostolic, Roman Religion is that of the Nation; the public powers will protect it and ensure that it is respected as an essential element of social order (...)". This meant that Colombia would not allow any other religion or cult contrary to Christian morals because of their possible subversive influence. Article 41 of the constitution restored the Church's control over education and its economic privileges through tax exemptions on the Church's real estate. This new constitutional order made the Catholic Church the central pillar of social order.

Liberal ideas contrary to the Catholic faith were responsible for chaos, anarchy, and disorder and hence prohibited in any educational institution. Education was again at the center of political debate (Silva, 1998). Conservative reforms placed higher education and public universities under direct government control, eliminating academic autonomy (Silva, 1998). The Concordat sealed ecclesiastical control over education and imposed compulsory classes in the Catholic religion with specific texts on faith, philosophy, and morals. The Concordat also established the right to denounce and exclude any teacher who might be suspected of religious or moral beliefs contrary to the official ones (Silva, 1998; Rodríguez, 2018). This new constitutional framework and an atmosphere of political and intellectual repression triggered a new era in Colombia's education system. Under the leadership of Caro, Rafael María Carrasquilla, and Manuel María Madiedo, conservative governments turned to ultra-conservative Catholic Hispanism. They dismantled the transformations of the liberal revolution in the 1850s and the 1863 political constitution.

The central government merged Colegio San Bartolomé, Universidad Nacional, and Colegio del Rosario (Mayorga, 2001) to guarantee its control over higher education. Presidential decrees determined textbooks and appointed professors. Public universities dismissed liberal professors, who began teaching in private institutions. Universidad Nacional dismissed Juan David Herrera, who became Professor of Biology and Forensics at El Exterando in 1887; Juan Manuel Rudas, president of El Rosario, and Santiago Pérez, both exiled, later joined El Externado (Rodríguez 2018, p. 415, 417). Other professors of political economy, like Galindo and Camacho Roldán, followed suit and were replaced by conservative figures who had participated in the elaboration and promulgation of the constitution.

Carlos Martínez Silva, Nicolás J. Casas, Miguel Abadía Méndez, and Alejandro Motta took over the courses between 1886 and 1899. Martínez Silva, former Secretary of the Treasury,[16] was a conservative ideologue who graduated from Universidad Nacional in 1868 and received a doctorate in law and political science in 1872 (Mayorga, 2001). Author of the *Treatise on Judicial Evidence*, he was well known for attacking Bentham and Bonnier. He actively participated in the public debate through his articles in several conservative newspapers (Martínez, 1926). Caro appointed Casas as professor of political economy at Universidad Nacional in 1889. Both appointments echoed the conservative newspaper *El Recopilado*'s (1888) concern for a wise choice of public servants because of their influence "on the good and stable progress of the morals and healthy customs of the country" that had to avoid university professors with "radical ideas ... dissociative of all society" (in Rodríguez, 2018, p. 291).

Liberal professors went to private universities such as El Externado and Universidad Republicana, founded in 1886 and 1890, respectively, and continued the instruction of liberal generations (Delpar, 1994, p. 325). These new institutions kept education free of religious control and provided the proper environment for teachers such as Camacho Roldán to introduce new ideas. Camacho Roldán had tried to introduce Comte's Positivism in his classes at Universidad Nacional when he inaugurated the chair of sociology.[17] With his departure, he took these ideas to El Externado, adding Herbert Spencer's theory, which became the most important reference, especially in jurisprudence theses (Rodríguez, 2018, p. 10). This approach to social phenomena found its place at this private university alongside the courses in political economy, where the liberal influence was still present.

Likewise, Aníbal Galindo found a place at Universidad Republicana. These universities were able to "bring together a prominent group of radical professors, banned from the universities where they had taught their courses, with students who had left *Rosario* and the *Universidad Nacional* as well as others who began their studies at *El Externado*" (Rodríguez, 2018, p. 292).

Liberal professors at private universities and conservative professors at public universities marked significant differences for their students. Students read Spencer, Bentham, Smith, Say, Locke, Kant, Darwin, Comte, and Marx, among others, at El Externado and Universidad Republicana. At Universidad Nacional, the 1898 book catalogs of the Law and Political Science Department include Bastiat, Leroy-Beaulieu, and Baudrillard (Rodríguez, 2018). Students' theses also show the difference between private and public universities. Whereas El Externado students wrote theses on political economy, interest in the field declined at Universidad Nacional. In 1890 and 1891, there were hardly any political economy theses presented at the latter, but at the former common topics were free trade, the study of the working class, taxes, and free banking.

In 1889, El Externado granted autonomy to teachers and eliminated all restrictions on teaching materials and syllabi. Universidad Republicana stated its mission as "raising the intellectual and moral level of youth, putting out the bonfire of hatred consuming this country" (Mejía Gutierrez, 2017, p. 163), and granted autonomy to professors. These private universities preserved the political economy course much as Pérez had taught it in 1880. Antonio José Iregui, professor at the Universidad Republicana, taught a similar course up to 1905, as shown in his notes for a "theoretical and practical course in political economy adapted to national needs." He claims to

have followed the flow of ideas, rectified by the experience of our distinguished Santiago Pérez, Miguel Samper and Camacho Roldán, from the first of which we have taken, due to the insurmountable form, a large part of definitions and concepts of his unpublished lectures his disciple collected.

(Iregui, 1905, p. 3)

Nevertheless, he introduced some novelty in the course. A typology and characterization of economic ideas divided economic thought into four schools, liberal, socialist, solidarity, and naturalistic, and three derivatives from the classical school, Marshall and Jevons's mathematical approach, Menger's psychological or Austrian approach, and Spencer and Schaeffler's bio-sociological approach. Iregui was a pioneer in introducing Spencer as a political economist; he was also the first to teach Marshall and to use Jevons to explain labor, Walras for utility, wealth, and rent, Menger on utility and wealth, Comte on the division of labor, and Marx to explain the socialist concept of capital, collectivism, and the socialist critique of capitalists' interests and profit. Iregui was convinced, as he claimed in his 1905 course, that "If we can claim for economic science the position of honor it deserves in national thought and the country's administrative opinions, if we restore confidence in the efficacy of economic principles, almost lost by skepticism [...] we will have reaped as a nation the most precious level of well-being and glory." The 19th century ended with a stark contrast between what students learned in private and public higher education institutions. Political economy courses lost their liberal bent in the latter and remained a haven for liberal thought in the former. These courses and the topics related to the field still interested students at El Externado and the Universidad Republicana but were substituted for analysis in canonical law and jurisprudence at Universidad Nacional.

1.5 Concluding Remarks

Even if there were no diplomas or programs on political economy during the 19th century in Colombia, courses on the subject were part of higher education plans from early on. Since the second decade of the 19th century, political economy had been taught in the leading higher education institutions, first in Bogotá and then all around the country. However, not only did the spread of such courses mark the importance of political economy as a modernizing discipline, those who were political economy students and teachers occupied high positions in national and local government. In an important exception to the political dynamics of the century, both liberals and conservatives were involved in teaching this discipline and mostly used Say's *Treatise* and *Course* as the primary textbooks. This changed with the *Regeneración* and led to a stark difference between public and private universities. The former appointed professors that restored Catholic ideals, and the latter hired the liberal professors fired from public institutions.

Archival documents show that the aim of education in political economy had to do with practical concerns regarding the design and implementation of economic institutions that would promote market economy and industrialization. This new economic organization required specific individual behaviors that promoted the necessary environment for creating national enterprises to insert the country into the international division of labor. Say's intention of producing textbooks to enlighten citizens of industrial societies fitted perfectly with this national objective, so it is relatively straightforward to understand why his texts were widely used and hardly ever contested as the primary bibliography in these courses.

Notes

1 We are grateful for comments and suggestions received on previous versions of this chapter, particularly those of participants at the Meeting of the Asociación Latinoamericana de Historia del Pensamiento Económico, and to the other authors in this book, especially Claudia Pico, for their comments during our author workshop.
2 The use of Bentham's and Destutt de Tracy's books was a permanent source of controversy during the 19th century in Colombia. The dispute in the controversy – recorded as the *Querella Benthamista* – was associated with Bentham but included Destutt de Tracy, establishing a direct connection between Bentham's utilitarianism and Destutt de Tracy's *idéologie*. Their detractors accused the books of a deleterious impact on public morality because of their materialist and sensualist philosophy, contrary to Christian and Catholic values (cf. Cortés Guerrero, 2006).
3 The Colombian National Library and the Central Bank's library (Biblioteca Luís Ángel Arango) have digitalized and made most of this archival evidence available online.
4 Ezequiel Rojas (1803–1873), a politician and writer, was considered by his contemporaries as the primary representative of utilitarianism in Colombia (Hurtado, 2015). He had among his students many who would later become the leaders of liberal radicalism in Colombia (Hurtado, 2017).
5 There are several texts tracing the transformations and ensuing debates around higher education in the country (cf. Jaramillo, 1974; Ahern, 1947/1991; Uribe-Urán, 2000; Cardona Zuluaga, 2007; Gaitán, 2010; Elías-Caro & Renán-Rodríguez, 2016; Rodríguez, 2018; Malagón Pinzón, 2019) but there is much less research on political economy, possibly because these courses were part of majors in jurisprudence. The first higher education program in economics was created in 1931 at the Pontificia Universidad Javeriana in Bogotá, followed by the Institute of Economics and Commerce at the Pontificia Universidad Bolivariana in Medellín. The first Economics Department, a product of the Instituto de Ciencias Económicas, was created in the Universidad Nacional in 1945, followed shortly by the Economics Department at the Universidad de los Andes in 1948, which incorporated the former BA program in industrial and commercial administration at the Gimnasio Moderno in Bogotá.
6 The *Treatise*, published in 1803, was translated and published in Spanish in 1807; a translation of the first volume appeared in 1804.
7 This section is based on Hurtado (2016), where a detailed account can be found.
8 Moreno y Escandón, a public official, had to leave the country in 1781 due to the colonial authorities' political arrangements with the Catholic Church to curb the Comunero's Revolt. His "'departure undoubtedly contributed to slowing down the projected reforms [to higher education], particularly the proposed creation of a public university. For over a decade, he had been the most active promoter of educational reform. [... Also creating] the first public library in New Granada in 1777.

He also pioneered the introduction and teaching of modern mathematical and astronomical theories" (Uribe-Urán, 2000, p. 105).

9 This debate also played an important role in the discussion about criminal law, as shown in Chapter 4.

10 The country's continual civil and political conflict during the 19th century, with several major open civil wars, proved this aim to be mostly wishful thinking.

11 As found in the chapters in Augello & Guidi (2012),

> all translations were adaptations. They contained terms, full passages, and sometimes entire parts that were omitted or replaced by original contributions more suited to the conditions and problems of the target country. Paratextual apparatuses like introductions, footnotes, and appendixes guided readers to apply what they read to their national situations. They warned them about the dangers of imitating ideological or practical patterns considered unsuited to their national character. Sometimes explicit translations were substituted by apparently original works that went from plagiarism to honest imitations and compilations from other sources.
>
> (p. 33)

12 This bookstore's catalogs show how courses, lectures, and books on political economy spread from elite education to the public. Besides Say's books, other French liberals are included between 1885–1898. By the end of the century, the catalog included socialist authors mainly dealing with political economy, sociology, and history.

13 Soto could not continue teaching his course after 1828 because he was accused of participating in the September plot against President Bolívar's life and forced into exile.

14 When he returned from exile after being condemned for having participated in the September plot, just as Francisco Soto did.

15 In addition to censorship, government officials used other methods to discourage reading books considered heretical. The Catholic Church used the Association of the Apostleship of Prayer to exchange "pernicious books for good books," and its campaign was so successful that in less than a year, about 1,700 volumes had been changed (Rodríguez, 2018, p. 421).

16 As Minister, Martínez Silva was accused of participating in clandestine monetary emissions in the National Bank, which ended in the bank's closure in 1893 (Kalmanovitz, 2017, p. 492). A special commission studied the case and noted in its report that the Minister of the Treasury had incurred abuse in authority because he was neither a legal nor statutory member of the Issuance Board and, therefore, had no opportunity to participate in its decisions. The Commission concluded that the Board incurred in-excess emissions three different times, and Treasury Minister Martínez Silva was held responsible (Hernández Gamarra, 2000).

17 Camacho Roldán, in the inaugural speech for the 1882 academic year at the Universidad Nacional, made the first reference to Spencer. He talked about

> a new science whose study refers to the laws that, through a man's social tendencies, preside over the historical development of collective beings called Nations: sociology. [...] Rousseau and Turgot, Condorcet and Gibbon, Kant and Auguste Comte, Spencer and Bluntschli, Buckle and Summer Maine, who have applied to the study of [social] phenomena the same procedure of observation and experience to which the physical and natural sciences owe their progress in modern times.
>
> (Camacho Roldán, 1882, pp. 2–3)

Bibliography

Ahern, E.J.G. (1991). *El desarrollo de la educación en Colombia· 1820–1850*. Digital-izaed by Red Académica, Universidad Pedagógica Nacional. (Original work published 1947).

Álvarez, A. (2016). Banca Libre, federalismo y soberanía monetaria regional en el siglo XIX en Colombia. In A. Álvarez & J.S. Correa (eds), *Ideas y políticas económicas en Colombia durante el primer siglo republicano*. Bogotá: Ediciones Uniandes, pp. 155–181.

Álvarez, A. (2017). From free banking to paper money: Ideas behind the building of a National Bank in Colombia at the end of the nineteenth century. In A. Cunha & C.E. Suprinyak (eds), *The political economy of Latin America Independence*. pp. 205–226. Routledge.

Augello, M. M., & Guidi, M. E. L. (eds). (2012). *The economic reader: textbooks, manuals and the dissemination of the economic sciences during the 19th and early 20th centuries*. Abingdon, Oxon; New York: Routledge.

Burbano-López, G. (2008). Colombia. In C. García Guadilla (Ed.), *Pensamiento universitario latinoamericano. Pensadores y forjadores de la universidad latinoamericana* (pp. 169–201). CENDES, IESALC-UNESCO, Bid & Co.

Camacho Roldan, S. (1882). *Discurso leído por Salvador Camacho Roldán, profesor de sociología de la Universidad Nacional, en la sesión solemne de distribución de premios a los alumnos, el día 10 de diciembre de 1882*. Bogotá. Imprenta de Echevarría Hermanos.

Cardona Zuluaga, P. (2007). *La nacion de papel: Textos escolares, lectura política: Estados Unidos de Colombia, 1870–1876*. Fondo Editorial Universidad, EAFIT.

Cataño, G. (1995). Los radicales y la educación. *Revista Credencial Historia, 66*. Available at: http://www.banrepcultural.org/blaavirtual/revistas/credencial/junio1995/junio2.htm

Correa Restrepo, J.S. (2001). Economía Política I Estadística de Santiago Pérez Manosalva. *Revista de Economía Institucional, 5*, 258–262.

Cortés Guerrero, J.D. (2006). Los debates político-religiosos en torno a la fundación de la Universidad Nacional de Colombia, 1867–1876. In R. Sierra Mejía (Ed.), *El Radicalismo colombiano del siglo XIX* (pp. 327–349). Universidad Nacional de Colombia.

Delpar, H. (1994). *Rojos contra azules: El partido liberal en la política colombiana 1863-1899* (Colección el liberalismo radical). Bogotá: Procultura.

Elías-Caro, J., & Renán-Rodríguez, W. (2016). *La educación superior en la provincia de Santa Marta y el Magdalena. Siglo XIX*. Universidad del Magdalena.

Gaitán Bohórquez, J. (2010). Agenda ilustrada y agenda republicana en la cuestión educativa neogranadina. *Revista Historia de la Educación Latinoamericana, 14*, 100–124.

Galindo, A. (1978). *Estudios Económicos y fiscales*. Biblioteca Popular de Economía, ANIF-COLCULTURA. Ediciones Sol y Luna. (Original work published 1870).

Hernández, A. J. and Tortorella Esposito, G. (2017). El liberalismo de Jean Baptiste Say, sus discípulos y la Economía Política en España. *Revista Empresa y Humanismo, XX*(1), 7–34.

Hernández Gamarra, A. (2000). Emisiones clandestinas. *Revista Del Banco De La República, 73*(874), 23–53.

Hurtado, J. (2015). Ezequiel Rojas: entre Utilitarismo e Ideología. *Economía, XXXVIII* (75), 151–174.

Hurtado, J. (2016). La economía política en los estudios superiores en la segunda mitad del siglo XIX en Colombia. Ezequiel Rojas, sus influencias y programas. In A. Álvarez and J.S. Correa (eds). *Ideas y políticas económicas en Colombia durante el primer siglo republicano* (pp. 35–67). Ediciones Uniandes-Editorial CESA, 2016.

Hurtado, J. (2017). Jean-Baptiste Say's social economics and the construction of the 19th century liberal republic in Colombia. In A. Mendes-Cunha & C.E. Suprinyak (Eds), *The political economy of Latin American Independence* (pp. 141–162). Routledge, Taylor and Francis Group.

Iregui, J.A. (1905). *Curso teórico y prático de economía política, adaptado a las necesidades nacionales.* Bogotá: Casa Editorial El Mercurio.

Jaramillo Uribe, J. (1974). *El pensamiento colombiano en el siglo XIX* (2da edición). Editorial Temis.

Kalmanovitz, S. (2017). Miguel Antonio Caro, el Banco Nacional y el Estado. In *Obra Selecta.* Bogotá: Penguin Random House.

López Castellano, F. (2009). La réception de Say et son influence sur l'institutionnalisation de l'enseignement de l'économie en Espagne (1807–1856), *Revue d'Histoire des Sciences Humaines,* 2(21), 127–150.

López Domínguez, L.H. (ed.) (1993). *La querella benthamista.* Bogotá: Biblioteca de la Presidencia de la República.

Malagón Pinzón, M. (2019). *Historia de la formación y la enseñanza de la ciencia administrativa y el derecho administrativo en Colombia (1826–1939).* Universidad del Rosario, Universidad de los Andes.

Mayorga, F. (2001). *Documentos para la historia del Colegio Mayor de Nuestra Señora del Rosario. La Ley 78 de 1890.* Documento Histórico, Bogotá: Universidad de Nuestra Señora del Rosario.

Mejía Gutiérrez, J. (2017). *La Universidad Republicana Y Laica De Colombia 1886–1924.* Bogotá: Escuela Superior de Administración Pública.

Meléndez, S. (2019). *La economía política como campo de batalla: la evolución de la formación en economía política durante la transición del liberalismo radical a la Regeneración (1885–1905).* [Memoria de grado Universidad de los Andes]. https://repositorio.Uniandes.edu.co/bitstream/handle/1992/45116/u830431.pdf?sequence=1&isAllowed=y

Ministerio de Gobierno. (1924). *Codificación nacional de todas las leyes de Colombia desde el año 1821, hecha conforme a la ley 13 de 1912.* Imprenta Nacional.

Pico, C. (2016). The teaching of political economy, circulation of ideas and economic performance. A review of the Colombian experience in the nineteenth century. In M. García-Molina & H.-M. Trautwein (Eds), *Peripheral visions of economic development: New frontiers in development economics and the history of economic thought* (pp. 286–305). Routledge.

Rodríguez, J.C. (2018). *La luz no se extingue: Historia del primer externado 1886–1895.* Universidad Externado de Colombia.

Silva, R. (1998). La educación en Colombia. 1880–1930. In *Nueva historia de Colombia: NHC. IV: Educación y ciencia, luchas de la mujer, vida diaria.* Bogotá: Planeta.

Soto, D. (2005). Aproximación histórica a la universidad colombiana. *Revista Historia de la Educación Latinoamericana* 7: 99–136.

Steiner, P. (2012). Cours, Leçons, Manuels, Précis and Traités. Teaching Political Economy in nineteenth-century France. In M.M. Augello & M. E. L. Guidi (eds) *The Economic Reader. Textbooks, manuals and the dissemination of the economic science during the nineteenth and early twentieth century.* Routledge, Taylor & Francis Group.

Tovar González, L. (2002). Ciencia y Fe: Miguel Antonio Caro y las ideas positivas. In R. Sierra Mejía (Ed.) *Miguel Antonio Caro y la cultura de su época* (pp. 33–55). Universidad Nacional de Colombia.

Universidad Nacional de los Estados Unidos de Colombia. (1870). Anales de la Universidad Nacional de los Estados Unidos de Colombia, vol. IV, no 22. Imprenta Gaitán, pp. 291–419.

Uribe-Urán, V.M. (2000). *Honorable lives: Lawyers, family, and politics in Colombia, 1780–1850*. The University of Pittsburgh Press.

2 Revolutionaries, Conservatives, and Reformists

The Political Economy of Debasement and Recoinage in New Granada 1780–1821

*James V. Torres**

2.1 Introduction

On September 21, 1819, a series of thorough, yet little explored reports explaining the rapid collapse of colonial rule in New Granada (present-day Colombia and Ecuador) flooded the office of the authorities in Madrid. The previous month, a small battle in a town two days away from Bogotá, the viceregal capital, had led to the flight of the colonial authorities and the expansion of republican rule across central New Granada. In two months, the revolutionaries attained what had been an elusive enterprise since the outset of the Independence Wars in 1810. According to the former director of the Viceregal Court of Accounts, "the calamity" of 1819 resulted, inter alia, from the Viceroy's lack of understanding of "monetary matters".[1] The Viceroy passed several orders in 1818 to receive at face value the coins issued by the Spanish and loyalist forces while receiving as "mere metals" the ones issued by the revolutionaries. This policy, according to the General Attorney of Bogotá's Royal Audience, Agustín de Lopetedi, failed since "venerable philosophers have taught us that any manipulation of currency is but a mirage as long as the intrinsic and extrinsic value of the coins diverges" (Ortiz, 1965, pp. 230–231).

After failing to enforce the 1818 decree, the Viceroy decided to undertake a more ambitious policy. Following the advice of a money committee (*comisión de moneda*), he enacted a general recoinage, paying at face value the coins submitted to the mints. Given the low metallic content of the old monies, the cost of the operation was to be covered with a new tax on urban wealth. The General Attorney concluded that "the streams of coins collected in the recoinage attested the last blow to a man who was already bleeding". The city councils of several cities of the kingdom informed that people commented in the *pulperías* (stores) that the currency change was but a "great theft". The former mint superintendent remarked that the Viceroy and his "clique", by refusing to

* Conversations with the contributors to this volume during the Workshop on the History of Colombian Economic Thought held at the Universidad de los Andes, Bogotá, in April 2022, helped me to improve an early draft of this chapter. I would also like to thank Jimena Hurtado, Andrés Alvarez, Daniel Gutiérrez, Ana Otero-Cleves, and John Tutino for their constructive comments.

DOI: 10.4324/9781003289241-3

undertake a piecemeal currency reorganization, ended up "unleashing a new revolution" (AGI, Santa Fe, 833).

The recoinage of 1819 was one episode of a long saga of monetary reforms in the Northern Andes. The late colonial money supply consisted of a heterogeneous set of gold and silver coins of different intrinsic values that promoted monetary segmentation. Paradoxically, the economies that provided the stable, widely appreciated coins that had oiled global trade for centuries, suffered from a lack of good-quality coins for internal trade. The fragmentation of the Spanish monetary union and the policies the authorities adopted during the different stages of the revolution exerted further challenges. Debasements, recoinages, and ill-fated experiments with fiat monies led to important changes in the nature and composition of the region's money supply. By the early 1820s a mosaic of coins from different ages and qualities was flowing across the region (Torres, 2021, pp. 350–370; Meisel, 1990, pp. 25–30; Barriga, 1969, pp. 186–187).

Economic and political historians have stated that the "monetary chaos" that stemmed from the Independence Wars was one of the drivers behind the poor economic performance of the region during the early republican years (Irigoin, 2009a, pp. 550–552). Recent literature, in contrast, has emphasized the need to develop statistical data not only to calibrate the composition and size of the money supply but also to understand the impact of the co-circulation of coins of different quality on the mechanics of trade (Torres, 2021, pp 350–370; Jaramillo, Meisel, and Urrutia 1997, pp. 447–448). This chapter contributes to these debates by perusing the ideological disputes regarding monetary policies and their imprints in the adoption of concrete mintage practices during the late colonial period and the Wars of Independence. In particular, the research examines debates between treasury officials, merchants, mint masters, and the military regarding the debasements and recoinages enacted between 1780 and 1821. This approach will allow us to contribute to the literature on the history of Colombian thought that has hitherto focused almost exclusively on late colonial and early republican reports of creoles, viceroys, and revolutionaries.[2]

The chapter argues, first, that these debates were embedded into the broader, global discussions regarding the financial transformations that followed the escalation of the Atlantic Wars after the 1790s. This was an era of monetary experimentation, the formation of currency committees, and the cementation of global bimetallism. New Granadans drew ideas and insights from international discussions and some of them were well-versed in theoretical insights such as David Hume's price–specie flow mechanism and early versions of the quantity theory of money. They used these insights to make sense of the fiscal and monetary structure of the Northern Andes, providing data on the distinctive denomination of coins issued in domestic mints, the diverging bimetallic ratios across the region, and the constraints and incentives created by the polymetallic nature of North Andean mines.

Secondly, the chapter states that the individuals involved in the debates tended to fall into three broad groups. The first privileged piecemeal improvements, emphasizing the need to avoid large debasements and the importance of gradual recoinages to preserve monetary stability. The second group, in contrast, advocated the use of monetary inflation to finance the armies and the need to undertake profound overhauls of the monetary regime. This clique focused on the incapacity of the colonial system to supply low denomination coins and on the need for liquidity to fuel economic recovery. The last group, finally, emphasized the need to restore monetary stability to enhance political sovereignty, disregarding the macroeconomic constraints and consequences of monetary policy. While the second and third groups exerted a larger imprint in the transformation of mintage practices, the presence of the reformists curbed the scope of some measures. This equilibrium helps to explain why monetary volatility in the region was not as prevalent as in other parts of the former Spanish Empire.

2.2 The Mechanics of Late Colonial Mintage

By the time Napoleon crossed the Pyrenees, unleashing a political transformation of Atlantic proportions, the monetary system of the Spanish Empire had experienced profound changes. Attempts at coinage modernization, fiscal stringencies, and macroeconomic challenges inserted Spanish monetary policy into the broader, worldwide trends of monetary experimentation during the Atlantic Wars (Irigoin, 2009a, pp. 560–561; Torres, 2021, pp. 65–78). In the United Kingdom, the financial burden of the wars led to the suspension of the convertibility of the notes of the Bank of England until 1821, fueling the debate over the nature and efficiency of commodity money systems (O'Brien and Palma, 2020, pp. 10–12; Palma, 2018, p. 235). In France, the disastrous experiment with the *assignats* shored up the return to convertibility under a bimetallic system, leading to the international consolidation of three monetary blocs (gold, silver, and bimetallic) whose bullion flows pivoted around the French ratio until the advent of the gold standard in 1871 (Flandreau, 2004, pp. 39–42). In China and India, the changes in the supply of coins in Spanish America had broader macroeconomic reverberations, while the United States adopted bimetallism with a fixed ratio that remained in place until 1834 (Redish, 2000, pp. 163–171; Irigoin, 2009b, pp. 210–215). This was an age of monetary experimentation in which renowned political economists and policymakers such as David Ricardo, Henry Thornton, Alexander Hamilton, and Richard Cantillon exercised their craft (Fetter, 1959, pp. 102–110; Perlman, 1986, pp. 750–755). Lesser known are the monetary ideas and practices that emerged during this era of change in Spanish America in general and New Granada in particular.

The toolbox of the Spanish American authorities was constrained by the very nature of the commodity money arrangements that had operated in the Empire since its inception in the sixteenth century. The reforming of these constraints was at the very core of the ideas and policies that emerged during the late colonial period. In the Empire, the ultimate monetary sovereignty and policy resided in the King, but concepts and advice of officials at the ministries (Treasury and Indies), viceroys, and the mint superintendents permeated royal decisions. In parallel to these officials, committees and corporate bodies proposed and examined policies in both Madrid and the Indies (Céspedes, 1996, pp. 159–180 and pp. 220–229; Torres, 2013a, pp. 78–89).

The basic system that governed the monetary structure of the Empire was bimetallism, a regime in which authorities issued coins of two metals (gold and silver) at a fixed exchange rate.[3] The divergences between the market and fixed bimetallic ratio, the relative supply of the two metals, and small divergences in mint policies determined the bimetallic composition of the money supply across the heterogeneous regions of the Empire. These differences triggered indirect and direct arbitrage operations of bullion exchange whose economic imprints have been recently documented (Torres, 2021, pp. 105–152). A free minting policy anchored the system, allowing private holders to sell unrestricted quantities of bullion at a set mint price expressed in N coins per quantity of metals. The authorities also defined the unit of account in which transactions were to be carried out and the number of units each coin was tendered. In this framework, a Spanish marc (230 g) of pure silver or gold was combined with copper to produce an alloy of F percentage fineness. The alloyed marc was then struck into N number of coins of face value V. The mint par, L, is the value of a marc of pure silver or gold in coins.[4] The basic minting equation can be expressed as follows:

$$L = V \cdot N / F \tag{2.1}$$

The authorities intervened in the monetary supply by changing the mint par through alterations in F, V, and N. During the Bourbon era, debasements were the main tool of intervention, albeit the degree and frequency of devaluation were incomparably fewer than in other early modern monarchies (Rolnick, Velde and Weber, 1996, pp. 790–793). Authorities carried out debasements through a combination of three methods: (1) lowering the fineness of the coin (a reduction in F); (2) increasing the number of coins per marc (an increase in N); and (3) increasing a coin's face value (changes in V). Naturally, the minting process entailed some costs (S) that the holders of bullion were willing to pay given the lower transaction costs of dealing with coins vis-à-vis raw metals. These costs encompassed both the fixed and variable costs of producing coins at the mint and the fiscal revenue (seignorage) obtained by the King in the process. In other words, this premium of coin over raw metals was expressed as the mint price (Q, the face value of the number of coins received by the holders from the mint) minus the mint par, a relationship formalized as follows:

$$Q = (1 - S) \cdot L \tag{2.2}$$

This equation shows that monetary interventions, if the authorities decided to preserve the commodity money regime, came in the form of changes in mint prices and parities. These changes faced important restrictions. For instance, changes in Q, F, and V altered the opportunity costs of bullion holders, stimulating smuggling and counterfeiting, while changes in S created fiscal challenges to the royal treasuries. As a member of Bogotá's Court of Accounts pointed out in 1797, "monetary matters cannot be addressed without causing other problems perhaps more serious than the current ones. Prudence and caution are the best guides to examine monetary proposals" (AGI, Santa Fe, 831). To these proposals, we now turn in the following sections.

2.3 Late Colonial Monetary Landscape

In the late colonial period, the currency of the Spanish American colonies experienced two debasements (1772 and 1786) and one adjustment in its bimetallic ratio (1786) (Hamilton, 1944, pp. 24–29; Torres, 2014, p. 121). By 1786, the bullion content of silver coins was 2.28% below the pre-1772 level and 4.5% in the case of gold coins. The bimetallic ratio was fixed at 16.61:1, 3.8% above its pre-1786 level, persistently overvaluing gold over silver vis-à-vis world markets (Redish, 2000, p. 277). This pattern, as recent studies have shown, created an opportunity for New Granada's producers to undertake profitable exchanges with silver-based economies (Torres, 2021, pp. 151–159). Clipped, sweated, and abraded coins known as *macuquinas* issued before the monetary reforms of the 1730s – in which the Crown started to take over the administration of the colonial mints and carried out a debasement – circulated extensively up to the end of the colonial period and beyond. Between the 1730s and the 1750s, hammered coins were still issued but at a lower bullion content than the old *macuquinas*. After the introduction of milled coinage that produced a coin known as *monedas de cordoncillo* (edge-marked coins), the quality of the new specie improved but the debasements of 1772 and 1786 altered its intrinsic content again. The Crown enacted a recoinage process in 1772 that could not absorb the old currency (Torres, 2014, p. 123). Therefore, the late colonial money supply was composed of a heterogeneous set of coins of different qualities and ages.

New Granada's monetary history diverged from that of New Spain and Peru in three broad aspects. First, the timing of its coinage modernization was slower than in New Spain but faster than in the South-Central Andes.[5] This modernization encompassed the production of milled coinage and the creation of a purchase fund that allowed mints to buy up to 80% of bullion bars on sight (Torres, 2014, p. 120). As in New Spain, this fund reduced the market power of bullion merchants.[6] Secondly, New Granada's mintage services were more decentralized, with two mints operating permanently after 1772 in Bogotá and Popayán (Torres, 2014, p. 125). Despite having a smaller population and a smaller bullion production, New Granada did not suffer from a centralized mintage service like New Spain. Lastly, the range of denominations issued in New Granada's mints was unusual in the context of the Empire, specializing in the issuance of gold coins and *cuartillos*, the coins of the smallest denomination that were useful for petty trade (Torres, 2013b, p. 196). The money factories of Mexico City, Lima, and Potosí only issued these coins after 1791 in the context of a huge debate about the shortage of small change.[7]

North Andean money supply was complemented with flows from neighboring viceroyalties. In a report about the currency of the viceroyalty, the Viceroy stated what other officials also reported continuously to the authorities in Madrid: most of the money supply was composed of Peruvian silver coins (*peruleras*) and a small amount of silver specie from Guatemala and Mexico City (Torres, 2013a, pp. 125–136). These inflows, however, were a matter of concern among North Andean authorities because they were composed chiefly of *macuquinas* whose bullion content was between 12–30% below its face value (Torres, 2014, p. 124). This devaluation created huge debates across the Empire. Authorities even called these monies the "authentic provincial currency of the colonies" in reference to the provincial coins issued in Spain with lower intrinsic value (AGI, Indiferente, 1769).

In several reports, royal officers from Bogotá and other provinces stated that the gap between the intrinsic and extrinsic value of the *macuquinas* segmented the monetary market. The situation seems to have reached notable proportions in the late 1790s (AGN, C., Mon., v. 3, ff. 902–960; v. 4, ff. 550–551; AGN, C., Misc., v. 94, ff. 578–579). In the business of merchants, bullion specialists, and tax farmers, these coins circulated by weight and not by tale (Silvestre, 1988, p. 462). The non-specialists – most of the wage workers, natives, and artisans – traded these coins at face value. This dichotomy raised a classic case of information asymmetry.[8] Treasury officials were also caught in this dilemma. Nicolás Tanco, the director of the Royal Post Office in Bogotá, pointed out that mail services were mostly paid in *macuquina*. Royal and viceregal decrees stated that these coins should be received at face value in the payment of taxes if the "columns and seals were still visible". Yet, when Tanco tried to pay his workers and contractors with old coins, they protested since "they are only traded by weight in the stores of the city" (AGN, C., Corr. Cund., v. 1, ff. 564–566).

In Cartagena, military officers complained frequently about the low quality of coins disbursed by the royal treasuries, with most store owners receiving Peruvian coins that flowed from Bogotá and Quito by weight and not by face value (AGN, C., Mil., v. 43, ff. 858–862). Reports of this sort forced the authorities to take measures. The Viceroy reiterated the old decrees that ordered the inhabitants of the kingdom to receive the *macuquinas* at face value (AGN, C., Mon., v.3, ff. 950–951). As expected, this measure was not enforced, and market segmentation was still operating up to 1810 in Bogotá, Popayán, Cartagena, and other urban centers (AGN, C., Mon., v.4, ff. 550–551).

The circulation at face value of undervalued coins provided fertile soil for the activation of Gresham's law, creating large profits for money changers and merchants. Debates have ensued about the extent to which bad coins (*macuquinas*) drove the good ones (*cordoncillo*) out or drove them to a premium (Torres, 2021, pp. 128–132). The fluctuation of premiums and the variety of coins shaped the microeconomic operation of merchants, royal treasurers, and businessmen, increasing transaction costs and promoting counterfeiting. As the viceroys and other officials reiterated, the main remedy to such a situation was a general recoinage, a policy impossible to achieve given the enormous gap between the intrinsic and extrinsic value of the coins (Torres, 2021, pp. 58–59). In the context of the financial stringencies of the Atlantic Wars, nobody dared to propose new taxes to cover the expenses of a recoinage. Worldly philosophers came up with audacious proposals. Though never implemented, these proposals allow us to distill some contours of the late colonial monetary thought.

2.4 Viceregal Money Doctors

Late colonial monetary policymakers and thinkers tended to fall into three broad groups. First, there was a conservative clique that advocated law enforcement, endorsing punishments to those who rejected trading at face value the old coins while proposing bans on the flows of Peruvian and Mexican *macuquinas* via Quito and Cúcuta. The second group, composed of moderate reformists, promoted piecemeal recoinages financed with modest debasements and new foundries to stop smuggling. Finally, the late colonial economic challenges fueled a circle of radical reformists who envisioned a deep overhaul of the monetary system, proposing large debasements and the adoption of paper money and copper coinage.[9] Despite their acute differences, the three groups shared a similar intellectual toolbox with three main elements: (1) the use of history and comparative analysis to back up specific claims; (2) the development of empirical methods to measure the money supply; and (3) the discussion of modern theories of money developed in Europe to organize their reasoning.

A good starting point to peruse the intellectual toolbox of the three groups is the analysis of the late colonial schemes to issue copper coins. The adoption of trimetallism was a policy contemplated since the early years of colonial rule but gained new momentum during the Bourbon era (Romano, 2004, pp. 293–294). In the early 1750s, a report written by Francisco Herrán, a resident of Cartagena, claimed that only copper coinage could solve the "scarcity of money of this kingdom", in particular the proper supply of small change (AGN, C., Contr., v.1 ff. 999–1000; AGI, Ultramar, 837).[10] Viceroy Sebastián Eslava and his advisers rejected Herrán's proposal by arguing that the range of coinage denominations was appropriate to the kingdom's price level. Most importantly, in their view, the adoption of such a policy would lead to "an alteration of the value of our goods, prompting the exportation of our [silver and gold] coins in favor of foreigners". They concluded that "the proposal reminds us of Lycurgus [of Sparta] who wanted to vanish of his republic gold and silver in favor of copper on the grounds that this vile metal will diminish the greed of the citizens" (AGN, C., Contr., v.1 ff. 999–1000).

The fear of inflation and specie outflows kept at bay further proposals in favor of copper coins. In the late 1790s, in the context of empire-wide debates about small change, the complaints about the quality of the *macuquinas*, and the lack of coinage in the growing economies of Cuba, Venezuela, and Puerto Rico, some policymakers revived the case for trimetallism (AGI, indiferente, 1767; AGI, Ultramar, 837). The treasurer of Havana's royal treasury, for instance, argued that the lack of small change and the variable intrinsic content of the old coins had hampered the expansion of trade across the Spanish Caribbean possession, inviting authorities in New Spain, New Granada, and Venezuela to support the injection of copper coins. Most officers and merchants in New Granada criticized these projects (AGI, Indiferente, 1767; AGI, Santa Fe, 831). The General Attorney Bogotá's Royal Court, José Antonio Berrío, stated that the issuance of copper "will alter the price of everything, as history has taught us throughout centuries". He provided comments on the great debasement in England during the reign of Henry VII and the negative effect of copper coinage in Spain on prices and manufacturing in the seventeenth century. Berrío elaborated an assertion in line with Hume's specie flow mechanism, emphasizing how coins of a third metal hamper the capacity of inflation/outflow cycles to correct trade imbalances (AGN, C., Contr., v.1 ff. 1000–1001).[11] Years after, José Ignacio de Pombo, a Popayán-born merchant who operated in Cartagena and wrote reports considered fine pieces of political economy, expressed a more elaborated explanation of the impact of specie flows on prices and trade:

> The abundance of money in an industrious and judicious country is as bad as its scarcity. The abundance elevates the value of wages, lands, productions, and industries, destroying them since they are now less competitive vis-à-vis the foreigner's production. That's what happened in Spain after the discovery of America, since the value of coins (el valor de los signos) surpassed the value of goods, and given the incapacity of the government to match both, the latter's price increased in the same proportion as the former. Foreigners, then, came and sold their wares at half the price and destroyed the Peninsula's agriculture and industry.
>
> (Pombo, 2010, p. 249)

Neither Pombo nor Berrío quoted Hume, but their analysis shows a certain exposure to the theories in vogue that critiqued the basic tenants of bullionism and mercantilism.[12] Bogotá's city councilors and trade deputies also seconded Berrío in attacking the prospects of copper coinage, pointing out that this measure "will cause a drainage of gold and silver coins, elevate our prices, restrict trade, and create poverty as the history of coinage in Spain has shown". In addition, the injection of coins of a third metal would alter the anchor of bimetallism: "In the current system, the exchange of gold for silver and vice versa is the main support of the internal trade of these kingdoms. With copper, dealers and landowners will be compelled to exchange copper for silver and silver for gold, altering the premiums between the two precious metals."[13]

Most officials and merchants who refused to endorse the issuance of copper proposed few changes to monetary matters. Even though recognizing the problems generated by the broad mosaic of coins circulating, they saw it as a lesser evil than the prospects of copper coinage or further manipulation of coinage. The failure of the 1772 recoinage also convinced most of them that without enough funds, any attempts at uniformizing the money supply would face resistance from coin holders. The visitor general Gutiérrez de Piñeres, who was less judicious in other financial matters, warned that "a forceful recoinage of the *macuquina* would cause dangerous reactions in this kingdom since it is widely used in internal trade". He recommended, instead, monitoring the silver flows from New Spain and Peru that entered the kingdom via Cúcuta and Quito (AGI, Ultramar, 837). Viceroys in the 1780s and 1790s issued several decrees enforcing the trading of coins at face value while regulating the flow of silver coins of the *situados*, the fiscal transfers that linked the different treasuries of the Empire. They struggled to enforce royal decrees that enacted that the Quito *situado* was to be transferred in full-bodied coins, with the merchants in charge of transporting the coins forced to deliver them in the same quality as received (Torres, 2013a, pp. 95–100).

The conservative stance dominated the discussions, but some moderate reformists emerged among the ranks of the Bourbon bureaucracy. Miguel de Santiesteban, the superintendent of Bogotá's mint, recommended in the 1750s subsidizing the issuance of *cuartillos* by exchanging silver bars for doubloons, diminishing seignorage given the higher average cost of producing small coins (AGI, Ultramar, 837).[14] Francisco Silvestre, former Antioquia governor and official of the viceregal court, proposed in the 1790s the creation of a fund whose proceeds were to come from small transit taxes on European merchandise to exchange *macuquinas* at face value in a process that was to be carried out over ten years (Silvestre, 1988, pp. 452–459).

Another source of monetary ideas and policies came exogenously, from the empire-wide projects to debase significantly silver coins, issuing a *moneda provincial* that was to circulate only in the Indies. The proposal, sponsored by reformist José de Galvez and intendants and treasurers from Caracas and Havana, sought to reduce the intrinsic value of silver coins by 30–40%, providing incentives to recast the *macuquinas* into milled coins and avoiding its flow to foreign colonies (AGI, Ultramar, 837; AGI, Santa Fe, 831).[15] Most authorities in New Granada opposed the project. Among them was the Count of Casa Valencia, a Popayán-born miner and former treasurer of the mint of that city. In the 1790s he was appointed chair of the Madrid Coin Committee (*Junta de Moneda*) that oversaw discussion of the Empire's monetary affairs. In his view, "any reduction in the intrinsic value of gold and silver coins would lead to the elevation of prices, limitless opportunities for counterfeiters, and the importation of foreign wares that will be correspondently cheaper". Echoing the reports of other officials, he stated that the problem was not the quantity but the quality of coins, since most colonies in the Caribbean enjoyed sizable trade surpluses. Building upon reports sent from Venezuela and other regions, he calculated that the money supply was roughly two-thirds of the value of exports plus the value of internal trade, a method that according to him was used widely in Europe. Valencia recommended enacting a general recoinage like the one carried out in England in the 1690s, with the creation of a bank providing the financial funds to cover the gap between the intrinsic and extrinsic value of the coins (AGI, Indiferente, 1767).

The *moneda provincial* plan also elicited a response from moderate reformists. Francisco de Zalamea, an official of Bogotá's mint, crafted two proposals to solve the monetary maladies of the kingdom without undertaking large debasements (AGI, Santa Fe, 831–832).[16] The first was the creation of a fund to purchase gold bars in Cartagena and other regions to tap the revenues from the smuggled bullion that flowed out to foreign colonies. These funds, in his view, would provide revenues to purchase full-bodied coins in New Spain. The second proposal consisted of an alteration of the mint's bimetallic ratios, debasing silver moderately to equilibrate Spain's ratio vis-à-vis the international level. As in the first proposal, the revenues from the debasement would facilitate the recoinage of the *macuquinas* while the reduction in mint par would lessen minting costs. Authorities in New Granada and Spain did not support either proposal. The lack of funds to establish the purchase funds and the rapid changes in international bimetallic ratios created uncertainty about small changes in mint parities. Some conservatives stated that additional debasements to those enacted in 1772 and 1786 would affect the confidence of merchants in colonial coins (AGI, Santa Fe, 831–832).

The Spanish authorities' incapacity to reform coinage fueled the emergence of radical proposals from local businessmen and intellectuals who included the coinage problem in broader critiques of colonial rule. Antonio Nariño, a Bogotá-based merchant who belonged to a clique of conspirators who eventually ascended to power after the 1810 revolution, was one of the most important exponents of anticolonial rhetoric. In 1797 he submitted a proposal to the Viceroy to overhaul economic policy in the kingdom. In his view, among the most important issues that impeded the economic expansion of the region was the ubiquitous presence of the *macuquina* and the "scarcity of [good] coins, since its quantity is not proportional to the internal exchange of the kingdom". He advocated the issuance of paper money and copper coins, accompanied by the issuance of bonds to solve the viceroyalty's financial problems. Nariño reasoned that the adoption of unbacked money would expand the money supply, encourage the exportation of the *macuquina*, and reduce the overreliance of the kingdom on gold as the main export commodity. The *de facto* demonetization of precious metals would fuel a short-term expansion of European and Asian imports and, in the medium term, once the reservoir of old coins ran out, merchants would be compelled to invest in export agriculture, creating new jobs and conduits of trade. The copper issuances would exert a similar effect, replacing the *macuquina* in small transactions, shifting the demand for copper, and transforming the region into a net exporter of this metal. In his words, "our mines in Moniquirá will be a new Potosí" (Nariño, 2010, pp. 49–65).

Regardless of the feasibility of his proposals, Nariño's case for money expansion was accompanied by an empirical and theoretical sophistication that reflects the intense intellectual milieu of late eighteenth-century New Granada. He documented the importance of paper and copper circulation in Europe and the United States while perusing episodes in monetary history such as Newton's role in English money reforms to back up his ideas. He developed basic statistics to calculate the region's GDP through consumption expenditure, showing a deep familiarity with the basic contentions of physiocracy and the quantity theory of money. In the late colonial period, Nariño and other radical reformers may have appeared as quixotic intellectuals in a world at change. Napoleon's invasion, however, transformed these *quijotes* into policymakers.

2.5 Transforming the Monetary Landscape

The Atlantic Wars reached a new, transformative force when French armies forced the abdication of Charles IV and the imprisonment of his legitimate heir, Ferdinand VII.[17] Immediately, the Spanish city councils (*cabildos*), which under imperial rule had operated as the microcosm of local politics, revolted against the French and established *juntas* to resume sovereignty after the *vacatio regis*.[18] In the colonies, several city councils followed suit, summoning similar *juntas* to claim sovereignty and autonomy. Economic and financial crisis after years of trade blockades and unpopular policies fueled the impact of political crisis, eliciting regional responses and opening an enormous breach between landed entrepreneurs, middle-scale merchants, and imperial authorities across the Atlantic basin (Adelman, 2006, pp. 106–10; Stein and Stein, 2009, pp. 52–53).

In New Granada, the creation of local *juntas* and the eventual removal of the Viceroy in 1810 led to a well-known mosaic of political alternatives that soon turned into open warfare. The confrontation gravitated around three broad blocks. Bogotá strove to revendicate its centrality and proceeded to create a central state, Cundinamarca, that absorbed some of the provinces in its environs. The states of Cartagena, Antioquia, Neiva, Pamplona, and Tunja, in turn, led a federalist counterpoint, the *Provincias Unidas de la Nueva Granada*, that managed to incorporate several other provinces in the western and eastern portion of the former viceroyalty.[19] Finally, the royalists were confined to two poles, Santa Marta and Panama in the Atlantic, and Pasto, Cuenca, and Guayaquil in the south.

The revolution brought profound changes in the fiscal and monetary structure of the viceroyalty. In Cundinamarca and the *Provincias Unidas*, authorities carried out a deep fiscal reform, eliminating some monopolies, indigenous tributes, and other levies considered damaging to economic growth. The loyalist regions were also forced to innovate, adopting *ad hoc* measures to attract popular support while accepting some of the liberal precepts of the Cádiz Constitution enacted in 1812. Given the soaring size of war expenditures and the shrinking flow of revenues after the reforms, the three blocks had to finance the war through monetary inflation. This opened a Pandora's box of financial experimentation, creating macroeconomic challenges that have been studied by generations of scholars.[20]

Even though the Northern Andes did not experience a mintage decentralization like the one that unfolded in New Spain in the 1810s, disputes over seignorage and debasement rates fueled attempts at creating new mints, while disagreements over fiscal flows led to the dislocation of the *situados*, with a profound impact on liquidity and trade connections (Torres, 2021, pp. 359–370). Not surprisingly, the first regions that resorted to monetary expansion were those that were affected by the end of Spanish fiscal transfers. Cartagena, for instance, issued unbacked paper money and copper coins early in 1812 (Meisel, 2019, pp. 266–269). Mompox also experimented with fiat money while Santa Marta became the mint center of the royalists in the region (Barriga, 1969, pp. 127–130). The mint officials in Santa Marta harnessed Mexican silver, via Panama trade, to issue debased silver coins known as *provincial legítima* or simply as *moneda de Santa Marta*. The authorities also authorized the minting of copper coins in *medios* and *reales* and formed a fund to buy silver in jewels and ornaments (AGN, EOR, Casa de Moneda, Box 11, ff. 46–53 and 107–110).[21] In the south, Popayán also joined the innovation pattern by issuing copper and silver coins of different intrinsic values.[22]

In Bogotá, the revolutionary authorities did not issue paper money or copper coins. However, in 1813, the authorities, headed by Antonio Nariño, decided to mint debased silver monies of 7 *dineros* (0.538 fine) called *moneda provincial de Cundinamarca* or *moneda de la China* (Barriga, 1969, pp. 145–148). Silverplate and the recoinage of the *macuquinas* sourced the bullion to issue the new coins. This operation was highly profitable since the old monies had higher intrinsic value than the new ones despite their weight loss (AGN, EOR, Casa de Moneda, Box 11, ff. 216–224 and 236). In parallel with the issue of these debased coins, the mint continued to issue silver *fuertes* according to the Spanish ordinances. Most of the *plata de cimiento* and the silver from mines were processed in this manner (Barriga, 1969, pp. 543–545). The Cundinamarca authorities adopted, then, a *de facto* dual approach to silver mintage that possibly helped to constrain the negative effects of monetary expansion.

The twilight of the first wave of revolutionary governments in the Northern Andes came in 1815. A year before, Ferdinand VII returned to the throne, abolished the liberal reforms undertaken by the Cádiz *Cortes*, and proceeded to assemble an army to restore his rule in the colonies. By that time, Captain General Francisco Montalvo, in the north, and the president of the Quito *Audiencia* Toribio Montes, in the south, had already made important inroads. In 1816 Ferdinand's army, the so-called Expeditionary Army led by Pablo Morillo, completed the task. The restoration of Spanish rule in the region, as Daniel Gutiérrez has pointed out, was short-lived because Morillo's leadership created a huge coordination problem with civilian authorities, weakened the legitimacy of the regime through arbitrary exactions of manpower and resources, and elicited an unprecedented spiral of violence (Gutiérrez, 2016, pp. 55–56).

After years of conflict, the monetary landscape that the restorationists found in 1816 was composed of a diverse set of coins of different metals. Morillo and Montalvo committed themselves to restore the pre-war monetary regime and proceeded to stop the issuance of debased coins and dismantle Santa Marta's mint (AGN, EOR, Casa de Moneda, Box 11, Folder 2 ff. 34–66; Montalvo, 1988, pp. 272–273). In addition, they blocked any other innovation in terms of the location of mintage facilities and prohibited the issuance of copper coins. The uniformization of the money supply, however, proved an insurmountable challenge. The restorationists managed to increase the purchase funds of the two mints and restored the quality of the new coins to the Spanish ordinances but lacked the resources to undertake a viceregal-wide recoinage process (Torres, 2021, pp. 396–401).

The monetary heterogeneity created huge challenges for the royal treasuries since they kept the old colonial decrees that made them receive coins at face value. Complaints soon started to emerge when the proceeds from taxes were made in coins of extremely low quality. Customs records started to differentiate between good and bad *macuquinas* and officials reported high rates of counterfeiting in their accounts (Torres, 2021, pp. 398–399). It is in this context that a new set of money doctors emerged to provide some solutions. Most of those solutions failed, creating little studied political consequences.

2.6 Monetary Ideas in the Context of Revolution and Counterrevolution

The intellectuals, businessmen, and officials who crafted monetary proposals during the late colonial period found in the Independence Wars fertile soil to put into practice their ideas. The conservative clique emphasized the negative impact of monetary inflation, documenting how the lack of sound money hampered market transactions. They not only proposed a return to the pre-1810 system, but also a revindication of the King's monetary sovereignty to undertake costly projects of recoinage. The reformists recognized the population's lack of confidence in the coins circulating, but they proposed gradual methods to combat monetary inflation and heterogeneity. The revolutionaries, finally, saw the monetary expansion as a new opportunity for economic and financial modernization, emphasizing how the new coins fostered market deepening and widening.

One of the well-known debates regarding monetary changes during the Independence Wars was the one between Antonio Nariño and Manuel de Pombo. The latter, a mint official and brother of José Ignacio de Pombo, opposed the former's attempt at monetary expansion (AGN, AAI, Guerra y Marina, v. 135, f. 90–94). As Roberto Junguito has rightly pointed out, Pombo was one of the first exponents of the advantage of having independent monetary institutions (Junguito, 2012, pp. 111–114). The sophistication and nature of his proposals, however, deserve further attention. In contrast to late colonial commentators, he opposed monetary innovation, invoking the impact of debasements on the local and international confidence in coinage, rather than elaborating on their impact on prices and bullion flows. Pombo advocated institutional modernization, with debasements and monetary changes enacted only under authorization by the legislative branch of government, condemning Nariño's executive powers in this regard.[23]

Pombo's critiques transcended the realm of ideas since he actively reported to the authorities in Cartagena and other ports about the quality of Bogotá's coinage while participating actively in the public debates about monetary matters. Naturally, he considered the circulation of old and debased coins an issue that should be solved since "legitimacy and stamp of the coins are the pillars of public prosperity". Yet, in contrast to the most conservative defenders of sound money, he advocated a slow recoinage financed with seignorage revenues. He pondered that proceeds from mintage services should not be "fiscal revenues to sustain the luxury of the Bourbons", but funds to help the modernization of the two mints and to fund the recasting of old coins (Barriga 1969, p. 298). His proposal constituted a moderate alternative amid a conservative backlash and a feverish drive to reform the colonial monetary system (Torres, 2021, pp 361–365). This moderate instance was also adopted, at least initially, by lawyers and businessmen connected to the government of the *Provincias Unidas*, such as Camilo Torres who contended with Nariño regarding monetary sovereignty and the need to put the two mints under the federal government which would guarantee the intrinsic value of coins.[24] These debates no doubt helped to temper the negative impacts of monetary manipulation.

Nariño, as stated above, argued in favor of monetary expansion not only to cope with the fiscal crisis but also to promote market deepening and eliminate monetary heterogeneity. The issuance of the *chinas* was publicized in the official press as the best mechanism to get rid of the *macuquinas* and encourage retail trade (Hernández, 1990, 365–375). Miguel de Pombo, a cousin of Manuel and famously known for his translation into Spanish of the US Constitution, proposed to the *Provincias Unidas* a project to issue copper coins using a similar argument to those of Nariño.[25] Pombo's proposal sought to solve four interrelated problems. First, the financial crisis of the revolutionary government. Second, the growing contraction of the money supply due to the "collapse of the Chocó mines and the obstruction of the trade that via Maracaibo and Guayaquil used to infuse silver pesos from Peru and Mexico". Third, the need to smelt the old *macuquinas* whose lack of intrinsic content had fueled counterfeiting. Finally, the need to provide small change.

In line with late colonial commentators, Pombo used history to support his proposal, providing insights into the positive effects of copper coinage on domestic trade in antiquity and the modern era. He also emphasized the success of copper issuances in Cartagena and Popayán. In the latter, argued Pombo, "the value of silver and gold coins were not affected by the circulation of copper ones". In Cartagena, the circulation of the *chinas*, in turn, provided "vital aid to their war efforts". He proposed the issuance of 500,000 silver pesos in different denominations at an estimated cost of 20,000 silver pesos in copper from Moniquirá. It is not clear how Pombo came up with this number but, in his view, this quantity was enough to revive trade since "half-million pesos in government expenditures are equivalent to the same amount in the pockets and expenditures of the population". The injection of copper, in addition, would help to "equilibrate" the kingdom's price level since the money demand of wars, the collapse of the mining, and the end of silver flows from Maracaibo and Guayaquil, had "unmatched the number of coins circulating and the value of the things".

Pombo's assumption about the population's confidence in copper issuances was criticized by conservatives and reformists alike. An anonymous proposal submitted to the *Provincias Unidas* in 1815 supported Pombo's project but with a key modification: the issuance of copper coins should be carried out by a bank that was to guarantee the exchange of copper for silver or gold at the holder's behest.[26] The anonymous writer emphasized that copper issuances had similar effects to those of unbacked paper money and constituted an attack on the "property rights" of the public. By indicating the failures of Cartagena's experience with paper money, he concurred with other contemporary commentators on the perils of unchecked emissions. Simón Bolívar, for instance, in his famous "Cartagena Manifesto", argued in 1812 that paper money issuances violated property rights, fueling popular support for the King's cause (1980, pp. 10–11). Thus, the bank's role in copper issuances was to channel the revenues from the new taxes enacted by the *Provincias Unidas* to create reserves of 30–50% to back up the issuance of copper coins. This would reinforce the population's confidence in the new coins while solving the financial problems of the government and remedying the lack of silver flows from Maracaibo and Guayaquil.

2.7 Recoinage and Sovereignty

By the time the restorationists affirmed their power in 1816, a plethora of coins of different qualities and ages dominated the New Granadan money supply. Right after being appointed in 1817, Viceroy Juan de Sámano received orders from Madrid to undertake a costly process of recoinage. The King saw the circulation of "revolutionary coins" as a threat to his sovereign power, since "issuing coins with the lawful stamps is the symbol of [his] supreme authority" (AGN, AAII, R.H., F, box 7, 1, f. 212). In 1818, Sámano assembled a coin committee (CC) (*comisión de moneda*) to craft proposals to carry out the King's orders. The CC was composed of the higher echelons of the viceregal bureaucracy, including members from the Royal High Court, the Court of Accounts, the Royal Treasuries, and Bogotá's mint. After years of warfare, several of the committee members were new in the kingdom while others were loyalists with little experience in policymaking.[27]

Before the CC started to exercise its craft, local authorities had already sent several complaints about the monetary maladies of the viceroyalty. The most common complaint was the difficulty in identifying counterfeit coins, given the variable intrinsic content of the monies issued by both royalists and insurgents. Local authorities proposed a mosaic of far-fetched solutions. In Cartagena and Mompox, the officials of the royal treasuries and the Post Office recommended deploying essayers to periodically identify the counterfeit monies across the river and seaports (AGN, AAII, R.H., F, box 7,1, ff. 192–196). In Honda, the city council proposed regulating the business hours of the stores (*pulperías*) to monitor the flow of coins (AGN, AAII, R.H., F, box 7, 1, ff. 192–196). Sámano and his clique tried a well-known but ineffective policy: the enforcement of the orders to receive legitimate coins at face value, disregarding their intrinsic content (Torres, 2021, pp. 406–408).

The CC acted more cautiously, collecting reports on the aggregate configuration of the kingdom's money supply. The reports were accompanied by suggestions that reflected once more the rich toolbox of monetary policymakers. Bogotá's mint superintendent, José Enriquez Guzmán, was the first to provide data on the money supply of the kingdom, identifying three broad categories of coins circulating (AGN, AAII, R.H., F, box 6, 3, ff. 200–203). First, the old *macuquinas*, including coins of Peruvian and Mexican origin. Second, "insurgent coins". And finally, the "Santa Marta monies issued by the order of the former Viceroy Francisco Montalvo", which also encompassed those introduced by the Expeditionary Army from Caracas and Maracaibo.

Regarding the *macuquina*, Enriquez suggested not undertaking a recoinage because the gap between their intrinsic and extrinsic value was on average 33%, a huge amount that the Treasury was not able to cover. He remarked how the gap created problems of monetary segmentation, but echoing late colonial assessments, this was a lesser evil given the fiscal crisis of the kingdom. As for the insurgent coins, he recommended paying them as if they were bullion since it was the population's fault they had received these "illegitimate coins". Monetary reform, then, in the view of the mint's superintendent, should focus on the third category, since it is "the most important currency of the kingdom, the cause of a widespread counterfeiter activity, and the target of foreign imitations" (AGN, AAII, R.H., F, box 6, 3, f. 202). Enriquez, however, recommended caution since the "alteration of the coin circulating (*signos en cirulación*) has well-known imprints on the price of all things". In his view, the collection of new taxes to fund the recoinage was a better choice than further altering "the kingdom's circulatory system".

The Court of Accounts, led by the veteran accountant Carlos Urisarri, provided more data and cautionary ideas to the viceregal authorities (AGN, AAII, R.H., F, box 6,3,f. 204–205). The kingdom, in his view, "was in constant agitation because of the circulation of bad coins". After compiling data from the archives, he calculated the face value of the coins to be smelted at roughly 1.5 million silver pesos, with the recoinage costs amounting to 750,000 silver pesos. Harnessing a method similar to that used in the late colonial era to calculate money supply by comparing exports and internal trade, he cautioned that a sudden recoinage could affect "the already weak commerce of this kingdom". Drawing examples from economic history, Urisarri advised instead lowering the coin's face value: "so, a coin of two reals should be received now at 1 real".[28]

Despite the cautionary suggestions of the reports, the CC decided to restore the monetary sovereignty of the King, no matter the cost. The Viceroy, famously known for his intransigency in other matters, followed the CC's advice. He ordered a direct tax of one percent to be levied on the value of all the properties of the viceroyalty to cover the cost of recoinage of the *provinciales* while the insurgent coins were to be bought as bullion (AGN, AA1, Historia, t. 25, f. 566–567). The two policies elicited critiques from local and provincial powers.[29]

By April 1819, the Viceroy had made up his mind and confirmed the recoinage and the collection of the direct tax. Three months later, roughly 740,000 silver pesos in *provinciales*, whose intrinsic value was approximately 412,820 silver pesos, had been funneled to Bogotá's mint (AHCM, SDa002).[30] In Popayán, the enforcement of the reform was weaker and only 17,819 silver pesos had been collected by late August (ACC, independencia, FyC, 799). The direct tax, in the meantime, failed to yield enough resources to cover the gap between the extrinsic and intrinsic value of the currency and, therefore, the recoinage of the old coins was extremely slow (AGN, C., Mon., t. 6, f. 799). Even though no data exist to measure the short-term macroeconomic effect of this measure, it is likely that the contraction of the money supply by this amount had important impacts on both prices and investments. Be that as it may, when Bolívar entered Bogotá in mid-August, he seized the coins collected and put them into circulation. In addition, he ordered that no innovation should be undertaken in monetary matters until the enacting of a constitution (Ortiz, 1965, pp. 246–249; Perilla, 2012, pp. 129–130). During the following two decades, no government dared to undertake a general recoinage. The meteoric military expansion of the revolutionaries in 1819 and 1820 was fueled, in part, by the liquidity released after Bogotá's fall and the unpopular policies of the last viceroy. Lopetedi, whose insights served to open this chapter, may have exaggerated his point, but the monetary decisions and ideas of the restorationists had unintended, yet deep political and economic consequences.

2.8 Final Remarks

The twilight of Bourbon rule in New Granada was an age of vibrant intellectual activity. Historians of Colombian economic thought have examined well-known reports of creoles, revolutionaries, and officials to study the emerging force of liberalism in the region, the growing critiques of Spanish colonialism and mercantilism, and the changing economic policies enacted by viceregal and republican authorities. Monetary ideas and policies, however, have remained poorly studied, with few scholars considering the synergy between intellectual discussions and concrete mintage practices. This chapter has engaged the literature by analyzing little-known reports crafted by a wide array of businessmen, mint and treasury officials, lawyers, and intellectuals in a context of political change and macroeconomic challenges. New Granadans were embedded not only into the expansive flow of ideas produced by worldly philosophers across the Atlantic basin but also into the financial transformations brought by the Atlantic Wars. Discussions about recoinage and debasements provided novel inputs to explore how problems of monetary experimentation and reform unfolded in New Granada's intellectual milieu.

The chapter found that monetary analysis has tended to rest on a toolbox of three main components. First, the use of history and comparative analysis to back up specific claims. New Granada's intellectuals and policymakers provided examples from the past to show how episodes of monetary experimentation and stability created problems and opportunities to guide economic reasoning. In addition, some commentators gathered data on monetary regimes in the United States and Europe, showing how other economies dealt with issues of the lack of small change and alleged specie scarcity. Second, New Granadans drew ideas from global monetary discussions and early modern economic theories to organize their proposals. Finally, some contemporaries developed methods to empirically calculate the region's money supply and other macroeconomic variables. Harnessing their experience as bullion merchants, miners, and mint officials, they creatively provided the empirical ground at a time when the development of statistical data was in its infancy.

The chapter also argued that the region's policymakers and intellectuals tended to fall into three broad groups. There was overlap and cross-pollination between the ideas of the three groups, but their ultimate conclusions and practices were distinctive. First, there was a conservative clique led by businessmen and officials in the higher echelons of the viceregal and republican bureaucracy. Despite recognizing the problem of monetary segmentation, they argued that the fiscal stringencies of the treasuries impeded a general recoinage. Instead, they advocated the enacting of laws forcing the receipt of coins at face value, the regulation of financial and bullion flows, and the rejection of changes in monetary regimes. When faced with the problem of monetary sovereignty after the 1810 revolution, this group decided to support a general recoinage through tax increases, severely affecting the political legitimacy of Bourbon rule.

A second group encompassed a small set of moderate reformists who advocated piecemeal solutions to the monetary maladies of the region. They opposed a deep transformation of the monetary regime, criticizing debasements, copper coinage, and other mechanisms of specie manipulation. Higher transaction costs, inflation, and loss of monetary sovereignty were the main reasons behind the rejection of monetary transformations. Yet, in contrast to conservatives, the reformists stated that recoinages were feasible despite the fiscal stringencies of both royalist and republican treasuries. They proposed an overhaul in seignorage and bullion taxation to provide funds to smelt the old and debased coins, advocating institutional independence of the mints vis-à-vis executive powers.

Finally, there was a small clique of radical thinkers and bureaucrats who proposed a deep change in the monetary regime, supporting debasements, trimetallism, and the issuance of fiat money. Though diverging on the mechanisms to achieve monetary expansion, radicals emphasized that such a policy would lead to the recoinage of the *macuquinas*, the provision of small change, and the expansion of economic activity. After 1810, when they became highly influential in the context of the Wars of Independence, radicals saw the financing of war via monetary inflation as a good opportunity to modernize the monetary regime.

The mélange of monetary ideas and policies reflected not only the sophistication and distinctiveness of New Granada's intellectual milieu but also how ideological discussions permeated monetary policies. The emerging radical ideas certainly pressed the authorities (both royalists and republicans) to craft concrete mechanisms to solve the monetary problems of the region. Conversely, once the radicals came to power, the presence of conservatives and reformists tempered the impact of monetary inflation. Once the loyalists struck back, in turn, popular reaction taught policymakers that the restoration of sound money was not a frictionless process. Ultimately, the monetary chaos survived several decades more, but the rich debates of the age contributed to starting the long-run tradition of sound monetary institutions in republican Colombia.

Archival Sources

ARCHIVO GENERAL DE INDIAS (AGI)
    Santa Fe: 831, 832.
    Indiferente: 1767,1769.
    Ultramar: 837.
ARCHIVO GENERAL DE LA NACION, COLOMBIA (AGN)
    Colonia (C.):
        Contrabando Cartas (Cont.): v.1, v.13.
        Correos Cundinamarca (Corr. Cund.): v.1.
        Milicias y Marina (Mil.): v.43.
        Miscelania (Misc.): v. 13, v. 94
        Monedas (Mon.): v. 3, v.4.
    Archivo Anexo I (AAI):
        Guerra y Marina: v.135.
    Archivo Anexo II (AAII):
        Real Hacienda (R.H.):
            Funcionarios (F.): box 6, 3; box 7,1.
    Enrique Ortega Ricaute (EOR):
        Casa Moneda: box 11.

ARCHIVO CENTRAL DEL CAUCA (ACC):
Independencia: FyC, 799.
ARCHIVO HISTÓRICO DE LA CASA DE LA MONEDA (AHCM)
Directores: SDa002

Newspapers

Correo de la Nueva Granada (Bogotá)

Printed Sources

Bolívar, S. (1980). *Escritos políticos*. Bogotá: El Áncora.
Hernández, G. (1990). *Archivo Nariño 1812–1814*. Bogotá, Presidencia de la República.
Montalvo, F. (1988). Instrucción sobre el estado en que deja el Nuevo Reino de Granada el Excelentísimo señor Virrey don Francisco de Montalvo, en 30 de enero de 1818 [...]. In *Relaciones e Informes de los Gobernantes de la Nueva Granada* v.3 (pp. 193–336). Bogotá: Banco Popular.
Nariño, A. (2010). Ensayo sobre un nuevo plan de administración en el Nuevo Reino de Granada [1797]. *Revista de Economía Institucional, 12*(23), 301–319.
Ortiz, S. (1965). *Colección de documentos para la historia de Colombia. V.2, época de la independencia*. Bogotá: Editorial El Voto Nacional.
Pombo, J. (2010). Informe del Real Consulado de Cartagena de Indias a la Suprema Junta Provincial de la misma [1810]. In *Escritos económicos: don Antonio de Narváez y don José Ignacio de Pombo* (pp. 223–364). Bogotá: Banco de la República.
Restrepo, J. (1860). *Memoria sobre amonedación de oro i plata en la Nueva Granada*. Bogotá: imprenta de la Nación.
Silvestre, F. (1988). *Relación de la provincia de Antioquia*. Medellin: Secretaría de Educación y Cultura de Antioquia.

Notes

1   The reports are in AGI, Santa Fe, 833 and 834. Some of them were published in Ortiz (1965, pp. 246–249 and 229–233). The Viceroyalty of the New Kingdom of Granada encompassed the territories of present-day Colombia, Ecuador, Panama, and Venezuela. By the late 1770s, the Captaincy of Venezuela was granted executive and judicial autonomy. For simplicity, we will use the terms "New Granada" and "the Kingdom" to refer to present-day Colombia. The capital of the viceroyalty, Santafé de Bogotá, was commonly known as "Santafé". Throughout this chapter we will use the term "Bogotá" to avoid confusion for readers not familiar with the history of the region.

2   The literature has focused on the emerging force of liberalism in the region, the growing critiques of Spanish colonialism and mercantilism, and the changing economic policies enacted by viceregal and republican authorities. See González, 1983; Rodríguez, 1989; Melo, 2015.

3   For the rules of the game of bimetallism, see Redish (2000, pp. 52–59) and Velde and Weber (2000, pp. 1210–1215).

4   Here I follow Nathan Sussman's model for preindustrial mintage activities (1993 and 1998). For New Granada see Torres (2013a, pp. 78–98; 2014, pp. 120–125).

5   Torres (2013b, pp. 79–82); for Mexico City see Soria (1994, pp. 28–29); for Lima and Potosí see Lazo (1992, pp. 105–108 and 180–188).

6 For the impact of the purchase fund in New Spain see Brading (2008, pp. 45–47) and Pérez (1988, pp. 140–141).

7 For this comparative approach, see Torres (2013b, pp. 198–200). For a rigorous analysis of the empire-wide discussions on the problem of small change, see Konove (2021).

8 For an application of asymmetry information analysis to monetary history see Dutu (2004, pp. 560–561).

9 Debates regarding monetary regimes in Europe also tended to fall into a three-fold set of ideological currents. See Rössner (2018, pp. 100–105).

10 As Angela Redish has suggested, contemporary complaints about coin scarcity due to an external drain referred not to quantity but to the quality of coins (1984, pp. 715–720). For New Granada see Meisel (1990, pp. 25–30) and Torres (2013a, pp. 59–63).

11 Berrío, who studied law in Bogotá, had extensive experience in the mechanics of finances and trade in the Indies, occupying key posts in the treasuries of Cartagena and Santo Domingo. See Restrepo (1954, pp. 483–484) and Burkholder and Chandler (1982, p. 47).

12 It is likely that the specie flow mechanism and other variants of the early quantity theory of money had been transmitted to late colonial commentators through the consultation of Adam Smith, whose works circulated in New Granada. The Salamanca School also provided important inputs. On Smith and Hume see Wennerlind (2000, pp. 77–80) and Curott (2017, pp. 324–326). On the Salamanca School and its imprints in the Atlantic world see Duve (2021, pp. 10–15). For the circulation of Smith in New Granada see Rodríguez (1989, pp. 94–96).

13 For the reports of the city council and the trade deputies see (AGN, C., Cont., v. 1, ff. 1002–1005) and (AGI, Ultramar, 837).

14 In terms of Equation (2.2) above, Santiestieban wanted to reduce S through bimetallic exchanges.

15 Some of these proposals sought to achieve this debasement by reducing F or N in Equation (2.1) above.

16 Before his appointment in the mint, Zalamea had traversed the Chocó mines as a gold merchant and magistrate, giving him firsthand experience of bullion flows. See (AGN, C., Misc., v. 13 ff, 91–120).

17 Recent literature has proposed a periodization to understand the collapse of the Empire that will be followed in this chapter: Interregnum (1808–1815), Restoration (1816–1820), and the Colombian years (1821–1830). See Gutiérrez (2010, pp 30–32); Gutiérrez (2016, pp. 29–31); Martínez (2018, pp. 15–21).

18 For a solid, empire-wide account of these years, see Chust (2007, pp.15–21).

19 On the magnitude of warfare during these years, see Pinto and Torres (2016, pp. 180–182).

20 For a broad overview of the fiscal transformation, see Pinto (2018, pp. 158–169).

21 Santa Marta authorities debased coinage through changes in both F and N in Equation (2.1) and changes in Q in Equation (2.2).

22 On the Popayán's copper coins, see Torres (2021, pp. 402–405). On the circulation of debased coins in the region, see the 1816 qualitative assessment of a former mint official (AGN, AAI, Guerra y Marina, v. 135, ff. 90–94).

23 Pombo's letter to Nariño was published in Barriga (1969, pp. 296–300).

24 See the missives of Torres and other lawyers in Hernández (1990, pp. 125–150 and 355–359).

25 See "Informe y voto de un diputado", *Correo de la Nueva Granada* Facsimile edition by Daniel Gutiérrez. Issue 16, Jan. 23, 1816. I want to thank Daniel Gutiérrez for sharing this reference with me.

26 See "Reflexiones económico-políticas un patriota", *Correo de la Nueva Granada* Facsimile edition by Daniel Gutiérrez, Issue 6, Nov. 14 1815.

27 For the changes in some of the echelons of the viceregal bureaucracy during the Restoration, see Gutiérrez and Torres (2021, pp. 285–289).
28 Urisarri, then, advocated a change in *V* in Equation (2.1) above.
29 See reports for Santa Marta, Cartagena, Honda, Mariquita, and Mompox in AGN, AA2, R.H, F, Box 6, Folder 3, f. 129–135 and 93–198.
30 The figures provided by this logbook roughly coincide with those provided by José Manuel Restrepo (1860, p. 13).

Bibliography

Adelman, J. (2006). *Sovereignty and revolution in the Iberian Atlantic*. New Jersey: Princeton University Press.
Barriga, A. (1969). *Historia de la casa de la moneda, v. 2*. Bogotá: Banco de la República.
Brading, D. (2008). *Miners and merchants in Bourbon Mexico 1763–1810*. Cambridge: Cambridge University Press.
Burkholder, M., & Chandler, D. (1982). *Biographical dictionary of audiencia ministers in the Americas, 1687–1821*. Michigan: Greenwood Press.
Céspedes, G. (1996). *Las casas de moneda en los reinos de indias, 1: Las cecas indianas en 1536–1825*. Madrid: Fabrica Nacional de Moneda y Timbre.
Chust, M. (2007). Un bienio transcendental. In M. Chust (Ed.), *1808: la eclosión juntera en el mundo hispano*. Mexico: Fondo de Cultura Económica.
Curott, N. (2017). Adam Smith's theory of money and banking. *Journal of the History of Economic Thought*, *39*(3), 323–347.
Dutu, R. (2004). Moneychangers, private information and Gresham's law in Late Medieval Europe. *Journal of Iberian and Latin American Economic History*, *22*(3), 555–571.
Duve, T. (2021). The school of Salamanca. A case of global knowledge production. In T. Duve, J. Egío, & C. Birr (Eds.), *The school of Salamanca: A case of Global Knowledge Production* (pp. 1–42). Leiden: Brill Press.
Fetter, F. (1959). The politics of the bullion report. *Economica*, *26*(102), 99–120.
Flandreau, M. (2004). *The glitter of gold. France, Bimetallism, and the emergence of the international gold standard, 1848–1873*. Oxford: Oxford University Press.
González, M. (1983). La Política Económica Virreinal en el Nuevo Reino de Granada: 1750–1810. *Anuario Colombiano de Historia Social y de la Cultura*, *11*, 129–186.
Gutiérrez, D. (2010). *Un Nuevo Reino: Geografía política, pactismo y diplomacia durante el interregno en Nueva Granada, 1808–1816*. Bogotá: Universidad Externado de Colombia.
Gutiérrez, D. (2016). *La restauración en la Nueva Granada (1815–1819)*. Bogotá: Universidad Externado de Colombia.
Gutiérrez, D., & Torres, J. (2021). *La compañía Barrio y Sordo. Negocios y Política en el Nuevo Reino de Granada y Venezuela, 1796–1820*. Bogotá: Universidad Externado de Colombia.
Hamilton E.J. (1944). Monetary problems in Spain and Spanish America 1731–1800. *The Journal of Economic History*, *4*(1), 21–48.
Irigoin, M. (2009a). Gresham on horseback: The monetary roots of Spanish American political fragmentation in the nineteenth century. *Economic History Review*, *62*(39), 551–575.

Irigoin, M. (2009b). The end of a silver era: The consequences of the breakdown of the Spanish peso standard in China and the United States, 1780s–1850s. *Journal of World History*, *20*(2), 207–243.

Jaramillo, J., Meisel, A., & Urrutia, M. (1997). Continuities and discontinuities in the fiscal and monetary institutions of New Granada, 1783–1850. In *Transferring wealth and power from the old to the new world: Monetary and fiscal institutions in the 17th through the 19th centuries* (pp. 414–450). New York: Cambridge University Press.

Junguito, R. (2012). Manuel de Pombo: precursor de la banca central independiente en época de la Independencia. *Ensayos Sobre Política Económica*, *30*(67), 104–127.

Konove, A. (2021). In search of a decent coin: The value of small change in Bourbon Spanish America. *Colonial Latin America Review*, *30*(4), 589–610.

Lazo, C. (1992). *Economía colonial y régimen monetario: Estructura e historia de la amonedación colonial (siglos XVII–XVIII)*. Lima: Banco Central de Reserva de Perú.

Martínez, A. (2018). *Historia de la Primera República de Colombia, 1819–1831*. Bogotá: Universidad del Rosario.

Meisel, A. (2019). La crisis fiscal de Cartagena en la era de la Independencia, 1808–1821. *Economía & Región*, *5*(1), 253–272.

Meisel, A. (1990). El patrón metálico 1821–1879', in *El Banco de la Republica: antecedentes, evolución y estructura* (pp. 3–55). Bogotá: Banco de la República.

Melo, J. (2015). Economistas y economía en la Nueva Granada, 1770–1810. In *La economía colonial de la Nueva Granada* (pp. 355–387). Bogotá: Fondo de Cultura Económica.

O'Brien, P., & Palma, N. (2020). Danger to the old lady of Threadneedle Street? The Bank Restriction Act and the regime shift to paper money, 1797–1821. *European Review of Economic History*, *24*(2), 390–426.

Palma, N. (2018). Money and modernization in early England. *Financial History Review*, *25*(3), 231–261.

Pérez, P. (1988). *Plata y libranzas: la articulación commercial del México borbónico*. Mexico: COLMEX.

Perilla, A. (2012). Financiamiento de los ejércitos en la guerra de independencia de Colombia. In H. Bonilla (Ed.), *Consecuencias económicas de la Independencia*. Bogotá: Universidad Nacional de Colombia.

Perlman, M. (1986). The bullionist controversy revisited. *Journal of Political Economy*, *94*(4), 745–762.

Pinto, J. (2018). *Entre colonia y república. Fiscalidad en Ecuador, Colombia y Venezuela, 1780–1845*. Bogotá: ICANH.

Pinto, J., & Torres, J. (2016). Guerra y fisco en la Nueva Granada, 1811–1824. *Revista de Economía Institucional*, *18*(35), 171–195.

Redish, A. (2000). *Bimetallism: An economic and historical analysis*. Cambridge: Cambridge University Press.

Redish, A. (1984). Why Was Specie Scarce in Colonial Economies? An Analysis of the Canadian Currency, 1796–1830. *The Journal of Economic History*, *44*(3), 713–728. doi:10.1017/S0022050700032332

Restrepo, J. (1954). *Biografía de los mandatarios y ministros de la Real Audiencia (1671–1819)*. Bogotá: Cromos.

Rodríguez, O. (1989). El pensamiento económico en la formación del estado Granadino, 1780–1830. *Historia Crítica*, *2*, 93–110.

Rolnick, A., Velde, F., & Weber, W. (1996). The debasement puzzle: An essay on medieval monetary history. *The Journal of Economic History*, *56*(4), 789–808.

Romano, R. (2004). *Mecanismos y elementos del sistema económico colonial americano, siglos XVI–XVIII*. Mexico: Fondo de Cultura Económica.

Rössner, P. (2018). Monetary theory and cameralist economic management, c.1500–1900 A.D.. *Journal of the History of Economic Thought*, *40*(1), 99–134.

Soria, V. (1994). *La Casa de Moneda de México bajo la administración borbónica, 1733–1821*. México: Universidad Autónoma Metropolitana.

Stein, B., & Stein, S. (2009). *Edge of crisis: War and trade in the Spanish Atlantic, 1789–1808*. Baltimore: Johns Hopkins University Press.

Sussman, N (1993). Debasements, royal revenues, and inflation in France during the hundred years' war, 1415–1422. *The Journal of Economic History*, *53*(1), 44–70.

Sussman, N. (1998). The late medieval bullion famine reconsidered. *The Journal of Economic History*, *58*(1), 126–154.

Torres, J. (2013a). *Minería y moneda en el Nuevo Reino de Granada. El desempeño económico en la segunda mitad del siglo XVIII*. Bogotá: ICANH.

Torres, J. (2013b). Sencillos y piezas de a ocho. El problema de la moneda de baja denominación en el Nuevo Reino de Granada en la segunda mitad del siglo XVIII. *Anuario Colombiano de Historia Social y de la Cultura*, *40*(1), 179–212.

Torres, J. (2014). Monedas de antiguo y nuevo cuño: envilecimiento y reacuñación en el Nuevo Reino de Granada en la segunda mitad del siglo XVIII. *Memoria y Sociedad*, *18*(36), 121–136.

Torres, J. (2021). *Trade in a changing world: Gold, silver, and commodity flows in the Northern Andes 1780–1840*, PhD thesis, Georgetown University, Washington D.C.

Velde, F., & Weber, W. (2000). A model of bimetallism. *Journal of Political Economy*, *108*(6), 1210–1234.

Wennerlind, C. (2000). The human paternity to Adam Smith's theory of money. *History of Economic Ideas*, *8*(1), 77–97.

3 Rhetoric and Practice

Protectionism and Free Trade in the Second Half of the 19th Century

Edna Carolina Sastoque

3.1 Introduction

Forty difficult years after independence from Spain, the mid-century liberal reforms in Nueva Granada brought new business and political opportunities. A new economic model was debated and implemented, and the recently created conservative and liberal parties were building new narratives against the background of classical liberal thought. The economic and political debate of the time has been traditionally presented as confronting the conservatives who defended "order" and therefore "protectionism"—and the liberals—who stood for "freedoms" and thus "free trade". This simplified view reflects the emergence of an alignment among interest groups that led to a cultural change and the confrontation between liberal and anti-liberal positions, the former taking inspiration from England and the United States and the latter from France and Prussia. However, the story is not that simple.

This institutional conflict also meant a generational change, with the first national leaders—educated in republican schools—coming to the fore. As shown in Chapter 1, these leaders had been exposed to a much broader array of foreign ideas than any of their predecessors (Martínez, 2001; Safford, 1989). They broke from the doctrine of monopoly and Spanish mercantilism and embraced *laissez-faire, laissez passer*, regardless of their political party. Their differences were not related to the convenience of free trade but instead to whether it should be applied to all aspects of social action.[1]

Most general liberal economic principles were widely accepted in Nueva Granada, except for those who rejected liberal anticlericalism and the artisans who fought against trade liberalization. These principles were not a monopoly of any sector. Nevertheless, the debate between protectionism and free trade played a role in the country's construction and the configuration of the political and social debate of that period. In this chapter, we explore two reasons: first, it is not always possible to separate this debate from the more general discussion about fully embracing *laissez-faire* in other spheres of social action; second, the multiple ways of producing and communicating ideas.

Tracing this specific feature of the debate confirms what we have found in the first two chapters and what will also be evident in the rest of this book: foreign ideas were not replicated without criticism. They permeated different

DOI: 10.4324/9781003289241-4

social circles, were adopted or discarded according to the specific context and produced heterogeneous forms of communication. Using primary and secondary sources, including the official records dating from 1846 through 1900, newspapers, books, and memoirs of those who actively participated in the debate, this chapter proposes a periodization of the free trade v. protectionism debate, by reconstructing the account of the actors and their positions.

The work of Adam Smith, Jeremy Bentham, Frédéric Bastiat, Jean-Baptiste Say, Anne Robert Jacques Turgot, David Ricardo, Thomas Malthus, John Stuart Mill, and Friedrich List, among others, inspired and fueled the national debate on what wealth was and how it was created (Samper, 1852; Murillo, 1853/1979; González, 1865/1981c, etc.). The debate was vital to understand how different economic systems, free trade, or protectionism would better suit the search for national prosperity. The history of the debate builds upon three aspects: first, the prominent grasp figures had of the scientific method and the theories and ideas at hand, and how they sometimes changed their minds toward more radical positions; second, the influence of political discussions on how the ideas were interpreted, transformed and applied,[2] and finally, the pressure by political parties to make people who were perceived as too radical moderate their views under threat of being accused of betrayal or censorship. Depending on the circumstances, the topic addressed, and the type of text, it is sometimes possible to perceive if there was a more prevalent aspect or if there was a mixture of them.

What were the issues addressed? Which were the prevailing techniques for communicating contending opinions? What did the parties seek? In order to answer these questions, this chapter explores three periods of the debate: (1) 1845–1863, self-education, travel, and opinion forming; (2) 1864–1885, towards a precise concept definition, expanding the ideological spectrum and developing pedagogy; and (3) 1886–1900, from moderate interventionism to protection policy. We then systematically review the reports of the Memoirs of the Ministry of Finance and the Treasury (1846–1900) as an example of rhetorical, legislative, and institutional commitment.

3.2 1845–1863: Between Self-education, Travel, and Opinion Forming

The intellectuals participating in the debate were liberal and conservative public officers, politicians, soldiers, professors, judges, and businesspeople. They were well traveled, some due to banishment or exile, others because of diplomatic appointments or studies, some due to a combination or all of these reasons. They were the object of admiration and envy, and their journeys abroad were momentous for their close social circles, as for their political, business, and even family ties (Cordovez Moure, 1893/1957; Safford, 1989; Martínez, 2001). These trips also offered them the opportunity to explore political economy beyond the course some had to follow in the university (see Chapter 1). They continued their economic education on their own through conversation, books, and newspapers.[3] As seen in Chapter 1, the central economic figures among the liberals were also professors of political economy: Ezequiel Rojas, Florentino González, Aníbal Galindo, and Miguel Samper. Some, like

Salvador Camacho Roldán and Santiago Pérez, were associated with radical liberalism, favored English liberalism, and showed significant concern for equality in the betterment of people's economic conditions with a more individualistic view. Mariano Ospina Rodríguez, Leonardo Canal, and Julio Arboleda were the central figures on the conservative side of the debate.

The most significant of the sources they consulted to build their own views was the importation of books for personal use or sale, which stimulated the appearance of bookstores, often owned by commercial houses, in the main cities.The channels of intellectual sociability used were diverse. Newspapers were one of the most used mechanisms in the debate of ideas; however, their circulation was limited, given the high rates of illiteracy and their regional character. Syllabi and notes for teaching political economy, with explanations of the doctrines, selected contents, and the order of presentation of the dissertations and postulates were also used to participate in the debate. Many intellectuals and politicians published brochures, books, and memoirs to socialize, clarify or defend their positions. Finally, correspondence was the preferred channel for tracing how ideas were received, adapted, transformed, and materialized.[4]

Florentino González was one of the first to openly advocate for free trade in the mid-1840s. He was Treasury Secretary (1846–1848) under Tomás Cipriano de Mosquera's administration and was instrumental in advancing the free trade agenda. González's 1847 law reform project was considered the first step towards free trade and integration with international trade (Ancizar, n.d./1985). His motivation was clear:

> Freedom for agriculture, freedom for mining, freedom for manufacturing and trade, this is the clamor that is heard everywhere. A rational clamor, a clamor based on the demands of the people, on the need for well-being for all of us who live on this earth.
>
> (González, 1847/1981a, p.592)

Manuel Ancizar (n.d./1985) backed this idea, asserting that free trade was not intended to serve the interests of the merchants; it also served those of agriculture:

> [...] With the moderation of the customs tariff, native producers have been invited to expand their companies, since by facilitating imports, domestic production is naturally stimulated by the increase in exchange rates and the drop in prices in foreign items interchangeable with ours. Consequently, the reduction of import duties is not considered a favor done to commerce but secondarily, and primarily to agriculture, which is perhaps the only thing that deserves the name of national industry in this country in relation to foreign trade.
>
> (p.38)

Immediately after the law was proclaimed, the artisans of Bogotá vetoed it.[5] The debate continued until 1853, when a protest against a new free trade bill turned violent: Florentino González, once again in the public eye as the instigator of the law, was the target of violent attacks from the artisans amidst confusing facts (González, 1981b).

The merchants and the incipient business community also participated in the debate. A heterogeneous commercial bourgeoisie showed the first traits of a class conscience—a mix of political realism and functional romanticism—to push for measures and take advantage of the trade opportunities arising from the exchange between internal and external markets. Over time, merchants distanced themselves from artisans, the former more interested in the greatest possible circulation of commodities and the latter in domestic production. This divide affected the internal politics of the liberal party, which materialized in two opposite factions: *Gólgotas* and *Draconianos* (Nieto Arteta, 1941/1962, p.112). Miguel Samper's defense of free trade and Manuel Murillo Toro's response to Samper illustrate the opposition between the two factions. In 1852, Samper wrote:

> Amid free competition, of absolute freedom of industry, the value of each of these services is fixed. A price born of supply and demand, free of all coercion, must be accompanied by equity and justice as a general rule. Such are the general laws that govern the formation and distribution of wealth.
>
> (Samper, 1852)

In 1853 Toro responded:

> Mr. Dr. Miguel Samper.
> Under the heading that heads this letter, you addressed to this newspaper an article that appeared in number 225 on November 26, and in which you make an effort to accredit the selfish and disastrous doctrine advocated by Juan Bautista Say and his entire school, which includes the simple formula of let do; or what is the same: let them steal, let them oppress, let the Wolves devour the Lambs [..].
>
> (Murillo, 1853/2011)

On many occasions, the artisans and *Draconianos* accused free traders—whom they dubbed rich—of selfishness and lack of patriotism. According to them, the rich and powerful backed a doctrine that would ruin national craftsmanship, showing no concern for domestic manufacturers.

These factions played an essential role in connecting national and regional politics. They brought local concerns and interests to national attention, making the liberal party an umbrella for representatives from diverse ethnic and social groups. These representatives came from regions with uneven development levels but used a common republican language (Loaiza, 2011; Sowell, 2006; Mayor Mora, 1997; Gutiérrez, 1995; Jaramillo Uribe, 1994; Kalmanovitz, 1994; Ocampo, 1990; Mejía, 1985). This wide array of positions ranged from a sense of lack of representation and targeted solutions in the national discourse to those akin to the radical liberal project. The socialization channels of these multiple and heterogeneous positions were also diverse, as shown in Table 3.1.

Table 3.1 Places for the socialization of ideas in the second half of the 19th century

No		Type	Purpose	Observations
1	Liberal Social Groups	Democratic Societies	Social movements that became mechanisms of liberal political identity and political education for their members.	A place for alliances and ruptures between the liberal elite and the artisan movement.
2		Masonic groups	Groups where elite members came together; some sought to reconcile liberal principles with those of the Catholic faith, and others opposed the Catholic Church.	Highly formalized and regulated groups for literate individuals searching for distinction, recognition, and freedom of expression.
3	Conservative Social Groups	Catholic Associations	Defense of the Catholic, Apostolic and Roman religion and the application of its principles in education.	Electoral and political support for candidates who would legislate in favor of the interests of the Catholic Church.
4		Artisanal Mutualism	Commonly known as Popular Societies, opposed to the Democratic Societies, they defended the prevalence of the Catholic Church. They resorted to guild mutualism and institutional attempts at self-education.	Based on the family organization, their network was smaller than Democratic Societies but still powerful in some regions.
5		Catholic Associated Offensive	Promotion of what might be called economic progress.	Using the press, associations, and education, they stated there was a false dilemma between modernity and tradition.
6	Attempts at Autonomous Social Groups	Artisan Party	Association of the artisan elite, independent from the traditional elites.	Promotion of protectionist policies.

Source: Loaiza, 2011.

Those groups more inclined towards protectionism were particularly active during election periods, publicly denouncing their political opponents for bringing dangerous foreign ideas ill-adapted to the nation's reality (Martínez, 2001, p. 89). The main points of controversy were: the high sensitivity of fiscal resources to customs revenues; the value of work enhancing the value of merit; the market as the best allocator of resources, and the need for many suppliers and demanders; the need for a growing population to provide labor and demand goods; increased commercialization of agricultural products; improving and building more roads; and stimulating credit and finding sources of capital.

The debate fluctuated, reinforcing and enhancing positions and factions. Political economy debates attested to the tension between theory and practice. Leopoldo Borda, Treasury Secretary, wrote in 1858:

> Although it is precisely like mathematics, the science of Political Economy varies in its applications, which explains why it is discussed so much globally and has received thousands of questions. This is the stumbling block of this great and challenging science, if its truths were like those of mathematics, everyone would accept them without opposition, and there would not be different schools, as there are none in mathematics. [...] However, what happens in practice is the opposite; interpretations and debates abound.
>
> (Borda, 1858, pp. 5–6)

In 1863, from exile in Chile, Florentino González asserted:

> [...] Indeed, I believe that those who have written about the science of the economy, from Adam Smith to Stuart Mill, have been the most useful workers of freedom, precisely because they have shown that it is the best means of developing wealth and distributing the goods the economy can provide among men. This great development of wealth, and its distribution, contributes most to a society's civilization. Consequently, whoever is a friend of civilization and steeped in the truths of the science of the economy can never be an enemy of freedom; but not because of this will he fail to understand the need to consider the conditions of society to make good use of it.
>
> (González, 1863/1981b, p. 310)

During these years, defenders of free trade presented it as the basis of development and the "legitimate child" of independence. Free trade gave the people the right to trade freely and freely offer their labor, and protectionism was considered old-fashioned (Samper, 1880/1984). Later, with the appearance of new actors, the delimitation of political and social affiliations, and the increase in competition for power, the new political parties introduced more external bibliography to the public debate.

3.3 1864–1885: Greater Definition of Concepts, Expansion of the Ideological Spectrum, and Development of Pedagogy

Free trade ideas gained more significant political influence with radical liberalism in power and the 1863 Constitution of Río Negro. The federal model, instituted in the Constitution, was functional to free trade, establishing that progress depended on the country's integration with the world economy. A virtuous cycle would ensue if citizens believed they would enjoy perfect freedom and security in their person and properties because they would work, save, accumulate, and extend their activity (Samper, 1869). In his 1864 opening lecture in the Political Economy course in Guatemala, Mariano Ospina Rodríguez stated:

> In the system of free competition,] the industry has developed unprecedentedly in history. Capitals multiply with prodigious speed; new inventions come every day to improve products and lower prices, reducing production costs; previously unknown arts and products increase the enjoyments of the rich and lessen the sufferings of the poor; trade opens new paths, and new markets widen its movement in all points of the globe [...] the power of man and nature extends and fortifies every day.
>
> (Ospina, 1864/1969, pp. 63–64)

Despite the explicit defense of free trade ideas in public policy, a third option emerged during this period. Rafael Núñez's election as President in 1880 brought the possibility of "moderate free trade", which attracted the moderate factions of both parties. This third option spoke for the need to combat abuses from the old legislation and establish order and freedom as the basic principles of a republic where business could flourish.

Following List, Núñez argued that the dominant economic discourse exaggerated the benefits of free trade and that not all countries that defended free trade practiced it. According to this position, countries used protectionist policies to build industry, and only after the consolidation of national industry did they implement free trade to participate in international trade. Questioning the historical knowledge of his opponents, Núñez criticized them for forbidding the implementation of policies that had worked for others. According to Liévano (1944):

> Núñez proposed two instruments: protection through customs tariffs, in which imported goods like those of national manufacture were heavily taxed; and the system of assuring starting factories the sale of at least part of their products, with the government buying them at good prices for a prudent period.
>
> (p. 374)

Aníbal Galindo (1880, p. 252) lamented this turn of events:

> With the *Confederación Granadina* ends the history of the economic school, or simply free trader, to whom freedom owes its most precious conquests, under the principle of laissez-faire, a principle despised and slandered for having already fulfilled its mission on Earth. In 1863 the history of the modern school of progress began for us, which, taking a little more pity of the misery of the greatest number than the rigidly doctrinaire school, assigns the Government the moral duty of accelerating the advent of a greater degree of well-being for the needy classes, using part of the community's resources to spread instruction and to overcome the material obstacles that hinder their economic and social development.

Despite these moderation efforts, the artisans took a more radical stance by demanding their representatives defend the increase of tariffs on foreign goods in the debates held in Congress in 1880:

> [...] Why have you allowed yourselves to be intimidated by the eternal exploiters of the poor people, those who have no God but gold and their pockets as their only homeland? Do you not see that the bankers, the monopolists, and the large-scale resellers have nothing to do with anything sacred other than their interests? That is why they have shouted until they were deaf against the bills of the national bank, the law of public order, and the reform of the customs tariff: a trinity that will save the country from anarchy, the plunder and misery in which those ruthless Colombians have it.
>
> (Muchos Artesanos, 1880)

Besides tariffs, education was another widely debated topic during the period. As a building block of national identity, education was expected to form a technically and scientifically trained elite capable of governing society (see Chapter 1) and use grammar, arts, and letters to make obedient and civilized citizens (Ramírez, 2015). Intellectual cosmopolitanism contributed to the expansion of the ideological spectrum and the development of pedagogy. The free trade vs. protectionism debate was enriched by these changes because both sides actively participated in education as teachers and authors of teaching material in political economy. Moreover, they turned to journalism and publication to make their ideas known beyond their intimate and close circles (Table 3.2).

The Catholic Church also contributed to the mobilization of ideas and the expansion of newspapers, publishers, and bookshops. The public debate included more economic issues considered critical for state building, and was further enriched by the potential benefits of regional diversity, consolidating an internal market, training in useful trades, and taking advantage of trading opportunities. These also introduced new publications and

Table 3.2 Sources that provoked ideas and theories in the development of the economic ideas of the elites 1864–1885

No	Type	Purpose	Observations
1	Treatises	Scholars and intellectuals proposed critical studies of foreign knowledge.	Authors intended to advance knowledge in the country through methodical, theoretical, and practical research.
2	Writings, studies, or notes on political economy	Disseminate and support public policy with theory.	Adapt theories to the specific context.
3	Manuals, lessons, elements, or compendia	Guide teaching, instructing, and putting policy recommendations into practice.	The development of experimental sciences and useful trades for the market made these texts very popular.
4	Catechisms	Didactic aimed at teaching unquestionable truths that proved useful for civic education.	These texts included dialogs that invited discussion to presentations of questions and answers meant to help memorize the creed.
5	Popular printed matter	Knowledge—and its transmission—that had reached a certain consensus around their postulates, methods, and ways of explaining and conceiving the truth.	Writers informed and transmitted those aspects of knowledge considered essential for society.
6	Other mnemonic strategies: include rhyme, poetry, comic strips, calendars, etc.	Conservation and transmission of oral knowledge.	Widely used, especially where written and printed texts were scarce.

Source: Chapter author.

communication channels with new aesthetic, stylistic, physical, and linguistic frameworks.

In 1872, Aníbal Galindo, on behalf of a moderate group of artisans from Bogotá, addressed a proposal to Congress requesting that resources be appropriated so that theoretical and practical chairs could be introduced in the School of Arts and Crafts. The aim was to promote mechanical arts and to provide the country with an enlightened, intelligent, and industrious working class.

Not yet twenty years ago, the artisans of Bogotá, imbued with the false ideas of the protectionist system, addressed the Congress of 1853, asking in the name of the protection of national labor for the law to reject foreign artifacts at customs, forcing to consume at a high price those of inferior quality manufactured in the country. In other words, they asked that the law impose, for the benefit of a few, an exorbitant, unfair, and prejudicial general contribution, whose infallible result would have been, like that of all premiums, to keep national labor stationary, removing the sting of foreign competition.

[...] Compare, Citizen Representatives, the immense space that good economic ideas have traveled and the amazing progress that all social classes have made in the school of free trade, for which the selfless and patriotic artisans of Bogotá ask you today. That document, which to the honor of the country should be translated and published in French, limits itself to asking you to give the working class the fair share it should have in the elementary, theoretical, and practical instruction, paid for with public funds, in order to be able to compete, in a free field, with foreign industry, for the market of our own country.

(Diario Oficial, No. 2507 of April 5, 1872)

The 1873 international financial crisis and political tension between the great powers tipped the balance towards protectionism. Núñez (1886) appealed to nationalistic feelings by showcasing, as we saw above, how more advanced countries implemented policies to protect their national economies rather than fully embracing free trade. From abroad, Samper (1880/1976) and others advocated for globalization.

As a result, moderate liberalism rose to power. The radical faction shrank under the control of a group of civil notables, primarily lawyers and merchants, engaged in the debate of whether increasing the production of agricultural goods for export would or would not bring prosperity to the greater part of the people.

3.4 1886–1900: From Moderate Interventionism to Protection Policy

Núñez and Caro came to power after the conservative victory in the 1885 civil war. The 1886 Constitution set out to build a new politically and administratively centralized socio-political organization as the nation's foundation. In 1886, with Executive Decree 449, new tariffs on imported goods and a new economic view advanced the protectionist agenda (Liévano, 1944). The *Regeneración* (Regeneration) had formally begun. Its rhetorical efforts focused on opposing the arguments of economic liberalism and advancing the need for state intervention. In addition to the problems of complete free international trade, economic freedom could not solve everything, and it would not guarantee fair or competitive wages or the adequate circulation of money through a free banking system. In practical terms, state intervention meant regulating trade, an active fiscal and monetary policy, and promoting national industry.

Núñez had already expressed his reservations on economic liberalism in an article on the promotion of industry published on November 25, 1883, where he quotes Mill:

Economic science has progressed in recent times given the comparative trials of new doctrines. In general, all absolute dogmatism is now discarded by sensible people. The English decided to abolish quarantines in 1850 on the grounds that there were no contagious diseases, but they did not take the advice for themselves. Modern economists, free thinkers, and liberals of the first force, like Mill, have modified some of the economic principles which were considered evangelical forty or more years ago by those who then carried the banner of progress. Here is what that great scientific thinker says:
The superiority of one country over another in a production branch often comes from having started earlier. There may be no inherent advantage or disadvantage on either side, but only superiority due to greater or lesser experience. The country that is inferior for the moment could still have internal conditions of greater efficiency, which only need enough safe development. It should also be noted that every production branch frequently advances whenever it is subjected to trials. However, it cannot be expected that individuals will be willing to take risks and incur the expense of the acclimatization of a new industry while having to endure the competition of entrepreneurs placed in more advantageous conditions. A protective right kept for a reasonable period will be, on occasion, the best means that a country can employ to facilitate the experiment.
(Núñez, 1883/1945, pp. 516–517)

Some radical liberals accused Núñez of betraying the liberal party, making alliances with conservatives, and becoming a conservative himself. On the side of free trade, impetuous voices could still be heard. For example, Juan A. Montoya (1887/2011) defended free trade in his thesis in law:

The protective system is based on the false principle that a nation's progress consists of producing everything it needs. Obeying this principle amounts to implanting forced industries in the country, using different procedures that prevent foreign competition with national products.
Free trade, for its part, maintains that progress is only possible if there is competition and cooperation between the different individuals that make up the nation and between the different nations that make up humanity.
[...] Protectionism diverts the natural course of labor and capital because, by protecting an industry, everyone will want to be privileged, and since not everyone has the same aptitudes and facilities for it, capital

and labor will not receive the benefits they could have in another industry. It burdens the consumer because there is no competition, as the producer does not have to reduce prices to the level of production costs. It suppresses natural expenses for labor and the improvement of products because it matters little to the privileged producers, knowing there is no competition for their products, whether they are of good or poor quality. The one who suffers is the consumer. Not because they are at the national level but because they deliver a cheaper product.

(pp. 98–100)

Notes from a student attending Santiago Pérez's political economy class also show the optimistic view of free trade that was being taught in universities:

The economic sophistry has consisted, in commercial matters, in merging these economic units into a factitious collective unit called the State or nation and supposing that as long as that factitious unit wins, it does not matter if the actual unit loses. That is why they usually say: it is better to buy expensive goods from a compatriot than cheap ones from abroad. There are no foreigners in political economy. Each buyer is interested in buying as cheaply as possible, and each seller is interested in selling as expensively as possible. What matters to the one who gives something is not that it goes far or near but that it provides more things in return, and what matters to the one who buys a thing is not that it comes from far or near but for it not to demand too many things from him.

(Transcribed by Correa, 2002, pp. 78–79)

Those on the side of protectionism claimed measures more appropriate to the national context that could better promote progress. The difficulty of expanding the agricultural frontier, labor shortages, and low levels of foreign investment and migration introduced rigidities to the economy, especially in the rural sector. Even if improving international commerce was strategic for national progress, these rigidities could not be ignored[6] (Arévalo, 2002).

Rhetoric became the main form of discussing and promoting economic theories and ideas. Those participating in the debate refined their discourse to convey their expert knowledge and delight, moving and persuading a broader audience through editorial pages. "Treatises" and "compendia" also became favorite outlets to transmit the most important lessons of economic theories and make them more palatable to the public. These carefully abridged publications intentionally weighed the order and scope of the contents (Cardona, 2019). Moreover, in 1887, a printing jury and a civil court were put in place. The first acted as a public censor, and the second was in charge of punishing subversive, seditious, obscene, or infamous actions.

During the last decade of the century, some conservatives still defended free trade and were skeptical about protectionist policies. Some expressed

[...]dissatisfaction with fiscal practices in a document of the Conservative Directory called "Bases of government and administration," published in 1897. Others, like House Representative Leonardo Canal,
opposed the promotion of industry and a proposal to reduce taxes on
imported merchandise in the electoral convention of 1897.

(Castro, 1984, p. 89)

From 1893 to 1900, opposition to government policy, first from the liberals and
then from the dissident conservatives, became more robust as a reaction to
Caro's reactionary and intransigent attitude in politics and economics. By the
end of the century, the debate had calmed down. Coffee production, in the
hands of "practical men", became an effective way to handle the complex integration of foreign trade and industrialization (Bergquist, 1981). Liberals also
moved from their fervent approval of free trade. In 1904, Rafael Uribe Uribe,
an influential leader of the liberal party, stated in a public lecture at Bogotá's
Municipal Theater:

[...] all Ibero-Americans have been victims of European publicists such
as Smith, Say, Bastiat, Stuart Mill, Spencer, Leroy-Beaulieu, and other
preachers of absolute free trade and the famous maxims of laissez-faire,
laissez-passer, a minimum of government and a maximum of freedom.
While in the new continent we have been applying these elucubrations for
three-quarters of a century, especially in economic matters, the countries
of those writers, France the first, have been pleased not to listen to them
and to practice the opposite. Hence, those doctrines have been there,
almost in everything, export literature, that we Americans have paid double the price of brand-new books and the opening of our markets to
European products [...] making them adopt a line of conduct that they
take good care not to follow.

(Uribe Uribe & Rafael, 1904/1974)

3.5 An Approach to the Legislative Debate

During the first period of the debate, newspapers were the preferred channel
for discussing economic ideas, but little of this discussion reached the public.
Few people could read, and newspaper circulation was limited, mostly regional,
and sometimes censored. The law was perhaps a more effective way of promoting ideas and interests. The legislative debate allowed people to promote their
interests and create business opportunities (Dávila, 2003). They did not need to
know how to read to engage in political and legislative debates, promote the
practical advantages or disadvantages of specific projects, or use their economic power to introduce and move laws favorable to their interests. Different
groups and individuals actively participated in appointing or removing public
officials, governors, and members of Congress. These groups participated in

the national debate because their plans aligned with the debates of the prevailing parties.

These debates can be traced in the records of the Ministry of Finance and the Treasury and the Ministry of Treasury and Promotion. A closer look at this archival material dating from 1846 to 1900 shows two apparently antagonistic economic schools of thought in competition. The first advanced an individualistic view, based on the principle that each person is the best judge of their own interests; the second, the socialist view, was based on the promising principle of solidarity. The first advocated for a limited government whose primary responsibility was maintaining harmony between the rights and interests of individuals or, which is the same, providing security. The second considered the state should actively participate in the economy rather than allocate resources to individual initiatives.

A third school can also be found in the records. The eclectic school favored the coexistence of the two former principles, giving each of them a more or less functional application, depending on the subject and the conditions for their applicability. For example, wherever the principle of association has acquired a great practical development within the sphere of individual action, public intervention should be reduced in private affairs. In the opposite case, the government should take over and guarantee the appropriate evolution of the economic and social environment. Only with the combination of the two forces would it be possible to break the material obstacles threatening economic development. Table 3.3 shows the most frequently mentioned topics during the period.

The intellectual debate increasingly became a pastime of wealthy intellectuals who found themselves linked to different issues of the period's economic activity. Most of the population participated in politics to a greater or lesser extent, according to their social and political characteristics, responding to inter-class tensions. A diversity of actors and topics overlapped in the debate:

a   Politicians associated an increase in commerce and money flows with economic health. Therefore, from a broadly civic stance, they promoted the formation of a consumer base.
b   The urban economy integrated capital flows from agriculture and commerce that would allow an increase in the consumption of imported goods and the possibility of participating in foreign trade.
c   Economic growth was slow and local markets continued to dominate.
d   Some people considered traditional artisans who refused to disappear, such as carpenters, tailors, small shopkeepers, etc., to be a stagnant sector. However, other artisans adjusted to the new conditions, and even others emerged in the new trades and incipient manufacturing activities closer to modern processes.
e   The poor or indigenous peasantry, considered in need of being educated and "civilized", was seen as a remnant of the tradition that blocked the development of progress.

Table 3.3 Debated topics

Promotion	In favor of free trade	In favor of protectionism
Government revenue diversification	The customs legislation was far from fulfilling its purpose, both in its substantive and adjective parts, due to its lack of simplicity, complicated operations, opacity, and slowness, making it difficult to proceed with business and collecting resources. Incomes suffered the most from the disruption of public order, which could reduce smuggling.	Income from customs tariffs was the country's main source of fiscal income, making it necessary to harmonize fiscal interests with those of the industry. An optimal rate of taxation had to be found.
Agricultural techniques	It would allow the improvement of agricultural techniques and lead to higher yields and better-quality food through the introduction of new crops, the improvement of their rotation, the arrival of scientific agricultural principles, and the use of new instruments and machines. Likewise, the arrival of foreign capital was expected with these measures, which would solve the financing restrictions for agriculture. Livestock development was also supposed to benefit from improved forms of cooperation in new agricultural systems, the introduction of "artificial" grass—which would support a more significant number of livestock—and the arrival of better breeding techniques.	They showed positive results, especially in commodities such as cotton, coffee, rubber, cocoa, etc. On the other hand, the export of tobacco and cinchona decreased, mainly because the English had already developed these crops, with greater productivity in their colonies.
Incipient industry	The protection discussed up to now for the national industry through certain customs franchises was sterile and powerless to give production all the impetus it needed. Additionally, the benefit the industry could receive was incomparably less than what it could obtain with the free importation into the country of as many reproductive items as it needed.	Although it is recognized that the diversification of exports brought positive consequences in some regions, in aggregate terms, it generated a modest and hesitant economic expansion. The most significant effect was observed in the dynamics of imports, which notably affected the interests of some activities—inputs, labor, and the nature of consumption: productive and unproductive.

(Continued)

Table 3.3 (Continued)

Promotion	In favor of free trade	In favor of protectionism
Internal trade	Nueva Granada could not claim to be equal in manufacturing production to the European powers because, even if it had the same knowledge and dispensed with its small population, it would lack capital, an essential element that the Europeans had in excess.	Trade relations created, sustained, and enlivened political relations so that the internal trade of a country was much more valuable than its foreign trade. The integration of the internal market gave cohesion to the various parts of the territory and the country's population.
Forms of Communication	The lack of good roads hindered the country's development and commercial and industrial movement. Without the help of foreign capital, it was impossible to improve to the level that the needs of the Republic demanded.	Although the importance and benefits that the arrival of foreign direct investment could bring were recognized, it was also recognized that the guarantees that the national government could establish and the material priorities that it established according to national interests were much more critical.
The Expansion of Banking	The arrival of foreign capital could stimulate the creation of mortgage banking since the scarcity of long-term resources did not seem to be an engaging activity for the first bankers. Nevertheless, the country did demand an immense amount of capital to develop activities linked to the agriculture industry.	Among the insufficiencies and adverse effects, it is worth mentioning the limited interest of these banks in incorporating new products and services into the local market. Their reluctance to take risks and the selectivity of their operations—which often resulted in an excessive concentration of their activities in certain geographical regions, market sectors, and products and services—all hindered progress.
The Exploitation of Undeveloped Land	It was hoped that free cultivation would change the face of the country's land and correct the immense regions enslaved by owners. These landowners had a vast territorial extension awarded to them, with the sole purpose of monopolizing fertile land or reducing the status of workers—who needed to occupy it for cultivation—to servants.	The Republic suffered enormous losses due to the abuse tolerated in the past by the exploiters of national forests.

Source: Constructed from archives of the Ministry of Finance and the Treasury (1846–1900) and the Ministry of Treasury and Promotion (1865–1877) (MSHT, 1846–1900; MSHF, 1865–1877).

f Generational changes meant that the intellectuals in the center of both parties promoted and defended movements that favored a more moderate and democratic spirit.

This diversity attests to the changing characteristics of the debate and the increasing appearance of disruptive and innovative ideas associated with what were identified as good practices leading to policy recommendations.

3.6 Conclusion

The free trade v. protectionism debate was instrumental in the socioeconomic construction of the country during the second half of the 19th century. The debate goes beyond the reductionist view of free trade liberals and protectionist conservatives. Within the two parties, factions and divisions emerged, hindering them from speaking with a single voice. Ideas and interpretations were widely discussed and often changed according to individuals' willingness to listen to opposing arguments when evaluating the feasibility of their application or the possibilities of communication. The debate became a vast and permanent field of study and application of knowledge and common sense. Knowledge of foreign markets, constantly evolving agricultural and industrial processes, the needs and resources of the country, the complicated science of changes, and the thousands of factors that contribute to making products cheaper or more expensive were all part of the debate.

Three groups participated in the debates, each advancing a different basic principle: the individualistic, meaning each individual is the best judge of their interests; the socialist, building from solidarity; and the so-called eclectic, which advocated for a more or less functional application of both points of view. All of them recognized the problems posed by the meager fiscal resources available. However, the controversies of free trade or protectionism were not limited to the issue of tariffs, but permeated the intersection with other vital issues.

Literary disciplines were cultivated as the heritage of the intellectual and political elite. In this period, the elite tried to write, communicate, and think in a contextual, rational, and informed manner. There was a shared belief that by forming and diffusing these ideas in daily life, it would be possible to achieve a greater benefit for our democracy, as it made people more enlightened, aware, and productive. New ways of transmitting new knowledge were needed to take over the old ways of thinking. The appropriation of ideas and their application to the national context was a social process of cultural production. Its forms and functions coincided with the political and economic needs of the construction of the nation-state.

66   *Edna Carolina Sastoque*

Notes

1 For Luis Ospina Vásquez (1987, p. 232), "The conservative party had declared itself unequivocally for the purest Manchester doctrines. Liberalism did not want to be less Manchester-like, it wanted to be more so, as in some of the reforms that they wanted to carry out in the [Sovereign State] of Santander." José A. Ocampo (1990) considers that, with some minor exceptions: "The reformism of the mid-century was much more determined under the government of José Hilario López, the transition to the "liberal model" began under a conservative government. This party also supported some of the liberal reforms, [...] and the momentum for change was maintained under the bipartisan government of Manuel María Mallarino (1855–1857) and the clearly conservative government of Mariano Ospina Rodríguez (1857–1861). Thus, it is perhaps not an overstatement to speak of a certain "consensus" of the elite regarding the economic model" (1990, p. 23).
2 "An example can be seen in the study of the genealogy of the speeches that fought for the liberation of the tobacco monopoly or in those that were waged around the tariff system since the fiscal needs showed the limits within which operated the purest conceptions of free trade and protectionism, and in practice forced their moderation" (Ocampo, 1990, p. 26).
3 As seen in Chapter 1, there had been a widespread controversy since the 1830s between supporters of English utilitarianism or Benthamism and those who considered these ideas contrary to religion. Burbano (2008) traces this controversy to the introduction of political economy and the use of texts by Say, Montesquieu, Destutt de Tracy, Condillac, and Mably, mainly in law and philosophy.
4 Analyzing the correspondence in the present day is challenging, since its conservation and availability depend on private archives and therefore the precise flow of sustained communication cannot be ascertained.
5 They had created the *Democratic Society* in 1846 to exchange knowledge and practices and develop political awareness to advance their interests.
6 Palacios (2002, p. 267) states:

> laissez-faire, laissez-passer liberals and Regenerationists supported the export model, with varying strength and the same unshakable faith in capitalist progress. The disagreements revolved around defining political relationships with the popular classes. The liberals, perhaps thinking of their urban artisan clientele, concluded that, by stimulating individual initiative, the free market would promote political democracy and social mobility. Conservatives and Regenerationists, thinking perhaps of their clientele of small independent peasants, argued that leaving the forces of the free market in play would weaken the principle of authority and the liberal and religious tradition without which it was impossible to build the strong state that the nation demanded.

Bibliography

Ancizar, M. (1985). *Escritos políticos*. Editorial Incunables. (Original publication date is unknown).
Arévalo, D. (2002). Sobre un Manual de Libre Cambio. In: *Economía política y estadística. Santiago Pérez* (24–42). Universidad Externado de Colombia.
Bergquist, C. (1981). Café y conflicto en Colombia 1886–1910. La Guerra de los Mil Días: Sus Antecedentes y Consecuencias. FAES.
Borda, L. (1858). *Hacienda Nacional*. Imprenta de Echeverria Hermanos.

Burbano, G. (2008). Colombia. In: C. García Guadilla (Ed.), *Pensamiento universitario latinoamericano. Pensadores y forjadores de la universidad latinoamericana* (169–201). Cendes, Iesalc-Unesco.

Cardona, P. (2019). Al alcance del pueblo: impresos populares y tradicionales retóricas en Colombia en la segunda mitad del siglo XIX. In: *El oficio del historiador. Reflexiones metodológicas en torno a las fuentes*. Universidad de los Andes, Universidad del Rosario y la Universidad Nacional de Colombia, Sede Medellín.

Castro, A. (1984). Industria y política económica del siglo XIX. *Cuadernos de Economía 6* (7): 83–107.

Cordovez Moure, J.M. (1957). *Reminiscencias de Bogotá*. Aguilar. (Original work published 1893).

Correa, J.S. (2002). Sobre un manual de libre cambio [Transcription of Santiago Pérez Manosalva's lessons]. In: *Economía Política y Estadística. Lecciones dictadas en la Universidad Nacional, 1830–1900* (23–53). Universidad Externado de Colombia.

Dávila, C. (2003). *Empresas y empresarios en la historia de Colombia, siglos XIX–XX, una colección de estudios recientes*. Naciones Unidas, CEPAL.

Diario Oficial (DO) No. 2,507 of April 5, 1872.

Galindo, A. (1880). *Estudios económicos i fiscales*. Imprenta H. Andrade.

González, F. (1981a). Bases del liberalismo económico. In: *Escritos políticos, jurídicos y económicos*. Instituto Colombiano de Cultura. (Original work published 1847).

González, F (1981b). Explicación y apología del liberalismo oligárquico. In: *Escritos políticos, jurídicos y económicos*. Instituto Colombiano de Cultura. (Original work published 1863).

González, F. (1981c). Introducción al gobierno representativo de John Stuart Mill. In: *Escritos políticos, jurídicos y económicos*. Instituto Colombiano de Cultura. (Original work published 1865).

Gutiérrez Sanín, F. (1995). *Curso y discurso del movimiento plebeyo (1849–1854)* (1st ed.). El Áncora Editores.

Jaramillo Uribe, J. (1994). Las Sociedades Democráticas de Artesanos y la coyuntura política y social colombiana de 1848. In *La personalidad histórica de Colombia y otros ensayos*. Bogotá: Segunda edición. El Áncora Editores.

Kalmanovitz, S. (1994). *Agricultura y Artesanía durante el siglo XIX. En Economía y Nación: una breve historia de Colombia*, Cuarta edición., 93–168. Bogotá: Tercer Mundo Editores.

Liévano, I. (1944). *Rafael Núñez*. Ediciones Librería Siglo XX.

Loaiza, G. (2011). *Sociabilidad, Religión y política en la definición de la Nación, Colombia. 1820–1886*. Universidad Externado de Colombia.

Martínez, F. (2001). *El nacionalismo cosmopolita: la referencia europea en la construcción nacional en Colombia, 1845–1900*. Banco de la República, Instituto de Estudios Andinos.

Mayor Mora, A. (1997). *¿De artesanos a técnicos? En Cabezas duras y dedos inteligentes* (1st ed.). Colombiano de Cultura.

Mejía, G. (1985). Las sociedades democráticas (1848–1854) Problemas Historiográficos. *Universitas Humanística 25–26*, 145–177.

Memorias de la Secretaría de Hacienda y del Tesoro [MSHT] (1846–1900). Available at: https://www.banrep.gov.co/es/libro-memorias-hacienda-tesoro

Memorias de la Secretaría de Hacienda y del Fomento [MSHF] (1865–1877). Available at: https://www.banrep.gov.co/es/libro-memorias-hacienda-tesoro

Montoya, J.A. (2011). El Libre Cambio. In: J.C. Rodríguez Gómez (ed.), *Tesis del primer Externado. 1886–1895*. Universidad Externado de Colombia. (Original work published 1887).

Muchos Artesanos. (1880). *La Reforma de la tarifa aduanera i la Cámara de Representantes*. Imprenta "La Reforma", May 22, 1880.

Murillo, M. (1979). *Obras Selectas*. Cámara de Representantes; Imprenta Nacional. (Original work published 1853).

Murillo, Manuel. (2011). Dejad hacer. *Revista de Economía Institucional 13*(25). (Original work published in *Neo-Granadino* magazine, year VI, 246, April 15, 1853, pp. 126–128).

Nieto Arteta, L. E. (1962). *Economía y cultura en la historia de Colombia*. Tercer Mundo. (Original work published 1941).

Núñez, R. (1886). Mensaje del Presidente Constitucional de los Estados Unidos de Colombia al Congreso de 1886. D. O. No. 1156, April 9. pp. 1132.

——— (1945). Fomento a la industria. In: *La reforma política en Colombia: colección de artículos y discursos publicados en El Impulso, El Porvenir de Cartagena y La Nación de Bogotá, entre 1879 y 1890*. Biblioteca Popular de Cultura Colombiana. (Original work published 1883).

Ocampo, J.A. (1990). Comerciantes, artesanos y política económica en Colombia, 1830–1880. *Boletín Cultural y Bibliográfico 27* (22), 20–45.

Ospina, L. (1987). *Industria y protección en Colombia*. Editorial Oveja Negra.

Ospina, M. (1969). Economía Política. In: *Escritos sobre Economía y Política*. Biblioteca Universitaria de Cultura Colombiana. (Original work published 1864)

Palacio, M. (2002). La Regeneración ante el espejo liberal y su importancia en el siglo XX. In: *La clase más ruidosa y otros ensayos sobre política e historia*. Editorial Norma.

Ramírez, M. (2015). El proceso económico 1880–1930. In: E. Posada (Coord.). *La Historia Contemporánea. Colombia. La apertura al mundo. Tomo 3 (1880–1930)* (pp. 137–199). Editorial Taurus.

Safford, F. (1989). *El Ideal de lo práctico. El desafío de formar una élite técnica y empresarial en Colombia*. Empresa Editorial Universidad Nacional-El Ancora Editores.

Samper, M. (1852). Dejad Hacer. Neo-Granadino, year V, 225, November 26 852, 295–296.

——— (1869). *Memoria del Secretario de Hacienda I Fomento para el Congreso Federal de 1869*. Imprenta de la Nación.

——— (1984). La protección. In: *Las Ideas radicales del Siglo XIX. Escritos políticos*. El Ancora Editores. (Original work published 1880).

——— (1976). Protección y libre cambio. In: *Selección de escritos*. COLCULTURA. (Original work published 1880).

Sowell, D. (2006). *Artesanos y política en Bogotá, 1832–1919*. Ediciones Pensamiento Crítico.

Uribe Uribe, Rafael. (1974). Socialismo de Estado. In: *El Pensamiento político de Rafael Uribe Uribe* (Antology). Instituto Colombiano de Cultura. (Original work published 1904).

4 The Role of Economic Thought in the Administration of Justice in Colombia in the Second Half of the 19th Century

Claudia Milena Pico, Edna Carolina Sastoque and Luis Eduardo Sandoval

4.1 Introduction

British and European 18th-century Enlightenment ideas became particularly influential in Colombia during the 19th century. As seen in the previous chapters, these ideas were brought to bear on national economic debates on fiscal, monetary, and commercial policies. In this chapter, we will concentrate on their influence on debates about the administration of justice. Cesare Beccaria and Jeremy Bentham were significant influences in the discussion about criminal legislation. Their influence can be seen in the opinions of several 19th-century intellectuals in the country, even beyond this discussion. This chapter explores the extent to which these economic ideas became the basis of the discussion on criminal legislation and led to modifications of normative provisions in the country.

Following Mackaay (2000), we argue that utilitarianism is a clear link between economics and law in the 18th and 19th centuries. This link can be seen in Beccaria's stance on the dissuasive effect of criminal sanction and Bentham's calculus of pains and pleasures. Beccaria, with Pietro Verri,[1] paved the way for utilitarianism and set the basis for Bentham's moral philosophy during the second half of the 18th century (Faucci, 2014). Bentham built upon Beccaria's ideas and both elaborated and adhered to the greatest utility principle, which they posit as the guiding principle of any country's legislative and economic design.

As with monetary (Chapter 2) and trade (Chapter 3) policy, criminal law was also the result of the combination of ideas, utilitarian in this case, and the goals and aspirations of the political forces organizing and disputing republican power throughout the century. Beccaria's and Bentham's utilitarianism represented an ideal of modernization that appealed to political figures and legislators in the country. This ideal had to be adapted to the national context, which meant its transformation through political and legislative debate. In this chapter, we trace this transformation.

The first step was the translation into Spanish of Beccaria's and Bentham's books. Ramón de Salas y Cortés, a Spanish jurist, translated Bentham's *Introduction to the Principles of Morals and Legislation* from Etienne Dumont's

DOI: 10.4324/9781003289241-5

French edition in 1823 and published an extended commentary on Beccaria's *On Crime and Punishment*, including the translation of excerpts in 1836. The second step can be found in the intellectual debate in the country. Ezequiel Rojas and Miguel Antonio Caro engaged in a lengthy discussion over utilitarianism (cf. Chapter 1) and its implications for the new republic in a publication on moral philosophy. Finally, these ideas found their way, albeit strongly transformed, into the criminal justice system and criminal legislation, as seen in the 1837, 1873, and 1890 national codes. We will follow these steps throughout the chapter.

In the first section, an analysis of Beccaria's and Bentham's works will show how colonial criminal legislation transitioned to one inspired by liberal principles. Proportional punishment, the guiding principle of justice administration found in Beccaria and Bentham, was debated in the early years of the Republic, prefiguring further developments that would lead to the national codes of 1837, 1873, and 1890. We discuss these codes in the second section, showing their rationalist influences and impact after promulgation. Finally, to better assess this impact, we present statistics on judicial processes and show how punishments and their proportionality varied, which further attests to the influence of the debate of ideas.

4.2 The rise of rationalism in criminal law: Beccaria and Bentham

According to Groenewegen (2002), "the third quarter of the 18th century marks perhaps the most important period in the history of economic thought, since it is at the end of this period that economics emerged as a separate and new science" (p. 3). Three economists were influential during the emergence of economics as a science: Adam Smith, Anne Robert Jacques Turgot, and Cesare Beccaria. The debates they promoted were influential in establishing the foundations of classical political economy; their contribution has in common the comprehension of political economy as the reproduction, distribution, and circulation of wealth. Beccaria understood political economy as: "[...] a part of the science of legislation and politics which is used to increase the opulence of the subjects and of the state" (Groenewegen, 2002, p. 28).

Beccaria's ideas emerge during the secularization of Italian society. This process had two main characteristics: reflection on individual rights and the establishment of limits to state power (Faucci, 2014). Both gave rise to a liberal conception of the state and set the conditions for institutional reforms that included the public administration and the administration of justice. The influence of the Enlightenment permeated multiple aspects of public life and led to the definition of common principles in political economy and law. In this section, we explore the reflections on criminal law as a part of the institutional change promoted by the emergence of political economy as a scientific field.

Cesare Beccaria (1738–1794) is recognized mainly as the forerunner of the classical Italian school of criminal law. This school attempted to limit the state's actions and prioritize the deductive method (Bernate, 2004). As Bressler

(2018) points out, Beccaria's work influenced the United States Constitution, the structuring of utilitarian rationality, and the notions of the civilizing process of nations.

Beccaria's book *On Crimes and Punishments* advances a liberal view in defense of the minimum limitations of personal freedom needed to enjoy security and protection:

> [...] indeed, each one does not want to put in the public deposit but the smallest portion possible, that one that is only enough to move the men to defend him. The aggregate of all these possible small portions of freedom forms the right to punish everything else is abuse and not justice; it is fact, not law.
>
> (Beccaria, 1764/2015, p. 20)

Beccaria identifies criminal behavior with damage, which generates a loss of well-being at the individual or community level. That damage motivates the action of the state. The state acts against three types of crimes: those against the nation, against individual security and happiness, and against the obligations of citizens.

Jeremy Bentham (1748–1832), the founder of modern utilitarianism, shares this principle in his definition of crime, public policy against crime, and choice of optimal punishment (Simon, 2009). According to Bentham, the utility principle allows the assessment of crimes, but more importantly, it is the guiding principle for legislation and all reasoning about human matters. This principle states that any action should be evaluated regarding its net utility: how much pleasure and pain it produces. Bentham proposes a table of pleasures and pains to assess actions, in general, and consider the gravity of criminal conduct, in particular:

> In morality or legislation, reasoning that cannot be translated by these simple terms of pain and pleasure is obscure.
>
> If you want, for example, to study the matter of crimes, which is the great object that dominates all legislation, this study will be nothing more than a comparison, a calculation of pleasures and pains: you will consider the crime or the evil of certain actions, [...] the motive of the offender, [...] the benefit of the crime, [...] the legal punishment to be imposed [...]. This theory of pains and pleasures is therefore the foundation of all science.
>
> (Bentham, 1823, p. 86)

Bentham's utilitarian principle implies a duality between pain and pleasure that links crime to the damage caused to society. Crime is related to the absence of the victim's consent and the absence of positive effects caused by the damage.

Beccaria and Bentham advance that legislation must be put in place to punish crimes. According to Beccaria, it is only the legislator, as representative of the social contract, that can establish laws to define criminal behavior and its appropriate punishment. There is no room for interpretation of the law; it should be followed literally to avoid any possible uncertainty. Therefore, the law must be written, a principle of proportionality of the sentence must be guaranteed, and crimes must be punished in proportion to the evil or pain they have caused. The law should follow a precise scale:

> [...] if there were an exact and universal scale of penalties and crimes, we would have a common and probable measure of the degrees of tyranny and freedom, and of the depth of humanity or malice of all nations.
>
> (Beccaria, 2015, p. 26)

Proportionality signals the margin of impunity, thus promoting or dissuading criminal behavior. However, Beccaria, like Bentham, was against physical punishment, especially the death penalty. Following Simon (2009), it is clear that

> Beccaria strongly disagreed with the death penalty for two reasons: first, the State cannot cause death. [...] Second, the deterrence caused by the death penalty is too costly. Such punishment produces an insufficient deterrent to crime, at the cost of a considerable amount of suffering [...].
>
> (p. 23)

Hence, Beccaria believed that the strictest punishments could generate short-lasting effects and that, although the state should severely punish the most serious crimes, the death penalty would not have the expected effect in preventing crime.[2]

The idea of proportionality goes beyond equating the benefits and costs of criminal behavior for the criminal. Beccaria and Bentham would agree and condemn the criminal law of the old regime based on physical punishment. Such punishment, argued Beccaria, was subjective because it depended on a specific moral system and had to consider the circumstances of the condemned. To avoid all subjectivity, Beccaria proposes the damage caused as the sole objective criterion that should be applied in criminal law.

Bentham would follow and refine this assessment, focusing on a marginal analysis that compared the damage criminal actions cause with the costs of preventing their occurrence. Simon (2009) synthesizes the analysis:

> The punishment must satisfy four requirements: it must act against very harmful actions, it must cause adequate deterrence, it must have a cost that must not be greater than the damage caused by the crime, and it must not have less expensive alternatives. [...] Bentham's theory applies the concept of marginal deterrence to avoid the possibility that crimes of different seriousness appear equivalent or are indifferent to criminals and prevent them from committing crimes.
>
> (p. 25)

Choosing the optimal punishment was crucial for both Beccaria and Bentham. Beccaria thought crimes should be punished with arrests and, in the case of the rich, the payment of fines should be avoided; Bentham recognized that detention was crucial. Bentham proposed the panopticon, one of his most well-known ideas, as a building that would materialize the possibility of surveillance and payment for committing a crime. The panopticon received much attention in the country and has an important place in the history of criminal law regarding the construction of prisons and surveillance centers (Romero & García, 2021).[3]

Beccaria and Bentham aimed at developing universal systems of criminal law administration. These could be put in place anywhere because they were built upon the principle of utility, that is, pleasure and pain, the universal motives of human action. José del Valle, a Guatemalan writer and politician, called Bentham "Legislator of the World" precisely because he intended, like Beccaria, to advance an objective and universal system far from any contingency or contextual specificity. In the next section, we will consider if this was possible in the Colombian case.

4.3 Moral philosophy and utilitarianism in Colombia

Beccaria's and Bentham's ideas directly influenced criminal law in Colombia during the second half of the 19th century. Their theories were fundamental in developing radical liberal ideas represented by authors already mentioned in this volume, like Ezequiel Rojas, Florentino González, and José María Samper. In contrast, conservative leaders were less prone to accept utilitarianism as a moral system, probably because of its opposition to Christian morality. This section describes the formation of ideas about the administration of justice in Colombia and its connections with the criminal law codes.

It is easy to identify the influence of Beccaria's and Bentham's ideas in the promulgation of penal codes in the country. Nevertheless, the Colombian penal system has specificities, mainly because the country moved between modernization efforts and the construction of national identity during the second half of the 19th century. There was a constant tension between the ideas of enlightened liberalism and conservative thought, whose primary social foundation was the old oligarchies and the clergy. New regional forces rose that supported different interests within the contending social forces.

Politicians, intellectuals, and legislators consulted penal codes from Great Britain, Spain, France, and the United States as sources of inspiration and criticism for national criminal law. A wide range of views can be found in the public debate, from the most radical positions to more moderate ones, some transferring ideas from abroad, others adapting them to the local context. As seen throughout this book, the debate inevitably transformed those ideas. In practice, many participated in the discussion of penal codes, drafting, and legislative approval. Presidents of the Republic, justice ministers, and Congress representatives, among others, made for a heterogeneous crowd seeking to unify criminal legislation that was permanently submitted to criticism, objections, demands, and reforms.

The first penal code for New Granada was promulgated in 1837. Even though it was an attempt to modify some colonial institutions, it retained penalties that included physical punishment. According to Marquez (2011, p. 73):

> [...] it was nothing more than a hybrid of legal utilitarianism, liberalism, and natural law that characterized penal institutions that ruled Colombia during the first half of the 19th century. The code guided the behavior of citizens against the State, a legally structured State with liberal ideas, in a society governed by Catholic morality.

One example of the influence of Catholic morality is found in the 30th article, which established that no sentence could be carried out on Sunday and that the convict had to be accompanied by officers of the judiciary and by a priest during the execution of the death penalty. The presence of Catholic symbolism was also important during an execution.

The Penal Code of 1837 went through a number of reforms over the following 20 years. These reforms are consistent with political changes and the ascent of liberals to executive power. During the second half of the century, intellectuals, politicians, and citizens engaged in detailed discussions about increasing the country's catalog of crimes and penalties. In a liberal move, citizens sought to transform the colonial institutions and set new penal and economic systems more adapted to the nascent republic.

For instance, José María Samper (1828–1888), a liberal leader, recorded in *Apuntamientos para la historia política i social de la Nueva Granada*:

> The Republic is incompatible with permanent armies; slavery; professional privileges; the death penalty; taxes on consumption and production; the prerogatives of the clergy and the military; rent-seeking monopolies; the restriction of the press; the supremacy of a religious sect and the existence of spiritual power; the attempted imprisonment of the citizen; in a word, with the old institutions of the monarchy. [...] Once an idea has been adopted as a principle of government and legislation, it is necessary to carry it forward, without hesitation, with all its consequences. The ruler who acts in another way, who fluctuates in fear due to the difficulties of the moment, fosters contradictory interests in society and lacks legislative harmony, the government is lost, and the ruler works his fall.
>
> (Samper, 1858, pp. 46–47)

Samper defended eliminating ancient-regime institutions, rejected outright physical measures or direct control, and advocated for a more liberal economy. Towards the end of the text, Samper concludes:

Of course, in the current state of our civilization and judging according to the new ideas that have emerged from the intellectual movement of the time, the codes of procedure and judicial organization sanctioned in 1834, and the criminal code of 1837, suffer from notable defects, contradictions, and gaps, obsolescence and extreme severity in the classification of crimes and the imposition of penalties.

(Samper, 1858, p. 270)

Another prominent liberal figure, Florentino González (1805–1874), professor of criminal law and political economy, amongst other roles, brought ideas from the French, British, and U.S. legal debates of the times. González used these debates to advance theoretical and practical discussions (Velázquez, 2012). In 1858 Florentino González wrote:

We have always been enemies of that barbaric penal legislation that has as its object to torment humanity, not to improve it, and we condemn the punishments that cannot have any useful result. [...] Of course, we are opposed to those punishment institutions in which man suffers and is corrupted at the same time because they are a source of future criminals more dangerous than those who entered. [...] The punishments for murder and robbery are insufficient to avoid these crimes, especially if we consider the state of the punishment institutions in the country. Criminals laugh at unsafe prison houses where they spend a little time, if they want, in idleness and often in merriment with their friends.

The judges are afraid of condemning men who can go out in a short time to exercise cruel revenge, and the extreme indulgence of the legislator, far from improving customs, gradually creates in society the idea that crime is not bad, assuming that the authority forgives him, or punishes him lightly. Personal revenge then takes the place of public justice and gives rise to a series of private reprisals that destroy security and, consequently, the social and business order.

(González, 1858/1981, p. 333)

Likewise, Ezequiel Rojas (1803–1873), as in other instances, explicitly defended and applied utilitarian principles to the assessment and reform of the legal system, and more specifically of criminal law. He extensively explained the correspondence between pain and pleasure and the good and the bad, stating that this standard was universal, absolute, and invariable. Following Beccaria and Bentham, Rojas had a utilitarian approach to studying crimes, underscoring the objective and rational dimension of crime (Rojas, 1868).

Despite Rojas's closeness to Bentham's ideas, his interpretations did not necessarily follow the English scholar's approach.[4] Nevertheless, Rojas became one of utilitarianism's most prominent defenders and promoters in his more than 45 years of university teaching. He tried to make the science of legislation conform to the science of useful means or utility. This science allowed Rojas to tackle what he considered fundamental questions for criminal law: Is punishment the appropriate response to crime? What sanctions can efficiently contribute to the eradication or control of criminal conduct? Although it is legitimate for the state to impose penalties to guarantee the citizens' rights, how much and which penalty should be used for this purpose? Rojas worked through these questions based on Destutt de Tracy and Bentham's work to justify the structure of the laws structure and the scale of the penalties.

These liberal views and Rojas's attempts came under direct attack, in 1868, from Miguel Antonio Caro (1843–1909), a rising young figure in the conservative camp. Caro took it upon himself to question the internal consistency of utilitarianism and, in particular, its application to a penal system. In a series of articles published in the newspaper *La Fe*,[5] Caro pursued this task by inviting his reader to ask a utilitarian thinker "with what right and to what purpose does public authority impose any punishment" (Caro, 1868, p. 139). After presenting the answer Caro thought the utilitarian thinker would give, he states:

> [...] we can conclude without minimal violence, that, given that when society imposes a punishment, it does nothing but accumulate evils on one individual to produce good for another one and, given that it has the right to do so, it has the right to accumulate pains, that is evils on an innocent person for the benefit of other individuals, good or bad, few or many; it has it to expropriate the solitary rich person to enrich many poor people, to assassinate a man whose meat promises good flavor, to satisfy numerous cannibals!... The consequence is frightening but logical. Then, let us not be surprised that utilitarian doctrine leads to all sorts of depredation and violence in the name of the general good. If those are the regular ideas [of a Utilitarian thinker], how can they not lead to such events?
>
> The right to punish, explained under the tenor of the utilitarian doctrine, is an atrocious injustice under another concept.
>
> (Caro, 1868, p. 139)

Caro questions the absolute character of utility since the practical without the good is the means without the end. He mainly questions two things: first, he says that human beings, according to Bentham, are under the empire of pleasure, thus they are not the owners of their actions; second, Bentham's principles distort the idea of governing. Bentham would advance that to govern is to educate, to perfect the individual and society; therefore, it is inconsistent with having laws that cause harm to an individual – applying a penalty – for the benefit of the common good. Caro concludes that the exercise of public power cannot be the ministry of terror, and, on the contrary, good government reconciles "justice and charity", thus verifying that beyond scientific arguments, the Christian faith should be the origin of our moral and civil judgments (Caro, 1869).

The debate on utilitarianism as a source for criminal justice in the country was framed during a period when federalism had been adopted as the political and economic organization of the Republic. This new model emerged between 1858 and 1863 and lasted between 1861 and 1885. Implementing and managing the new model made the country's legal culture[6] more complex, since each sovereign state created a new legal system in criminal matters and, consequently, many enacted their codes. In general terms, the penal system in most states was a power rooted in the citizens and aimed at controlling state activity.

Federalism responded to the ideals of radical liberals, who, once in power, promulgated the Constitution of Rionegro in 1863. A main pillar of this constitution was the safeguarding of individual rights. The Constitution, in Article 15, stated:

> The essential and unmovable basis of the Union between States is the recognition and guarantee by the General Government and the Governments of each one of the States, of the individual rights belonging to the inhabitants and transients of the United States of Colombia.

The first five individual rights directly related to criminal law are:

1 The inviolability of human life, under which the General Government and those of the States commit to avoid enacting the death penalty in their laws.
2 Not to be sentenced to corporal punishment for more than ten years.
3 Individual freedom has no limits other than the freedom of another individual; that is, the faculty of doing or omitting anything that would not result in harm to another individual or the community.
4 Personal security; in such a way that it is not attacked with impunity by another individual or by the public authority; nor be imprisoned or detained but for criminal reasons or correctional punishment; nor tried by commissions or extraordinary courts; nor punished without being heard and defeated in court; and all this by pre-existing laws.
5 Property; not being deprived of it, but by punishment or general contribution, following the laws, or when required by some serious reason of public necessity, judicially declared and prior compensation.

Ten years later, the radical liberals enacted Law 112 of 1873, the country's second Penal Code. The combination of the classical[7] and positivist[8] schools allowed continuity with the previous penal code. However, it also marked a rupture, such as the elimination of capital punishment, the establishment of a broad recognition of individual rights and guarantees, and the expansion of considerations on crimes to property and patrimony (Aguilera, 2002). The maximum punishment for crimes was 120 months imprisonment, that is, ten years; murder, desertion, and violation of the Constitution were the crimes with the longest prison term.

Nevertheless, in practice, the radical liberal project encountered significant management and application difficulties. This was due to the sociopolitical reality of the nation, characterized by constant civil wars and electoral instability (Uribe & López, 2006), which generated a sense of permissibility and disorder.[9] In 1883, Rafael Nuñez, future President of the Republic and former defender of absolute freedom, addressed the question in a document examining whether national politics had become true chaos.

> Precisely. The general absence of principles has made individual interests overlay everything, and mistrust prevails. Not having faith in anything that depends on someone else, each person seeks, on her account, what suits her, and in that search, they do not hesitate to use any means, no matter how prohibited [...] The word order is anarchic... instead, it is every man for himself.
>
> (Nuñez, 1885, p. 545)

The 1863 Constitution and the 1873 Penal Code led to such a state of discontent that after two civil wars – in 1876 and 1884 – a radical change in the legal order came with the rise of the conservatives to power and a new constitution proclaimed in 1886, ending federalism and establishing a centralized republic. Caro, who participated in the drafting of the new constitution and later became vice-president (1892) and president (1894) of the Republic, stated that liberalism in the radical era amounted to a: "[...] political system that, by not distinguishing the good from the bad the true from the false, in the moral and dogmatic order, grants the same social rights to good and evil, truth and error" (Caro, 1989, pp. 172–173). As seen in previous chapters, the *Regeneración* meant a complete break with radical liberalism. For the conservatives now in power, criminal law was no longer to limit the exercise of power; it would become an element of power itself, a tool to govern seeking to protect it, especially the state, from the actions of the individual. Article 29 of the new constitution stated:

> The Legislator will only impose capital punishment in cases defined as more serious, the following legally proven crimes: treason against the Homeland in a foreign war, parricide, murder, arson, robbery, gang, piracy, and certain military crimes defined by the laws of the army.
>
> (CRC, 1886, Art. 29)

The increased crime and what was considered a loss of moral authority led to a third national criminal code, issued in 1890.[10] The most important change in this code was the focus on preventing crimes instead of punishing the offender (Cancino Moreno, 1990; Bernate, 2004). According to Aguilera (2002), this criminal code:

> [...] returns to the old division between corporal and non-corporeal punishments, hardens the forms of punishment by restoring capital

punishment and by extending the time of the various penitentiary punishments. The return of capital punishment with the method of execution intended to intimidate common criminals who had lost "sensitivity and conscience" but ended up being applied to the occasional criminal and with greater emphasis on the political criminal.

The reform had its detractors. More severe punishments, the primacy of authority, and punitive justice were met with opposition. Echoes of this opposition can be found in Felipe Forero's and Ramón Gonzalez's Jurisprudence theses at the Externado University in 1892. Forero's criticism was directed at the penal code, the legislators, and Bentham:

> The laws have almost completely lost sight of this essential point of punishment because the legislators believed they found in intimidation the most powerful lever available to a Government to direct the conduct of the people. Led by this error, they have set all their attention on the exemplary nature of the penalty, as evidenced by the definition that the Roman jurisconsults have given of it and according to which the penalty is an evil of passion that the law imposes for the evil of action, or more clearly, an evil that the law does to the delinquent for the evil that he has done with his crime. Bentham has also said that for the penalty to be effective, its evil must outweigh the price of the crime.
> These concepts make it clear to us that both the Roman jurisconsults and Bentham did not have a complete idea of the nature and purpose of punishment; since, in them, the tendency to the theory of intimidation is manifested palpably, a theory currently condemned by science.
> (Forero, 1892, p. 364)

Gonzalez Cuellar claimed:

> Once the crime has been committed, the theory of correction does not see in the delinquent an incorrigible being, devoid of rights or subject to capricious action, but rather a more or less dangerous individual, susceptible in any case of modifications employing an adequate treatment. Therefore, the seriousness of the crime is not in the magnitude of the damage caused as in the perversion of the agent, perversion that is measured by the probabilities of the repetition of the act.
> (González, 1892, p. 687)

In the following years, Medardo Rivas[11] (1893) and Arturo Quijano[12] (1898) also participated in the debate calling for the modernization of criminal jurisprudence in Colombia. The debate showed the prevailing tensions associated with constructing a nation-state. Regardless of theoretical and ideological affiliations, people discussed the scope of social control and the administration of justice. More importantly, they discussed the tensions between legal and legitimate, between what was cultural and what was political, between public and private, between the state and the population, and between morality and legislation.

The *Ley de Caballos* (Law 61, 1888), one of the most important criminal regulations of the time, is an example of the complexity of the debate raised during the *Regeneración*. The law established how the President of the Republic could face threats to public order from associations against the regime (Diario Oficial, 1888, p. 35):

1 To administratively prevent and repress crimes and offenses against the State that affect public order, being able to impose the penalties of confinement, expulsion from the territory, imprisonment, or loss of political rights for as long as is deemed necessary.
2 To prevent and repress, with the same penalties, conspiracies against public order and attacks against public or private property that involves, in his judgment, a threat of disturbance of order or the aim of instilling terror among citizens.
3 To erase from the ranks those soldiers who, by their conduct, become unworthy of the government's confidence in the opinion of a Magistrate.

> Article 2. The President of the Republic shall exercise the right to inspect and monitor scientific associations and educational institutes and is authorized to suspend, for the time he considers convenient, any Society or Establishment that, under scientific or doctrinal pretext, is the focus of revolutionary propaganda or subversive teachings.
> Article 3. To be put into effect, the measures taken by the President of the Republic under the power that this law confers to him must be definitively agreed upon in the Council of Ministers.
> Article 4. The penalties under this law do not exempt the convicts from the responsibility that corresponds to them before the judicial authorities under the Penal Code.

Caro used this law to persecute the new constitution's political opponents, which led to a wave of exiles, confinements, expropriations, and persecutions against the press. One of the most controversial points in the law was the subjectivity in the definition of the infraction and its gravity. The *Ley de Caballos* was a clear example of the rupture of Colombian conservatism with utilitarian ideas and its replacement with a system consistent with the moral premises of the Catholic church. It is also evident that political programs were imposed over Bentham's and Beccaria's universalistic ideas on criminal law.

The debate on the proportionality of penalties and their legal character was perceived as a significant advance for criminal law. It gave the legislator a central role because this figure determined clearly and precisely which behaviors were harmful and established the corresponding punishment. However, these principles were implemented so that the sense of increasing unrest was associated with what were seen as authoritarian and unjust practices.

Even if traces of Beccaria's and Bentham's ideas can be found in the penal code during the radical era, this is hardly the case in 1837 and 1890. These penal codes included physical punishments and established punishment and sanctions that limited or were contrary to individual freedoms. These changes in the codes reflect the debates and tensions of constructing a modern society where political power was disputed, and material restrictions loomed large.

4.4   The administration of justice in practice: a statistical approach

The previous section explained the differences between the 1837, 1873, and 1890 penal codes. The Penal Code of 1837 attempted to overcome the colonial regime's ideas but failed to accomplish a modern liberal conception. In contrast, the 1873 code was closer to liberal ideals and used Bentham's and Beccaria's principles mainly on restricting physical punishment. A new penal code was promulgated during the conservative government, which aimed to erect a social order far from utilitarian principles and consistent with Catholic charity. The remaining question is whether those legislative changes led to a difference in the execution of crimes.

Statistics can tell us whether the penal codes had any real effect. Part of building the state had to do with reliable statistics. At the time, there was an explicit effort to expand, unify and standardize statistics into a national system. Many statistics were produced with judicial information. However, the data quality was affected by the rapid change from federalism to centralism and the public financial and administrative capacities. We take three years, 1850, 1874, and 1882 as reference points to see the impact of the 1837 and 1873 codes.

Figure 4.1 shows the incidence of crimes in 1850, when the 1837 code was in force and when the first liberal reforms were starting to gain traction.

The most common crimes were theft and injury, typically punished with corporal punishment. The incidence of serious crimes was less frequent. Prison sentences could not exceed eight years. These statistics suggest that the preservation of some colonial measures did not cause an increase in more severe crimes. Contrary to Beccaria's premise, severe corporal punishment proved to be a deterrent that prevented more serious crimes from being committed. However, this conclusion must be drawn with caution because the data do not capture the motivations of those convicted, the circumstances of the crimes, or their levels of gravity.

The 1837 Penal Code included corporal and non-corporal punishment. In Adarve's (2012) words:

Corporal punishments were the following: death, forced labor, imprisonment, seclusion in a workhouse or prison, expulsion from the Republic's

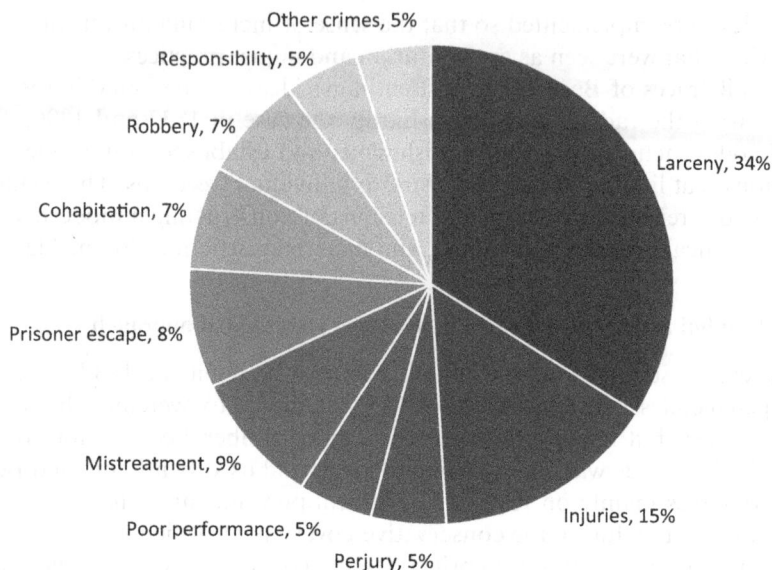

Figure 4.1 Percentage of crimes committed in 1850 in the Republic of Nueva Granada.
Source: General Archive of the Nation, Republic Fund, 1850.

territory, confinement in a particular parish district, canton, or province, and banishment from a particular place or district. The non-corporal ones were: express declaration of infamy; deprivation of political and civil rights, of some of them, or the suspension thereof; subject to surveillance by the authorities; disqualification or suspension from employment, profession, or public office in general, or in a specific class; deprivation of employment, pension, profession or public office; arrest; judicial warning; obligation to post good conduct bond; fine and loss of some effects whose amount is applied as a fine [...].

(p. 54)

Figure 4.2 presents the proportion of crimes committed after the promulgation of the 1873 Penal Code, when radical liberalism was in power and a strong anti-clerical feeling prevailed:

In this case, it is not surprising to find a higher incidence of crimes associated with authority and public order since it was a period of growing institutional instability, divisions between states, and threats of civil war. This situation may also explain the higher incidence of fights. Even though the Penal Code of 1873 had a liberal inspiration and, in principle, could lead to changes in crimes, the truth is that it preserved patterns observed when the code of 1837 was in force.

Figure 4.3 presents the proportion of crimes committed in 1882 after the rise of the conservatives to power. Homicide rises, and theft becomes less

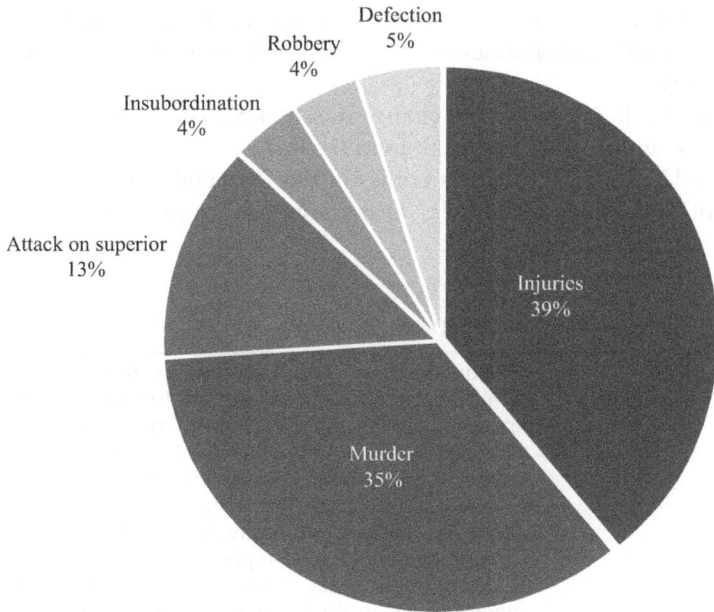

Figure 4.2 Percentage of crimes committed in the United States of Colombia 1874.
Source: General Archive of the Nation, Republic Fund, 1874.

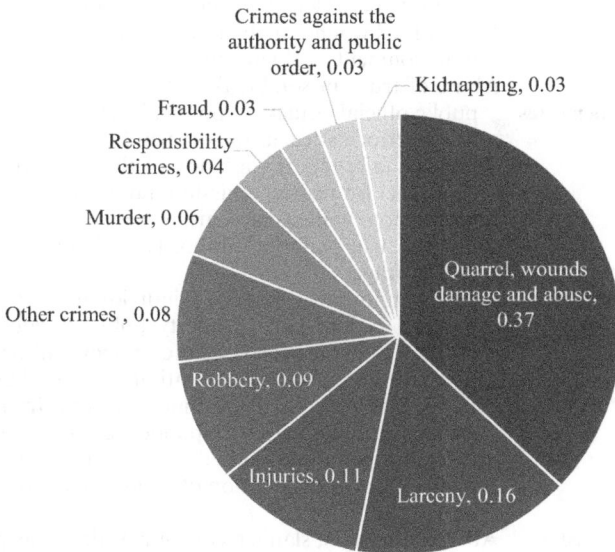

Figure 4.3 Percentage of crimes committed in 1882.
Source: General Archive of the Nation, Republic Fund, 1882.

frequent. The change from liberals to conservatives might explain the increase in insubordination and attacks on superiors, which reached 20% of all registered crimes.

Finally, Table 4.1 shows the change in sentences between the 1873 and the 1890 codes, with less severe penalties in the former.

Of the 12 acts established as crimes in the 1890 code, six were related to a breach of good faith in business. Other conduct relating to the violation of religious dogma became crimes.

Table 4.1 Changes to sentences between the 1873 and 1890 codes

Crimes with an increase in penalties	Abortion, obscenity, youth corruption, embezzlement, threat to authority, murder, riot, damage to property, indecent assault, assisting an escape, causes of responsibility against public officials, minting of gold-silver coins, cutting of copper or other coins, counterfeit currency circulation, damage to third-party property, crimes against modesty and good customs, poisoning, fraud, rape, falsehood, forgery, rent fraud, false report, letting a prisoner escape, injury to public officials, homicide, theft, arson, public incontinence, insults, insubordination, disrespect for justice, the introduction of fake gold and silver currency, the introduction of false currency other metals, mistreatment, negligence in the performance of one's duties, loss of a process, perjury, malfeasance, prostitution of a daughter, fraudulent bankruptcy, rebellion, sedition, theft of public documents, theft and destruction of public documents, attempted murder, attempted theft, attempted poisoning, attempted wounding, bigamy, violation of terms of imprisonment, and violence.
Crimes with a reduction in penalties	Abuse of trust, prison break-in and assault, attack on a public official, attack on political rights, desertion, poor work performance, using force and violence to a woman, giving a false report, violation of the Constitution, disrespect for justice, omission, taking a horse without permission, malfeasance, armed resistance to authority, fighting, usurpation of authority, and violation of freedom and suffrage.
Crimes with penalties unchanged	Child abandonment, attack on individual liberty, smuggling, damage to third-party property, public revenue fraud, crimes against property, failure to obey authority, dispossession, arbitrary detention, the illegal exercise of public employment, drunkenness at work, fraud, loss of public funds, loss of correspondence, child exploitation, extortion, failure to fulfill duties, resistance to acts of justice, improper retention of funds, and correspondence violation.
Crimes condemned in the 1890 Penal Code but not in the 1873 code.	Adultery, bawdry, slander, conspiracy, delays as prefect, prohibited games, embezzlement of public funds, mutilation, loss, curtailment and exchange of parcels, parcel theft, and use of someone else's property.

These figures do not show substantial changes in types of crimes or their incidence throughout the century. As Bernate (2004) and Adarve (2012) have noted, the changes in codes did not lead to significant changes in criminal behavior. Some variations are observed, but they can be attributed to the political changes of a century where struggles for defining state power were the norm.

Despite the change in the philosophical foundations of the codes, there is no evidence of significant changes in crime patterns. The crimes that were prosecuted were mainly in response to political priorities and environmental conditions associated with public order and government priorities. Debates on the utilitarian foundations of criminal law featured constantly in 19th-century Colombia; however, they remained in the ideological sphere and did not transcend law enforcement.

4.5 Conclusion

Studying the evolution of criminal law, crime, and penalties allow us to establish that the history of economic ideas also permeated criminal matters. There was no evidence of the mechanical transfer of European texts to the American world in the production of criminal laws and the administration of justice. The Colombian experience of justice administration shows the incorporation of the system's own needs imposed by the country's historical, economic, political, and social circumstances in the second half of the 19th century.

It is possible to identify the influence of Beccaria's and Bentham's utilitarian tradition in the content of the penal codes, and an interest in its application in the classroom. However, the reflections of moral philosophy in Nueva Granada and the transformation of the political and social environment throughout the 19th century account for the specificities that contextualized and distanced those debates and the penal codes from the normative conditions advanced by Beccaria and Bentham.

There was a normative dimension in the design of criminal codes in Colombia based on economic thought and a positive dimension of law enforcement and adaptation to the 19th-century context of Nueva Granada. The character of this dimension was more idiosyncratic, close to the political beliefs of the authors and governments, and based on principles that, although utilitarian, are not exhaustive in this tradition.

Despite the regulatory changes, no relationship was observed between the severity of the penalties contained in the penal codes and the incidence of some crimes. It was more the dynamics of public order and the social tensions characteristic of the second half of the 19th century that dictated the crime patterns of the time.

Archival Sources

General Archive of the Nation, Republic Fund, 1850, 1874, 1882.

Notes

1 Beccaria and Verri were part of the Milanese school and made important contributions to the economic theory of civil society. As described by Porta (2016, p. 99), they contributed with: "[...] an institutional notion of competition, conceived as a process embedded within civil society."
2 In line with modern economic analysis of the law (Goldman, 2017), Beccaria advanced that an effective punishment equals the damage the crime caused. We find an echo of this idea in Anglo-Saxon legal thought: "[...] a person will carry out an illicit act to the extent that she estimates that its potential benefits will outweigh the expected costs" (Goldman, 2017, p. 17).
3 In Colombia, the building of the Museo Nacional in Bogotá is inspired by the panopticon and was built originally as a prison.
4 There is a documented debate dealing with this connection between Bentham and Rojas in Colombian historiography. Jaramillo (2011) advances that Rojas's reasoning sometimes lacks logic and that he adds elements of liberal doctrines that do not necessarily correspond to Bentham's. In contrast, Hurtado (2016), tracing the discussion about Bentham's and Tracy's texts being compulsory in higher education in the second half of the 19th century, considers that, despite the controversy, their influence and promotion are undeniable, not only in the programs of political economy courses but also in other aspects of social life. See Chapter 1 for more on this.
5 These articles became the basis for the book "Study on Utilitarianism", published in 1869.
6 Understood as the set of techniques – both expository and interpretive – which were learned, used, and modified by practitioners and theoreticians of law, as well as the ideological background set of values, principles, doctrines, conceptual systems, and reasoning elaborated and shared by jurists.
7 The classical school has its foundations in natural law and understands the criminal as a subject who enjoys free will and, therefore, must be responsible for their actions.
8 The positivist school of criminal law maintains that the offender's behavior is determined (by biological, social factors, etc.), so the state's punishment is based on the dangerousness of the perpetrator and not on the seriousness of the act.
9 Aguilera (2002) argues that by then, both liberals and conservatives agree that there was an increase in crime, which was attributed to the "relaxation of customs", the weakening of the principle of authority, impunity, and the bad example set by the unjust and violent acts carried out by the government.
10 Law 23 of 1886 established a commission to prepare a penal code project that would amend the errors and fill in the gaps in the current law. The commission members were all jurists: Demetrio Porras, Clodomiro Tejada, Luis Carlos Rico, and Juan Pablo Restrepo were Councilors of State (Bernate, 2004).
11 Medardo Rivas (1825–1901) is considered a pioneer of educational reform in Colombia. During his political career, Rivas promoted legislation changes on slavery abolition and women's education. He was a constant contributor to the daily newspaper *El Siglo* and participated in the publication of the liberal party's founding manifesto.
12 Arturo Quijano (1873–1935) wrote the first thesis published in Colombia that addressed the history of criminal law as a central theme.

Bibliography

Adarve, L. (2012). La ejecución de las normatividades penales en Colombia: 1888–1910. *Estudios de Derecho*, 68(153), 50–67.
Aguilera, M. (2002). Las Penas. *Revista Credencial*. https://www.revistacredencial.com/historia/temas/las-penas

Beccaria, C. (2015). *Tratado de los delitos y de las penas.* Madrid: Universidad Carlos III. (Original work published 1764)

Bentham, J. (1823). *Tratados de legislación civil y penal.* (B. N. Colombia, Ed.) Mason e Hijo Bogotá.

Bernate, F. (2004). El código penal colombiano de 1890. *Estudios socio-jurídicos, 6*(2), 537–558.

Bressler, J. (2018). The economist and the enlightenment: how Cesare Beccaria changed Western civilization. *European Journal of Law and Economics, 46*(2), 275–302. doi:10.1007/s10657-016-9546-z

Cancino Moreno, A.J. (1990). *Las instituciones penales colombianas y su evolución a partir del código de 1837.* Bogotá: Universidad Externado de Colombia.

Caro, M. (1868). Principios de la moral. Refutación del sistema egoísta, In: *La Fe,* Bogotá, June 10, 1868, Trim I, No. 6, pp. 43–45; June 27, No. 7, pp. 52–53; July 11, No. 9, pp. 69–70; August 22, No. 15, pp. 117–117; August 29, No. 16, pp. 122–125.

Caro, M. (1869). *Estudio sobre el utilitarismo.* Editorial Biblioteca Nacional. Bogotá. https://catalogoenlinea.bibliotecanacional.gov.co/client/es_ES/search/asset/86726/0

Caro, M. (1989). *"Libertad de imprenta". Estudios constitucionales y jurídicos (segunda serie).* Bogotá: Instituto Caro y Cuervo.

Constitución Política de la República de Colombia (CRC). (1886). Bogotá: Universidad Externado de Colombia.

Diario Oficial. (1888). DO. Bogotá: No. 7.399, Bogotá, 29 de mayo.

Faucci, R. (2014). *A history of Italian Economic Thought.* Routledge, Taylor & Francis Group.

Forero, F. (1892). *El determinismo del Derecho Penal.* Bogotá: En Tesis del primer Externado 1886–1895. Universidad Externado de Colombia. 2011.

Goldman, D. (2017). Análisis económico del derecho penal y del derecho penal liberal: confluencias y bifurcaciones. *Revista Derecho Penal y Criminología, 38*(104), 13–74.

González, F. (1981). *Escritos Políticos, Jurídicos y Económicos.* Bogotá: Biblioteca Básica colombiana.

González, R. (1892). "Teorías Penales y sus instituciones". *Tesis del primer Externado 1886–1895.* Universidad Externado de Colombia. 2011. Bogotá.

Groenewegen, P. (2002). *Eighteenth century economics: Turgot, Beccaria, Smith and their contemporaries.* New York: Routledge.

Hurtado, J. (2016). La economía política en los estudios superiores en la segunda mitad del siglo XIX en Colombia. Ezequiel Rojas, sus influencias y programas. In J.S. Correa & A. Álvarez (Eds.), *Ideas Políticas en Colombia durante el primer siglo Republicano.* Bogotá: Universidad de los Andes y Colegio de Estudios Superiores de Educación (CESA). pp. 35–67.

Jaramillo, J. (2011). *El pensamiento colombiano en el siglo XIX.* Bogotá: Alfaomega.

Ley 112 del 26 de junio de 1873 (n.d.). Código Penal de los Estados Unidos de Colombia (CPEUC). Bogotá: Universidad del Rosario.

Ley 19 del 19 de octubre de 1890 (n.d.). Código Penal de la República de Colombia (CPRC). Bogotá: Universidad del Rosario.

MacKaay, E. (2000). History of law and economics. Available at: https://papyrus.bib.umontreal.ca/xmlui/bitstream/handle/1866/86/0029.pdf

Márquez, J. (2011). Control social y construcción de Estado. El código penal de 1837 y su influencia en la legislación criminal del Estado Soberano de Bolívar: 1870–1880. *Historia Caribe, VI* (18), pp. 65–87.

Nuñez, R. (1885). *El agua en el vino.* Colombia: En la Reforma política en Colombia. Imprenta de la Luz.

Porta, P. (2016). Free trade and protectionism in primary export economies. In M. García-Molina & H.M. Trautwein (Eds.), *Peripheral visions of economic development: New frontiers in development economics and the history of economic thought*. Routledge.

Quijano, A. (1898). *Ensayo sobre la evolución del derecho penal en Colombia*. Bogotá: Imprenta Medardo Rivas.

Rivas, M. (1893). *Conferencias sobre jurisprudencia criminal y reflexiones contra la pena de muerte, hechas en la Universidad Republicana*. Bogotá: Imprenta de Medardo Rivas.

Rojas, E. (1868). *Filosofía moral* (Biblioteca Nacional ed.). Bogotá: Imprenta de la Nación. https://catalogoenlinea.bibliotecanacional.gov.co/client/es_ES/search/asset/180254/0

Romero, S., & García, M. (2021). Prisiones en el siglo XIX colombiano: un balance historiográfico. *Revista de estudios históricos, 74*, 205–237.

Samper, J. (1858). *Apuntamientos para la historia política i social de la Nueva Granada*. (B. Nacional, Ed.) Bogotá: Imprenta el Neogranadino. https://catalogoenlinea.bibliotecanacional.gov.co/client/es_ES/search/asset/75406/0

Simon, F. (2009). Criminology and economic ideas in the age of Enlightenment. *History of economic ideas, 17*(3), 11–39.

Uribe, M.T. & López, L. (2006). *Las palabras de la guerra: un estudio sobre la memoria de las guerras civiles en Colombia*. Bogotá: La Carreta Histórica.

Velázquez, M. (2012). *La ciencia Útil. Una reconstrucción de las conciencias jurídicas procesales en Colombia y América Latina*. [Doctoral dissertation, Universidad de los Andes, Bogotá.

5 Fiscal Reform and the Origins of Social Spending in Colombia 1850–1886

Edwin López-Rivera[*]

5.1 Introduction

During the colonial period in Latin America, the Catholic Church was the principal provider of social welfare services, controlling almost every charitable organization under Christian charity. Although the Church's prominence in the charitable sphere remained after independence in the first half of the 19th century, one crucial aspect in creating the new states was the effort of governments to centralize power and take control over social services (Sanborn, 2005, p. 5). In the Republic of New Granada, now Colombia, the liberal government of José Hilario López (1849–1853) started a formal separation process between State and Church, in which the former began to provide social services that religious organizations had previously offered. In Colombia, as in many other Latin American countries such as Argentina, Brazil, Uruguay, and Mexico, the idea of public charity progressively replaced the notion of Christian charity, impacting the fiscal organization of these countries both in centralized and decentralized government levels (Sanborn, 2005, p. 6). The division between these two approaches to charity and their impact on the public provision of social welfare services was not immediate. It introduced a dynamic of competition and often cooperation between religious and government authorities. For example, although religious orders maintained responsibility for administrating the Charity Hospital in Popayán, a city in the country's southwestern region, the local government would pay for part of hospital expenses after 1863 (Velázquez, 1995). In Bogotá, the country's capital, the San Juan de Dios hospital experienced a similar budgetary arrangement (Restrepo, 2011). These two examples suggest the existence of some spaces for cooperation between the Church and the state at the local level, contrasting with the bitter political tensions between the central government and the Catholic Church since López's government.

The 1863 Constitution established the United States of Colombia (1863–1886), a federalist republic based on liberal principles created from the

[*] The author thanks Carlos Brando for helpful comments on a previous version during the "A History of Colombian Economic Thought" workshop at the Los Andes University in April 2022. All errors and omissions remain the exclusive responsibility of the author.

DOI: 10.4324/9781003289241-6

union of the Nine Sovereign States: Cundinamarca, Antioquia, Magdalena, Santander, Tolima, Bolívar, Cauca, Boyacá, and Panama. Under the terms of this constitution, the federal government fulfilled specific tasks in foreign defense, education, and the opening of interstate communication routes. The states had to organize their tax structure to finance their current expenses – bureaucracy, justice, and local police. Local governments also had to allocate resources to promote economic growth, such as education, infrastructure, and public charities, which started in 1850 with the fiscal decentralization law issued that year. The federal government, states, and municipalities began to create organizations such as Societies of Public Charity (*Sociedades de Benefi- cencia Pública*) to manage hospitals, hospices, and lazarettos, among others.

Central and local governments also passed legislation to create specific taxes and contributions to fund these organizations. According to National Budget Laws, the central government's average budget allocation in public charity and hospital administration was 8.3% in 1855–1861 and 1.2% in 1863–1885. Along with this public funding, discussions about who should be deserving of chari- table assistance from the government began to permeate the public debate on poverty and labor productivity in a period in which the Colombian economy was slowly inserting itself into the globalization of the 19th century.

Since the late colonial period, Bourbon governments had attempted to cen- tralize power and gain greater control over the provision of social services traced back to the period of the Bourbon Reforms at the end of the colonial period (Alzate, 2007). However, the liberal governments of the nascent republic of Colombia in the mid-19th century took a more determined step towards a secular state and gaining greater control over care of the sick and the treatment of poverty. This chapter studies the ideas of contemporary politicians and lib- eral intellectuals who supported the creation and public funding of Societies of Public Benefit to replace the Church's role in caring for the poor and the sick. It will also seek to analyze the impact of these ideas on the fiscal organization of local and national governments at this time. The sources will be tax and spending budget laws, treasury reports from provincial and federal govern- ments, newspaper articles, and writings by contemporary officials and observers.

The chapter consists of three sections. The first part presents the develop- ment of the idea of Christian charity at the end of the colonial period and the early years of the republic. The second section analyzes the role of public char- ity in the tax reform of the mid-19th century in Colombia, inspired by liberal ideas. The third part presents the operation of the new tax structure and the materialization of the idea of public charity in the budget allocations of the states that formed the United States of Colombia. The chapter ends with some conclusions.

5.2   Christian charity and the state-building process

The emergence of the Enlightenment in the 18th century introduced the ideas of democracy, citizenship, productivity, rationality, and the value of information gathering. It was an important source of inspiration for Colombian reformers. These ideas partially inspired the Bourbon public health reform during the late colonial period (Alzate, 2007) and spanned across the 19th century, inspiring Republican reformers to develop their ideas about poverty reduction, public health, sanitation, and productive workers in the future of the new country. After independence, Republican governments sought to build legitimacy among the population by providing state services such as justice, defense, health, and education. However, the different visions of how the new Colombian state should be organized led to bitter political conflict between elites organized around two political parties, liberals and conservatives, which frequently ended up in a military conflict that determined tax and budget priorities for governments, leaving expenditure on social services such as health and education (Sotomayor, 1997) in second place. The 1832 Constitution, however, was the first to include *beneficencia* or public charity. Concerns about poverty, welfare, and public health began to be a recurring topic in the writings of government officials and intellectuals after independence in the first half of the 19th century.[1]

One of the most significant obstacles that reformers of the Colombian state encountered in the post-independence period was the Church's important role in the administration of hospitals, charity organizations, and public health. The Catholic Church had been an integral part of political and social control during the colonial period, so the modernizing process undertaken by the Republican governments sought to minimize the influence of the Church in society. Although the state sought to take over some of the tasks traditionally carried out by the Church, especially in education and health, the state's fiscal weakness left a significant void for the Church and private charitable organizations to keep providing social services such as health care.

Since colonial times, the Church had been a significant actor in the protection of vulnerable populations such as elders, women, and children. Tithes and credit arrangements such as *censos* and *capellanias* were the primary sources of income the Church used to finance its clerical, educational, and hospital activities, even after independence. Religious orders continued to administer hospitals and train future generations of doctors, especially at the Universidad del Rosario's medical school. The Church had a significant role in establishing ideas and attitudes to disease and healing that changed gradually over time with the introduction of Western scientific ideas.

The emerging idea of beneficence or public charity took up the need to classify poverty, as had been done in colonial times. The establishment of the Real Hospicio de Santafé in 1790 exemplifies the materialization of health reforms in New Granada, supported by the Viceroy Jose Manuel de Ezpeleta. This hospital operated with a doctor, chaplain, manager, and two assistants, and it was financed by donations and some colonial funds. Its primary purpose was the classification and resocialization of beggars and people in need, distinguishing between "truly poor" people and simple loafers who took advantage of the work of others (Tierney, 1959, p. 55). Thus, an incipient notion of the "deserving poor" was introduced, people who were in poverty because of social and individual wrongs, that is, too old, disabled, or too sick. Only "deserving" poverty[2] was to be assisted with public policies, whereas idleness should be punished as a primary source of "undeserving" poverty. In this new approach, Catholic ideas such as "love of neighbor" (or *amor al prójimo*) and Christian charity were to be reconverted by the state into "public utility". Without departing totally from the Catholic doctrine, the Bourbon state reformulated the idea of "Catholic charity" and introduced the notion of "enlightened charity" (Ramírez, 2006, p. 127). Disease was a source of "deserved poverty" that the enlightened state should combat, not only with administrative measures but also by incorporating the scientific innovations in treating disease that were taking place in Europe at the turn of the 18th century.

Enlightenment philosophy paved the way for the Industrial Revolution by changing European political and economic systems and guiding its social organization and productivity considerations. Some aspects of the ideological and scientific revolution merged with elements of the Enlightenment, generating an "industrial Enlightenment" that gave rise to the new technologies of the Industrial Revolution (Mokyr, 2007). Utilitarianism emerged in philosophy, wielding its claims for the welfare of society, and changing the relationship between the state and the citizens, also conceived as workers. Capitalism and modernization required laws reflecting the new relationship between the states and the people about improving working conditions, hours of work, wages, and safety. The French Revolution also played an important role in the changes that were taking place in the Western world. The individual was supposed to become part of the state, which gave him a privileged position. It also reflected the changes in how the state interacted with the people at the onset of industrial capitalism. The materialization of this relationship implied a change in tax and public budget allocation priorities.

The constitutionalist movement began in the world of law, influencing the whole of Europe. In Spain, it was capitalized with the Cadiz Constitution, which inspired the Neogranadine process. The process of nation formation that started before independence was based on the creation of specific identities in Spain and Spanish America, using historical narratives and institutions in which colonial intellectuals went beyond mirroring or contesting European ideas. It also put forth audacious and original critiques of European epistemologies, resulting in substantially new ideas about democracy and modernity. Thus, despite military efforts to expel the Spanish from American territory, the heritage that had already been accomplished could not be denied, so the Iberian influence on the notions of sovereignty, federalism, and public administration, as well as on the drafting of the constitution, was present.

The Bourbon health reforms introduced at the end of the colonial period were a central part of this shared heritage. This reform was part of a civilizing project that sought to form healthy, obedient, and productive subjects based on specific practices linked to the canon defined by enlightened values. In New Granada, the reforms had to do, essentially, with establishing measures to combat epidemics within the organization and sanitation of the urban space (Alzate, 2007). Thus, the reforms sought to break the vicious circle between poverty and poor health conditions in the kingdom's subjects.

The incipient development of modern medical science in the early 19th century also pointed to the relationship between poverty and health conditions. In Europe, many scholars began to relate social conditions, such as housing, hygiene, and economic and urban planning, to health status. In other words, health was no longer going to be conceived as an isolated fact but as a part of the whole that affected society.[3] Public health as a legislative object resulted from social demands to improve the quality of life and work. It was increasingly becoming assumed that the desirable goal of protection from disease should apply, in principle, equally to all citizens of a nation-state. Secondly, the even more ambitious goal of positive human health improvement was becoming imaginable (Riley & Simone, 2003). European thinkers formulated proposals to improve public health through the intervention of the physical and social environment, considering for the first time that these should emanate from the state. Meanwhile, contemporaries were also faced with contradictory evidence that the world's first industrial revolution seemed to be having anything but obvious health benefits for most of the population (Szreter, 2003). In other words, the Enlightenment brought about democratic principles, the social contract, and the importance of the individual over the collective, setting the basis for new improvements in humanitarianism (Riley & Simone, 2003).

After independence, the 1821 Constitution set the foundational principles of the new republic of Colombia constituted by current Colombia, Ecuador, and Venezuela. However, even when freedom of belief was enshrined in the first Constitution, the Catholic Church kept its power over land, financial matters, health of the poor, and education. After the dissolution of Colombia in 1831, the political environment between the separation of first Colombia and the emergence of the Republic of New Granada was affected by conflicts between the opposing tendencies associated with conservative and liberal ideas. Although liberal ideas proposed a model of the state where priority was given to freedom, equality, and less interference by the state in the life of individuals, those somewhat utopian ideas are widely discussed by various authors, even though these principles were enshrined in the Constitution of 1832 (Blanco, 2007). However, the slow introduction of liberal ideas into the institutional structure of the new state paved the way for a greater separation of the Church from the affairs of the state, one of the most prominent political discussions during the 19th century.

For the second half of the 19th century, the tensions between the old visions of Christian charity and the new concerns about productivity converged in the need to relieve the conditions of poverty of the population. Poverty and public charity were two central concerns in Colombia during the mid-19th century, openly discussed in the press and in important writings of the time, such as *La miseria en Bogotá* published originally in 1867 by Miguel Samper (1969). These social concerns arose from the visibility of poverty in the main urban centers and because of the fear, often expressed, that the country was approaching the situation of European pauperism that ended up in uprisings, such as those of the Paris Commune (Martínez, 2001). Both public and private charities were founded to help the poor and produced guidelines to mitigate the problem of poverty and control social unrest. The key ideas that guided the practices developed by the state and institutions to address the problem of care for the underprivileged in the second half of the 19th century and the first half of the 20th century in Colombia revolved around three notions: charity, social action, and public assistance.

The notion of charity is linked to the precepts of Catholic Christianity. During the colonial period, the Spanish monarchy provided protection and support for evangelization and the organization of the Church; education and the few existing health and welfare facilities were administratively delegated to the Church. The political rupture represented by the Spanish-American independence meant the possibility of rethinking the relations of the new nations in formation with the Holy See. The new rulers, with respect for religion, wanted to maintain control over the Church – the patronage – without guaranteeing its situation of privilege or monopoly. Therefore, one of the great political discussions of the first half of the 19th century was about the place and function of the Church in society. On the other hand, the Catholic Church wanted to free itself from state control. However, simultaneously, it wanted to maintain its privileged situation and monopoly over other religious denominations (Martínez, 2001).

5.3 Public charity and fiscal reform

The middle of the 19th century was a period of liberal reforms in Colombia and other countries in Latin America – reforms that aimed to reduce the burden of the colonial legacy on its institutions. The first fiscal reforms were undertaken during the government of General Mosquera, between 1845 and 1849, to dilute the monopolistic, controlling, and authoritarian state and give way to one that would promote favorable policies for economic development and encourage exports and the development of free enterprise. These reforms also included the confiscation of mortmain,[4] local governments control of clerical funds, and the expulsion of Catholic orders such as the Society of Jesus. The reforms produced tensions between Church and state that mainly impacted the provision of those services traditionally delivered by the Catholic Church: education, hospital administration, and the care of the poor. The controversy was centered on the differences between Christian and public charity, which were considered mutually exclusive practices in the broader discussion of the secularization of the state and the development of a form of public administration controlled by civilians and managed independently of the Church and its hierarchies. The reforms impacted the funding and administration of facilities for the poor that depended on a religious association or community. However, in some cases, local governments also had some involvement. Initially, these facilities were entirely owned by municipal governments.

Hospitals, hospices, and even schools managed by religious communities were progressively transferred to local governments. In some cases, the communities were called upon by governments to establish contracts or different kinds of agreements to manage these facilities. These arrangements implicitly expressed the inexperience of the governments and the fact that the Church had accumulated long experience in this area. The debate on the ideas of public and Catholic charity vanished before the fact that the Church and the local governments had to cooperate in managing charitable facilities. The notion of charity was revitalized and returned to the forefront, strengthened by the renewed presence of the Church and the social forces that supported it (Arrom, 1997).

Having managed to create a system of care for the poor in the hands of local governments, the reforms contributed to transforming the traditional notion of charity in the direction of public charity or beneficence. Regardless, by force of circumstances, this meant entering into agreements with religious institutions and communities for its administration. The difference with the previous period, when the Catholic order independently managed these facilities, was that the state created specialized establishments and offices for that purpose and committed itself to a program of economic aid for the institutions, imposing some level of control over religious orders. Institutional aid before 1870 was little and concentrated in large urban centers, essentially in establishments such as hospitals, caring for the sick poor, and exceptionally the House of Refugee of Bogotá, founded in the late 18th century as a hospice. After 1870, changes in institutional aid were observed, mainly the foundation and creation of more specialized establishments, especially in the most significant urban centers, trying to ensure the dominance of the establishments and the responsibilities of local, regional, and national governments.

The most outstanding efforts of institutional aid during the liberal governments focused on education. The field of education was separated from that of charity, and the Board of Public Instruction was created with responsibility for promoting education, mainly free primary schools. Apart from the education houses, the health and protection houses were also important establishments for institutional assistance. These establishments were promoted by municipal and regional governments, created by secular societies, and promoted by Church authorities or, in some cases, by religious congregations. In this time frame, the capacity to house the poor grew. During this period, institutional aid to isolate and lock up the poor was firmly established in the main Colombian cities, as in most Latin American countries (Martínez- Vergne, 1999). Most large cities had a shelter for the indigent that also provided care for people with mental health issues and orphans, founded with public resources through municipal or departmental authorities. The new facilities that private organizations or individuals created were complementary to the efforts of the state, which were always limited.

In 1887 the Central Board of Hygiene and Departmental Boards of Hygiene were established in each state. These boards were promoted and administered by physicians responsible for setting out plans and ideas about public health in the country. Before these organizations were established, public health action was taken only in emergencies, such as epidemic events. Most of the social assistance activity took place in urban large and medium-sized environments. However, the activity was much more concentrated in the Colombian cities that showed more significant growth and dynamism. This geographical distribution of social assistance was surprising given that, by this time, the population in Colombia lived mainly in the countryside (Castro, 2001). The concentration of social assistance in urban areas was also a constant in Europe, where attention to the poor population had from early on mainly been focused on the cities (Jutte, 1994), where poverty was possibly more visible, more "dangerous," and more pressing than in the countryside.[5]

The creation of public charities to serve the poorest and most needy was a fundamental transformation in the organization of the state and an expression of the government's interest in playing a more active role in these critical aspects of the public sphere. Nevertheless, the development and operation of these organizations required fiscal resources. In the context of liberal reforms, in 1852 the state decreed the decentralization of taxes, rents, contributions, and expenses proposed by the liberal intellectual Salvador Camacho Roldán and its leading promoter, the future president Manuel Murillo Toro. The new law sought to abolish the taxes of the old regime and replace them with modern taxes. Taxes such as tithes and fifths that used to be the primary funding source for Church activities were transferred from central to provincial governments in the hope that local government could eliminate them more easily than the central government (Melo, 2007).

Other taxes, such as those on liquor, tolls, and gold smelting, were transferred to the states, which, on the expenditure side, had to pay for the local judicial system, regional communication channels, and the salaries of priests and others in charge of Catholic ceremonies. Camacho Roldan estimated that the total value of the rents transferred was more than 530,000 pesos, while the expenditure for which the provinces were now responsible amounted to some 435,000 pesos (Melo, 2007). These reforms were the first step towards Colombian federalism, established thirteen years later, and in practice, determined the behavior of public finances for the following three decades. Between 1851 and 1857, there were a series of modifications from the old colonial income system to one more in line with the justice and equality of Republican institutions.

These inaugurated a period in which the governments of the different states composing the new pseudo-federal country created taxes, contributions, offices, and spending items to finance sanitation activities in cities, hospital administration, and disease containment in the event of epidemic outbreaks. This process developed fully with the federal constitution of 1863. The new *carta magna* organized the country into nine states (Cundinamarca, Antioquia, Magdalena, Santander, Tolima, Bolívar, Cauca, Boyacá, and Panama) with autonomy over their constitutions and congresses, taxes, and bureaucratic organization. This constitution arose as a solution to the conflicts that had plagued the territory since independence, looking for a middle ground between the excessive local-ism that had caused the previous wars and the attempt to build a stable nation and political order, a task that had been pending since independence (Lewin, 2008). The constitution gave the states greater autonomy to determine their tax revenues and manage their expenditure. It ordered the regional administra-tions to establish a productive tax system that would promote their region's economic development. In addition, it limited the specific functions of the national government to fields such as defense, education, and the opening of roads.

5.4 Government spending and taxation on public charities in a decentralized context

One of the reasons for establishing federal systems was the decentralization of the collection of income from the treasury, which considered the particu-larities of each territorial unit into which the country was divided and made the provision of public goods more consistent with the preferences of the inhabitants of each state. In a federal system, the citizens were supposed to feel closer to the politicians they elected, allowing the local government to exercise better control over the population. At the same time, they were to influence public spending, forming a virtuous circle of consensus taxation that financed the works and satisfied the majority's preferences. In centralism, the opposite was supposed to happen: the leaders were not very dependent on the citizens, they tended to oppress them with taxes, and the spending was inefficient (Lewin, 2008).

It was usual for centralism to decree taxes without legislative approval, thus violating the golden rule of political liberalism that representation was what gave legitimacy to taxation. In the Colombian case, the tendency to capture the bulk of taxation with the import tariff reflected the political inclination to resort to a relatively invisible burden on citizens and enlist the support of man-ufacturing or artisanal sectors that benefited from the protection of local pro-duction. The rejection of direct taxation and property tax reflected, in turn, the great prerogatives acquired by the Creoles, even under Spanish rule, by the King's grants of large tracts of land, considered a privilege graciously granted by the now Republican state which distributed them in a more disorganized and general manner than the Crown, and exempt from any obligation. If dur-ing the colonial period the most observant landowners had paid their tithes to maintain worship and the care and educational organization managed by the Church, this practice ceased with the republic after the manumission of mort-main in 1863 (Rojas, 2004).

The strengthening of local finances after 1850 was remarkable, mainly due to the export boom, whose volatility also weakened them. With the beginning of the Regeneration, political and fiscal centralization was implemented. In 1870, Camacho Roldan, proud of the system he had promoted, pointed out: "the fiscal situation of the States has taken consistency; the sectional administration has become more rigid; the income product is today three and a half times higher than in 1857 and 1863, probably as well" (Memoria de Hacienda, 1870). Fiscal organization differed among states. While Santander, Boyacá, Cauca, Tolima, and Cundinamarca opted for direct contribution, the remaining states maintained a fiscal system that taxed production and consumption, highlighting the rights of consumption and income from alcohol. However, it is necessary to emphasize that indirect contribution was the central collection source in all states, even those that opted for direct contribution (Melo, 2007). In 1874 the income from direct contribution corresponded to 40% of the total, and in 1877 it was 60% (Archivo Departamental de la Gobernación de Boyacá, 1877, p. 77).[6] In any case, the most important taxes in most states were indirect, and the participation of these was high and growing during the period.

As part of the fiscal autonomy that local governments enjoyed under the terms of the 1863 Constitution, the states that were created earmarked taxes for spending on public charity. The State of Cundinamarca, for example, created the following taxes and contributions to finance the Department of Public Charity (Departamento de Beneficencia):

- *Impuesto para Lazareto*
- *Mitad del impuesto de registro y anotación*
- *Impuesto de beneficencia*
- *Impuesto sobre sitios de juego*
- *Derechos sobre las casas y sitios de juego*
- *Rentas del Lazareto (de Agua de Dios), Hospital de la Caridad, Hospicio de Bogotá, de los asilos de indigentes y casas de locos, del Hospital San Juan de Dios*
- *Donaciones y contribuciones voluntarias para asilos y hospicio de Bogotá*
- *Mortuorias (para lazareto)*
- *Subvención nacional para lazareto*
- *Junta General de Beneficencia*

States and even the central government transformed their fiscal structures, and some states, such as Cundinamarca and Panama, also created *Juntas de Beneficencia*, or charity boards. The tax reform also paved the way for transforming public expenditure to reflect the realities of the local public administrations and the priorities and aspirations of liberal governments. One common task that the states undertook was to build roads and infrastructure, as reflected in public budget allocations between 1856 and 1899: around 27% was allocated to the Department of Public Works, which was the most significant expense during this period. On average, the remaining expenditure (public debt, government, justice, interior, public instruction, treasury, and war) was financed by 10% of the total. The Public Charity Department received 4% of the budget on average (Figure 5.1); however, budget allocation for issues such as vaccination campaigns and medical care can be found in the budgets allocated to

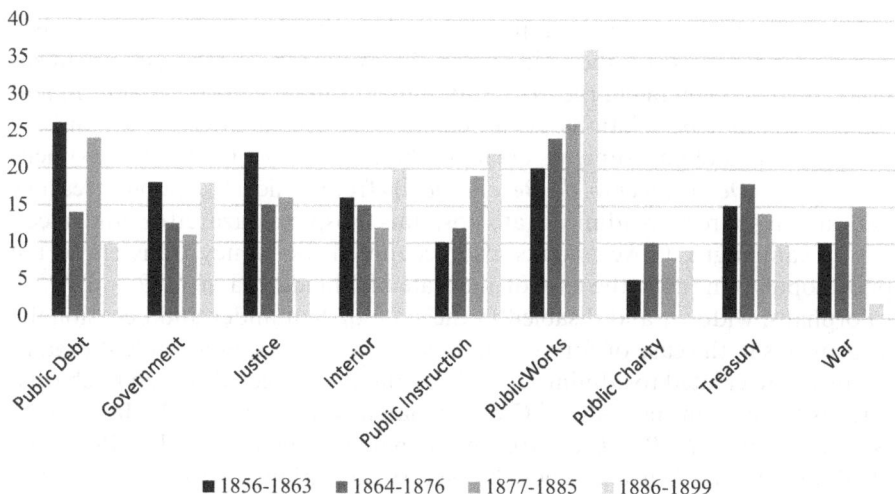

Figure 5.1 Budget allocations between 1856 and 1899.

Source: Federal and states budget laws (1856–1899) and Annex 1.

government and interior. Governments also allocated resources for the construction and improvement of hospitals, but they were accounted for in public works budgets.

With the expulsion of some religious orders during the liberal period, groups of citizens who were members of the economic elites established charitable organizations, with Catholic inspiration, to continue providing care to the poor and needy in the cities. These organizations, which promoted home medical visits to poor populations, were primarily run by the wives of conservative politicians, political allies of the Catholic Church. Two examples were the *Congregación del Sagrado Corazón de Jesús* (1873) and *Sociedad Protectora de Niños Desamparados* (1883). These organizations not only had charitable purposes inspired by Church doctrine but also harbored political objectives.[7]

Elites and incipient business people also may have aimed to keep the working classes healthy to maintain their productivity in the early years of Colombian capitalism. An additional hypothesis is that by keeping vulnerable populations healthy, elites reduced the likelihood of becoming ill themselves during epidemic episodes. Other mutual and charitable organizations also emerged to care for women, children, the elderly, and workers in need during the beginnings of Colombian capitalism. The actions of these charitable organizations were intended to maintain the presence of Catholic principles in the public sphere and among poor populations in the hostile environment for the Catholic Church created by liberal radicalism. However, these practices were also based on principles that precede modern Catholic social teaching, such as life and dignity, solidarity, choice for the poor and vulnerable, and dignity of work for the incipient working class in the Colombian regions.

These charitable societies responded to the reforms introduced by the liberal governments to fill the void left by the expulsion of religious organizations that had been in charge of the administration of schools, hospitals, and the care of poor populations. As a first step, the central government and the nine federal state governments created a budget item called the Department of Charity (*Departamento de Beneficencia*), from which the public treasury allocated resources to administrate hospitals, hospices, lazarettos, and vaccination campaigns. Governments also accounted for money transfers to the poor population (as in the case of the state of Magdalena in 1869 and 1870), to orphans, widows, and disabled in the state of Santander and occasionally as pensions in the case of former soldiers. In some cases, independent organizations were created to administer and execute the budget allocated to charity. Such is the case in the state of Cundinamarca, which created Public Charity Boards (*Juntas de Beneficencia*), and Panama, which created a Board of Health (*Junta de Sanidad*). These budgetary allocations varied among states; however, all states include allocations for "public charity" in their expense reports (Annex 5.1).

Spending requirements at all levels of public administration grew in practically all the states by the 1880s due to investments in public works and railroads (Figure 5.1), causing states to turn increasingly to the national treasury (Ocampo, 1984). This generated a deep deficit in the central government between 1880 and 1883. National transfers and aids were interpreted as "a reappearance of centralism and a weakening of the local energy that had been tried to promote with the mid-century decentralization" (Ocampo, 1984, p. 355). In the specific case of Antioquia, the expenditure was calculated in expense budgets that were classified into expense departments for the liquidation and recognition of the credits to the creditors and the ordering of the payments (Table 5.1).

Table 5.1 Antioquia's expense departments

Spending departments	1859	1867
Public debt	Acknowledgment and payment of any type of debt incurred by the state/department.	
Government	Personnel and material expenses of the legislature, the Governor's Office, the Department Prefectures, and other public administration employees in the executive branch.	Personnel and material expenses of the Assembly, Governor's bonus and personnel and material expenses of the territorial subdivisions (prefectures, mayors' offices, and townships), and per diems
Justice	Personnel and material expenses of the State Superior Court, the Circuit and Parish Courts, the employees of the Public Ministry and the wardens of the Circuit prisons.	Salaries of prison staff and support and transfer of unionized and poor prisoners.

(Continued)

Table 5.1 (Continued)

Spending departments	1859	1867
Interior	Expenses related to official prints, prisoners' conduct, maintenance of poor prisoners, and order and health police.	Expenses related to printing, personnel, and material of the printing house, the Guardia Civil, and the Gendarmería.
Treasury	Expenses related to the personnel and material of the General Accounting Office, the General Administration of the Treasury, the other collection offices, the Post Office Administration, and other expenses of the administration, collection, and accounting of income and contributions.	Expenses related to the personnel of the Secretary of the Treasury, the General Administration of the Treasury, the General Office of Accounts, and the Municipal Collectors; personnel and material of the Post Office Administration; personnel of the Registry Offices and related.
Public Instruction	Expenses for personnel and materials of the State College [later University] and other educational establishments that the State supports.	Personnel and material expenses of the secretary of the branch; salary of the undersecretary; personnel and material of the University of Antioquia.
Charity	Aid to charity hospitals and pensions granted by the legislature.	Subsidy to hospitals, charities, and societies.
Public Works (Development)	Expenditure on personnel and materials for correctional facilities, construction, repair, and improvement of public buildings, roads, and circuit prisons.	Expenses related to the Antioquia Railroad and the Junta de Caminos, acquisition, refurbishment, and improvement of public buildings and departmental roads, and related.

Source: Estado de Antioquia, Law of December 16, 1859, and Estado de Antioquia, Ordinance July 27, July 15, 1896.

Decreasing revenues and rising spending were putting pressure on state finances by the 1870s. In the case of spending on public charity, the state of Antioquia, for example, went from being responsible for maintaining hospitals to subsidizing charitable organizations' activities (Table 5.1). Although this illustrates a certain level of cooperation between the government and private agents, it also increased pressures on the budget. The fiscal crisis that manifested itself in other states added to the discontent on the part of conservative sectors and led to the end of liberal radicalism in the early years of the 1880s.

5.5 Conclusion

In the mid-19th century, the government of the New Granada Republic undertook significant reforms to promote the separation between the State and the

Catholic Church, which had been instrumental in the relief of the poor during the colonial period and the early years of the republic. The liberal governments of New Granada also looked to reduce the burden of the fiscal colonial legacy on its institutions. The first fiscal transformations were undertaken during the government of General Mosquera, between 1845 and 1849, to dilute the monopolistic, controlling, and authoritarian State and replace it with one that would promote policies favorable for economic development and encourage exports and the development of free enterprise.

Local governments and even the central government adopted earmarked taxes. Some also created *Juntas de Beneficencia*, or charity boards, to set public policy on attention to the poor. The contrast between the *Juntas de Beneficencia* and the budget allocations of the *Departamentos de Beneficencia* on the one hand and private organizations on the other represents the debate between public and private charity that marked public concerns about care for the poor population in the 19th century.

After 23 years of the radical federal system established in the liberal constitution of 1863, a political coalition of moderate liberals and conservative leaders won the 1884 Colombian general election. The elected president was Rafael Núñez, a moderate liberal transformed into a leading coalition member who sought to abolish the reforms introduced by the liberal party in the 1863 Constitution, including fiscal federalism. Different state governments, led by radical liberals, resisted militarily the new policies that threatened their political

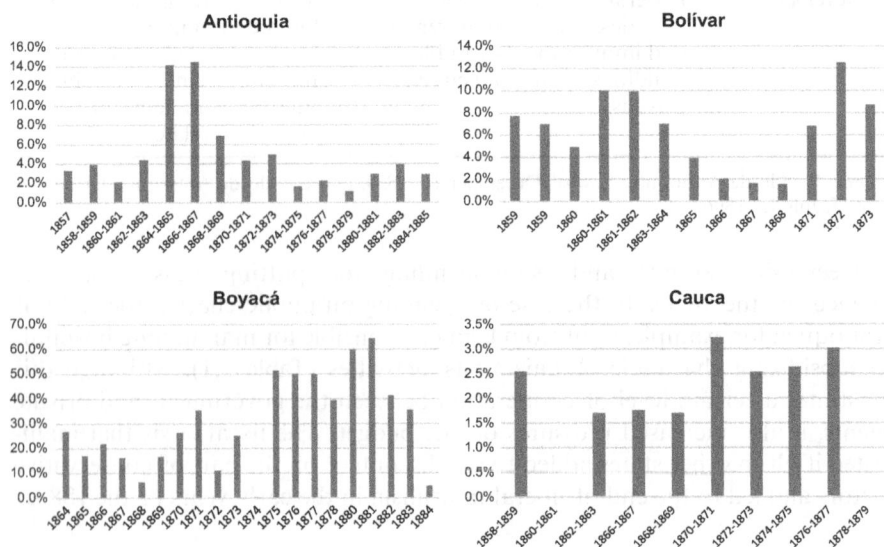

Annex 5.1 Evolution of the expense in public charity as a percentage of the total expenditures.

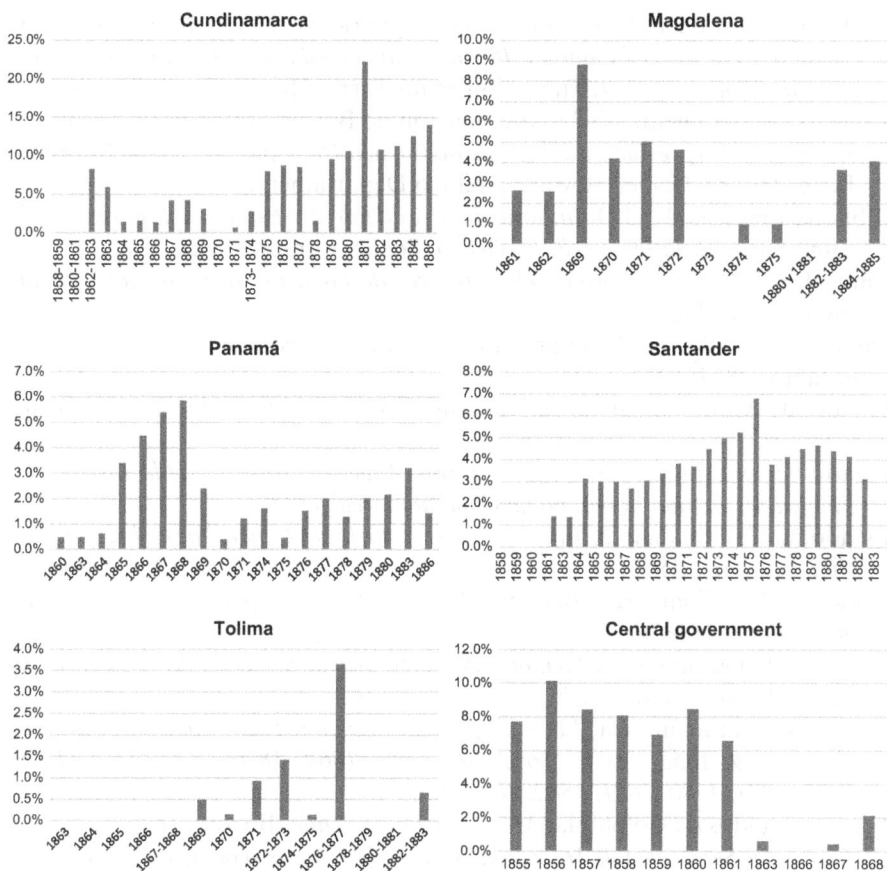

Annex 5.1 (Continued)

and taxation autonomy. The federal government eventually stopped the local rebellions, taking control of the state governments and repealing the old constitution, replacing it with a new one in 1886. The new constitution introduced a series of reforms that reduced taxes and the budgetary autonomy of the regional entities known as *departamentos*, or departments, under the new constitution. It centralized the fiscal administration in Bogotá, which became the country's and the department of Cundinamarca's capital.

Archival Sources

Archivo Departamental de la Gobernación de Boyacá. *Informe del Presidente del Estado 1858–1868.*

Archivo Departamental de la Gobernación de Boyacá. 1886. *Informe del presidente del Estado Soberano de Boyacá a la Asamblea Legislativa en sus sesiones de 1868.* págs 3–4. Tunja. Imprenta Torres Hnos y Cía., en Boyacá.

Archivo Departamental de la Gobernación de Boyacá. *Informe del Secretario de Hacienda al presidente del estado de Boyacá 1877.* pág 77. Tunja. Imprenta Torres Hnos y Cía, en Boyacá. Archivo Departamental.

Biblioteca Nacional. 1870. *Informe del Presidente del Estado de Santander a la Asamblea Legislativa de 1870: parte 6.* Socorro: Imprenta Del Estado.

Camacho, J. (1890). *Informe del secretario de hacienda al señor gobernador.* Imprenta del Departamento.

Departamento de Cundinamarca Leyes de presupuesto de rentas y gastos de los años: 1887–1912.

Estado de Cundinamarca, *Informe del secretario de Gobierno de Cundinamarca,* 1863.

Estado de Cundinamarca, *Tercer Informe Anual del director de la Instrucción Pública del Estado Soberano de Cundinamarca,* 1873.

Estado de Cundinamarca, *Informe del secretario de General al Gobernador de Cundinamarca,* 1873.

Estado de Cundinamarca, *Decreto 130 de 1878 sobre liquidación de gastos del presupuesto de 1879.*

Estado de Cundinamarca, *Memoria del secretario de hacienda del Estado soberano de Cundinamarca,* 1879.

Estado de Cundinamarca, *Leyes de presupuesto de rentas y gastos de los años: 1857, 1859, 1863, 1864, 1866, 1867, 1868,1869, 1870, 1874, 1875, 1876, 1877, 1878, 1880, 1881, 1882, 1883, 1884.*

Estados Unidos de Colombia, *Memoria de Hacienda,* Bogotá, 1871.

Memoria del Secretario de Hacienda del Estado Soberano del Cauca. 1877.

Informe del Secretario de Hacienda del Estado Soberano del Cauca a la Lejislatura. 1881, 1883, 1869, 1871, 1872, 1873, 1875.

Informe del Secretario de Gobierno del Estado Soberano del Cauca a la Lejislatura. 1881, 1883, 1869, 1871, 1872, 1873, 1875.

Informe del secretario de hacienda del Estado Soberano del Cauca a la lejislatura en sus sesiones ordinarias de 1873 (Bartolomé Castillo). Popayán, Imprenta del Estado, 1873.

Provincia de Bogotá, *Informe del gobernador de la Provincia de Bogotá 1856,* Presupuesto provincial de gastos para el servicio del año económico de 1856 a 1857.

Sánchez, S. (1898). *Informe del secretario de hacienda al señor gobernador.* Imprenta del Departamento.

Notes

1 Antonio Nariño, one of the first ideologues of Colombia's independence, considered the role that social assistance and public charity should have in the new republic. Nariño, president between 1811 and 1813, considered that "Giving only to the

needy is paying a debt to humanity and a right to society. Giving comfort to families and distributing charitable relief is the perfection of public charity." On these premises, he created the Particular Board of Charity, with a statute that had to be adhered to by the General Board, made up of twelve gentlemen who "will be honored with the title of Fathers of the Poor" and an advisory group of ladies who were distinguished with the name of Sisters of Charity, in the manner of the religious congregation founded in Paris in 1635 by Saint Vincent de Paul for the practice of charity among the poor. Hernández de Alba (1973), On the poor (Thoughts or notes for memory on the poor, pp. 9–10); On beneficence (Chaptal in his letter to the prefects, pp. 11–14). Lost original from the National Library, section 1, no. 12137. Anselmo Pineda Fund. Only the transcript made by Guillermo Hernández de Alba is preserved.

2 On deserving poverty, the *Decretum Gratiani*, a collection of canon law written in the 12th century, introduced a whole theory around the ideas of the "deserving" and "undeserving" poor (Tierney, 1959, p. 55). This terminology would later be used intensively, particularly in the rise of the welfare state in Europe and the United States. See Alice O'Connor (2009). *Poverty Knowledge: Social Science, Social Policy, and the Poor in Twentieth-Century U.S. History*. Princeton University Press.

3 Moris and Titmuss demonstrated that the incidence of such "individual" afflictions as juvenile rheumatism, rheumatic heart diseases, and peptic ulcer varied according to changing social conditions, such as unemployment. See Ann Oakley (1996). *Man, and Wife - Richard and Kay Titmuss: My parents' Early Years*. Harper Collins.

4 The mortmain were real estate, furniture, vehicles, and census (mortgage loans) that could not be sold or redeemed; therefore, they were out of the market. Almost all the goods included in the mortmain extension were those controlled by the clergy, which derived tremendous economic and political power. The radical wing of the liberal party that governed between 1863 and 1876 promoted reforms to eliminate obstacles of the old regime to advance production; the most important was the manumission or disentailment of mortmain.

5 It is highly possible that there was more informal aid in the rural areas – very little is recorded in the official archives – or that aid institutions were strengthened and consolidated if they maintained closer links with the political power established in the capital.

6 Report written by the Finance Secretary to be read by the President of the State of Boyacá 1877, 77.

7 The formation of societies for charitable purposes raises the question of whether the actions of these organizations are motivated by altruism or selfishness. In *Leviathan*, Thomas Hobbes argues that selfishness is fundamental to human nature and thus affects behavior, thereby questioning the human's supposed 'social nature.' If this is so, then a human being interested in the association does so out of personal, particular interest and not necessarily out of benevolence towards others; they do not do it out of charity (Peña, 2017). For Hobbes, civil societies are not mere groups; they are alliances, and loyalties and pacts are necessary to achieve them (Hobbes, 1642/1984). Although individuals find loneliness annoying, associations are only sought for selfish purposes, which can end up being common, to the extent that there are loyalties and pacts around specific issues, such as protection from the influence of the Church in Colombian society in the mid-19th century.

Bibliography

Alzate, A.E. (2007). *Suciedad y Orden: Reformas Sanitarias Borbónicas En La Nueva Granada 1760–1810*. Colección Textos de Ciencias Humanas. Escuela de Ciencias Humanas.

Archivo Departamental de la Gobernación de Boyacá. (1877). Informe del Secretario de Hacienda al presidente del estado de Boyacá 1877. Tunja. Imprenta Torres Hnos y Cía, en Boyacá. Archivo Departamental.

Arrom, S.M. (1997). ¿*De la caridad a la beneficiencia? Las reformas de asistencia pública desde la perspectiva del Hospicio de Pobres de la Ciudad de Mexico, 1856–1871*. (Instituciones, actores sociales y conflicto político 1774–1931).

Blanco, J. (2007). De la gran Colombia a la Nueva Granada, contexto histórico-político de la transición constitucional. *Prolegómenos X*(20): 71–87.

Castro, B. (2001). *Charity and Poor Relief in a Context of Povery: Colombia 1870–1930*. Oxford University Press.

Memoria de Hacienda. (1870). República de Colombia.

Estado de Antioquia. Law of December 16, 1859.

Estado de Antioquia. Ordinance July 27, July 15, 1896.

Hernández de Alba, G. (1973). Nariño, Precursor de la asistencia social. Una faceta desconocida. Sesquicentenario de la muerte de Nariño. Bogota. Beneficencia de Cundinamarca.

Hobbes, T. (1642/1984). *Leviatán o la materia, forma y poder de una república eclesiástica y Civil*. Fondo de Cultura Económica.

Jutte, R. (1994). *Poverty and Deviance in Early Modern Europe*. Cambridge University Press.

Lewin, Alfredo. (2008). Historia de las Reformas tributarias en Colombia. In Eleonora Lozano (Ed.) *Fundamentos de la tributación*. Ediciones Uniandinas, Temis.

Martínez, F. (2001). *El Nacionalismo Cosmopolita. La referencia europea en la construcción nacional en Colombia, 1845–1900*. Banco de la Republica e Instituto Frances de Estudios Andinos.

Martinez-Vergne, T. (1999). *Shaping the Discourse on Space. Charity and its Wards in Nineteenth-Century San Juan, Puerto Rico*. Texas University.

Melo, J. (2007). Las vicisitudes del modelo liberal 1850–1899. In J.A. Ocampo (Ed.) *Historia económica de Colombia*. Planeta.

Mokyr, J. (2007). *The Enlightened Economy. An Economic History of Britain 1700-1850*. Yale University Press.

O'Connor, A. (2009). *Poverty Knowledge: Social Science, Social Policy, and the Poor in Twentieth-Century U.S. History*. Princeton University Press.

Oakley, A. (1996). *Man and Wife: Richard and Kay Titmuss: My parents' Early years*. Harper Collins.

Ocampo, J.A. (1984). Centralismo, descentralización y federalismo en la historia colombiana. In J.A. Ocampo & S. Montenegro (Eds.) *Crisis Mundial, protección e industrialización* (345–366). Ensayos de historia económica colombiana.

Peña, E. (2017). La dificultad entre la caridad y la filantropía: un aspecto a revisar en el marco de las acciones voluntarias en Colombia. *Panorama 11*(20), 61–74.

Ramírez, M.H. (2006). *De la caridad barroca a la caridad ilustrada. mujeres, género y pobreza en la sociedad de Santa fe de Bogotá, siglos XVII y XVIII*. Universidad Nacional de Colombia.

Restrepo, L.S. (2011). *El Hospital San Juan de Dios, 1635–1895: una historia de la enfermedad, pobreza y muerte en Bogotá*. Universidad Nacional de Colombia, Sede Bogotá, Facultad de Ciencias Humanas, Departamento de Historia, Centro de Estudios Sociales-CES.

Riley, J. & Simone, S. (2003). *The Eighteenth-Century Campaign to Avoid Disease*. Macmillan.

Rojas, A.M. (2004). *I*mpactos monetarios e institucionales de la deuda pública en Colombia 1840–1890. *Borradores del CIE* 2813.

Samper, M. (1969). *La miseria en Bogotá*. Universidad Nacional.

Sanborn, C. (2005). Philanthropy in Latin America: historical traditions and current trends. In C. Sanborn & F. Portocarrero (Eds.) *Philanthropy and Social Change in Latin America*. The David Rockefeller Center Series on Latin American Studies, Harvard University.

Sotomayor, H. (1997). *Guerras, enfermedades y médicos en Colombia*. Juan N. Corpas.

Szreter, S. (2003). *The Population Health Approach in Historical Perspective*. Cambridge University Press, American Journal of Public Health.

Tierney, B. (1959). *Medieval Poor Law: A Sketch of Canonical Theory and Its Application in England*. University of California Press.

Velázquez, M.C. (1995). *Hospital Universitario San José de Popayán: restrospectiva histórica*. Hospital Universitario de Popayán.

6 Overtones of a Novel Political Philosophy

Mariano Ospina Pérez and Catholic Social Thought in the Rise of Public Banking in the 1930s

Carlos Andrés Brando

6.1 Introduction

This chapter argues that in the early 20th century, a novel political philosophy started to take hold among influential political leaders – a philosophy that distanced itself from liberalism, which, having enjoyed broad inter-party elite support since the 1840s, had dominated the visions of state, economy, and society for approximately half a century. One of the prominent figures to closely observe the tenets of the newly emerging system of beliefs was Mariano Ospina Pérez, a versatile, pragmatist, conservative party politician and entrepreneur who from the 1920s took it upon himself to re-engineer the nation's banking system to reduce the cost of agricultural production and widen access to credit to small- and medium-size rural producers. In doing so, Ospina procured a more just society, closer to the principles and practices of Catholic Social Thought (CST), which he praised and identified with. We will argue that through the foundation of the publicly owned Agrarian Credit Bank (ACB) in the early 1930s, Ospina managed to embed CST values in a financial institution that grew in importance to shape the structure of the nation's banking system for decades to come. CST justified state action to protect and defend the poor from injustice and exploitation. Core notions associated with CST, such as social solidarity and justice, nurtured the conceptions around the purpose and design of the Bank at the time of its foundation and came to define several of its distinct features once in operation. The history of the influence of CST upon the development of banking and finance is uncharted territory. In this respect, the chapter seeks to offer new grounds for reflection and controversy, whilst contributing to the literature dealing with the often underprivileged relations between finance and religious thinking.

The chapter is divided into six sections. The first reviews the dominant prevailing system of beliefs (liberalism) prior to the emergence of CST and notes precedents of the doctrine on public figures in the late nineteenth and early twentieth centuries. The second traces and examines Ospina's political philosophy. It analyzes the most important intellectual influences on his thinking and considers his views on what is natural to humanity and what are the limits and the subjects of public policy. The next details his normative proposals and

DOI: 10.4324/9781003289241-7

opinions on the role of the state in production and distribution, with an emphasis on banking and credit issues. The fourth section concentrates on the background to the ACB and analyzes its purpose. The fifth examines its design, focusing on its capital and governance structure; and the last section considers ACB's policies and the distinctive CST-related values that they represent and that came to define it.

6.2 Precedents: Rafael Núñez and Miguel Antonio Caro

State interventionism during the liberal-led Radical era (1853–1886) was mostly out of favor. In the "temple of omni-mode liberty", the idea that governments' interference ought to be minimal, "for their actions only provoked misery and suffering to the peoples", remained an influential element of the dogmatic economic liberalism that tended to prevail (Posada-Carbó, 2011, p. 164). *Laissez-faire* ideals punctuated policy-making, from free banking and extreme federalism to the elimination of monopolistic privileges and the expropriation of church land. Even if dogmatism did not go unchallenged, and several (liberal) thinkers and politicians moderated their principles and practices, the state largely remained a force in check.[1] According to Safford, the first significant departure from economic liberalism occurred with Rafael Núñez. His administration stepped up commercial protectionism and "brought the national government into banking and note issue, theretofore a strictly private activity" (Safford, 1988, pp. 58–59). Correa claims that Núñez's government, in addition to defending state intervention, reoriented fiscal and monetary policies – the former meaning the strengthening of revenues and the latter the creation of an organization that served as stimuli for credit activity and a tool for economic development (Correa, 2016, pp. 226–227).[2]

Núñez called for the introduction of paper money and for this purpose created the National Bank in 1880. It was conceived of as a mixed bank tasked with extending loans to the least developed economic sectors (small agricultural producers and artisans), as well as managing credit documents for the conversion, unification, and amortization of internal debt (Álvarez, 2016, pp. 176–177; Romero, 1991, pp. 28–29). In practice, it operated as a (public) bank of issue and above all, according to Romero, as "fiscal assistant" to the government (Romero, 1991, p. 39). Deposits and loans with the intended public were few and far between, not least because it hardly branched out beyond Bogota, and when it did (Barranquilla), it languished, lending quasi-exclusively to commercial ventures on thin capital. Ocampo (1994, p. 21) has noted that the National Bank ended up financing public expenditure via secret and illegal emissions, and when the scheme was uncovered Congress rushed to declare its closure.[3]

The short-lived experiments of the "monetary Regeneration" started by Núñez and continued by Miguel Antonio Caro in the 1890s proved reassuring for liberalism in the long run, however.[4] For Safford (1988, p. 59), their failure allowed for the stigmatization of state-led economic policies well into the

1940s.[5] This constituted part of the historical legacy of the Regeneration years. We take issue with this view and pause to locate the contribution of our analysis in the literature and to highlight (however broadly at this stage) the distinctive nature of Ospina's economic thinking, when set against the precedents of both Núñez's and Caro's ideas and ideologies.

First, the fact that publicly owned banks emerged in the 1920s/30s indicates that the accuracy of Safford's interpretation around the hegemonic endurance of economic liberalism into the early 20th century needs to accommodate developments in the banking and financial sectors that, at the very least, qualify his view. What is most interesting within this tension is that the ideological force competing for influence in the public institutional arena was neither socialist nor a strain of positivist thought but CST. Secondly, it may seem at first that Núñez, Caro and Ospina shared significant intellectual ground and principles, for they all sought to create and maintain a more active and stronger state in the economy, specifically in the financial sphere. No doubt, the three criticized dogmatic liberalism but beyond it the differences were greater than the similarities.

Núñez had been a radical liberal who in his later years probably found in the Catholic church the means to secure the moral bases he deemed necessary to bind society together, and thus provide the order from which liberty and justice were derived (Posada-Carbó, 2003, pp. 103–104). Religion was not so much a temple for the soul but a tool for political mobilization. Regarding currency, his concern lay with the financing of an increasingly larger and stronger state (Álvarez, 2016, pp. 176–177). With this objective in mind, the choice of paper money over commodity money with intrinsic value (possibly gold since silver was falling out of fashion) made sense as a more flexible and achievable strategy. The greatest historian of Colombian social and political thought, Jaime Jaramillo (1996, p. 327), suggested that even though Núñez remained a critic of liberalism he was not capable of elaborating an alternative conception of the state to that of liberalism itself – where society was the sum of individuals which, enjoying universal suffrage, constructed a representative state.[6] Núñez found CST useful and quoted Leo XIII to justify the intervention of the state to protect the common interest from abuse by the powerful.

Caro's thought diverged from this. His conception of society was probably closer to Hobbes'. Men did not find happy and equitable solutions to their differences out of their own impulses – far from it. To protect the weak from the strong, the state was endowed with a mission to propend for justice. Caro rejected Kantian individualist doctrine, which dispossessed the state from all moral content, reducing it to serve as the guardian of private property (Jaramillo, 1996, p. 341). In his political philosophy, the state ought to intervene as a response to the commoditization of man's labor and its subsequent pauperization. Money was an element of credit and a social bond, whose capacity for circulation ultimately depended upon the legal force the state could endow it with, and in turn, on the support and moral solidarity that the community provided to that state (Jaramillo, 1996, p. 377). Caro stood for free credit for the financing of useful social ends and against usurious banking. He shared with Núñez the rejection of metallist theses and the support of the state theory of money, which almost inevitably led to the state's permanent right of issue (Jaramillo, 1996, p. 326).

Caro's political philosophy distinctively moved away from Núñez's in one structural respect. Unlike the latter, Caro opposed the individualist and representative society–state duo. Instead, as Jaramillo has argued, Caro conceived the idea of the state as one emerging within a corporativist or organicist society that granted legal status to entities such as the family or the Catholic church. Consequently, it sought "to establish a qualification of the suffrage", according to social status and individual qualities (Jaramillo, 1996, p. 326). The corporativist and organicist conception distances Caro's thought from Núñez's but brings Ospina's closer.

Unlike Caro, Ospina was no dedicated treaty-like writer, therefore the corporativist elements of his thinking must be looked for in sparse documents. Motivated by his anti-individualist *laissez-faire* and "class struggle" postures, Ospina clearly stressed the role of *gremios* in the organization of society. In the historical account of the conservative party's achievements, a speech delivered in 1939, he advocated for the defense of the worker and for fair pay, not through revolutionary struggle, but via the "harmony and collaboration of all classes and guilds". Thus, he advanced the need to give the country a "corporativist organization of truly democratic and republican features" (Ospina Pérez, 1978f, pp. 168–169). According to Henderson, Ospina managed to embody his technical and corporativist ideas in the party's *Programa* of 1931, following its national convention (Henderson, 2006, p. 290). Concrete proposals of this kind may be appreciated in his short writing on the organization of the Republic's Congress. There, he recommended division of labor and specialization to make this organ more serious, accurate and effective. Congress, Ospina claimed, should create a specified number of permanent commissions, staffed exclusively with competent and specialized members. Advised by experts from outside the legislature, all congressmen could attend the meetings but only the relevant minister and the members of the commissions and the projects' authors could participate (Ospina Pérez, 1978h, pp. 25–26). To criticisms that such organization limited democratic liberties and restricted parliamentary initiative, Ospina responded categorically: "EITHER DEMOCRACY ADJUSTS ITS ACTIVITIES TO THE LAWS OF TECHNIQUE OR IT SHOULD PREPARE ITSELF TO LOSE ITS HEGEMONY IN THE GOVERNMENT OF PEOPLES".[7]

On monetary matters Ospina's stance was the opposite of Caro's, however. Caro endorsed the theory of state money proposed by George Knap and William Jevons, and almost naturally accepted the state's exclusive privilege of right of issue and paper money.[8] Ospina was a metallist, a staunch supporter of the gold standard even amidst the crisis of the 1930s. The monetary chaos of past times, he stated, had been overcome thanks to the establishment of a monetary system tied to convertible notes into gold on demand and at par value (Ospina Pérez, 1978f, p. 157). Credit should bear an interest. However, advances to small agricultural producers in particular could be offered at lower than commercial rates.

As can be seen from the above, there were stark differences in the criticisms of liberalism shared by Núñez, Caro and Ospina. We should also note here that neither the first nor the second were successful (perhaps not even genuinely interested) in establishing a national bank of credit intending to serve agricultural producers by supplying cheap credit, as Ospina was, and as will be shown below. The fact that a study by Hernandez (aforementioned) on the historical origins of Colombian central banking examines closely both the Banco Nacional and the Banco Central (prior to the Banco de la República) strongly attests to this.

6.3 Ospina's Political Philosophy: Leo XIII and not Lenin

The foundations of Ospina's social thought lay in property, family and fatherland.

> Recognizing the right of private property [...], it is accepted that such right ought to be limited by State intervention only when demanded by morality, salubriousness, and public good. When our enemies posed the thesis that property is a social function, which in fact and logically turns the State into the master of absolutely everything, and the owners into simple employees and public servants, easily dispossessed or replaceable, we present a more realistic postulate, more modern and more constructive, and sustain that property is not a social function, but an individual right, which has social functions [...] we mean to say that the property of the product of work and the goods acquired with it, is an essential natural right, and a key element of progress, of independence and freedom, only subject to those limitations determined by motives of the common good.
>
> (Ospina Pérez, 1978, p. 152)

Not only was private property a natural right, but it was through it that a nation's order and stability was to be pursued:

> The desire to possess even the essentials for life and welfare, is a fundamental characteristic of human nature.
>   If peoples can establish an area of property and control even if it were over a few square meters and over a modest room, in the cities or over a plot of land, a house, a harvest or some heads of cattle ... they experiment with it a sense of stability, of security, of welfare and equilibrium, whose effects on the political and social order is pleasant to imagine. Instead of destroying property right, it should be extended and democratized, preserving its social function, without suppressing its character

and natural individual right. The general orientation should be that of creating more and more owners in the cities and in the countryside.

(Ospina Pérez, 1978, p. 215)

In his analysis of the "social question", Ospina concluded that economic imbalances, social injustice, and workers' discontent were the legacies of industrialism, urbanization and the corruption of morality that characterized the 19th century. Further, he argued: "Rural workers, attracted by the mirages of mills and the movements of the cities, started to abandon the work on the land in masses… and disproportionately increased the supplies of labour to industrialists…" (Ospina Pérez, 1978g, p. 180).[9] Revolutionary solutions, however, he confronted directly:

Marx and Engels, in their famous Communist Manifesto appeared in 1848, raised in aggressive and violent manner the flag of workers revindications, based on the destruction of the existing social and economic order as a reaction against the thawing results of the liberal theses. The theories of the Manchester School, founded on the "laissez-faire", the absolute economic freedom, including for salaries and working conditions […] only produced the growing enrichment of the few next to the misery of masses of workers; work vilified, the salary devalued to its maximum, human dignity does not exist in the great industrial concentrations, the antagonism between entrepreneurs and workers seems fatal and inevitable.

(Ospina Pérez, 1978, p. 180)

For Ospina, the answer lay with the Pope: "the sublime encyclical from Leo XIII, small of body and pinched of flesh, with the sweetness of his semblance and the softness of his voice, but terrible in the truth, untamable in the justice, unbreakable in the spirit Christian, and prophetic and illuminating in concept." The Pope spoke to the world in terms that are "always wise, always new, and nowadays more than ever essential and providential", Ospina continued (Ospina Pérez, 1978g, pp. 180–181). In *Rerum Novarum*, Leo XIII led the way and sourced the answers.

Ospina's economic analysis around a "humane, and truly real concept that does justice to what a salary is and what it should be" also relied on the Encyclical. There the Pope was "clear, illustrative and Christianly-inspired" (Ospina Pérez, 1978c, p. 215). According to it, nature dictated that workers' remuneration must be enough to support the wage earner and his family in reasonable and thrifty comfort. If this is not achieved, and the worker, be it from necessity or for fear of worse evil, accepts such conditions, then he is the victim of injustice (Finn, 2010, p. 148).[10] Importantly, faced with this situation the worker has a rightful claim to justice. Since God created the material world to meet the needs of all, and this is a natural law, a second level of justice is due to right this wrong. Within CST, the solution is to go beyond commutative justice, that is, beyond the legal obligations agreed between the parties to a contract, and into distributive justice – the kind of justice that relates to the proper order between the community and its members. In this case, the employer must provide a fair wage to the worker that meets his needs and those of his family; if the former does not, he will be falling short of the Christian moral standards to which all community members are subject (Finn, 2010, p. 154). The specific section of the Encyclical where commutative justice is shown not to be sufficient to conform to natural law, was well known to Ospina – and he quoted it at length.[11]

In the context of combating the rise of living costs for the worker and his family, which erodes nominal wages, Ospina establishes that the causes leading to this situation ought to be addressed by the state. The bias toward intervention in favor of the countryside, cooperatives, and monetary stability is evident:

> Regarding the currency, it corresponds to the State maintaining the relative and possible stability of its purchasing power, avoiding where circumstances permit, brusque changes, so as to defend not only the workers and the employees, but in general, the great number of middle-class people who live off a fixed rent […]
>
> Relative to the intermediaries, which often are efficacious collaborators in the mechanism of the national economy, they must also be overseen by the State, to avoid abuses […] whilst it is also needed to promote cooperatives of various sorts with the purpose of reducing the overcharge between the cost of production of the good and its selling price for the consumer […]
>
> The cost and quantity of our national agrarian production is at this moment the principal problem of our economy, which is affecting radically all social classes, city dwellers and countryside residents, industrial production, the living costs of peasants, the urban to rural migration, the defense of the race, in one word, the nationality itself. Here too, the State has immense responsibilities to assume …
>
> (Ospina Pérez, 1978, pp. 217–218)

One of Ospina's biographers, Jaime Sanin, regards the range and importance of the institutional work accomplished by Ospina in a lifetime of public service largely dedicated to promoting and defending agrarian production and rural workers, as unique. Sanin suggests that what best distinguishes Ospina's profile from other politicians is his conception of the state's function regarding agriculture. A counterfactual, in which Ospina would have passed away at the beginning of the 1920s, forces us to rethink what would have become of the Agricultural Secretary of Antioquia, the Ministry of Agriculture, the Agricultural Mortgage Bank (AMB), the ACB, the Institute for Colonisation and Land Parceling, the Colombian Agricultural Institute, the Institute of Natural Resources, or in the case of the Federación Nacional de Cafeteros (FNC), which was created before he managed it, its defining features (Sanin, 1978, pp. 106–107).[12] Not in vain, Ospina himself once claimed: "I was the man of the coffee-growers, and Manuel Mejia was the man of coffee" (Alvear 1992, p.107). In fact, in line with his political campaigning during the 1940s, once elected to head the executive power, official documents of visible interests called him "president of the peasants" (Bustamante, 2017, p. 101), a label that stood the test of time.

The most critical influence on Ospina's thinking on the state was perhaps the bishop of Mainz, Wilhelm von Ketteler, who pioneered a study on the "labour question" and whose works are said to have inspired *Rerum Novarum*. Leo XIII admitted this and called him his "great predecessor" (van Keersbergen, 1995, p. 219).[13] Serving as president of the German national convention of Catholics, von Ketteler proposed legal protection against physical and financial exploitation, and state administration of welfare arrangements for all classes of society (van Keersbergen, 1995, p. 218). On the state, Ospina referenced him directly:

> ... as Monsignor von Ketteler, the wise bishop of Mainz, stated: "The State has no right to remain indifferent when it comes to the working classes. The theory of letting do is declared bankrupt, for it has conducted society to the edge of the abyss. A double mission pertains to the State in relation to the poor; help them organize in corporative associations and protect them and their families against all innocuous exploitation. These words, which gave the final blow to the economic School denominated liberal or Mancunian, which preached the theses of laissez faire, contained a complete action programme for the legislative corporations and for the executive power.
>
> (Ospina Pérez, 1978, p. 218)

Clearly, von Ketteler and Ospina shared the notion of state intervention to protect the poor from exploitation. The nature of this exploitation might come from physical or financial relations. In the aftermath of the 1929 crisis, Colombian peasants suffered the latter kind at the hands of informal moneylenders who advanced credit against harvest at usurious interest rates. Based on the same logic of righting the wrong described above on the issue of wages, we argue that distributive justice was called for in the case of rural producers signing exploitative contracts with speculators. This took place through state intervention via the institutionalization of credit sourced from a public development bank, the ACB. This bank charged low interest rates, and its organization and operation integrated corporativist and cooperative elements, as will be detailed below. Ospina's adherence to von Ketteler's and Leo's XIII social thought suggests a close link between his banking activities and the notions held by key figures in CST, which he much admired.

Finally, Ospina's political philosophy demanded action. Choosing between parties and political economies turned into duty amidst turbulent times when he proclaimed the following words in a speech given for *Juventud Católica* in 1929. He remarked:

> The times we live are of exceptional gravity and any minute lost can be decisive in the long run. Neutrality and inertia are a crime and can only be adopted by the coward or the unconscious. It is necessary to gather at the base of one of the two flags: the red, of the revolution or the white, of peace, progress and conciliation. The law of concentration imposes: Lenin or Leo XIII ...
>
> (Ospina Pérez, 1978, p. 134)

6.4 Banking Credit: Nationalize, Decentralize and Democratize

Ospina's thinking on credit can be appraised through his congressional speech at the Senate in August 1933. Analyzing the country's banking and financial problems, his statements on the democratization, nationalization, and decentralization of credit illustrate what he understood each of these concepts to mean, and how the country ought to proceed to promote their development.

Ospina declared himself against the idea of nationalization of credit derived from government control of the issuing institute, as mutual complacency between the two would inevitably lead to the undermining of healthy currency and of distributive justice in credit matters. Instead, he provided an alternative to the trusting the state with the ownership and direction of the national banking system. His concept evolved around the search for an equilibrium between the intervention of government and that of "productive forces", particularly at the helm of the bank of issue, and regarding credit oriented towards production – as opposed to credit aimed at speculation. In his own narrative, the first step towards the nationalization of credit had been taken in 1924, with the creation of the Agricultural Mortgage Bank, in which he had a major role. The second came with the foundation of the ACB, designed to increase the financing share of agrarian output – which according to him stood at a meager 5% of national production, and until then had been concentrated in the hands of commercial banks. "For those dedicating their lives to rural endeavors the ACB provided worthy financial support", Ospina argued, unlike that offered by speculators, intermediaries, and usurers, who raided their efforts. Another step towards credit nationalization materialized with the creation of the Central Mortgage Bank – even if amidst the urgent need to provide relief to debtors, part of its benefits had been watered down. Finally, the functioning consolidation of General Deposit Warehouses, which acted as ancillary credit institutions, taking products under custody, and issuing discountable pledge bonds, furthered the nationalization path. Thanks to the Ospina-led FNC of the early 1930s, these entities were serving not only coffee growers but producers of wheat, rice, sugar, cocoa, tobacco, and so on, none of whom was then forced to sell their products at "surrender" or "sacrificial" prices during adverse market conditions.[14] In Ospina's political philosophy, the nationalization of credit had achieved concrete institutional manifestations through bold state intervention: specifically, via the foundation of (largely) publicly owned and managed banking entities. Further, the AMB and the ACB intended to cater for agrarian producers who possessed large rural estates but also for small-scale growers who did not and could only offer pledge as guarantee. In both these cases, the corporativist aspect through the role played by the FNC featured prominently, be it as initiator, lobbyist, facilitator, shareholder and/or operator.[15]

As noted above, Ospina's main preoccupation lay with the agricultural sector, and it was those laboring in the countryside that these entities targeted as clients. In the case of GDWs, they supported the same kind of producers, yet a principle of solidarity propended by the FNC (whether genuine or alleged) allowed non-coffee growers to benefit from the credit transactions that pledge bonds facilitated. Ospina resorted to "national solidarity" as the common denominator by which his efforts and those of the FNC concerning the ACB and GDWs, had braced Colombian agriculturalists at large and not only those associated with the Federation or the production of coffee (Ospina Pérez, 1978a, p. 34; 1978e, p. 57). A final comment notes that two of the four institutions examined by Ospina dedicated their businesses to financing long-term capital investments (AMB and BCH) and another two concerned themselves with short-term credit (ACD and GDWs). For him, the underlying determinant of the success (or failure) of any institutional venture was with its organization along carefully planned and efficient criteria, rather than on the nature of its ownership or trade.

On the issue of decentralization Ospina referred to the unfortunate allocations of loans that the recently founded Central Mortgage Bank (CMB) had been conducting. He focused on an insufficiently even distribution of resources amongst the nation's regions from this bank and contrasted it with the services that the ACB offered (Anales del Senado, p. 296).[16] Ospina seems to have used a shortcut in this argumentation. The CMB had been created in 1931 for the purpose of relieving both debtors and private banks (commercial and mortgage ones) in the context of a deflationary spiral that was freezing their portfolios, increasing the number of overdue/unpaid obligations and worryingly contracting credit. Therefore, to a significantly large extent the allocation of CMB's credit merely reflected the distribution of the non-performing portfolios of the banks it assisted. In the case of private mortgage banks (Banco Hipotecario de Colombia and Banco Hipotecario de Bogota), we know that their geographical concentration of business heavily privileged the state of Cundinamarca.[17] The ACB, on the other hand, was rapidly expanding through the nation's rural areas in line with its mandate. Nonetheless, and to correct such bias, Ospina announced he intended to introduce an article in the bill providing for a more "reasonable and equitable" allocation of loans by the CMB (Anales, p. 296). In our view, decentralization of credit for Ospina meant taking credit to the regions, even the most remote of rural outposts, and away from Bogota and its peripheral zone of influence.

By the democratization of banking credit, Ospina first meant wider access. His aspirations on this were clear and specific: "… internal credit should be enjoyed by both the large and the small producers; it should serve the well-to-do and the not well-to-do" (Anales, p. 296). Further, he noted that nearly 20,000 small coffee owners or producers regularly had to travel from their land and from small towns to state capitals to obtain credit from usurers at high interest rates for either harvesting or expansion. Because of this, *seccionales de crédito* or credit cooperatives were called for, since these could play the role of small agricultural banks, scattered throughout the agrarian municipalities of the country (Anales, p. 296). Ospina singled out coffee growers in his democratization scheme, and it also turned out to be the case that ACB's preferred clients tended to be landowners (if small ones). This implied that over time an important segment of the rural population tilling the land under a wide range of legal arrangements, such as *colonato, aparcería*, and *anticresis*, would benefit only marginally from access to the resources of the ACB.

6.5 The Agrarian Credit Bank: Background and Purpose

Social demands for banking institutions purposefully designed to cater for the credit needs of agrarian producers had been registered before the crisis. The Colombian Society of Agriculturalists (SAC), an influential, private-interest association had commissioned studies on both cooperative and pledge credit, and was particularly vocal in recommending Congress and the Ministry of Industries to passing laws creating development banks to serve the peasantry Revista Nacional de Agricultura (RNA, 1928, p. 322; RNA, 1929, p. 139). In July 1929, the Society's president stated during the 2nd National Agrarian Congress:

> … what is being missed is that great institution of agrarian credit [which] offers short-term capitals at low interest rates to cultivate the land, to process its fruits and to defend the farmer from the ambushes of the speculator, which sizes every opportunity to buy the harvest at a low price […] the Society believes in the attention that you will put […] to fill this void with the creation of Agrarian Credit Banks that meet such necessity, not as a business, but as a service to Agriculture.
>
> (RNA, 1929, pp. 24–25)

In fact, during the 1st National Coffee Congress in 1920, the emerging National Federation of Coffee Growers (FNC) had also examined the issues of agrarian banks and pledges (Revista Cafetera, n.d., p. 22).[18] Similarly, in 1927 and in the context of the 2nd Congress, a special commission called on commercial banks to organize exporting sections and requested the Ministry of Finance to present a project to the Congress of the Republic reforming the public mortgage bank, enabling this entity to offer short-term loans against agrarian pledges (FNC, 1939). It was during the 4th

Congress, however, that the future nature and scope of the Agrarian Credit Bank were first conceived and defined. The FNC and its general manager, Ospina, set to work towards the creation of an agrarian credit organization designed to lend to agriculturalists, and especially to small-scale coffee producers under the system of agrarian pledge and the most favorable possible conditions (FNC, 1939, p. 81). Further, the FNC approved the subscription of up to 20% of the paid-up capital of the Bank, provided the following conditions were met: first, that the entity conveyed complete trust regarding the reliability and efficacy of its functions; second, that the effective start-up capital passed the $2 million pesos threshold; and lastly, that the Federation appointed a representative to the board of directors of the new institution.[19]

Soon after, acting in his double capacity as representative of the FNC and congressman, Ospina wrote, presented, and defended in Congress the project that provided the basis of the law that would establish the ACB a year later.[20] The institutional purpose of the newly emerging organization is best captured through a review of the law's explanatory memorandum. Ospina and associates noted:

> All the authorities on economic and financial affairs ... have reached the unanimous conclusion, that one of the first necessities is to supply cheap capital, and in favourable conditions, to the agriculturalists [...] The FNC, which recently gathered in this city [Bogotá], cared about studying in great depth not only the problems of the coffee industry, but also those related to agriculture and the national economy, reaching the conviction that our fundamental problem in regards to production, is that of providing capital, in adequate form and at a modicum interest; mainly, to small producers, who are nowadays victims, in all of the country's regions, of the scarcity of resources and of usurious interests...
>
> (Anales, 1930–1931, p. 1078)

The memorandum included an observation signaling that neither private commercial banks nor the publicly owned Agricultural Mortgage Bank (AMB) could solve the problem Ospina posed – for these entities concerned themselves with the financing of exporting and commercial operations and with long-term loans.[21] Ospina concluded his intervention with a warning that more than six million Colombians who lived off the land expected Congress and the national government to help them. A later biographer of Ospina recalls that during the parliamentary debates, the congressman exhibited contracts over anticipated harvest sales carried out by small-scale farmers, demonstrating that they were paying interest rates close to 100% per year.

As revealed by both the origins of the Bank in the producer associations' demands and the concrete initiative presented by Ospina, its creation served a clearly specific and targeted purpose. The ACB intended to lend to small agricultural producers, especially to coffee growers. Unlike existing banking institutions, it would concentrate on conducting short-term loans against agrarian

pledge. In so doing, the Bank would reach a large segment of the rural population, which was being exploited by moneylenders and speculators through the
charging of exorbitant interest rates – widely considered usurious. In other
words, the bank served the short-term needs of a (largely) previously excluded
sector. It did so to protect the recipients from financial exploitation and from
unjust contracts.

6.6 The Agrarian Credit Bank: Design (Capital)

Concerning the nature and the design of the Bank it seemed to have been clear
from the start that such an institution could not be conceived as a private venture. Insistence on offering loans at low and/or subsidized interest rates, as well
as on its developmental purpose and bias towards a spirit of service (as opposed
to business- or profit-oriented criteria), suggests it was bound to be publicly
owned. In fact, the legislative project proposed that the Bank function annexed
to the mostly state-owned AMB – albeit with its own capital and independent
legal representation.[22] Ospina's initial formula envisioned a bank of mixed
ownership, with the state as main partner and a private sector partaking
through the relevant sectoral associations – coffee growers and agricultural
producers in line with his corporativists preferences – as well as commercial
banks and members of the general public (Anales, 1930–1931, p. 1077). The
ACB, as a national-level development bank of mixed ownership intending to
lend to the masses of small-scale agricultural producers that constituted the
backbone of the peasantry, was certainly the first of its kind in the banking
history of Colombia.

   Criticisms surrounding concrete aspects of the Bank's operations, rather
than against the idea of founding this type of institution, rapidly emerged. The
minutes of the Central Bank's board of directors reveal a long list of observa-
tions: pursuing summary criminal procedures against the improper handling
of the guarantee; reinforcing the pledge with an additional mortgage; the
inconvenience of having the ACB receiving deposits; and the "anti-banking"
practice of fixing determined proportions of the Bank's investments in any one
class of obligations. It also stressed the benefits of increasing banks' representation on the board (Banco de la República, 1931, pp. 1756–1757).

   The ACB's authorized capital was set at $10 million pesos. To open for busi-
ness, 30% needed to be subscribed and 15% paid in cash. The government at
first committed to acquire stocks worth $3 million, whilst the FNC and the
AMB would subscribe up to $400,000 pesos each. No amounts were specified
as to the shares authorized for private banks or individuals (Anales, 1930–1931,
p. 1077). According to this shareholding participation, the draft bill contemplated changes in the governance structure of the Bank's parent organization,
the AMB. The latter's board of directors would have two additional members:
the Minister for Industries representing the government, and the FNC director-general – at the time, Ospina himself.[23] Functioning as a separate entity, the
governance structure would feature a general manager and a board of

directors consisting of seven members: three appointed by government, two by the subscribing banks, one by the FNC, and another by private interests (Article 23). In view of the lack of enthusiasm from private bankers for the newly emerging bank, the same law provided a conditional clause affecting its governance structure. If bankers failed to join, the ACB would operate annexed to the AMB and need not have its own general manager. In this case, the AMB's board of directors would be reorganized so as to feature three additional representatives; the Minister for Industries, the general manager of the FNC, and another to be decided upon by an entity to be established in the contract (Article 23).

After several changes to the board's configuration, which reveal the ambitions of different groups to have a voice and vote in the ACB, it would be the President who appointed its general manager and all five members, one of whom would represent the FNC, another the SAC, and a third the National Federation of Industrialists.[24] As with the previous legislation, this board ultimately meant a majority of private directors.[25] A later decree gave the Central Bank powers to appoint another, and finally, in 1933 a law ordered the opening of a credit section for mining and added another director – to be chosen by government from the organized mining associations.

How did investors pay for stocks, and how much did they contribute? Declarations notwithstanding, the paid-up capital of the ACB on 30 June 1932 stood at $2,500,000 pesos. The main shareholder of the Bank, the government, had stated it would pay dividends accruing to the nation from the shares it possessed at the central bank. In fact, using these dividends as collateral, it intended to obtain a loan to pay in cash for the bank's stock.[26] By October 1931, however, the origins of the government's resources had partially shifted. The Minister of Finance, in accordance with the Central Bank, opened a credit line for $5 million pesos with which Olaya hoped to establish the Bank "immediately".[27] Ultimately, the bulk of the resources with which the government paid for the ACB's stock came from an advance that the Central Bank extended late in 1931, resulting from an agreement whereby in exchange for the exploitation of several terrestrial salt mines the Central Bank channeled the cash needed to the government (Banco de la República, 1931, p. 1928–1933).[28]

For its part, the FNC honored its promise to subscribe $50,000 pesos, soon after the government's contribution materialized. It did not, however, meet its commitment to continue doing so (in annual installments) until the $400,000 pesos that the National Coffee Congress had agreed to was reached (FNC, 1939, p. 81).[29] Neither private banks nor the Central Bank acquired stocks to any significant degree.

Finally, individual private investors (*particulares*) subscribed stocks worth $46,000 pesos during 1932. According to Arias, the intention of the ACB was to have this type of investor as the principal supplier of the Bank's capital, and for that reason, $6,100,000 pesos in stocks (equivalent to 61% of the authorized capital) were nominally allocated as "D-class shareholders" – expecting them to become co-owners (Arias, 1961, p. 79).[30] In our view, this is a difficult argument to sustain for two reasons. First, in the draft bill passed by Ospina and associates, the authorization to acquire stocks for individual investors came last in the allocation order, and this right was shared along with the savings sections of commercial banks – with no specific distributions between them mentioned (Anales, p. 1077). However, if the share expected to be paid by *particulares* equaled the proportion once discussed for private banks, the figure would have been $150,000 pesos, or up to 5% of the authorized capital (Banco de la República, 1931, pp. 1756–1757). Second, if indeed *particulares* were to become prime investors of the ACB, a provision to eliminate their representation in the directorship of the AMB, as was effectively contemplated, made for a flagrantly obvious contradiction of purpose in the Bank's design (Anales, 1931, p. 1077).

Figure 6.1(a) and (b) provides a reasonably plausible comparison between the expected distribution of shareholding capital around the time the ACB's bill was being passed through Congress and the allocations effectively realized a year after it opened for business (December 1932). Three differences are worth noting. First, no bank, private or public, ended up subscribing shares from the ACB. Second, measured by shareholders, the ACB became in practice a state-owned bank – effective public participation at 96.5% vs. an expected 73%. Finally, the FNC, which through Ospina had been the key interest group

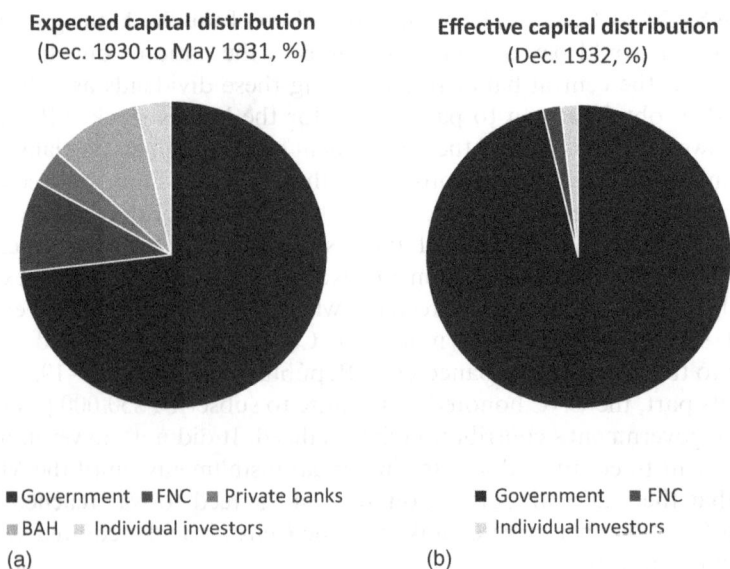

Expected capital distribution
(Dec. 1930 to May 1931, %)

Effective capital distribution
(Dec. 1932, %)

■ Government ■ FNC ■ Private banks
■ BAH ▦ Individual investors

■ Government ■ FNC
▦ Individual investors

(a)

(b)

Figure 6.1 (a) and (b) Agrarian Credit Bank: Capital distributions by shareholder, expected and effective.

Sources and note: 1(a) author's elaboration from Anales de la Cámara de Representantes. Proyecto de Ley, 1930–1931, No. 121 a 239, p. 1077, articles 3 to 5 and Banco de la República. AJDBR, Main office, Act No. 620, 18 February 1931, p. 1757. 1(b) from Revisoría Fiscal de Instituciones Oficiales de Crédito, 1946, p. 176.

behind its foundation, decided to remain a marginal investor – with a share of 1.9% vs. an expected 9.8%.

6.7 The Agrarian Credit Bank: Policies and Values

The Bank's policies and orientation regarding clientele, operations, pricing and expansion strategy, as initially conceived in the draft bill by Ospina, and as further shaped by him when serving as one of its first directors, point to its institutional values. Therefore, we next turn to examine these issues. The borrowers of the ACB had been identified by Ospina in various opportunities:

> The small agriculturalist, the peasant, who does not come to the senate's and chamber's stands, who does not organize political rallies or popular demonstrations in the great cities, who does not have access to the dailies' editorials, who does not talk, does not scream and does not write, but who works from sunshine to sunset tilted over the furrow, is the great victim of usury in our country. Our philanthropists and financiers alarmed themselves by city practices of a few pawnshops that lend money at three or five percent a month, but ignore that the peasant who has to sell in advance his harvest at half its price, is paying fantastic interest rates of ten or twenty per cent a month.
>
> (Ospina Pérez, 1978, p. 51)

Recalling his own deeds, later as President of the Republic, he stated:

> Amongst the modest initiatives I had presented to Parliament … was that of the Agrarian Credit Bank, destined to liberate the rural worker from the claws of usury. Because some years ago, credit supported those people in the same manner in which the rope supported the hanging man … those were the terrible days of usury…
>
> (Ospina Pérez, 1978, p. 51)

Ospina's and his associates' legislative project made clear who the Bank's clientele would be. Against the orthodox banking practices of the day, they targeted and specified its borrowers in a way that came to characterize the ACB's loan policy for many years. The bill established that: a) at least a third of the loans extended should be directed at small agricultural producers, that is individuals borrowing up to $1,500 pesos per loan, or at agrarian credit cooperatives, which would distribute the sum received from the ACB amongst individual loans that would not exceed $1,500 pesos each; and b) no less than a third of the loans would be made against agrarian pledge based on coffee (Ospina Pérez, 1978b, p. 51).

It is evident that whatever Ospina's plan for the ACB had originally envisioned, once the project left the lower house, changes in terms of its organization and around its potential clientele occurred. As laws and decrees piled over his draft, the Bank suffered two modifications that seemed to alter its intended purpose and initial design. The first came in 1932, as noted above, when the Bank opened an industrial credit section, and the second the following year, when it inaugurated a mining one. Even though a significant proportion of the Bank's capital was allocated to the industrial section and the broad range of operations it was authorized to conduct, credit to industry from the ACB remained minimal. This was even more so for mining.[31] The reasons for failing to serve non-agrarian clients have not been established. In my opinion, emphasis on pledge operations, as well as on short-term lending, and clearly defined limits on the size of individual loans probably made ACB's credit products unattractive to most of the potential industrial and mining borrowers. In Ospina's view, the industrial and mining *addenda* were more nominal than real, and during the time he remained associated with the Bank, he ensured this was so, for large allocations to industry or mining would have represented a move away from the main objective (Sanin, 1978, p. 222).

On the operations side of the Bank, it is necessary to stress the lending terms and the nature of the credit. From the Bank's inception, emphasis was laid on the short-term needs that ACB's loans would meet. Ospina and fellow representatives put this clearly in the law memorandum:

> It is also evident that to the agriculturalist of few and medium means, as most Colombian agriculturalists are, it does not suffice to boost his production, knowing that he will not face competition from imported foodstuffs, but that he needs to count on the indispensable resources to farm his property and sustain his family, whilst the harvest arrives. Neither the Agricultural Mortgage Bank nor other mortgage banks, nor the commercial banks resolve the problem which I am referring to. The benefits of the mortgage banks have not arrived, and it's very hard for them to arrive in the current state of affairs, to the small agricultural producer.
>
> (Ospina Pérez, 1978, pp. 33–34)

Mortgage banks operated with long-term horizons against real-estate guarantees that were rather difficult for small rural producers to match. Commercial banks concentrated their business in large cities and ports, where the financing of international trade proved a lucrative and relatively safe venture. Ospina was right to notice that no bank catered for the needs of small agriculturalists, whose location, collateral, and lending terms did not align with the interests of the existing banking industry. His draft bill established a maximum period of two years for credit operations conducted against agrarian pledge. This was the financial product *par excellence* of the ACB, and one that Colombian agriculturalists would soon turn to in growing numbers.

The guarantee or collateral, agrarian in nature, against which pledge credit was advanced by the Bank, included a wide range of items appropriate to the typical possessions of the peasantry: tillage tools, riding harnesses, machinery in general, animals of any kind and their produce, property utilized for rural exploitation, timber, and mining and industrial products of national origin (Franco, 1961, p. 36). Thanks to the advocacy of Ospina and Julio Lleras as members of the Bank's board, loans against current and future harvests were also deemed acceptable. The former declared in a meeting of the then recently inaugurated board: "For no reason am I in favour of closing the doors to farmers requesting money for planting."

Another distinct feature of the Bank's lending practices concerned its pricing policies. As soon as the Central Bank determined the interest rate of 5% at which it would rediscount obligations with agrarian pledge, ACB in turn fixed its active rate at 7%. By 1933 this had been reduced two points, thanks to the positive responses from the Central Bank to the Bank's requests to lower the rediscount.[32] By all means and purposes, the interest rate that the ACB charged for its short-term credit operations were lower than those applied by private banks.[33] ACB's loans were subsidized loans. Its pricing policies were not determined by the market. In this sense, the Bank was a developmental institution. Did this feature affect its profitability and sustainability?

Tensions are self-evident as any answer is sought after. On the one hand, the foundation of the Bank had contemplated the possibility that individual investors would subscribe part of its capital and thus, become shareholders. This implied that the ACB should operate with financial criteria that would guarantee certain profit margins, which in turn would lead to the distribution of dividends at regular intervals. In other words, the Bank would be managed as a capitalist organization, even if administered by the state. On the other hand, however, discussions around the developmental nature of the Bank's activities figured repeatedly in reports issued by the official regulator, in which the profit-making motive was often removed from any performance assessment.[34] Within the Bank itself as well, controversies surrounding its developmental status and low levels of profitability drew frequent criticisms.

Finally, the geographical expansion of the Bank's operations and its organization were closely intertwined. Ospina aspired to bring institutionalized banking credit to small rural producers facing usurious rates at the hands of informal moneylenders. Often, those most affected by these practices were located in the most remote of places – furthest away from commercial centers and urban-based, private banking services.[35] To widen the Bank's scope and fulfill its mandate, at its very first meeting the board designated a special commission to study the alternatives and issue recommendations.[36] The commission was integrated by the director-general of the FNC (Ospina) and the then representative of the Central Bank. Part of the dilemma hinged on whether to undertake the expansion directly with the Bank's own branches, agencies and offices, or to accomplish it indirectly through a system of locally based credit cooperatives serving as intermediaries between the Bank and individual producers, particularly in remote areas.[37] The example provided by the US in this regard won the day, and Decree 849 of May 1932 instructed the Bank to promote the constitution of credit cooperatives to facilitate the extension of its activities throughout the nation's territory.[38] As reported by the Minister of

Industries, the reception of the cooperatives was immediate. By 1934 co-ops in Bolívar, Cundinamarca, Valle, and Magdalena had intermediated resources, and these transactions accounted for over 10% of the Bank's total loans (Chaux, 1934, pp. 53–54). In short, rural credit cooperatives now figured in the domestic financial landscape, as a form of organization that brokered resources for the ACB.

Summarizing, Ospina's Catholic-inspired duty to help defend the poor from financial exploitation, a belief clearly held by CST, encouraged him to reconfigure Colombia's banking system around the time of the Great Depression. Writing, debating, and passing laws in the Republic's legislature, as both congressman and director-general of the FNC, he became a central figure in the rise of publicly owned banking institutions. First, he helped to found the AMB, then came the GDWs and the ACB. The ACB was probably the first developmental bank to exist and endure in the country's history. By design, it was a bank of credit that catered primarily to the short-term credit needs of small agricultural producers, especially coffee growers.

The ACB represented and entailed a wide array of values and practices closely linked to CST. At its most basic, this was a state-owned bank that prevented the continuous exploitation of rural workers by moneylenders. In other words, we conceive this as a state institution that enshrined distributive justice. Second, the Bank did this partly through an organization whose corporativist origins clearly identified with an association of producers, the FNC, which had been largely responsible for the creation of the Bank and held institutionalized representation in its governing body throughout its existence. Third, the promotion of credit cooperatives to expand the reach and scope of the ACB, so that it could offer its financial services in distant regions, speaks to the democratic intentions of ensuring access to credit for all the persons needing it, and to the solidarity principle around which these types of small and local entities organized themselves and intended to be managed. The credit cooperatives that liaised with the ACB also represented the first institutions of this kind in Colombia.

Primary sources

Anales de la Cámara de Representantes, 1930–1931.

Anales del Senado, 1933.

Banco de la República, Actas de la Junta Directiva, Oficina Principal, 1931, 1932.

Caja Colombiana de Crédito Agrario, Industrial y Minero. Libro de Actas de la Junta Directiva, Tomo 1, 1931–1933.

Caja de Crédito Agrario, Industrial y Minero de Colombia. Antecedentes Actas de la Junta Directiva, 1938.

Federación Nacional de Cafeteros, Compilación Cafetera, 1939.

Ministerio de Industrias y Trabajo. Memoria del Ministerio de Industrias y Trabajo al Congreso Nacional, 1934.

Revisoría Fiscal de Instituciones Oficiales de Crédito, Informe, 1942, 1943, 1946, and 1949.
Revista Cafetera, n.d.
Revista Javeriana, 1941.
Revista Nacional de Agricultura, 1928, 1929.
Superintendencia Bancaria. Informe presentado por el superintendente al señor Ministro de Hacienda y Crédito público, 1931, 1932 and 1933.

Notes

1 For an informed revisionist view, see Posada Carbó (2011, pp. 173–175).
2 Abel argues that the National Bank was the outcome of Núñez's certainty on the urgent need for credit centers that could secure economic growth; see Abel (1987, p. 44).
3 Others have stressed the political aspects of the National Bank, especially its increasingly centralizing nature; see Palacios and Safford (2002, pp. 256–257); and Correa (2016, p. 229).
4 The term is used in Correa (2017, p. 92).
5 Another bank founded by the state was Banco Central. This took place under General Reyes' administration in 1905. In the aftermath of the 'War of 1000 Days', its original purpose was to change old paper money and convert it into metal-backed money. As in the case of the National Bank, its nature soon shifted, and the privilege of issue was abolished. It continued operating until the mid-1920s as another private, commercial bank; see Avella (1987, pp. 39–41), and Hernandez (2001).
6 The next paragraphs rely heavily on Jaramillo (1996).
7 Capital letters in the original. Saether has linked Ospina and the creation of the National Federation of Coffee Growers in the 1920s with corporativism; see Saether (1998), *passim*. Ospina was co-founder of this association.
8 According to Jaramillo (1996), he also followed the Thomist theses on credit and the interest of money; fn. 42, p. 386.
9 In this longing for the preservation and reinforcement of rural-based socio-economic development, Ospina was no different than other leading politicians of the time. Patiño (1981) has shown that the electoral platforms of the three presidential candidates running for office in 1930 included this as a major aspect of their future governments.
10 In Ospina's own analysis of the salary, he stresses the need to think about the worker in his own social and family context (Ospina Pérez, 1978, p. 214).
11 See his text published for a faith-based university journal: "El Pensamiento Político y Social de León XIII" (1941).
12 Four philosophical principles, according to Alvear (1992, p. 79), guided Ospina's consolidation of the FNC during his tenure: growing market share in world markets, the establishment of developmental credit for the social promotion of small producers, the provision of a basic peasant infrastructure, and cooperation with other producers.
13 See, especially, his 'Christianity and the Labour Question'.
14 This section borrows heavily from Ospina's speech (see Anales del Senado, 1933).
15 In the case of GDWs, the FNC founded, owned, and managed several of these, especially along the so-called "coffee-axis" region.
16 By 1938 the ACB displayed 63 points of service, most located in rural areas (Caja de Crédito Agrario, Industrial y Minero de Colombia, 1938, pp. 961–963).
17 See for instance Superintendencia Bancaria, 1931, 1932, and 1933.
18 Luis Montoya Santamaria and Julio Gaitán presented the projects on these topics, respectively.

19 For further details, see FNC, 1939, Articles No. 5, 6, 7, and 8, pp. 81–82.
20 The session took place on 29 December 1930. Fellow proponents of the project were Julio Zuluaga, Antonio Salgar de la Cuadra and Carlos M. Pérez.
21 Drake notes that the commercial banks operating in the 1920s left both small agricultural and industrial producers marginalized from the bulk of the benefits that their credit offered; see Drake 1989, p. 43.
22 At least until the growth and development of the new entity called for its separation, which occurred a year after its foundation.
23 Article 2. A conditional clause, in the case that the government were to buy the stocks owned by the private sector in the BAH, stipulated the removal of the representative of private shareholders, and his replacement with another from the agricultural societies of the country. Government would establish the selection process for this member.
24 The National Federation of Industrialists was a relatively weak, private-interest group based in Bogota, that fizzled out in that same decade.
25 This time three out of five came from private bodies. Under Law 57, four out of seven did.
26 Article 6. Government recognized the need to agree on the procedures with the directives of the Central Bank to carry out such operation.
27 Decreto Legislativo No. 1754, 1931, Article 1. The above credit would also finance public works, cancel the Treasury's outstanding services, and complete its contribution to the Caja Colombiana de Ahorros.
28 The total sum amounted more than $15 million pesos. This arrangement shifted the previous relationship between the Central Bank and the government, for this was the first time that the CB committed to lend long-term funds to it; see Meisel, 1990. The advance represented nearly 4% of the GDP of 1932.
29 Only in 1934 did it contribute another $10,000 pesos, totaling $ 60,000 pesos, a figure which was not altered again until at least 1947.
30 The highest proportion of the Bank's capital owned by this class of shareholder was reached in 1933, when another $10,010 pesos from this source were added; see Revisoria Fiscal de Instituciones Oficiales de Crédito, 1946, p. 176, Cuadro 1.
31 Data from the Revisoría Fiscal de Instituciones Oficiales de Crédito indicate that less than 10% of the Bank's investments were channeled to these sectors combined between 1932 and 1940; see Table 49.
32 See for instance Banco de la República, 1932, p. 1968, and pp. 2180–2181.
33 Lacking data for the 1930s, we rely on evidence for the 1940s on interest rates compiled by Salazar (1996), appendix.
34 See anual reports from Revisoría Fiscal de Instituciones Oficiales de Crédito, 1942, 1943, 1946, and 1949.
35 Antonio García maintained that often the highest interest rates were charged in the most "isolated of regions"; see Arango (1977), p. 105.
36 See Caja de Crédito Agrario e Industrial 1931–1933, Actas I a 137; Act No. 1, pp. 2–3; and Act No. 2, p. 5.
37 A first discussion was recorded in LAJD, Tomo 1, Act. No. 5, pp. 12–14.
38 Decree 849 of 11 May 1932, articles 5–11. This norm also decided the legal regime governing co-ops and the conditions in which they could conduct credit operations with their members and with the ACB.

Bibliography

Abel, C. (1987) *Política, Iglesia y Partidos en Colombia*, Bogota: FAES-Universidad Nacional de Colombia.

Álvarez, A. (2016) 'Banca Libre, Federalismo y Soberanía Monetaria Regional en el Siglo XIX en Colombia' in Álvarez, A. and Correa, J.S. (eds) *Ideas y Políticas Económicas en Colombia durante el Primer Siglo Republicana*, Bogota: CESA and Ediciones Uniandes.

Alvear, J (1992) 'La Vida Ejemplar de Mariano Ospina Pérez', s. n.

Arango, M. (1977) *Café e Industria: 1850–1930*, Bogota: Carlos Valencia Editores.

Arias, J. (1961) *El Crédito a través de la Caja Agraria*, Bogota: Caja Agraria.

Avella, M. (1987) *Pensamiento y Política Monetaria en Colombia, 1886–1945*, Bogota: Contraloría General de la Republica.

Bustamante, L. (2017) 'Entre tintas azules y rojas. Representaciones de liberales y conservadores en *Relator* y *Diario del Pacifico durante la Republica Liberal*' (undergraduate dissertation).

Correa, J.S. (2016) 'Moneda y Nación: Política Económica y los Debates sobre el Estado, 1865–1889' in Alvarez, A. and Correa, J.S. (eds) *Ideas y Políticas Económicas en Colombia durante el Primer Siglo Republicana*, Bogota: CESA and Ediciones Uniandes.

Correa, J. S. (2017) *Moneda y Nación: Del Federalismo al Centralismo Económico (1850–1922)*, Bogota: CESA.

Drake, P. (1989) *The Money Doctor in the Andes: The Kemmerer Missions, 1923–1933*, Durham and London: Duke University Press.

Finn, D. (2010) 'The Unjust Contract' in Finn, D. (ed.) *The True Wealth of Nations*, Oxford: Oxford University Press.

Franco, A. (1961) *El Crédito a través de la Caja de Crédito Agrario*. Bogota: Departamento de Investigaciones Económicas de la Caja Agraria.

Henderson, J. (2006) *La Modernización en Colombia: Los Años de Laureano Gómez, 1889–1965*, Medellin: Editorial Universidad de Antioquia.

Jaramillo, J. (1996) *El Pensamiento Colombiano en el Siglo XIX*, Bogota: Planeta.

Hernandez, A. (2001) 'La Banca Central en Colombia: Banco Nacional (1880), Banco Central (1905), Banco de la República (1923)' in *Credencial Historia*, No. 135. https://www.banrepcultural.org/biblioteca-virtual/credencial-historia/numero-135/la-banca-central-en-colombia

Meisel, A. (1990) *Banco de la República: Antedentes, Evolución y Estructura*' Bogota: Banco de la República.

Ocampo, H. (2001) *Mariano Ospina Pérez: El Presidente*, Medellin: Camara de Comercio de Medellin.

Ocampo, J.A. (1994) 'Regímenes Monetarios Variables en Una Economía Preindustrial: 1850–1933' in Sanchez, F. (ed.) *Ensayos de Historia Monetaria y Bancaria de Colombia*, Bogota: Tercer Mundo Editores and Fedesarrollo.

Ospina Pérez, M. (1978a) 'La Caja de Crédito' in Plata, F. (ed.) *Mariano Ospina Pérez: Obras Selectas*, Medellin: Editorial Bedout.

Ospina Pérez, M. (1978b) 'La Redención Económica Está en el Campo' in Plata, F. (ed.) *Mariano Ospina Pérez: Obras Selectas*, Medellin: Editorial Bedout.

Ospina Pérez, M. (1978c) 'El Problema Social Colombiano' in Plata, F. (ed.) *Mariano Ospina Pérez: Obras Selectas*, Medellin: Editorial Bedout.

Ospina Pérez, M. (1978d) 'Paz Cristiana, Justicia Económica y Equilibrio Social' in Plata, F. (ed.) *Mariano Ospina Pérez: Obras Selectas*, Medellin: Editorial Bedout.

Ospina Pérez, M. (1948) *La Nueva Economía: Llamamiento a la Concordia Nacional*, Bogota: Imprenta Nacional.

Ospina Pérez, M. (1978e) 'Nacionalización, Democratización y Descentralización del Crédito (26 Aug. 1933)' in Plata, F. (ed.) *Mariano Ospina Pérez: Obras Selectas*, Medellin: Editorial Bedout.

Ospina Pérez, M. (1978f) 'Reivindicación Histórica de la Obra del Régimen Conservador' in Plata, F. (ed.) *Mariano Ospina Pérez: Obras Selectas*, Medellin: Editorial Bedout.

Ospina Pérez, M. (1978g) 'El Pensamiento Político y Social de León XIII' in Plata, F. (ed.) *Mariano Ospina Pérez: Obras Selectas*, Medellin: Editorial Bedout.

Ospina Pérez, M. (1978h) 'La Organización Técnica del Congreso Nacional' in Plata, F. (ed.) *Mariano Ospina Pérez: Obras Selectas*, Medellin: Editorial Bedout.

Palacios, M. and Safford, F. (2002) *Colombia: Fragmented Land, Divided Society*, New York and Oxford: Oxford University Press.

Patiño, A. (1981) *La Prosperidad a Debe y la Gran Crisis, 1925–1935*, Bogota: Banco de la República.

Posada-Carbó, E. (2003) *El Deasfío de las Ideas: Ensayos de Historia Intelectual y Política en Colombia*, Medellin: Fondo Editorial Universidad EAFIT and Banco de la Republica.

Posada-Carbó, E. (2011) 'La Tradición Liberal Colombiana del Siglo XIX: de Francisco de Paula Santander a Carlos Arturo Torres' in Jaksic, I. and Posada-Carbó, E. (eds) *Liberalismo y Poder: Latinoamérica en el Siglo XIX*, Santiago: Fondo de Cultura Economica.

Romero, C.A. (1991) 'La Regeneración y el Banco Nacional' in *Boletín Cultural y Bibliográfico*, 28:26, pp. 27–39.

Saether, S. (1998) 'Café, Conflicto y Corporativismo: Una Hipótesis sobre la Creación de la Federación Nacional de Cafeteros de Colombia en 1927' in *Anuario Colombiano de Historia Social y de la Cultura*, 26, pp. 134–163.

Safford, F. (1988) 'The Emergence of Economic Liberalism in Colombia' in Jacobsen, N. and Love, J. (eds) *Guiding the Invisible Hand: Economic Liberalism and the State in Latin American History*, New York: Praeger Publishers.

Salazar, N. (1996) *Historia Monetaria y Financiera de Colombia, 1940–1970*, Bogota: Fedesarrollo

Sanin, J. (1978) *Ospina Supo Esperar*, Bogota: Editorial Andes.

van Keersbergen, K. (1995) *Social Capitalism: A Study of Christian Democracy and the Welfare State*, London: Routledge.

Part II
The Short 20th Century

7 Becoming Economic Experts

Philanthropic Foundations and the Internationalization of Economics in Colombia During the 1960s

*Andrés M. Guiot-Isaac**

7.1 Introduction

Although there was a long tradition of economic thought and practice in Colombia before, the premise that experts on economic affairs require a specialized academic training was specific to the second half of the twentieth century. Political economy had been taught in faculties of law (Hurtado, 2016, see Chapter 1 of this volume) and engineering (Mayor Mora, 1984) since the early nineteenth century, but for most of Colombia's republican history economic analysts and policy makers were generalists without specialized training in economics – with some notable exceptions (c.f. Jaramillo, 2006). The approach of these men to economic science was more pragmatic than academic and their knowledge of economic issues stemmed mainly from their close practical experience dealing with private and public affairs. As economics became institutionalized in higher education in the mid-twentieth century (Kalmanovitz, 1993; Bejarano, 1999; Palacios, 2005), the figure of the economic expert as a specialist with a specific disciplinary training began to take shape. The professionalization of economics in Colombia should not be seen, however, as a teleological progression from the domain of non-specialists to that of experts. It was rather an open-ended process, influenced by both the legacies of pre-existing professional traditions and the selective appropriation of international disciplinary trends.

This chapter studies how the internationalization of economics during the 1960s shaped the economics profession in Colombia and its relationship with academe and the state. To do this, I examine the role philanthropic foundations, particularly the Rockefeller and the Ford Foundations, played as sponsors of economic education and research at the Universidad Nacional (*Unal*), the Universidad de Los Andes (*Uniandes*), and the Universidad del Valle (*Univalle*). What began as experimental programs in the 1940s within an established Faculty of Law and a sui generis commercial school gradually evolved into the

* Part of this chapter was written while the author held a bursary from the *Programa Colombia Científica, Pasaporte a la Ciencia Doctorado* in contribution to the *Foco Sociedad, Reto 2: Innovación social para el desarrollo económico y la inclusión productiva* and an Oxford Global History of Capitalism Project studentship. In the earlier stages of this research, the author was part of a project that received financial support from the Vice-chancellery of Research and the Centro de Estudios sobre Desarrollo Económico (CEDE) of the Universidad de los Andes.

DOI: 10.4324/9781003289241-9

economics departments of *Unal* (Hernández Gamarra and Herrera, 2002), Colombia's main state-funded university, and *Uniandes* (Álvarez et al., 2019), the first institution of higher education that was both private and secular. The third department of economics examined in this chapter opened its doors in the late 1950s at *Univalle*, a regional university funded by the state but administered by local business elites (Offner, 2019). Even if the economics departments at *Unal, Uniandes*, and *Univalle* were not at that time the only ones of their kind in Colombia – or even the first that granted degrees in economics (Montenegro, 2017) – they offered for contemporaries a clear alternative to what Jorge Ruiz Lara, Colombia's first PhD in economics, dubbed the prevailing "French system" of "training economic lawyers"(Ruiz Lara, 1958, p. 2). These were also the programs that US-based philanthropic foundations like the Rockefeller and the Ford selected in the 1960s to implement an internationalization strategy that proved successful in changing the face of economics departments in other Latin American countries.

If by comparative standards the creation of academic economics departments occurred rather late in Colombia, this is less true of the valorization of economists' expertise outside universities. Only after World War II did governments across the world begin to develop permanent staffs of economic experts and to rely routinely on professional economists for external advice. While in the post-war period economics departments supplied this expertise to a great extent in the United States (Bernstein, 2001, pp. 128–132), this was not necessarily the norm elsewhere. Until the 1960s, the demand for economics graduates in Great Britain outside universities was rather low (Tribe, 2021, p. 372). Government positions in France were staffed for most of the twentieth century by mathematicians and engineers who received on-the-job training in economics while working for the state (Fourcade, 2009, pp. 205–207). In Colombia, the picture was mixed. From the 1960s onwards, academically trained economists were actively recruited to work for the state but often found themselves sharing the workspace with other professionals – mainly engineers (Mayor Mora and Zambrano, 2016, p. 384) – in the planning department, the central bank, and the Ministry of Finance. As members of a relatively new profession, Colombian economists had to compete and even cooperate with an established tradition of autodidact economic lawyers and engineers.

To distinguish their expertise from that of other professionals with experience in economic affairs, economists in Latin America used "internationalization as a strategy of professionalization"(Montecinos, 1996, p. 284). Colombian economists, unlike those from other Latin American countries like Chile and Brazil (Fajardo, 2022), developed relatively weak links with the UN Economics Commission for Latin America (Villamizar, 2012). In the absence of a strong and established local *cepalino* community, US philanthropic foundations, namely the Ford and Rockefeller Foundations, were from the outset the central players in the creation of an institutional basis for the internationalization of economics in Colombia. Additionally, without a deeply rooted nationalist tradition of economic thought like in Mexico (Babb, 2001), the assimilation of the dominant disciplinary trends of the United States into Colombian economics departments was less prone to conflict between communities with opposing epistemic views about the economy and society. One must thus be cautious about making broad generalizations about the effects of philanthropic foundations' internationalization strategies based on the experiences in other countries, like that of the infamous story about the Chicago Boys in Chile (Valdés, 1995). As recent comparisons with the Ford sponsorship of economics in Brazil showed (Suprinyak and Fernández, 2021), similar internationalization strategies yielded divergent results when they were applied in different institutional contexts. If anything, as this chapter seeks to illuminate, the Chilean case was more likely the exception than the rule.

7.2 The Rockefeller and Ford Foundations as sponsors of economic education and research in Colombia

It was not by chance that US-based philanthropic foundations became one of the main sponsors of economics in Colombia after the Rockefeller Foundation allocated its first grant for the creation of the Centro de Estudios en Desarrollo Económico (CEDE) at *Uniandes* in April 1958 (c.f. Álvarez, et al., 2019, pp. 53–56). Within the Rockefeller and the Ford Foundations, the end of World War II led to an internal re-examination of their grant policies. After sponsoring "basic" research in economics during the interwar period, the Rockefeller's Social Sciences Division turned its attention to the problems of less developed countries (Geiger, 1993, 99).[1] In 1957, the Rockefeller appropriated its first three grants to develop economics departments and economic research centers in Latin America.[2] These grants, particularly the foundation's flagship program in the Universidad Católica de Chile (Valdés, 1995, pp. 127–32), became a referent for the projects the Rockefeller sponsored in Colombia. Yet, the influence of the Rockefeller's previous experiences was less pronounced in *Uniandes* than it was in *Univalle*, where the infamous collaboration between the Católica and the University of Chicago provided both a model and the manpower for the creation of the Centro de Investigaciones sobre Desarrollo Económico (CIDE) in Cali (Table 7.1).

From its first incursion in Latin America in 1960, the key priority for the Ford Foundation was to change the face of higher education in the region. In an exploratory report commissioned by Ford to survey the developmental problems in Latin America, a group of prominent social scientists based at the University of Yale identified the overall "weakness of university education" as one of the most pressing issues in the region.[3] During the 1960s, Ford became the main sponsor of "general education", attempting to break with the compartmentalization of the professions that allegedly characterized typical Latin American universities.[4] Transcending the understanding of the university as a "loose federation of schools and faculties" became reformers' motto in the first half of that decade (Wickham, 1973, p. 22). *Uniandes* and *Univalle* assumed the leadership of this top-down university reform project when they submitted a

Table 7.1 Rockefeller and Ford grants to economics departments in Colombia, 1958–1971

Recipient	Donor	Grant duration	Visiting professors	Fellowships
Uniandes	Rockefeller	1958–1964	2	11
	Ford	1968–1971	1	3
Univalle	Rockefeller	1963–1967	8	11
Unal	Ford	1968–1971	4	8

Sources: Rockefeller Foundation (1958, 1959, p. 195, 1960, 1962, pp. 162, 186, 1963, pp. 202–203, 1964, pp. 117, 134, 1965, p. 136, 1966, p. 145); Ford Foundation (1968, p. 130); Facultad de Economía, "Second Report"; Reed Hertford, "Final Report – Evaluation: National University, Faculty of Economics and CID", 8 January 1973, R3402, GF/FFR. NB: The table excludes grants for the development of programs in agricultural economics and business management.

joint proposal to Ford for creating basic studies programs that would contribute to the integration of academic units and to counter the professionalizing trend in higher education. In 1961 Ford appropriated its first grants in Colombia to both universities for the development of a "school of basic studies".[5] By promoting the integration between academic departments, these initial Ford grants had an indirect but important influence on the education of economists. At *Uniandes*, for instance, the resulting School of Arts and Sciences strengthened the mathematical training of economists in the economics department, exposed economics students to humanities subjects, like economic history, and facilitated cross-fertilization with students from other departments.[6]

Ford's integrationist aspiration also found an expression in the creation of the Division of Human Sciences at *Unal* in 1966, which merged the economics department with six other departments in the social sciences and the humanities, including sociology.[7] By rationalizing university administration, the so-called *Reforma Patiño* attempted to institutionalize the academic profession, or as one participant put it, to "create the profession of university professor as such" (quoted in Briceño, 1988, p. 144). As commentators argued in the late 1950s and early 1960s,[8] the absence of full-time professors, with proper remuneration and opportunities for career development in universities, contributed to the low academic standards of economics education and the general absence of a research culture in local economics departments. The *Reforma Patiño* was thus welcomed with enthusiasm by young professors and the student movement (Briceño, 1988, pp. 114–15; Archila, 2012, p. 80; Hernández Gamarra, 2020, p. 108). It also offered Ford, as Lauchlin Currie wrote in a report dated August 1966, a unique opportunity "to bring about a truly major reform in the largest university of the country". In his capacity of director of the division's new interdisciplinary research center, the Centro de Investigaciones para el Desarrollo Económico y Social (later known as CID),[9] Currie urged the foundation to sponsor the creation of a "Graduate School or Schools in the Social sciences, forwarding integration at a more advanced level".[10] Although this idea never came to fruition, in 1968 Ford appropriated a grant to *Unal* to support the staffing of the economics department and the CID for three years. Simultaneously, *Uniandes* received a Ford grant with funds earmarked for three fellowships to strengthen the teaching capacities of its graduate program in economics.

Between 1958 and 1971, the Rockefeller and Ford Foundations appropriated grants to the economics departments of the three universities to strengthen education and research in economics. These grants shared two underlying assumptions. First, foundation officials expected that promoting academic research through the creation of specialized centers such as the CEDE, CIDE and CID would have positive effects on the education of local economists. Besides becoming hubs for producing local knowledge about economic development, research centers were considered a solution to retaining full-time faculty. Second, Ford and Rockefeller grants were grounded on the idea that fostering exchanges with economics departments in the US would raise the academic standards of both economic research and education in Colombian universities. Those exchanges included prolonged stays by visiting professors and the allocation of scholarships to Colombian economists for studying abroad. The Ford and Rockefeller Foundations gave at least 33 fellowships to students from the three universities to pursue graduate studies in the United States (Annex 7.A1).

Foundation officials considered both disciplinary and area expertise when they brokered connections between their grantees and economic departments in the US. The two foundations, particularly the Rockefeller, relied on the networks of scholars, academic departments, and research centers they had built after three decades sponsoring economic research in the US. In the post-war period, those networks expanded to include Latin Americanist specialists based in US universities, a by-product of the area studies initiatives financed by Ford (Delpar, 2008, pp. 159–62). The strong disciplinary orientation that characterized the collaboration between the Universidad Católica in Chile and the University of Chicago (Valdés, 1995, pp. 145–46) was not a common characteristic of all the programs in economics that philanthropic foundations sponsored in Latin America. In some cases, such as the long-lasting cooperation between Brazilian universities and Vanderbilt University sponsored by Ford, the "area interest" predominated over the disciplinary focus (Suprinyak and Fernández, 2021, p. 914). Overall, the programs that Rockefeller and Ford funded in Colombia offered a nuanced picture. As I show below, no single collaboration left an indelible mark in the profession comparable to that which Chicago and Vanderbilt left in the Chilean and Brazilian cases.

Philanthropic foundations were not the exclusive patrons of economic research and education in Colombia during the 1960s. The Alliance for Progress not only created a state demand for economic expertise to negotiate foreign loans and coordinate public investments, but also made available financial resources for training economists through the Agency for International Development (AID).[11] The projects that philanthropic foundations sponsored in Colombia intersected those funded by US government agencies,[12] but this overlap does not imply they were mere instruments of US soft power, as Parmar (2012) suggests. Rather both foundations operated within a broader funding ecosystem that was intellectually anchored in shared assumptions about the association between technical education, modernization, and development (Solovey, 2013, p. 115; Gilman, 2003, p. 16). To a certain degree, the consensus that underlay the cooperation between different US donors was that the formation of a new technocratic elite would be a catalyst for economic and social change.

7.2.1 From the "Chicago Boys" to the "Rover Boys": The Rockefeller at Univalle

Created in 1958 at the request of regional business elites (Mayor Mora and Zambrano, 2016, pp. 45–46), the economics department at *Univalle* was the newest of the programs the philanthropic foundations sponsored. The dynamism of the Cauca Valley in the 1950s captured the attention of the Social Sciences Division of the Rockefeller Foundation, which throughout the 1960s invested heavily in the development of this state-funded regional university. In 1962, a Rockefeller envoy observed that *Univalle*'s economic department was remarkably well staffed by Latin American standards but suffered from a lack of leadership after its founder and dean, Antonio Posada, resigned in reaction to student strikes.[13] In search of guidance, the Rockefeller turned to the University of Chicago, building on its previous experiences with the Universidad Católica de Chile and the Universidad del Cuyo, a state-funded regional university in the province of Mendoza, Argentina.[14] Between 1963 and 1968, Rockefeller sponsored three Latin American PhD candidates from the University of Chicago to teach at the Universidad del Valle: Sergio de Castro (1963–1964), Luis Arturo Fuenzalida (1965–1967), and Alberto Musalem (1968).[15] Fuenzalida was also the first director of CIDE (1965–1966). Six students from *Univalle*, out of the eleven that received Rockefeller scholarships, pursued PhDs at the University of Chicago (Table 7.4, Annex).

The Rockefeller experience at *Univalle* demonstrated how similar strategies of internationalization yielded different outcomes depending on the local institutional context. The collaboration between *Univalle* and the University of Chicago was short-lived and the scholarship program did not produce the same results of the Rockefeller projects in Chile and Argentina, despite visiting professors' active attempts to build a Chicago school in Cali. Prospective candidates were subjected to intense preparation, overseen by Fuenzalida and other visiting professors, that aimed to prepare them for graduate study in Chicago. Among other tasks, this preparation included reading Stigler's *The Theory of Price* and resolving all the problem sets in that book (Mayor Mora and Zambrano, 2016, pp. 443–44). De Castro recognized that given their career expectations, his students in Cali, who came from diverse socioeconomic backgrounds, "suspected theory" and preferred instead to be taught "how to DO specific things which will allow them to perform something of concrete value to the economy". Yet, he expressed the conviction that with the proper training they could be persuaded that Chicago's theoretically driven approach was "'the kind of Economics'" that was right for them.[16]

In May 1965, the Rockefeller hired Arnold Harberger as short-term consultant to assist the graduate training of Colombian students in Chicago.[17] Harberger was expected to stop in Cali on his way to Chile and Argentina to interview candidates but cancelled his trip at the last minute and rescinded his contract.[18] Fuenzalida, Harberger's former student, personally selected four students to pursue a PhD in Chicago. The information registered in their application form indicates that these students did not necessarily come from privileged backgrounds. Three of them attended state-funded high schools before enrolling in *Univalle*, a marker of social mobility at the time. Unlike other Rockefeller fellows, none of them reported having previous experiences in the US.[19] A Rockefeller officer expressed that he had "mixed feelings about these boys",[20] but he was reassured that the economics department at Chicago was prepared for the job: "They take inadequately trained material and turn out well-trained people and maintain the standards at the output level. This, Al [Harberger] is prepared to do for Cali."[21] Two years later, all four candidates had left Chicago without even qualifying for a master's degree. Harberger remarked in the graduate record of one of these students that their level of English was a major difficulty, adding in a coldly hand-written note that their "poor background" and "inadequate intellectual capacity" were also to blame for their bad performance.[22] In the Rockefeller's reports and correspondence, the group of students from *Univalle* were referred to as the "Rover Boys at Chicago", an allusion to Arthur M. Winfield's early twentieth-century popular juvenile series, which narrated the pranks of a group of untamable youngsters at a military boarding school.[23]

These prejudiced remarks obscured how misguided had been the attempt to use the collaboration between the University of Chicago and the Universidad Católica as a model for *Univalle*. The case of the Rover Boys also illustrates how exceptional the experience of the Chilean Chicago Boys was. Due to their different life experiences, the students from *Univalle* faced higher barriers than the Chilean Chicago Boys in assimilating to student life in Chicago, as they faced bigger difficulties surmounting the language barrier, navigating an alien academic culture, and relocating their entire families to a new country.[24] The students from *Univalle* also expressed concerns about the type of economics education they received at Chicago and expected the Rockefeller to facilitate their transfer to Harvard after the first year of studies.[25] This expectation was probably nurtured by the experience of Antonio Urdinola, later Minister of Finance (1998). A graduate of *Uniandes*, Urdinola received a Rockefeller fellowship in 1963 to study in Chicago in his capacity as professor at *Univalle*. After passing his winter exams with solid marks, Urdinola requested a transfer to Harvard, arguing there were no faculty in Chicago who specialized in his field of interest, the "dynamic aspects of economic growth".[26] As a Rockefeller officer registered at Harvard, Urdinola would "be able to work the kind of economics that he believes fits the situation in Colombia much better than the work he was doing at Chicago".[27] Harvard's research program on the quantitative aspects of economic growth in the 1960s was more amenable to address the development issues that interested Colombian students than Chicago's strong mathematical emphasis on microeconomics.[28]

The Rockefeller and *Univalle* soon understood that Chicago-style economics was not the way to go in Cali. After 1967, the economics department at *Univalle* turned its attention away from a general program in economics to focus on its pioneering Ford-sponsored business management graduate degree and its agricultural economics program, which continued receiving Rockefeller support until the early 1970s.[29] It was in shaping these fields and not precisely that of economics that philanthropic foundations had a lasting impact at *Univalle*.

7.2.2 *Sponsoring applied research in economic development: The Rockefeller at* Uniandes

In contrast to the program at *Univalle*, Rockefeller's internationalization strategy at *Uniandes* appeared to be, from the foundation's perspective, more successful in achieving its goals. Nine of the eleven Colombian students from *Uniandes* that Rockefeller sponsored to pursue advanced studies in the United States obtained a graduate degree. The Rockefeller fellows from *Uniandes* had a higher endowment of social capital to begin with than those from *Univalle*. Only one of them had attended a state-funded high school. The rest had completed secondary education either in renowned private high schools in Bogotá and Barranquilla, or in private academies in the US. Jorge Ruiz Lara (U. Illinois, BA, 1954) and Miguel Urrutia (Harvard, BA, 1961)[30] had obtained their undergraduate degrees from US universities. Given their shared backgrounds and previous experiences, *Uniandes* fellows were arguably better equipped to confront the language and cultural barriers that were constitutive, not merely accessory, of the academic exchanges that philanthropic foundations promoted between economics departments in Colombia and the United States. To smooth the transition, the Rockefeller sponsored Colombian economists to attend a summer school in the Economics Institute of the University of Colorado, Boulder, which attempted to give foreign students an opportunity to improve their English, strengthen their theoretical foundations and meet other international students.[31]

Rockefeller fellows were expected to rejoin the economics department at *Uniandes* after completing two years of studies at master's level, even if some attempted to pursue a PhD. Jorge Ruiz Lara (U. Illinois, 1961) and Miguel Urrutia (Berkeley, 1967) were the only fellows who succeeded in obtaining a PhD. Only exceptionally did the foundation consider extensions for doctoral studies. The rejection of Eduardo Wiesner's application to extend his scholarship to pursue a PhD at Stanford illustrates why.[32] As a Rockefeller officer explained to dean Gómez, before attempting to obtain a PhD abroad, the department should encourage students like Wiesner to "get a tour of research and teaching which is long enough to bring them to grips with the problems in their home setting".[33] This position, which considered country-specific knowledge as important as disciplinary expertise, was consistent with the focus given to the national problems of economic development at CEDE since its creation.

To direct CEDE in 1958, the Rockefeller hired John Hunter, who was at the time the "Latin American specialist" at the Economics Department of Michigan State University. A PhD from Harvard (1949), Hunter had published various pieces on foreign trade and investment in Latin America during the 1950s.[34] One of his colleagues at Michigan State considered Hunter "to be closer to Arthur Lewis than most of the American development writers".[35] Hunter and his successor at CEDE, Wallace Atherton, who specialized in labor economics,[36] had a long-term impact on the center's applied and empirically oriented research on economic development (c.f. Sánchez et al., 2008). From its very first research contract with the Ministry of Economic Development, CEDE made it one of its main occupations to produce "basic economic data" that both researchers and policymakers could then use for economic analysis.[37]

Upon their return from the United States, the Colombian students funded by Rockefeller built on that legacy of applied economic research. From 1962 to 1971, CEDE was directed by four former Rockefeller fellows: Ruiz Lara, Urrutia, Ortega and Isaza Botero. In a memorandum dated October 1966, the Center was portrayed as a "pioneer" in applied fields such as labor economics, demographic studies, and urban and regional planning. CEDE researchers conducted the first periodical city-level survey on employment in Bogotá,[38] with support from the Rockefeller and the central bank, and later expanded its coverage to six additional cities in collaboration with the planning department. With the applied studies produced at CEDE, the memorandum argued, the economics department at *Uniandes* achieved political influence, positioning unemployment as a top issue in the economic agenda of the President (then candidate) Carlos Lleras Restrepo (1966–1970).[39]

While Rockefeller grants helped the economics department at *Uniandes* build closer links with the state through the data and analysis produced at CEDE, some external observers cast doubts on their impact on the institutionalization of economics in universities. The tension between building an academic community of economists, on the one hand, and responding to the state demand for economic expertise, on the other, became patent with the early experience of the first graduate program in economics in Colombia, the *Escuela de Economía Para Graduados* (later *Programa de Economía para Graduados*, PEG), after its creation at *Uniandes* in 1964.[40]

According to dean Wiesner (1965–1968), the economics department envisioned the creation of the postgraduate program as a solution to "the urgent demand that Colombia had—and still has —for a select group of well-trained economists at the graduate level"(Wiesner Durán, 1965, p. 2). With sponsorship from the US Agency for International Development, four professors from the University of Minnesota visited the economics department between 1964 and 1967 to design the curriculum for the graduate program and conform a faculty "trained in the techniques of modern economic theory".[41] The PEG's curriculum (Table 7.2) initially placed a strong emphasis on theoretical and mathematical economics, in line with contemporary disciplinary trends in the US (Orozco-Espinel, 2020). Given that the graduate program also aimed at the education of a "governing cadre" (Wiesner, 1965, p.2), the PEG's curriculum evolved to integrate policy-oriented subjects taught by government employees (Table 7.3). Until the late 1970s, the PEG was the only alternative for receiving advanced training in economics locally, which accentuated the protagonism the economics department at *Uniandes* acquired in the profession during the 1960s.

The professors who visited Colombia to teach at the PEG voiced their criticisms of the Rockefeller grants, which they argued had done little to raise the

Table 7.2 Curriculum of the *Programa de Economía para Egresados*, 1964

Preparatory	First semester	Second semester	Third semester
Economic Theory	Macroeconomics I	Macroeconomics II	Economic History II
Mathematics I	Microeconomics I	Economic History I	Elective*
English	Statistics I	Statistics II	Elective*
	Mathematics II	Elective*	Thesis
	Elective*	Thesis project	

Source: Lauchlin Currie, "Informe del visitador Lauchlin Currie sobre la Escuela para Graduados, Universidad de Los Andes," 5 April 1964, Informes, Rectoría (I/), UADA.

* The list of electives included: History of Economic Doctrines, Econometrics, Mathematical Economics, Labour Economics, International Economics, Public Finances, Monetary Economics, Public Services, Private Firms and Public Control, Demography

Table 7.3 PEG's roaster of courses** and professors, 1970

First semester (January–May)	Summer (June-July)	Second semester (August–December)
Applied Mathematical Analysis (Manuel Ramírez)	Monetary Theory and Policy (Enrique Low*)	Advanced Economic Analysis (Manuel Ramírez)
Statistics (Dionisio Ibañez*)	Public Investments (Guillermo Perry*)	Econometrics I (Eduardo Sarmiento)
Microeconomic Analysis (Roberto Junguito)		Fiscal Theory and Policy (Enrique Low*)
Macroeconomic Analysis (Max Rodríguez)		

Source: Facultad de Economía, "Segundo informe anual de la Facultad de Economía presentado a la Fundación Ford," 1970, I/UADA, 6–7.

* Visiting professors from the planning department.
** Elective courses: Economic Doctrines (Álvaro López Toro), Labor Economics (Miguel Urrutia, visiting professor from the Monetary Board).

academic standards of economics education at *Uniandes*. Minnesota professors had a low opinion of locally trained economists, who according to Larry Saajstad from the University of Chicago were inadequately prepared for the "heavy emphasis on theory, mathematics and statistics" that the Minnesota group gave to the *PEG*.[42] Visiting professors also took aim at the Rockefeller's internationalization strategy. According to Buttrick, the nature of *Uniandes* as an elite private university and the criteria Rockefeller officers used to shortlist candidates – such as students' English proficiency – combined to benefit students from advantaged socioeconomic backgrounds to receive advanced training in the US.[43] For these students, the prospect of becoming full-time university professors, a position that was poorly remunerated and did not enjoy public recognition, was highly unattractive. Hence, once Rockefeller-sponsored economists joined the faculty at *Uniandes*, they were "not highly motivated for either research or teaching" but were instead "more concerned with their social status".[44] Fellows used their international degrees and research record at CEDE to leverage positions in government, leading to a high turnover of faculty in the economics department which did not cause particular concerns to dean Wiesner.[45] Instead of making big efforts to retain personnel, Wiesner reached an agreement with the Population Council to finance demographic research in the economics department and offer a new round of scholarships for prospective researchers and teachers.[46]

To some extent, the strong bonds the economics department at *Uniandes* developed with the state through CEDE was a curse in disguise for developing an academic community with exclusive dedication to research and teaching as the Rockefeller had expected. As one foundation official put it, at a time when economic expertise was in high demand in government, the one-way flow in the rotation of personnel between universities and the state was a "constant danger" for the consolidation of an academic community at the economics department.[47] The early experience with internationalization at *Uniandes* created a path-dependent trajectory in the subsequent evolution of the economics department and its research center, which from early on positioned them as hotbeds for government economic experts.

7.3 University reform and the rebellious youth: Ford at the Universidad Nacional

Several factors explain the relatively late involvement of philanthropic foundations in the economics department at *Unal*. While *Uniandes* and *Univalle* represented the type of "modern" universities that the Ford and the Rockefeller Foundations expected to make exemplary models for the region, to their eyes *Unal* suffered from the ailments of the "traditional" Latin American university, caught in a struggle for control between the state, and the professorial and student bodies. At first, the philanthropic foundations abstained from appropriating funds to social science departments at *Unal*, with the notable exception of Ford's grants to Fals Borda's sociology program.[48] When dean Álvaro

Daza asked Ford in 1964 to support the department's Centro de Investigaciones Económicas (CIE), CID's immediate precursor, the foundation rejected
this request, alluding to Ford's existing obligations with the "graduate school
of sociology" and the "political and economic problems which confront the
University".[49] In the 1960s, the frustration of the youth with the National
Front political arrangement grew steadily (Leal Buitrago, 1981) – particularly
in state-funded universities. As the decade progressed, the student movement
radicalized and its leaders adhered to anti-government organizations (Archila,
2012, p. 84). Student strikes in state-funded universities, often displaying
anti-imperialist banners, became more frequent, which must have led Ford officials to consider with extreme care financing further projects in *Unal*.

It was not until Currie linked the staffing needs of the economics department to Ford's interest in general education and interdisciplinary research, that
the foundation considered sponsoring economics at *Unal*. In the field of economics, Ford had hitherto privileged investing in the on-the-job training of
economists and from 1963 sponsored a technical assistance mission from Harvard's Development Advisory Service (DAS) in the planning department.[50]
According to the testimony of former student Alcides Gómez (Hernández
Gamarra and Herrera, 2002, p. 435), Currie's brief tenure as dean of the economics department and the integration of the department into the Faculty of
Human Sciences were catalysts for the transformation of economics education
at *Unal*. While economics students suddenly had the opportunity to take
classes with Currie and Harvard professors from the DAS mission, like Karsten
Laursen and Lester Taylor, they read neo-Marxist and French structuralists
social thinkers with their peers from the Human Sciences Division on campus.

Although Currie's tenure was brief, the transformation of the economics
department continued under the deanship of his successor Bernardo García.
García had obtained his undergraduate degree in economics from the University of Louvaine (1964) and was a PhD candidate from the École de Hautes
Études in Paris. He initiated a program to staff the faculty following an internationalization strategy that resembled the one previously adopted by the
departments at *Uniandes* and *Univalle*. Yet, this faculty training program did
not rely exclusively on sending students to pursue graduate degrees in US universities, as some of the brightest students went instead to European and Latin
American institutions.[51] The appointment in 1967 of the economist Jorge Méndez as rector of *Unal* added credibility to the university's commitment to
strengthening its economics department.

Given its prolonged involvement in the planning department, Ford appeared
to be more receptive than the Rockefeller to the symbiotic relationship that
developed during the 1960s between economics departments in universities
and state institutions. When Ford's regional officers presented to the board of
trustees a grant request to fund the programs at *Uniandes* and *Unal*, it began
by recognizing that there was "already [an] important linkage among the
national planning agency" and those universities. Not only had the government "in the past five years recruited its key planning personnel by raiding the

economics staff of the two universities" but it was also starting to "look to the universities as a source of basic, policy-oriented research studies".[52] By the late 1960s, the legitimacy of economics as a source of expertise for informing and formulating government policy was beginning to settle. State institutions like the planning department, the Ministry of Finance and the Monetary Junta actively sought economists from the leading economics departments of the country to advise the government on key policy issues.[53] Ford's grants took as their point of departure the ground covered by a decade of Rockefeller sponsorship of economics education and research.

To coordinate the Ford grants, the foundation hired Albert Berry (PhD, Princeton, 1963). This was Berry's second visit to Colombia, where he had been in 1962–1963 to conduct research for the Economics Growth Center at the University of Yale, of which he was assistant director when the Ford approached him. Berry and CID's new director Roberto Arenas (1967–1970) proved to be successful community builders. Citing the "acute" need for economists in government and state institutions' growing demand for policy-oriented research, Berry advocated in favor of strengthening the research center at *Unal*. In his view, CID had a "good chance to be, right from the start, a better economic center than Los Andes because, unlike CEDE, it would not have to start from scratch but rather from CIE's previous experience and institutional capacities".[54] With Ford's support CID could, according to Berry, build a strong academic community in a relatively short period of time. Following Berry's advice, Ford covered the salary supplements of five "Colombian collaborators" to work at the center for three years.[55] It also sponsored two Latin American visiting professors, one of whom was the Argentinian Guillermo Calvo (then PhD candidate at Yale), and granted eight scholarships to pursue doctoral studies in the US. *Unal* committed to provide four additional scholarships. Berry got personally involved in the center and the economics department. He taught several courses at the department and the center's researcher training program, and interviewed prospective scholarship candidates. He also co-coordinated two pioneering research projects on the economic effects of urbanization and the distribution of agricultural income.[56]

In 1972, Ford officials concluded that, due to reasons relating to timing and "problems of design", the grant to the economics department at *Unal* "satisfied neither party to it".[57] This grim assessment was informed by the final grant report written by Reed Hertfort, who replaced Berry as adviser and taught agricultural economics at the department. Hertford's report outlined how student demonstrations, and the "hard-handed" response of the government, was affecting the work at the economics department and the research center. While the dilemma philanthropic foundations faced in other Latin American countries during the second half of the 1960s was whether to continue sponsoring economic research in universities that were under the grip of military dictatorships, in Colombia this question was posed by the reinvigoration and radicalization of the student movement.

From the very beginning of Lleras Restrepo's administration (1966–1970), relations between the government and the student movement were fraught. One of the main issues of contention for mobilized students was the "imperialist" intervention of foreign powers in higher education, which they perceived in the involvement of US-based philanthropic foundations in both private and state-funded universities. Shortly after Lleras Restrepo became president, radicalized students sabotaged a ceremony he was presiding over on university premises with Nelson Rockefeller as special guest. The president responded by enacting a decree that dissolved the student directory in *Unal* and removed students' representatives from the university's governing body (Hernández Gamarra, 2020, p. 121). A student demonstration in *Univalle* that in 1969 denounced the involvement of philanthropic foundations in that university sparked a new wave of protests that extended to both private and state-funded institutions across the country. Young professors supported the demonstrations, demanding a bigger say in university affairs (Briceño, 1988, p. 205). Against this background, Hertford reported that teaching at the department was constantly being interrupted due to either student strikes or government decisions, and class attendance remained low. Between 1968 and 1971, the university had seven rectors and the CID had four directors. This administrative instability impacted the continuity of the center's research projects. After Arenas Bonilla resigned as CID's director in June 1970, research activities at the center stalled.

The denouement of Ford's and Rockefeller's involvement in state-funded universities in the 1960s revealed to both foundation officials and university reformers the limitations of attempting to build academic communities in Colombian universities based on imported conceptions of academe that were not easily translatable to the local institutional context. In the 1970s, Ford shifted its attention to the sponsorship of independent economic research centers across Latin America, like Fedesarrollo in Colombia, thus closing the chapter of the big philanthropic foundations' institution-building efforts in universities.

Even if the Ford grant to the economics department at *Unal* did not yield the results foundation officials anticipated, it had unexpected outcomes that helped to shape the economics profession in Colombia. The short-lived experience of the CID in the late 1960s laid the foundations for the formation of an academic community mainly composed of alumni from Colombia's biggest state university. Of the eight Ford fellows, only Antonio Hernández (ABD, Rice) and Luis Eduardo Rosas (PhD, 1973, U. Brown) carried on pursuing doctoral studies.[58] While Hertford reported that only one of the eight Ford fellows joined the faculty at *Unal* upon their return, in the mid-1970s former CID researchers and their students became integrated into the economics department at the Universidad Externado de Colombia.[59] This group formed the basis of the professorial body at the Universidad Nacional when the Faculty of Economic Sciences was re-established in 1978 (Hernández Gamarra, 2020, pp. 138–139, 148–149).

Ford's grant at *Unal* also allowed a more diverse group of economists, both in terms of their socioeconomic origins and their intellectual outlook, to penetrate some of the institutional sites where Colombian technocrats legitimized their expert authority in the last quarter of the twentieth century. Hertford considered that Ford's internationalization strategy, despite its shortcomings, had not been an utter failure because "all [Ford fellows] are productively employed in Colombia and some are making rather significant contributions to policy research and management".[60] In 1970, García recruited some of his former students to form a research group (SEPROCOL) at the National Statistics Department to produce empirical socioeconomic analyses.[61] After leaving CID, Arenas was appointed by Pastrana to head the National Planning Department and hired former researchers at Unal's economic research center to join the technical staff. Currie and Berry served as Arenas' advisers. Only months before Ford received Hertford's report, Rosas replaced Arenas as director of the planning department. He directed the institution between 1973 and 1974. Thus, in an ironic twist, the two main programs in economics that Ford sponsored during the 1960s converged, at the exact moment when philanthropic foundations were crowding out from the sponsorship of economics in Colombian universities.

7.4 Conclusion

While the professionalization of economics in Colombia responded to the state's demand for experts on economic affairs during the 1960s, it was also driven by a deliberate internationalization strategy that aimed at building an academic community of economists in local universities. Philanthropic foundations' grants to fund scholarships, visiting professorships, and local research centers brought Colombian economists closer to the dominant trends in the increasingly US-centered economics discipline. The Rockefeller and Ford Foundations, together with US AID, fostered partnerships between local departments of economics and academic programs in the US that by contemporary standards had fairly heterogeneous approaches to economics, such as Chicago, Minnesota and Harvard. Arguably none of these institutional collaborations left a durable and indelible mark on the economics profession in Colombia, at least to the extent that scholars have documented for Chile and Brazil. The only attempt to build a school with a strong disciplinary identity at *Univalle* utterly failed. Instead, individual economists like John Hunter and Wallace Atherton at *Uniandes*, and Lauchlin Currie and Albert Berry at *Unal* left a bigger imprint in these departments by setting the direction of research agendas and building communities of technically literate but policy-minded economists. Philanthropic foundations' internationalization strategy yielded an unexpected and ironic outcome: the economics profession strengthened its position in key state institutions at the expense of building solid academic communities in universities.

Annex

Table 7.A1 Colombian economists who received fellowships from the Rockefeller and Ford Foundations to pursue graduate studies abroad

Sponsor	Name	Termination date	Degree pursued	Degree obtained	University
Universidad de Los Andes					
Rockefeller					
1	Jorge Ruiz Lara	1961	PhD	PhD	University of Illinois
2	Miguel Urrutia	1966	PhD	PhD	UC Berkeley
3	Hernán Mejía	1964	PhD	ABD	University of Oregon
4	Eduardo Wiesner	1962	MA	MA	Stanford University
5	Guillermo Franco	1962	MA	MA	University of Pennsylvania
6	James Ternent	1963	MA	MA	University of Oregon
7	Francisco Ortega	1964	MA	MA	Vanderbilt University
8	Max Rodríguez	1965	PhD	MA	Vanderbilt University
9	Giovanni Ciardelli	1966	PhD	MA	University of Minnesota
10	Roberto Villaveces	1964	MA	—	Harvard University
11	Rafael Isaza Botero	1964	MA	—	University of Oregon
Ford					
12	Jorge García	1976	PhD	PhD	University of Chicago
13	José Giordanelli	1972*	PhD	No information	London School of Economics
14	Darío Bustamante	1972*	PhD	No information	Princeton University

Universidad del Valle					
Rockefeller					
1	Antonio J. Urdinola	1966	PhD	ABD	Harvard University*
2	Enrique Low-Murtra	1969	PhD	ABD	Harvard University
3	Nohra Peñaranda	1964	MA	MA	University of Pittsburgh
4	Juan Manuel Torres	1964	MA	—	Duke University
5	Jaime Mejía	1965	MA	—	Wayne State University
6	Univalle fellow	1966	PhD	—	University of Chicago
7	Univalle fellow	1967	PhD	—	University of Chicago
8	Univalle fellow	1967	PhD	—	University of Chicago
9	Univalle fellow	1967	PhD	—	University of Chicago
10	Univalle fellow	1968	PhD	—	University of Chicago
11	Gustavo Argáez	1970	PhD	—	Harvard University
Universidad Nacional					
Ford					
1	Luis Eduardo Rosas	1973	PhD	PhD	Brown
2	Antonio Hernández	1970	PhD	ABD	Rice
3	Jaime Tenjo	1972	PhD	MA	Brown
4	Humberto Gallego	1972	PhD	—	Vanderbilt University
5	Hector Melo	1970	PhD	MS	NSSR
6	Miguel Neyra	1970	PhD	MS	Rice
7	Gustavo Jiménez	1971	PhD	MS	Rice
8	Rodrigo Manrique	1972	PhD	MS	Vanderbilt University

Sources: Fellowship cards, Social Sciences/Humanities, box 7, Record Group 10.1, Series 311, FF/RFR; Facultad de Economía, "Second Report"; Reed Hertford, "Final Report", FFR. The names of the fellows from Univalle who did not obtain the degree at Chicago have been excluded to protect their identity.

Archives

Archivo Central Histórico de la Universidad Nacional de Colombia. Actas del Consejo Directivo. (CD/ACHUN)

Ford Foundation Records. National University of Colombia- Development of Economics Training and Research. Grants L-N, Reel 3402, Rockefeller Archive Center, Sleepy Hollow, NY. (GF/FFR)

Ford Foundation Records. Catalogued Reports, Rockefeller Archive Center, Sleepy Hollow, NY. (CR/FFR)

Rockefeller Foundation Records. Fellowship Files, Social Sciences/Humanities. Record Group 10.1, Series 311, Rockefeller Archive Center, Sleepy Hollow, NY. (FF/RFR)

Rockefeller Foundation Records. Project Files. Record Group 1.2, Series 311, Rockefeller Archive Center, Sleepy Hollow, NY. (PF/RFR)

Population Council Records, Accession 1, Record Group 1, Grant Files, Grant # D64.85 - University of Los Andes, Colombia: Salary Expenditures for Demographic Program. Rockefeller Archive Center, Sleepy Hollow, NY (PCR)

Unidad de Administración Documental, Universidad de Los Andes. Actas del Consejo de la Facultad de Economía. (FE/UADA)

Unidad de Administración Documental, Universidad de Los Andes. Gimnasio Moderno (GM/UADA)

Unidad de Administración Documental, Universidad de Los Andes. Informes, Rectoría (I/UADA)

Notes

1 The Ford Foundation's program area on Economic Development and Administration "assumed the Rockefeller mantle" in recognition of its historical leadership in the field (Geiger, 1993, pp. 99–100).

2 The Getúlio Vargas in Brazil, and the Universidad Católica and the Universidad de Chile. See Rockefeller Foundation (1957, 193, 195, 202).

3 James W. Fesler, Albert O. Hirschman, Sidney W. Mintz, Robert Triffin, Henry C. Wallich, Lloyd G. Reynolds, "A Report to the Ford Foundation concerning Program Possibilities in Latin America," 30 June 1958, Catalogued Report 000066, (CR/FFR).

4 See Atcon (1966[1958]).

5 R. Frodin, J. L. Morrill, J. H. Rushton, "Recommendations for Aid to Higher education in Colombia", January 1961, Catalogued Report 000012, CR/FFR.

6 The faculty from the School of Arts and Sciences taught students from the economics department general courses in calculus and linear algebra and a specific course in "calculus for economists". See "Memorando Daniel Peñaranda a Consejo Académico de la Universidad," Acta #83-65, Actas del Consejo Académico Facultad Economía (FF/); "Tentative request for a grant to the Ford Foundation for the Consolidation of the School of Arts and Sciences of the University of the Andes," 6 December 1966, Informes rectoría (I/), UADA.

7 Acuerdo Número 71, Acta no. 22, 18 May 1966, CS/ACHUN.

8 H. K., Allen and J. F. Bell, "Final Report on The University of the Andes and The University of Cauca," RAC records, 311S, box 78, folder 739, p.2. See also Hunter and Ternent (1960, 191–94) and Ellis, Cornejo, and Escobar Cerda (1960, 1–3).
9 Created under Acuerdo 47, 1966, Consejo Superior Universitario, CS/ACHUN.
10 Lauchlin Currie, "The Possibility of a breakthrough in higher education in Colombia," 17 August 1966, R3402, GF/FFR, 4.
11 As I will show in Section 7.3, the AID sponsored the graduate program at *Uniandes*.
12 For example, Ford, US AID and the IADB supported the on-the-job training of economists in the planning department, which goes beyond the remit of this chapter.
13 "Report of Robert S. Smith on a visit to Cali" 3-12 October 1962", box 78, folder 720, RG 1.2, 311S, PF/RFR.
14 For the Project Cuyo see Sjaastad (2011).
15 De Castro and Fuenzalida had been Rockefeller fellows from the Universidad Católica, while Musalem participated in the Cuyo project. Alberto Núñez (PhD candidate, Chicago), from Panama, arrived with Ford support. "Allocation # 27, RF61153", 15 August 1963, box 75, folder 712; "Allocation #71, RF64095," 2 August 1965, box 75, folder 714; Reinaldo Scarpetta to Roger Biringer, 8 February 1969, box 75, folder 715, RG 1.2, 311S, PF/RFR.
16 De Castro to CMH, 17 February 1964, box 75, folder 712, 1.2, 311S, PF/RFR.
17 Memorandum of Consultation Agreement – Harberger, 18 May 1965, box 74, folder 706, 1.2, 311S, PF/RFR.
18 Recision of Consultation Agreement – Harberger, 30 July 1965, box 74, folder 706, 1.2, 311S, PF/RFR.
19 Box 123, folder 2192; Box 129, folder 248; box 139, folder 2253; box 155, folder 2434, 10.1, 311S, FF/RFR.
20 De Rycke to Hayes, 30 March 1965, box 129, folder 2148, 1.2, 311S, PF/RFR.
21 Davidson (RKD) to DeRycke, 8 April 1965, box 133, folder 2192. 10.1, 311S, FF/RFR.
22 Arnold Harberger, "Evaluation of Graduate Study," box 129, folder 2148, 10.1, 311S, FF/RFR.
23 JMD's diary notes, May 1966, box 129, folder 2148, 10.1, 311S, RFR.
24 Transcript of telephone interview with Greg Lewis, 5 January 1965, box 133, folder 2192, 10.1, 311S, FF/RFR.
25 Excerpt from GHS diary, 9–19 August 1965, box 133, folder 2192, 10.1, S 311, FF/RFR.
26 Urdinola to Compton, 2 April 1964, folder 2476, box 159, 10.1, 311S, FF/RFR.
27 Interview with JPP, 18 June 1964, box 159, folder 2476, 10.1, 311S, FF/RFR.
28 For applied research on economic development at Harvard, see Syrquin (2018).
29 Karsten Laursen and Lester D. Taylor, "Economics at the Universidad del Valle, Cali, Colombia," 30 October 1967., Reel 3395, GF/FFR. See also Offner (2019, 139–142, 144–171).
30 Director of the National Planning Department (1974–77) and general manager of the central bank (1993–2005).
31 See, for example, "Appointment to attend Economics Institute for Foreign Graduate Students," box 154, folder 2427, 10.1, 311S, FF/RFR.
32 Wiesner was Urrutia's successor as director of the National Planning Department (1978–81) and the first fellow appointed as Minister of Finance (1981–82).
33 CMH to Gómez, 7 December 1963. Box 161, folder 2498, 10.1, 311S, FF/RFR.
34 Curriculum Vitae, John M. Hunter, April 1959, box 78, folder 740, R.G, 311S, FF/RFR.

152   *Andrés M. Guiot-Isaac*

35 Martin Bronfenbrenner to Everett Hagen, 3 December 1957, box 78, folder 740, 1.2, 311S, PF/RFR.
36 Wallace Atherton CV, 13 May 1960, box 78, folder 742, 1.2, 311S, PF/RFR.
37 From the start CEDE specialized in producing basic economic statistics. According to Atherton, "such an emphasis has been essential in a country where many basic economic data are either absent (e.g. personal income distribution) or unreliable and conflicting". Wallace N. Atherton, "Third Annual Report," 1 September 1961, CEDE/Universidad de Los Andes, mimeo, 5.
38 See Franco Camacho (1965).
39 Memorandum, "The Activities of CEDE and the Rockefeller Foundation," 5 October 1966, box 69, folder 746, 1.2, 311S, PF/RFR.
40 Currie identified this tension in his evaluation of the graduate program. Economists in developing countries like Colombia were, according to him, typically called to address policy issues that required urgent solution, which needed "intuitive judgement" and left "very little margin for the use of advanced statistical techniques." In his view, economics students developed that intuitive judgement by learning economic theory and history. Lauchlin Currie, "Informe del visitador Lauchlin Currie" I/UADA.
41 "Agreement between The Universidad de Los Andes and the University of Minnesota to Establish a Graduate Program in Economics," 12 June 1963, folder 745, box 79, R.G 1.2, 311S, PF/RFR.
42 This was why the PEG mostly attracted engineering students, who excelled in the program, according to the coordinator of the Minnesota collaboration Jhon Buttrick. Diary Notes by Rondo Cameron, 17 November 1965; RKD Diary, with Larry A. Saajstad, University of Chicago, 6 May 1966, box 79, folder 746, 1.2, 311S, PF/RFR.
43 "Confidential Report on Los Andes-Minnesota project", 22 December 1965, box 69, folder 746, 1.2, 311S, PF/RFR.
44 Diary Notes by Rondo Cameron, 17 November 1965, box 79, folder 746, 1.2, 311S, PF/RFR.
45 Wiesner to Davidson, 16 February 1966, box 79, folder 746, 1.2, 311S, PF/RFR.
46 "Demographic grant. Universidad de Los Andes", box 60, folder 992, IV3B4. 3a, S2, Population Council Records.
47 JMD diary, visit to Los Andes, 01 September 1966, box 79, folder 746, 1.2, 311S, PF/RFR.
48 Rusthon et al. "Recommendations for aid to higher education", 16–18.
49 Daza to George Schyler, 6 April 1964; Schuyler to Daza, 13 May 1964, R3402, GF/FFR.
50 For a summary of the grants the Ford gave to the Harvard DAS group to assist development planning in Colombia see K.N. Rao to James R. Holmes, "Formal closing of the Grant Series 63-547," n.d., R4248, GF/FFR.
51 According to García (2002, p. 441), 17 students received scholarships during his tenure to pursue graduate studies abroad, which presumably included the eight Ford fellows. The economics department also introduced a system of teaching assistants to screen prospective candidates and financed language courses. Alberto Corchuelo obtained a graduate degree in development economics from ESCOLATINA in the Universidad de Chile (1970), while Gabriel Misas and Alcides Gómez both obtained a master's degree in economics from the University of Louvain in 1970 and 1971.
52 David E. Bell to McGeorge Bundy, Request No. ID-204, 16 July 1968, R3402, GF/FFR.
53 The recruitment of economists in government goes beyond the scope of this chapter, but it suffices to add that former Rockefeller fellows Antonio Urdinola, Miguel Urrutia, Eduardo Wiesner and Jorge Ruiz Lara had occupied advisory and directorial positions in those institutions.

54 Albert Berry to William Cotter, 2 April 1968, R3402, GF/FFR.
55 Between 1968 and 1971, the CID used Ford funds to hire four Colombian economists with doctoral studies in the US: Antonio Hernández (ABD, Rice), Humberto Camargo (ABD, Yale), Pablo Salazar (ABD, Georgetown) and Francisco Thoumi (PhD, Minnesota). Reed Hertford, "Final Report-Evaluation, PA68-759", 8 January 1973, R3402, GF/FFR, p.6.
56 CID, report "Ford Foundation grant No. 68-759," 17 February 1972, p. 47, R3402, GF/FFR
57 John C. Farrell, 19 February 1972, "Closing Grant 68-759," GF/FFR.
58 Decades later, Hernández was appointed General Comptroller (2002-2006). Rosas would become director of the planning department (1973–74) and head of ILPES (1974–78).
59 Among them, Antonio Hernández, Homero Cuevas (MA, 1974, McGill), Jesús Antonio Bejarano (MA, Development Economics, 1974, U. North Carolina), and Luis Bernardo Flórez (MA Development Economics, 1977, Hague International Institute of Social Sciences).
60 Reed Hertford, "Final Report-Evaluation, PA68-759", 8 January 1973, R3402, p.16–17, GF/FFR.
61 Interviews with Salomón Kalmanovitz (13 January 2020) and Gabrel Misas (13 May 2022).

Bibliography

Álvarez, A., Guiot-Isaac, A.M. and Hurtado, J. (2019) 'La formación de una tecnocracia pragmática: los inicios de la formación profesional de economistas colombianos', *Revista Desarrollo y Sociedad*, 82, pp. 41–71.

Mauricio Archila (2012) 'El movimiento estudiantil en Colombia: Una mirada histórica', *Observatorio Social de América Latina*, 31, pp. 71–103.

Atcon, R.P. (1966) *The Latin American university; a key for an integrated approach to the coordinated social, economic and educational development of Latin America*. Bogota: *ECO Revista de la Cultura de Occidente*.

Babb, S.L. (2001) *Managing Mexico: Economists from nationalism to neoliberalism*. Princeton, NJ: Princeton University Press.

Bejarano, J.A. (1999) 'La profesionalización en economía', in Bejarano, J.A. and González, J.I. (eds) *Hacia dónde va la ciencia económica en Colombia: siete ensayos exploratorios*. Universidad Externado de Colombia, Bogotá.

Bernstein, M.A. (2001) *A perilous progress: economists and public purpose in twentieth-century America*. Princeton: Princeton University Press.

Briceño, R.C. (1988) *University reform, social conflict, and the intellectuals: the case of the National University of Colombia*, PhD thesis, Stanford University, Palo Alto, CA.

Delpar, H. (2008) *Looking South: the evolution of Latin Americanist scholarship in the United States, 1850–1975*. Tuscaloosa: University of Alabama Press (Ebook central).

Fajardo, M. (2022) *The world that Latin America created : The United Nations economic commission for Latin America in the development era*. Cambridge, MA: Harvard University Press.

Ford Foundation (1968) *Annual Report*. New York.

Fourcade, M. (2009) *Economists and societies: discipline and profession in the United States, Britain, and France, 1890s to 1990s*. Princeton: Princeton University Press.

Franco Camacho, G. (1965) *Investigaciones sobre desempleo en Colombia*. Bogotá: Uniandes, Facultad de Economía, CEDE.

García, B. (2002) 'Tres debates en la Escuela de Economía 1958, 1968, 1972', in *Búsquedas y logros desde la academia*. Bogotá: Universidad Nacional de Colombia, pp. 438–444.

Geiger, R. L. (1993) *Research and relevant knowledge: American research universities since World War II*. New York; Oxford: Oxford University Press.

Gilman, N. (2003) *Mandarins of the future : modernization theory in Cold War America*. Baltimore; London: Johns Hopkins University Press (Collection: New studies in American intellectual and cultural history).

Hernández Gamarra, A. (2020) *Relatos de los oficios y los días*. Bogotá: Universidad Nacional de Colombia.

Hernández Gamarra, A. and Herrera, B. (2002) *Búsquedas y logros desde la Academia: 50 años Facultad de Ciencias Económicas*. Bogotá: Universidad Nacional de Colombia.

Hunter, J.M. and Ternent, J.A.S. (1960) 'The teaching of economics in Colombia', *Journal of Inter-American Studies*, 2(2), pp. 189–196.

Hurtado, J. (2016) 'La economía política en los estudios superiores en la segunda mitad del siglo XIX en Colombia. Ezequiel Rojas, sus influencias y programas', in Álvarez, A. and Correa, J. S. (eds) *Ideas y políticas económicas en Colombia durante el primer siglo republicano*. Bogotá: Ediciones Uniandes, pp. 35–57.

Jaramillo, M. (2006) *Esteban Jaramillo: indicador de la economía colombiana*. Bogotá: Taurus.

Kalmanovitz, S. (1993) 'Notas para una historia de las teorías económicas en Colombia', in *Historia social de la ciencia en Colombia*. Bogotá: Tercer Mundo Editores, pp. 15–65.

Leal Buitrago, F. (1981) 'La frustración política de una generación. La universidad colombiana y la formación de un movimiento estudiantil 1958–1967', *Desarrollo y sociedad*, 6, pp. 299–325.

Mayor Mora, A. (1984) *Ética, trabajo y productividad en Antioquia : una interpretación sociológica sobre la influencia de la Escuela Nacional de Minas en la vida, costumbres e industrialización regionales*. 1st edn. Bogotá: Tercer Mundo.

Mayor Mora, A. and Zambrano, C. (2016) *Economistas Antiguos y Modernos, Gigantes y Enanos y su Enseñanza en Colombia*. Bogota: Universidad Autónoma de Colombia.

Montecinos, V. (1996) 'Economists in political and policy elites in Latin America', *History of Political Economy*, 28(supplement), p. 279.

Montenegro, Á. (2017) 'Los albores de la economía en Colombia', *Revista de Economia del Rosario*, 20(2), pp. 307–324.

Offner, A.C. (2019) *Sorting out the mixed economy: The rise and fall of welfare and developmental states in the Americas*. Princeton: Princeton University Press.

Orozco-Espinel, C. (2020) 'How mathematical economics became (simply) economics: The mathematical training of economists during the 1940s, 1950s, and 1960s in the United States'. *Center for the History of Political Economy at Duke University Working Paper Series*, No. 2020-11.

Palacios, M. (2005) 'Knowledge is power: The case of Colombian economists', in Fitzgerald, E.V. K. and Thorp, R. (eds) *Economic doctrines in Latin America : origins, embedding and evolution*. Basingstoke: Palgrave Macmillan, pp. 182–216.

Parmar, I. (2012) *Foundations of the American century: The Ford, Carnegie, and Rockefeller Foundations in the rise of American power*. New York: Columbia University Press.

Rockefeller Foundation (1957) *Annual Report*. New York.

Rockefeller Foundation (1958) *Annual Report.* New York.
Rockefeller Foundation (1959) *Annual Report.* New York.
Rockefeller Foundation (1960) *Annual Report.* New York.
Rockefeller Foundation (1962) *Annual Report.* New York.
Rockefeller Foundation (1963) *Annual Report.* New York.
Rockefeller Foundation (1964) *Annual Report.* New York.
Rockefeller Foundation (1965) *Annual Report.* New York.
Rockefeller Foundation (1966) *Annual Report.* New York.
Ruiz Lara, J. (1958) 'La enseñanza universitaria de las ciencias económicas en Colombia', in *Primer Congreso Nacional de Economistas. Memoria.* Bogotá: Sociedad Colombiana de Economistas, Ediciones Uniandes.
Sánchez, F. et al. (2008) *Historia del Cede. 50 años de investigación en economía 1958–2008.* Bogotá: Universidad de los Andes-CEDE.
Sjaastad, L. (2011) 'Programa Cuyo: a short history'. *Documentos de Trabajo Universidad del CEMA*, No. 448.
Solovey, M. (2013) *Shaky foundations: The politics-patronage-social science nexus in cold war America.* New Brunswick, NJ: Rutgers University Press.
Suprinyak, C.E. and Fernández, R.G. (2021) 'The 'Vanderbilt Boys' and the modernization of Brazilian economics', *History of Political Economy*, 53(5), pp. 893–924.
Tribe, K. (2021) *Constructing economic science: the invention of a discipline 1850–1950.* New York: Oxford University Press.
Valdés, J. G. (1995) *Pinochet's economists: the Chicago School in Chile.* Cambridge: Cambridge University Press.
Villamizar, J. C. (2012) *La influencia de la Cepal en Colombia 1948–1970*, PhD thesis, Universidad Nacional de Colombia, Bogotá.
Wickham, R.S. (1973) *University reform in Latin America: A case study of the University of Valle, Cali, Colombia*, PhD thesis, Berkeley University, Oakland CA.
Wiesner Durán, E. (1965) 'Los Estudios de Posgrado en Economía', *Ponencia presentada a la III conferencia Latinoamericana de Escuelas y Facultades de Ciencias Económicas.* Mimeo.

8 Employment Missions in Colombia

Discovering Informality, 1949–1985

*Andrés Álvarez, Sofía Meléndez, Ricardo Peña
and Marta Juanita Villaveces-Niño*

8.1 Introduction

2020 marked the beginning of an economic crisis associated with the Covid-19 pandemic that brought back onto the agenda a historical and structural characteristic of labor markets in Latin American economies: high levels of informality. With informal employment figures close to 50% (DANE, 2020), the debate in Colombia aimed to assess the structural causes of persistent informality, the obstacles within the economic system to the creation of formal jobs and dealing with a labor market with frequent transitions between formality and informality for workers (Levy & Cruces, 2021).

However, this topic is far from new. Historical employment data show the existence of unprotected (i.e., without a legal contract) employment at around 30% in the 1960s when the concept of informality had not yet been coined. In the 1970s, informality was measured, and unprotected or informal employment was found to be around 50%, which increased to 58% at the end of the 1980s (López, Henao & Sierra, 1987).

The first diagnosis of the particularities of employment can be traced back to 1949 when the first comprehensive World Bank[1] Mission came to Colombia, even though the concept of informality was not yet used in economics. What would later be called informality referred to the precariousness of jobs in traditional rural economies and the salient presence of low-income and low-productivity jobs in the growing urban areas. The economic missions that followed also addressed precarious employment and emphasized the coexistence of a so-called "traditional" sector with "modern" employment.

This duality in the job market continued to appear in subsequent missions that also aimed to explain its causes, focusing mainly on the transition to industry and the modern economy in the context of urban population growth. The economic missions discussed in this chapter share a common interest in addressing the labor market, which was described at the time as a market transitioning from a traditional to a modern economy.

Initially, the idea of transitional conditions in the 1950s and 1960s was described as the evolution from rural employment with low productivity and low incomes to the modernization of the productive system. Low-quality

DOI: 10.4324/9781003289241-10

employment was seen as transitional, as it would adjust once the structural change occurred. However, the extensive migration from rural to urban areas kept this "transitional" as a (too) long-lasting process, and low-quality employment in urban areas persisted. This transitional employment was called under-employment or disguised underemployment in urban economics, sharing the features of low income and low productivity. Again, this employment was diagnosed as temporary, suggesting the dynamic transition from underemployment to full employment.

In the 1980s, underemployment proved to be persistent rather than transitional, raising the question of what was needed to correct it. Labor policies faced the challenge of assessing why a situation seen as transitory proved to be persistent and accounted for half of the labor force. In 1985 the employment mission stated that by creating the conditions for structural change, growth in investment and export dynamics would absorb informality. Almost 40 years later, informality persists and constitutes most of Colombia's employment. What was diagnosed as a transitional situation in the 1950s turned out to be a structural characteristic of the labor market. Furthermore, the missions that repeatedly suggested it would be a transitional situation were unable to acknowledge that informal employment was, and continues to be, a structural feature of underdeveloped economies like Colombia, more likely to be addressed by the current analysis of structural heterogeneity (Dvoskin, 2022).

The International Labor Organization (ILO) adopted the term "informal sector" as a renewal of the concept of "traditional sector" (Benanav, 2019). There was, however, a previous effort to address the reality of unemployment in developing countries present in the modern and traditional economy before they constructed the idea of informal employment. In this chapter, we aim to study how the successive missions of experts, their diagnostics, their conceptual frameworks, and their policy recommendations unveil the evolution of the concept of informality in the public debate in Colombia.

We focus on four economic missions during the second half of the 20th century. The four missions at stake share an interest in the general conditions of economic development and their incidence on the labor market's performance. Our analysis starts with the World Bank Mission of 1949. Then, we address the Mission of the Economic Commission for Latin America and the Caribbean (ECLAC or CEPAL[2] in Spanish/Portuguese) in 1954 and 1959, the Employment Mission of the ILO in 1970, and the Employment Mission led by Hollis Chenery in 1985 (Chenery 1986). We trace the concept of informality in each mission, their recommendations to tackle this issue, and the links between them. We also analyze to what extent the different ways in which each mission tackled the presence of a form of labor informality were related to the contemporary theory of development and employment.

This chapter also aims to contribute to the contemporary debate. In particular, this analysis can help to provide a better understanding of the prevailing phenomenon of informality, offering sharpened responses to the long-lasting failures of the labor market and, thus, of social inclusion.

8.2 The context of each economic mission

Colombia received about ten economic missions[3] involving international experts during the course of the 20th century. In many cases, the governments in office initiated these missions. In other cases, local economic and political actors called for them. Some were also somehow imposed by external actors. In all three cases, the missions played a crucial role in signaling the country's commitment to orthodox prescriptions in managing its public policies.

Following the first Kemmerer mission (1923), which would conclude with the creation of one of the first modern central banks in Latin America, and a profound reform of fiscal control institutions, Colombia tried to offer an image of a disciplined country to attract both credit and foreign investment. Some missions would also play an essential role in the search for consensus amid difficult political-economy disequilibria. Such is the case of the 1949 IBRD mission, which came just after the outbreak of social unrest that followed the assassination of a presidential candidate with significant popular support. Finally, it is also important to point out that the scope of the first missions (Kemmerer, Currie, CEPAL) was more extensive, including the goal of developing institutional capacity through technical assistance to shape a local technocracy (see Chapter 7). By the end of the century, the participation of national experts in some missions, for example, the Chenery mission, allowed an increasingly sophisticated local knowledge to be put into action, counting on the support and credibility of renowned international experts. In all cases, beyond the legitimate concerns to solve the significant structural problems of the economy, the missions played a strategic role in creating a political consensus to make the reforms viable.

Between the IBRD mission (1949) and the Chenery mission (1985), the country witnessed the first peak of its industrialization process, which had begun by 1930 after the first boom of coffee exports[4] but began to decline around 1961 (see Echavarría et al., 2006). Throughout the following decades, the country went through successive waves of moderate to deep macroeconomic crises (balance of payment and fiscal deficits), coping with massive unemployment and consolidating the informal segment of the labor market. The latter gained momentum during the 1970s, resulting in the two main international missions focused on the labor market: the ILO mission (1970) and the Chenery mission (1980).

8.2.1 The IBRD mission (Currie): A first comprehensive mission for development

In 1949, the IBRD sent a mission to Colombia to make a comprehensive survey of the state of development and the functioning of the economic system. This was neither the first IBRD mission nor the first international expert mission to arrive in Colombia. However, in terms of its goals, it was the most ambitious mission that the IBRD had so far carried out in the developing world, and thus also the most ambitious to be carried out in Colombia.

The mission leader, Lauchlin Currie, was a well-known scholar on macroeconomic questions. Before being appointed director of the IBRD mission, Currie had been part of the team that would accompany the implementation of the New Deal in the United States and the implementation of essential reforms to the Federal Reserve System (Sandilands, 2018, pp. 55–56). However, development problems had become his main interest since he was introduced to the work of Rosenstein-Rodan and Nurkse, among others (Sandilands, 2015). His visit to Colombia changed his development vision and transformed him into a policy advisor with an audible voice for almost 40 years in Colombia (Álvarez et al., 2020). His initial involvement led to the mission being known as the Currie mission.

The report of this rapid (less than half a year) but ambitious mission contained the first fully comprehensive analysis of the country's state of development and precise policy recommendations. It described a country in full transition, with forms of industrial production that were beginning to gain strength and develop a modern sector. However, a considerable part of the country was disconnected from this modernity. The mission focused on the existence of several bottlenecks blocking the spread of modernity. The most significant ones were the lack of infrastructure to connect the broken geography of the country, the lack of investment in capital in the countryside, the low level of consumption, and the low effective demand related to the low income levels of the population.

8.2.2 CEPAL: From technical support to a General Development Plan

In the early 1950s, CEPAL was developing a new methodology to enhance the planning experience in Latin America. In the context of rising urbanization, the extension of suffrage, a newly created or expanded state-sponsored welfare system (Love, 2018), and demographic transition, the modernization of the state was fundamental. Planning became an essential tool to fulfill this challenging task. The new CEPAL methodology evaluated and communicated possible economic trajectories based on the existing structure. The planning – or programming – technique developed by CEPAL was intended to be "neutral enough to bring about decisions that would foster the transparency and efficacy of political powers" (Arana, 2020, p. 56) and aimed not only to study the state of Latin American economies but also to train their economists in economic development.

The first CEPAL mission to Colombia resulted from a series of analyses and projections of economic development that the institution's Executive Secretariat[5] had launched throughout Latin America. With the cooperation of the Colombian government, through the Economic and Fiscal Planning Committee, a group of economists from the Secretariat[6] came to the country in March 1954 to begin preparatory work. They took five months to gather most of the primary material and later wrote the report in Santiago de Chile. CEPAL officials had access to the statistical material available in the country and were also able to come into direct contact with numerous public officials, representatives of private economic activities, academia, and experienced people from various sectors (Secretaria de la Comisión Económica para América Latina, 1957, p. 1).

The work carried out by the Secretariat of the Commission did not amount to a development program for Colombia. That program came with what could be considered the second CEPAL mission at the beginning of the 1960s. The first report, intended to "continue methodological research in terms of analysis and projections, trying to make the most out of the specific background on the Colombian economy" (Secretaria de la Comisión Económica para América Latina, 1957, p. 1), was entitled *The Economic Development of Colombia*. It consisted of a global analysis of the historical development of the Colombian economy and its main characteristics, as well as a detailed analysis of each of the main sectors of economic activity, primarily industry and agriculture. The second part presented alternative projections about future economic growth. The report pioneered the consolidation of Colombian economic statistics, and to this day it serves as a documentary base for studying the country's economy in the first half of the 20th century (Arévalo Hernández, 1997; Villamizar, 2012).

An Argentinian economist, Manuel Balboa,[7] led the second CEPAL mission (Arévalo Hernández, 1997) a few years later. The mission produced the "Plan General" analyzing Colombia's economic structure and development experience between 1950 and 1959. It used this information to set a series of development targets for the next decade. The Plan was part of an effort to meet the requirements to request and obtain global external financing for development programs and was carried out in conjunction with the National Council for Economic Policy and Planning and the Administrative Department of Planning and Technical Services. Moreover, the Plan made Colombia one of the first countries to complete a comprehensive economic and social development plan and present it for review to the Committee of Nine under the provisions of the Punta del Este Charter.

Law 19 of 1958 expressed the need to "submit the economy to rigorous planning". This law was inscribed in what would become known as "the era of planning", which occurred in the same ten-year plan. The convenience of a certain degree of state intervention in the economy was indisputable. However, it should obey technically pre-established and consistent objectives (Departamento Administrativo de Planeación y Servicios Técnicos de Colombia, 1961). Three documents following this notion were published in 1961: the six-part Ten-Year Plan (1960–1970)[8], a four-year investment plan, and a study of industry. Unlike the report of the first mission, which was limited to a diagnosis of the performance of the Colombian economy between 1925 and 1953, the General Plan offered specific recommendations on economic growth, industrial development, expansion of the welfare state, public finances, population, and workforce. The Quadrennial Investment Plan was even more explicit and detailed in stating what was needed to carry them out.

8.2.3 ILO: A multilateral view of employment

In 1967 the ILO launched the World Employment Program, which envisioned country missions to study the causes of unemployment and draw up national and international plans of action to tackle the issue. President Carlos Lleras Restrepo proposed to the ILO's director, David Morse, that Colombia be the first country to receive one of these missions.

At the time, the country had experienced considerable economic growth without reducing its unemployment rate. "Unbalanced growth" had disproportionately benefited specific sectors, leaving labor-intensive ones behind, unable to absorb workforce growth due to population growth and internal migrations to cities.

Arrangements were made for a high-level mission of international experts to visit the country in early 1970 with the explicit task of making short-term and long-term policy recommendations to the president to ensure growth would go hand in hand with high levels of productive employment (ILO, 1970, p. 3). The final report, "Towards Full Employment," was published that same year.

From the outset of the mission and in the final report, it was clear that economic growth was necessary but insufficient to solve the employment problem. Active state planning and public policy were necessary to direct growth to productive employment. Economic growth should be promoted in labor-intensive economic sectors that could absorb population growth. According to the mission, to achieve a 5% unemployment rate by 1985, 5 million new jobs would be needed. The goal was ambitious, considering that the mission estimated that the workforce stood at 6.5 million by 1970. At the current rate, the mission warned, only 1.5 million jobs would be created in the following 15 years.

Dudley Seers, director of the Institute of Development Studies at the University of Sussex, was appointed director of the mission. Altogether, the Colombian mission had 27 experts, primarily European and Latin American, who worked closely with the Ministry of Labor, the National Planning Department, and the Research Centre for Economic Development (CEDE) of the Universidad de los Andes, amongst others. They visited the country for five weeks and wrote their report over the following three months.

Seers' experience in development economics included his work under Michael Kalecki in the United Nations, where he collaborated with other development economists, including Thomas Balogh, Paul Streeten, and Hollis Chenery. He was profoundly influenced by structuralism after his work at CEPAL with Raúl Prebisch, Osvaldo Sunkel, and other Latin American economists (Jolly, 2009).

Seers saw clearly, as stated in the mission's report, that unemployment in the developing world was inherently different from unemployment in the developed world. He strongly disagreed with the view of economic growth as the sole objective of development policy, advancing that "development" corresponded to creating the necessary conditions for human personality real-ization (Seers, 1972). In Seers' work, including the ILO employment mission, employment, health, and education, were considered as ends and not just means for growth (see Seers, 1963).

8.2.4 Chenery: The quest for an independent mission

By 1984 the unemployment rate had reached 13.2%, about 3 points above the average for the 1970s. In 1985, Eduardo Pizano, an economic advisor to Presi-dent Belisario Betancur, stated the need for an economic mission to address the complex unemployment situation in Colombia. Pizano suggested Hollis Chen-ery from Harvard University as the chief of the mission in order to preserve independence from the government. Chenery had previously been vice presi-dent of the World Bank, and his work focused on the patterns of economic development in underdeveloped countries. In his previous work with Moshe Syrquin (Syrquin & Chenery, 1989), *Patterns of Development*, he had focused on macro features showing growth was related to demand and productivity, which affected employment and incomes. Roberto Junguito, Finance Minister, agreed with Pizano's suggestion.

Chenery's mission was invited 14 years after the ILO mission. Colombia was still suffering from the stagnation of industrial growth as a share of GDP and low job creation (Echavarría, 1999). The backlash from Mexico's default on foreign debt impacted all Latin American economies, plunging them into uncertainty. With lower levels of foreign debt than its Latin American neigh-bors, Colombia avoided default but faced a drop in GDP in 1982. More unem-ployment and loss of purchasing power followed.

Chenery continued the 1970 World Bank report (Junguito-Bonnet, 2016). Dragoslav Abramovic, the chief economist of that report, argued that the eco-nomic growth of the 1960s was explained by the increase in fixed capital invest-ment (19% of GDP) and available external resources due to the increase in coffee exports. According to the report, sustainable growth would depend on reaching full employment, defining strategic incentives for agriculture, and agrarian reform.

The Chenery mission report was published in 1986. Colombian economists José Antonio Ocampo, Manuel Ramírez (national coordinators), and Juan Luis Londoño, technical secretary, contributed to the report. The diagnosis was that causes of unemployment had changed between the 1970s and the 1980s. Massive urban migration in the 1970s and the dynamics of economic activity in the 1980s explained labor market disequilibrium.

The four missions (Currie, CEPAL, ILO, and Chenery) aimed to give a mac-roeconomic vision of the country to assess its development path. They all believed that development in underdeveloped economies could not be analyzed the same way as in the developed world. Development and structural change were context dependent and should be addressed as such.

As time passed, missions moved from a more orthodox and linear vision of development to precise economic planning. They proposed integrating short- and long-term strategies and, by the last mission, economists were advocating for a combination of macroeconomic and institutional variables for growth and development.

8.3 Uncovering informal employment since 1949

Since 1949, the notion of informality has been part of a large set of reports on the Colombian economy, from a notion associated with employment in traditional sectors (mainly rural) to employment with precarious incomes and lack of state regulations. All the reports considered that informality would fall as the economy grew in productive sectors, with public and foreign investment mainly in urban areas. More than 70 years later, informality remains a characteristic feature of the country's economy despite growth in modern sectors.

The academic explanation of unemployment and underemployment during the 20th century pointed to the allocation of productive factors and structural change, and moved to market frictions. Many important theoretical debates occurred during that time, including those on development and growth. Each mission responded to different theoretical positions that mostly replicated the change in the scholarly debate.

CEPAL and Arthur Lewis (1915–1991), the 1979 Economics Nobel Laureate, marked the discussion during 1950, arguing that dualism and unbalanced growth led to factor substitution and a crowding of labor in traditional sectors (i.e., agriculture). The discussion focused on open vs. disguised (or undercovered) unemployment rather than on disguised employment, making factor allocation a greater problem than precarious forms of employment.

The major transformation, and the renewal of the emphasis on precarity, came from the ILO under the influence of a more heterodox analysis. Instead of concentrating on the lack of aggregate demand and microeconomic frictions in the labor market, as Keynesian macroeconomic theories, the ILO and some *Cepalinos* focused on social security and legal contractual labor relationships.

During the 1980s, with the emergence of the search-and-matching theoretical approach in labor economics, frictional unemployment and mismatches became a central problem. Macroeconomic imbalances continued to be considered an important cause of mass unemployment, but structural informality was conceived as the consequence of labor costs and low productivity. This conception was apparent in the analysis of the Chenery mission.

8.3.1 The IBRD (Currie) mission: The bottlenecks of development

In the aftermath of one of the highest levels of internal confrontation and political struggles (1948), the country was beginning to return to the path of growth and consolidating its nascent industry. However, modernization was far from reaching the whole territory. The IBRD mission aimed to understand why. The comprehensive diagnosis of the Currie mission did not contain a detailed analysis of the determinants of unemployment, but it showed the heterogeneity of labor productivity between regions and sectors.

The IBRD (Currie) mission followed theories that viewed development as a linear process and, in the 1940s and 1950s, were included in the common denominator of modernization theory (Dvoskin, 2022). Industrialization played a central role in the natural transition from traditional to modern economies, going through different predetermined stages (Harriss, 2013). Development came with the adoption of modern capitalist relations, and internal obstacles caused underdevelopment, independently of relationships between countries (Phillips, 1977). The leading sectors would drive growth, modernizing the economy and creating quality jobs that would absorb the unoccupied or under-occupied labor force.

According to the mission, duality was a feature of the country's development process. On the one hand, coffee exports had fostered industrial progress; on the other, low technological development and productivity in agriculture explained Colombia's economic and social problems. The main block to development was the country's economic and geographic disconnection. Therefore, creating productive linkages was paramount for integrating backward economic sectors with modern high-productivity sectors.

As well as geographic disconnection, Currie pointed to the low levels of human capital and the significant educational gaps as another main bottleneck for development. Modernization and an industrial take-off would require an educational transformation to prepare workers for the mechanization and industrialization of natural resource exploitation.

Even if the mission did not explicitly mention the presence of undercovered underemployment, it noted the low wage levels, especially for the displaced population, and the relative loss of importance of agricultural production. Self-consumption forms of production in more than half of the rural areas accounted for the lack of an integrated national market and participation in the international market.

According to the Currie mission, low levels of labor productivity had to do with a floating labor force migrating to the cities, with low levels of health and education, to participate in an incipient labor market. This contrasted with urban labor's potential capacity to absorb these industry workers, boosted by the potential private savings due to the coffee booms. The Colombian paradox was the lack of a qualified labor force rather than the economy's inability to create quality jobs.

About ten years later, in 1961, Currie would recognize that the IBRD mission had failed to identify the presence of a "disguised" form of unemployment:

I suppose that for most of my life I have known the meaning of the expression "disguised unemployment." However, it was not until 1961 that I suddenly understood its significance concerning the Colombian problem. *Half of the unemployed Colombian labor force* was the key to all the analysis in Operación Colombia.

(Currie 1993, p. 337, our emphasis)

Operación Colombia, published in 1961, was Currie's most ambitious project for a comprehensive development plan. The plan acknowledged that a form of disguised underemployment was already significant when the IBRD mission was in Colombia. Disguised low-quality jobs with low productivity levels, high income instability, and little connection with the modern economy were now endemic. The causes were already present in the IBRD mission's first diagnosis. The small size of the national market and the low level of industrialization in agriculture explained disguised underemployment. In 1974, Currie related this phenomenon to a vicious circle of inequality and underdevelopment:

> So we can add another vicious circle: small market - little degree of industrialization - sparse urban population - extremely poor rural population -small market ... This is another aspect of the circle of great inequality - small market for mass consumption products - high levels of *disguised unemployment* - weakness of the element of attraction in labor mobility - growing inequality.
>
> (Currie 1974, p. 62, our emphasis)

This more elaborated and precise diagnosis built upon the IBRD report and proposed a two-stage strategy to attack the problem. First, voluntarist policies promoting infrastructure and construction as the leading sectors would absorb unemployment. Second, investment in agriculture was needed. Both, according to Currie, would break the vicious circle, enabling the transition from high disguised unemployment to high levels of formal employment, meaning high levels of employment in a modernized economy.

8.3.2 CEPAL: A diagnosis from a Latin American point of view

The internal labor market was not on the list of main issues for CEPAL's first diagnostic (1954–1957). There was, however, a concern about the difference in income levels per inhabitant in different population sectors related to the labor market's capacity to absorb the impact of a growing population (Secretaría de la Comisión Económica para América Latina, 1957, p. 27). Furthermore, the diagnosis contained a first intuition about what would later be called "informality." Also, unemployment was less of a concern than underemployment, and there was a vague idea of the duality between productive workers and underemployed workers, between "large-scale companies" and "companies with a very high number of small establishments and artisan forms of production" (1957, p. 262).

CEPAL calculated that the gap between the earnings of agricultural workers and those of the manufacturing industry was relatively small between 1925–1953. This was seen as a sign of the reduced amount of capital available per worker employed in manufacturing. More importantly, CEPAL considered that the recent industrialization process made this a transitory situation that would be solved by accelerating the industrialization rate: "it is to be expected that, with the growth of the average amount of capital per active inhabitant, the group of artisanal workers is gradually absorbed and incorporated into the industrial activity" (1957, p. 29). However, the low wages of many workers should be countered to increase the population's income and stimulate consumption demand from working families.

The General Plan, published in 1961, extended the labor market analysis. The Plan stressed the lack of reliable data to analyze the labor market. The industrial census available only had information on workers' occupations, the employer's economic activity, and the employee's position within the company. It said nothing about employment and productivity levels, since many people participated in "sporadic and low-income" activities. The situation worsened because different definitions could not be compared across statistical sources. The industry census only accounted for workers in industrial establishments, omitting unemployed, self-employed, family workers, and all those working outside those establishments. Only the 1951 population census included "data on the economically active population according to internationally recommended definitions" (1961, p. 15). However, while the first CEPAL mission had focused on the 1945 Industrial Census, the General Plan's calculations managed to include other workers besides those employed in industrial establishments.

The General Plan divided the economically active population into two large groups according to their position: a) contracted workers[9] and b) workers in another situation.[10] The Plan calculated that barely 6% of the active population was in the first category. The second category was divided between the self-employed and unpaid family helpers, who accounted for around 32% of the active population. The mission posited the existence of an inverse relationship between the number of family helpers and self-employed workers, and industrialization, since the presence of industries "allows family members to find paid work" and "the low fertility levels of highly industrialized countries influence so that the number of possible family workers is lower" (1961, p. 29).

According to CEPAL, the low-income groups were not limited to agriculture. In urban areas, partly because of rural migration, the higher-productivity sectors were unable to absorb all the incoming population, so workers were mainly engaged in construction, personal services, and small businesses. Oversaturation of available job opportunities explained the "inflation-occupation," as the phenomenon was called, in the cities.

8.3.3 ILO: Full employment as a goal

"Towards full employment" comprehensively describes the different dimensions of unemployment in the country, quantifying (to the extent the available data allowed) the magnitude, trends, and characteristics of each dimension. Although the term "informality" is absent from the text, the depiction of the different dimensions tries to encompass the different modalities of work in Colombia at the time (both in rural and urban settings).

The mission defines the "employment problem" in three dimensions: first, the lack of employment opportunities; second, the lack of reliable income for a large share of the labor force, and finally, unemployment and underemployment as an unutilized potential productive resource (ILO, 1970a, p. 15). Employment should be an end in itself, not just a desirable by-product of economic growth. Therefore, the ultimate goal of policy should be to create jobs that are "socially productive and yield enough income for a reasonable standard of living" (OIT, 1970, p. 16).

The mission estimated that 25% of the active urban labor force fell into one of the following categories (1970, p. 18): (i) open unemployment (persons without work and searching), (ii) disguised unemployment (persons without work and probably not searching due to high levels of unemployment), (iii) open underemployment (persons working less than 32 hours per week and looking for longer hours), and (iv) disguised underemployment (persons working less than 32 hours per week, willing to work longer hours if possible).

Underemployment was low. Labor legislation and unions made employers extend hours instead of hiring more people, and self-employed workers with low productivity worked longer hours to increase their income (ibid, p. 22). Moreover, a significant share of urban workers earned less than the minimum wage, and many could not afford sufficient or healthy food or adequate housing on their incomes.

There were no statistics for the rural sector, making it almost impossible to provide policy recommendations. Nevertheless, the mission found that the situation of rural workers was heterogeneous across regions and rural employment was cyclical depending on growing and harvesting seasons producing cyclical migration. This made defining "active labor force" and "unemployment" difficult.

The mission found that rural workers had low incomes even compared to the minimum wage in rural areas, mainly due to the uneven distribution of land. 40% of rural families owned less than two hectares, and 6% none (ibid, p. 24). The uneven distribution and the inadequate provision of public services made rural families subsist at the bare minimum, accelerating urban migration. The uneven distribution of land and the small sizes of their property hindered labor productivity, producing a large share of disguised underemployment. Productivity could be increased if these workers worked the vast amounts of adjacent underused land.

The ILO mission argued that it was not the workers' characteristics that were the leading cause of urban and rural unemployment, but rather the disequilibrium between labor demand and supply due to economic growth. The workers' "characteristics are important, but as determinants of who are unemployed, not of why unemployment exists" (ibid, p. 27). On the labor supply side, the report identified four main elements: population growth, migration, changes in the structure of participation (more women entering the labor force), and education (mainly the expansion of secondary and tertiary education). Land distribution and increasing urban migration made absorbing this growing labor supply into productive employment impossible.

Urban employment had not grown enough because the urban economy adopted capital-intensive techniques, with no use for unskilled labor; income was highly concentrated, and high-income groups consumed imported goods; limited foreign trade made investment insufficient, and labor legislation favored overtime work rather than the creation of new jobs.

The mission remarked how detailed Colombian labor legislation was under the *Código Sustantivo del Trabajo*, dating from 1950, and the transition phase of the social security system (ibid, p. 415). Social security would cease to be the employer's liability and would become a service provided by the state.

8.3.4 Chenery: The causes of informality (macroeconomics and institutions)

Chenery begins his mission report by analyzing informal employment. Contrary to the assumptions of the previous missions, informal employment and underemployment did not decrease with the growth of modern sectors. However, in the second half of the 1970s, employment increased, unlike what happened in Europe or the United States. Demographic changes, including natural growth, migration, and the growing number of women entering the labor force, were noticeable (Chenery 1986).

Like the other missions, this report also identified massive rural-to-urban migration since the 1950s and the inability of the urban productive sector to absorb all the labor force as the leading causes of informal employment. This excessive labor supply made people find jobs in marginal and poorly paid occupations that grew in participation. In 1972 the ILO Kenya report had defined this situation as informality (Bangasser, 2000). The Chenery mission was the first to use the term informality and openly address informal employment in Colombia.

Informality, or this "marginal employment," accounted for half of the employment in urban areas, mainly in medium and small cities, in 1985. The report tried to define informality better to include marginal employment, and sub-employment and disguised unemployment of small businesses with subsistence economic activities. Informality was defined as the employment of self-employed workers, family helpers, domestic service, small employers, and micro-enterprises with less than ten employees. Formal employment included workers with a legal contract, independent professionals, and public and private organizations with more than ten employees (López, 1986). Informality was associated with small-scale activities and was highly flexible to economic changes (Ocampo & Ramírez, 1986), hence capable of absorbing increasing labor supply, especially of unskilled younger or elderly workers.

Flexibility in prices (income) or quantities (employment) marked the difference and interconnection between the formal and informal sectors. At a microeconomic level, an individual decision to find a subsistence income connects the production of supplies and goods, allowing some productive processes to be subcontracted. At a macroeconomic level, informality is a dynamic situation that responds to cyclical variations in output and income distribution. Ocampo & Ramírez (1986) state that the informal sector is, on the one hand, a structural limitation of the modern wage system to cover all workers, and on the other, a symptom of the cyclical variability of the Colombian economy. This view opened a new academic field to tackle the issue.

The contrast and interconnection between the formal and informal sectors would be further explored. López et al. (1987), as well as Ayala (1986), suggested the coexistence of a modern capitalist economy working in accordance with legal provisions, and another economy, accounting for 55% of urban employment (82% of the informal labor force), operating on the fringes of legal regulations, with no taxes or contributions, and little to no access to social security (López et al., 1987). Following a common narrative in the 1970s and 1980s, Ayala (1986) found that informality resulted from the integration of non-capitalist production relationships with capitalist forms of production, enabling the reproduction of the labor force with wages that did not reflect productivity.

The formal and informal sectors were economically connected and legally and politically disconnected. Their interaction resulted from excessive labor supply and insufficient labor demand in the formal/modern sector, meaning people had to find a way of living without state support and legal regulation. Informal labor had low value added and productivity levels but allowed the pressure on formal wages to be reduced (Ayala, 1986). This non-capitalist sector provided a popular and massive market for formal goods, moving income from non-capitalist to capitalist sectors. According to this view, even if informality was a lag in the evolution of industrial and capitalist labor markets, it contributed to the capitalist and formal sectors. Informal labor participated in producing goods and reproducing workers, formal and informal, through their informal and family networks that crossed both sectors.

The size of the informal sector proved the state's inability to regulate real economics (López et al., 1987). There were two ways out of the problem: As the previous missions had stated, modernity would overcome informality, or a neo-economic and legal integration would transform informal employment into formal employment.

8.4 The evolving notion of informality throughout the missions

The diagnosis and analysis of the Colombian economy from the first IBRD mission in the late 1940s to the Chenery mission in the 1980s led to an understanding of the labor market that uncovered and conceptualized informal employment.

This process had two elements that were common to all the missions: The topics that allowed informality to be discovered, and the policy recommendations to overcome it. The analysis of sector productivity, the study of worker types in Colombian legislation, and the link with social security were the main issues that enabled informality to be conceptualized. Informal employment was prevalent in low-productivity sectors with unregulated or unlegislated employment categories and no access to social security. This characterization led all the missions to recommend different policies, assuming that informality was a transitory phenomenon that would become marginal once the issues of productivity, legislation, and access to social security were solved.

Despite this apparent continuity between missions, there is almost no reference to previous missions in their reports. Only the Chenery mission incorporated some policy elements from the ILO mission and part of the 1970 World Bank mission's economic analysis. Nevertheless, the common elements remain attesting to the shared diagnosis of the Colombian labor market and the increasing expert awareness of informality.

8.4.1 Unveiling informality through economic sectors, labor typologies, and social security

Informal employment or informality were not concepts used in economic theory and methods in the 1950s. The approach to a particular form of employment, depending on the sector, income, or legal conditions, came about as the nuances of employment in Colombia and other developing countries were better understood. The analysis of labor markets and the patent reality of unemployed workers' search for income sources made it possible for experts to try to come to grips with informality. The interaction between the development model, legislation, and social security were the key elements of this analysis that led to conceptualizing informality.

Each mission also faced its own contextual challenges. The Currie mission faced a lack of data or categorization of employment, and like the first CEPAL mission, linked rural employment with precarious income and low productivity. The same did not happen in the urban economy because modern productive sectors would create "quality jobs."

The legal typology of employment in the 1950s made any work relationship not mediated by a labor contract invisible. Decree Law 3743 of 1950 defined labor as a free relationship between two persons, one of them performing a paid activity or service for the other with a labor contract between them. Thus, anyone working without a contract was not considered a worker. To account for a large number of people in the country that were left out of the legal category of workers, the mission used the terms *disguised employment* or *sub-employment*.

The CEPAL mission included the categories of workers with contracts and those without contracts or self-employed in its diagnosis. The ILO, in turn, using income levels, added the categories of unemployment, open and disguised underemployment. Informality was first used in the Chenery mission to account for workers with labor contracts and self-employed workers that complied with micro-enterprise legislation.

The four missions went beyond unemployment (non-occupied persons who search for work), reporting sub-employment, low-productivity work, and insufficient income. All the missions recognized that a significantly large share of the labor force made just enough to get by, and remained in poverty. The Currie mission highlighted the labor productivity and human capital heterogeneity across sectors and regions, even if low productivity and low remuneration were extended throughout the country. The CEPAL mission made a more thorough categorization. It divided the economically active population into contracted workers[11] and non-contracted workers, the latter subdivided into self-employed and family care workers. The mission also highlighted the "inflation-occupation" phenomenon caused by people migrating from rural areas unable to find jobs in high-productivity sectors. The ILO mission classified employment as workers with or without an employment contract and urban and rural employment. Within these latter categories, the mission differentiated by income level and between open and disguised employment and open and disguised underemployment. "Disguised" qualified workers who, for lack of opportunities, could not work longer hours or find a job.

The Chenery mission used CEPAL's employment categories with and without a contract and explicitly used the terms formal and informal employment. It also introduced a structural component affecting frictional and non-frictional employment and a cyclical one, affecting mainly informal workers, explained by macro global disorders and internal economic policies (Tejada & Latorre, 1988).

The ILO[12] and the Chenery missions also analyzed the link between employment and social security to reveal informality because, from the 1930s, access to health, pensions, and other social benefits was tied to having a labor contract, thus being a formal employee.[13]

Both missions recommended broadening social security due to the loss of family protection associated with urbanization and the hiring costs for employers. The Chenery mission, in particular, recommended making the hiring process less burdensome and reducing social security costs associated with formal contracts as a way to promote the creation and maintenance of formal employment. CEPAL, on the other hand, recommended increasing the minimum wage to promote consumption and internal demand.

8.4.2 Possible ways to overcome informality

Even in the absence of a difference between the formal and informal sectors in the missions' reports, all of them shared the view of an unstable transitional duality. The reports account for different forms that lead to different theories of this duality, but this analysis is what allows unveiling and identifying informality. In the Currie mission, the duality points to the coexistence of a low-productivity economy in the larger part of the country that involves most of the population and a developing economy in the industrial sector. This mission focuses on a floating workforce that migrated to the cities and, because of their low incomes and poor access to health services and education, had low productivity levels. The CEPAL mission report follows in this characterization of duality between productive workers and underemployed workers, between "large-scale companies" and "companies with a very high number of small establishments and artisan forms of production," of "insufficient income" and "sufficient income" workers.

The ILO mission report highlighted the duality between the urban and the rural labor force, open and disguised unemployment, open and disguised underemployment, and finally, earners of adequate and inadequate income. Finally, the Chenery mission presented the duality between rural and urban areas and was the first to use the concept of formal and informal workers. The latter included marginal employment, underemployment, and disguised unemployment. The Chenery mission pushed the analysis to include the interaction between the informal sector and the formal economy throughout the economic cycle. The Chenery mission's report described duality as the coexistence of a modern, capitalist, and formal economy and an informal one, with no labor regulation or arbitration, no contribution to social security, and no social security protection.

Each mission named the duality differently, but they all agreed it was transitory, and economic development, economic growth, or the reduction of unemployment would reduce the gap between the two sectors. Hence, for all missions, there was a macroeconomic solution. Economic growth would lead to the absorption of this marginalized, low-income labor force. However, the ILO mission report warned that growth alone would not solve the problem. Growth had to be sustained and promoted in specific labor-intensive sectors.

Regardless of their overall agreement, the missions differed in certain details. The source of economic growth was one of those details. For the Currie mission, like CEPAL, the most important source of economic growth was increasing internal demand. CEPAL prioritized the consolidation of a solid national industry.[14] The Currie mission also insisted on the modernization of Colombian agriculture and, more importantly, on the geographical and economic integration of the country and the development of specific industrial sectors along with improving health and education to boost human capital accumulation. The Chenery mission recommended increasing foreign exchange inflow in the long term, promoting exports followed by import substitution, especially in capital goods, increasing investment and savings rates, and public investments with a higher distributive effect involving more national labor. The ILO, in particular, underscored that rapid growth had been accompanied by rising unemployment and "by the widening of gaps between rich and poor and between town and country" (1970b, p. 5). This mission's specific recommendation was that employment should be taken as an objective of development and not a by-product of growth.

Whereas the Currie and CEPAL missions focused on macroeconomic solutions, the ILO and Chenery missions also included institutional transformation. According to the ILO, non-salary costs should be lowered to promote employment, and labor regulations should be adjusted to encourage the creation of new jobs. The Chenery mission recommended reforming labor legislation that could lead to a more equitable social security system, reducing non-salary costs, and simplifying hiring processes.

8.5 Conclusion

Informality is a common and structural feature of the Colombian labor market. Coming to this conclusion meant more than half a century of economic analysis of the national economy. Tracing international missions unveils the struggles of economic theory and expert knowledge to understand informality as a multiform and persistent phenomenon. Furthermore, informality might be functional to developing economies rather than a mere stage in their development. The reports of the international missions since 1949 show that experts' misconceptions about informality led them to deal with it as a residue in the process of development that would shrink with "modernization" and growth.

However, the long-lasting nature of the phenomenon challenged the diagnosis, especially the policy recommendations from mission after mission. Since the Currie mission emphasized the need for modernization of the agricultural sector and a leading sector, growth and unemployment reduction was supposed to absorb informality. Policies were mainly macroeconomic. However, informality proved to be deeply related to institutional and rule design rather than a pure transitory level of unemployment.

Only the Chenery mission in 1985 attempted to build upon the results of the past missions. It continued to underscore the role of growth and internal demand and expected the "natural" absorption of informality. The report used the word informal for the first time to characterize a dual economy. Today this duality persists, but rather than identifying two distinct sets of labor conditions, it characterizes a constant interaction between the two sectors, with workers going from one to the other without a social security system capable of dealing with this circulation.

The law that currently regulates the social security system, Law 100 of 1993, follows the mission's understanding of two separate sectors with distinct labor conditions. The formal system includes workers with a legal labor contract or enough income to join the system. In contrast, the informal sector includes workers without enough income who access the social security system through solidarity mechanisms. According to the law, these workers are "peasants, indigenous and independent workers, artists, athletes, community mothers" who need these solidarity mechanisms to integrally "access the system and its benefits," including health, through the subsidized regime (article 157), and pensions, through the mechanisms of the Pension Solidarity Fund (article 13). This shows that the solidarity mechanism contained in the 1991 Constitution, later developed in Law 100 of 1993, was intended for a limited group of workers, not for half or more than half of the labor force.

The quest to understand and tackle the high level of informality continues today. In 2022 a new employment mission offered a new diagnosis and recommendations on the issue. The Levy–Maldonado mission aimed at presenting a different way to understand informality and recognized that any labor market reform required a more structural strategy focused on a new social contract redefining social security without forgetting informality as a structural characteristic of the labor market that should be linked to the general institutional arrangement of the Colombian economy.[15]

Notes

1 The International Bank of Reconstruction and Development (IBRD) at the time.
2 Henceforth, we will refer to the ECLAC as CEPAL.
3 Beyond the four missions we analyze here, there were five other missions: two Monetary Missions led by Walter Kemmerer (1923 and 1931); the "Economy and Humanism" mission led by the French priest L.-J. Lebret (1954–1956) centered mainly on education and social reforms; the first Fiscal Mission led by Richard Musgrave (1968–1971); the World Bank's "Economic Growth of Colombia: Problems and Prospects" mission, led by Dragoslav Avramovic (1970–1972); the Mission on Decentralization and Local Fiscal Autonomy, led by Eduardo Wiesner and Richard Bird (1981).
4 Jaramillo-Echeverri et al. (2015) offer an alternative narrative on the mechanisms behind the launching of industrialization during the 1930s–1940s. They underline the role of the Great Depression and the Second World War.
5 In compliance with Resolution 48 (V) on programming technique approved in April 1953.
6 The Executive Secretary at that time was Raúl Prebisch (1950–1963), head of the Mission from the Secretariat of the Commission (ECLA, 1955).
7 Manuel Balboa, born in 1917, attended the Universidad Nacional del Litoral in Rosario (Argentina), where he graduated as a public accountant in 1938. He first joined the Central Bank of the Argentine Republic (BCRA) as the Head of the Department of Economics and as the Head of Financial Affairs. He was also one of the main advisors of the Economics Affairs Ministry of Argentina. As his work turned towards programming, he joined CEPAL in 1955, leading the programming technique reports for Argentina. He worked for CEPAL for 20 years, where he was later named Head of the Economic Development and Research Division and Deputy Executive Secretary (Monti, 2008).
8 1) An analysis of the Colombian economy in the last decade, 2) the development program's goals, 3) the population and workforce, 4) the balance of payments, 5) an analysis of industrial development, and 6) the development of public finances.
9 By contractual workers, the report referred to the group of employers and "wage and salary workers" (p. 29).
10 These workers were also referred to as "non-contracted," "remnant" workers, or those "who work on bases other than contractual."
11 According to CEPAL, these workers accounted for 6% of the labor force at the time.
12 In the ILO report, social security is absent from the body of the document but appears in one of the annexes.
13 Social security legislation determined that access to pensions and health services depended upon the existence of a labor contract. In 1968, Decree 3135 social security defined the same rules for private and public workers with labor contracts.
14 The CEPAL report also studied agriculture and identified a problem of excess labor supply. Land tenure problems were linked to insufficient income for smallholders and rural wage earners. CEPAL recommended land redistribution, technological innovation in small farms, and improving marketing and social assistance to avoid excessive urban migration.
15 See Álvarez and Villaveces (2021), document for the Levy–Maldonado mission for a discussion on the historical evolution of the attempts to reform the labor market in Colombia since the 1930s.

Bibliography

Álvarez, A., Guiot, A., & Hurtado, J. (2020). "The quarrel of policy advisers that became development experts: Currie and Hirschman in Colombia". *History of Political Economy* 52:2, pp: 275–306.

Álvarez, A. & Villaveces, M. J. (2021). "El rompecabezas de la protección social en un mercado laboral con alta informalidad: análisis de un siglo de reformas en Colombia". Working paper. *Documento CEDE* No. 55.

Arana, M. (2020). The ECLA technique of programming and economists in Argentina in the mid-twentieth century. *CEPAL Review*, 131, 55–68.

Arévalo Hernández, D. (1997). "Misiones económicas internacionales en Colombia 1930–1960". *Historia Crítica*, 14, pp: 7–24.

Ayala, U. (1986). "Hogares, participación laboral e ingresos". In: J.A. Ocampo, & M. Ramírez (Ed.), *El problema laboral colombiano*. Servicio Nacional de Aprendizaje, Departamento Nacional de Planeación y Contraloría General de la República.

Bangasser, P. (2000). "The ILO and the informal sector: An institutional history". *Employment Paper* 2000/9, ILO.

Benanav, A. (2019). "The origins of informality: The ILO at the limit of the concept of unemployment". *Journal of Global History*, 14: 1, 107–125.

Chenery, H. (1986). "El problema laboral colombiano: diagnóstico, perspectivas y políticas. Informe Final de la Misión de Empleo". *Economía Colombiana*. Revista de la Contraloría General de la República. Serie de documentos: separata no. 10, agosto-septiembre de 1986.

Consejo Nacional de Política Económica y Planeación (Colombia). (1960). *Colombia: Plan cuatrienal de inversiones públicas nacionales, 1961–1964* (December 1960).

Currie, L. (1961). *Operación Colombia*, Biblioteca de Estudios Económicos, Sociedad Colombiana de Economistas, Bogota.

Currie, L. (1974). *Desarrollo económico acelerado*. Editorial Fondo de Cultura Económica.

Currie, L. (1993). "The Theory of Growth", *Cuadernos de Economies*, XIII: 18–19, pp: 377–390.

DANE. (2020). Gran Encuesta integrada de hogares, Mercado Laboral. Available online (03/03/2023) https://www.dane.gov.co/index.php/estadisticas-por-tema/mercado-laboral/empleo-y- desempleo.

Departamento Administrativo de Planeación y Servicios Técnicos de Colombia. (1961). Plan general de desarrollo económico y social.

Dvoskin, N. (2022). *Heterogeneidad estructural, subdesarrollo y dependencia. Los entramados histórico-teóricos del desarrollismo tardío latinoamericano*. Mimeo.

Echavarría, J. J. (1999). *Crisis e industrialización: Las lecciones de los treinta*. Tercer Mundo Editores - Banco de la República.

Echavarría, J. J., Villamizar, M., & González, J. (2006). "El Proceso Colombiano de Desindustrialización", *Borradores de Economía*, No. 361, Banco de la República de Colombia.

Economic Commission for Latin America (ECLA). (1955). *Annual Report* (10 February 1954–10 May 1955) (ECOSOC Reports). Economic Commission for Latin America (ECLA).

Harriss, J. (2013). *Development theories*. International Development Research Centre.

ILO. (1970a). *Towards full employment, a programme for Colombia*. ILO Geneva.

ILO. (1970b). *Summary towards full employment, a programme for Colombia*. ILO Geneva.

Jaramillo-Echeverri, J., Meisel-Roca, A., & Ramírez-Giraldo, M. T. (2015). "The great depression in Colombia: A stimulus to industrialization, 1930–1953". *Borradores de Economía*, No. 892, Banco de la República de Colombia.

Jolly, R. (2009). "Dudley Seers (1920–1983): His contributions to development perspectives, policy and studies". Institute of Development Studies, Mimeo.

Junguito-Bonnet, R. (2016). *Historia económica de Colombia en el siglo XX*. Editorial Universidad Sergio Arboleda.

Levy, S. & Cruces, G. (2021). "Time for a new course: An essay on social protection and growth in Latin America". *UNDP LAC Working Paper* No. 24. Background Paper for the UNDP LAC 2021 Regional Human Development Report.

López, H. (1986). "La Misión Chenery: una invitación a pensar en el mediano y largo plazo.", *Lecturas De Economía*, 20: 20, pp: 153–175.

López, H., Henao, M. L., & Sierra, O. (1987). "Sector informal: entroque económico y desconexión jurídico-política con la sociedad moderna". In: J.A. Ocampo & M. Ramírez (Eds), *El problema laboral colombiano*. Servicio Ed.

Love, J. L. (2018). "CEPAL, economic development, and inequality". *History of Political Economy*, 50: S1, pp: 152–171.

Monti, A. (2008). "In memoriam: Manuel Balboa". *Realidad Económica*. Revista de economía editada por el Instituto Argentino para el Desarrollo Económico (IADE), 236: 236, pp: 126–128.

Ocampo, J.A. & Ramírez, M. (1986). "Principales conclusiones y recomendaciones de la Misión de Empleo". In: H. Chenery (Ed.), *El problema laboral colombiano: diagnóstico, perspectivas y políticas. Informe Final de la Misión de Empleo*. Economía Colombiana: Revista de la Contraloría General de la República. Serie de documentos: separata no. 10, Aug–Sept 1986.

Phillips, A. (1977). "The concept of 'development'". *Review of African Political Economy*, 8, pp: 7–20.

Sandilands, R. (2015). "La misión del Banco Mundial a Colombia de 1949, y las visiones opuestas de Lauchlin Currie y Albert Hirschman". *Revista de Economía Institucional*, 17: 32, pp: 213–232.

Sandilands, R. J. (2018). "Albert Hirschman, Lauchlin Currie, la teoría de los 'eslabonamientos' Rosenstein Rodan y el 'gran impulso' de Paul Rosenstein-Rodan". *Revista de Economía Institucional*, 20: 39, pp: 53–68.

Secretaria de la Comisión Económica para América Latina. (1957). *El desarrollo económico de Colombia (III; Análisis y proyecciones del desarrollo económico)*. Naciones Unidas. Departamento de asuntos Económicos y Sociales.

Seers, D. (1963). *The limitations of the special case*. Institute of Economics and Statistics, Oxford. Bulletin Vol. 25 No. 2.

Seers, D. (1972). "What are we trying to measure?". In N. Baster (Ed.) *Measuring development: The role and adequacy of development indicators* (pp. 73–89). Frank Cass.

Syrquin, M. & Chenery, H. B. (1989). "Patterns of development, 1950 to 1983", World Bank - Discussion Papers 41, World Bank.

Tejada, N. & Latorre J. R. (1988). *Misiones de empleo en Colombia: una visión comparativa*. Misión OPIT, 1979-Misión Chenery, 1986. *Lecturas de Economía*, 25–26, pp: 173–200.

Villamizar, J. C. (2012). *La influencia de la CEPAL en Colombia, 1948–1970*. Doctoral Thesis, Universidad Nacional de Colombia. Facultad de Ciencias Humanas.

9 The Failed *Cepalino* Connection in Colombian Economic Thinking

Juan Carlos Villamizar

9.1 Introduction

Economic ideas in Colombia and Latin America in the last hundred years have gone roughly through three phases. The first, at the beginning of the 20th century, was characterized by the existence of a primary export model based on the theory of comparative advantage, in which Latin American countries specialized in the production of raw materials and European countries in manufactured goods. Economic policy seemed to closely follow the paradigm of economic liberalism, also known in the country under the slogan *laissez faire, laissez passer*.[1] The second phase, known as the development paradigm, adopted import substitution and placed the economy under state guidance. This paradigm deepened the economic crisis of the 1930s and continued until the 1980s. A new stage of economic liberalism began in the 1970s with the oil crisis and the increase in world prices and unemployment. The neoliberal paradigm meant tariff reductions in foreign trade, restructuring national external debt, and reducing state structures, which led to the current globalization period.[2] In Colombia, this last phase was adopted much later than in other countries.

In this chapter, we will focus on two specific moments in the competition between economic paradigms and their proposals for economic growth in Colombia related to the discussion and feeble acceptance of ideas from the Economic Commission for Latin America and the Caribbean (ECLAC). As Kalmanovitz shows in his contribution to this volume (Chapter 11), after a somewhat failed attempt by the likes of Alejandro López, Luis Nieto Arteta, and Antonio García Nossa, to implant the ideas of the German Historical School, Karl Marx, John M. Keynes in the first half of the 20th century,[3] *cepalino* ideas were discussed in the 1950s and 1960s but overturned by Lauchlin Currie's resource efficiency approach. In the1980s and 1990s, the Washington Consensus and what has come to be identified as the neoliberal paradigm took hold of economic public policy.

Two main reasons explain why the economist lawyers and *cepalino* ideas were unsuccessful in Colombia. On the one hand, the capitalist order calls for a particular type of knowledge in which calculation, precision, and economic

DOI: 10.4324/9781003289241-11

order are paramount. On the other hand, the institutional setting designed by the victorious countries after World War II, including the Bretton Woods system, the World Bank (WB), the International Monetary Fund (IMF), and the General Agreement on Tariffs and Trade (GATT), required specific economic knowledge. Both meant that countries had to develop an economic bureaucracy capable of participating in specialized exchanges with other countries and centers of global power. This economic bureaucracy gave professional, technically trained economists a privileged position. Even if ECLAC could offer this technical economic bureaucracy, the Colombian government leaned towards the WB and the IMF. The United States had accused *cepalinos* of having communist sympathies and inclinations during the 1950s and 1970s. In the context of the Cold War, this accusation inclined the balance toward other sources of technical economic practice and training (Villamizar, 2013; Ocampo, 2013). The most successful project along these lines was the strengthening of the neoliberal paradigm, in which, theoretically, the only driving force of the economy is the free market, led by a group of economists who define themselves as technical and, in theory, detached from political struggles and interests.

In what follows, we will retrace how Lauchlin Currie's approach to resource efficiency triumphed over the proposals of ECLAC in the 1950s and 1970s. By the end of the 1990s, the rise of the neoliberal paradigm and the training of orthodox economists led to market-oriented economic policies and closer relations between economists and political power, excluding any possibility for the ECLAC paradigm.

9.2 The debate on development (1950–1979)

The end of World War II and the creation of the new international economic system (IMF, WB, GATT) meant a new course for economic thought. The top priority was rebuilding the economy after the war and promoting economic development. International aid was vital. Through the Marshall Plan (1947–1952), the United States invested around 13 billion dollars in Europe. The United Nations created regional economic offices in Asia, Europe, Africa, and the ECLAC in Latin America in 1948 (Toye & Toye, 2004).

The reconstruction efforts and the discovery of the so-called Third World between 1950 and 1979 gave rise to the debate on development that would set out the path of economic thought at the time. In Colombia, the discussion on development, which sometimes led to specific policy actions, involved three overall diagnostic studies and two development plans.[4] We have already encountered in this volume the World Bank's mission to Colombia, better known as the Currie mission, in 1949 (see Chapter 8). Urbanization and industrialization would lead to a smaller part of the population being employed in the agricultural sector, with industrial employment taking the lead, and to a progressive land tax to promote efficient exploitation. Currie's vision emphasized efficient labor, capital, and land use.

In 1957, Raúl Prebisch directed ECLAC's comprehensive study, *Análisis y proyecciones del desarrollo de Colombia*. Using a center–periphery framework that led to the deterioration of trade in Latin America (Love, 1980; Ocampo & Parra, 2007), the study proposed a massive industrialization plan funded through international cooperation, increased tax collection, and economic integration to boost economic growth.[5] ECLAC proposed expanding arable land (ECLAC, 1957, pp. 155–156), new investments in agriculture, and an increase of 400,000 workers in the field. Annual productivity increases in agriculture would liberate around 500,000 workers that the industry could absorb (ECLAC, 1957, p. 221). The low and uneven transmission of technological change due to the asymmetries between the periphery and the center led *cepalinos* to propose specific import-substitution scenarios for the industry. Import substitution would promote the industrialization needed in developing countries such as Colombia to gain from the technological change in the center (Ocampo & Parra, 2007, p. 157).

Louis Joseph Lebret, French priest and sociologist, directed the third comprehensive study, *Estudio sobre las condiciones del desarrollo de Colombia*, in 1958. The study seconded ECLAC's economic analysis and underscored the need for education, health, and nutrition improvements. It was the first major sociological study on Colombia to point out that development required "the leading groups [to accept] a relative decrease in their privileged position" (Lebret, 1958, p. 118).

None of the reports proved influential for economic decisions during the conservative government of Laureano Gómez (1950–1953), the dictatorship of Gustavo Rojas Pinilla (1953–1957), or the liberal administration of Alberto Lleras Camargo (1958–1962).

Other economic plans followed in the next decade. ECLAC prepared the *Ten-Year Development Plan* in 1961 to comply with the Alliance for Progress agreements between the governments of Colombia and the United States and ECLAC. The same year, Currie wrote *Operación Colombia*, answering President Lleras Camargo's request to evaluate ECLAC's plan. Finally, in 1971, Currie directed the Four Strategies Plan as conservative President Misael Pastrana's development program. ECLAC and Currie proposed two development paths for a country devastated by violence with low growth levels. ECLAC recommended industrializing Colombia through import substitution and creating regional trade agreements. Currie aimed to promote the efficient use of resources (land, capital, and labor) through exports, a leading sector of the economy, and the industrialization of the countryside.

The three diagnoses and the 1961 and 1971 plans that followed became the source of economic debates during the 1960s and early 1970s. The most important debate involved Currie's assessment of ECLAC's Ten-Year Plan. Currie argued that ECLAC's recommendations would lead Colombia to a dead end. According to Currie, *cepalinos* missed the significance of the technical revolution in agriculture, associated with large economic units and large-scale agricultural exports, when they proposed small and medium-sized agricultural properties.[6]

Currie's criticism also advocated for policies he had already recommended as early as 1941 as an economic adviser to US President F.D. Roosevelt. At the time, Currie proposed a massive transfer of American peasants to the city to perform more productive activities in industry (Sandilands, 1990, p. 106). He was to follow up this idea in the 1950 WB report and again in 1961 in the critical assessment of ECLAC's plan contained in *Operación Colombia*.[7] Currie's plan for Colombia meant transferring at least 700,000 peasants in two years to the cities to work in the new industries, leaving the countryside free to make large-scale, capital-intensive investments. Currie suggested that ECLAC mistakenly believed the world would support Latin America through foreign loans. However, he forgot that the Marshall Plan had been Europe's way out of the destruction of World War II.[8]

Currie's ideas would have to wait a few more years. Carlos Lleras Restrepo (1966–1970) tried to implement some *cepalino* policy recommendations during his administration. A common market, similar to Central America's, was formed through the Andean Pact. Decree Law 444 of 1967 regulated foreign trade through the exchange regime, and an evasive agrarian reform was sought.[9] The reforms led to a development model that combined industrial protection with export promotion. The next government, with President Misael Pastrana, shifted from Lleras Restrepo's development plan and charged Currie with the design of a new plan.[10] Finally, after 20 years of living in Colombia, his chance had come.

The development plan Currie drafted in 1971 presented four strategies. First, the promotion of a leading sector of the economy, urban housing building, which would absorb the larger share of unskilled labor coming from the countryside. Second, the promotion of exports. Third, instead of transferring peasants to the city, the country's urbanization would absorb the labor surplus and the ideal capital resources in rural areas, producing a more efficient allocation of sources and raising aggregate demand. Finally, more progressive taxes would promote income redistribution.

Las cuatro estrategias (The Four Strategies) (1972–1974) tipped the economic debate towards Currie's side, although his idea of moving peasants to the city and the proposal for a progressive land tax were not implemented. Even if governments had accepted the creation of the Andean Pact, the regulation of foreign trade, and the adoption of industrialization by substitution of imports, these measures benefited an oligopolistic and traditional business sector and left aside the main *cepalino* theses. The Colombian elites, including economists, did not adopt the center–periphery view, the unequal international exchange, or the need for foreign aid to fund development programs. Currie's idea of urban housing building as the leading sector received wide support because it created low-paying jobs and a housing financial mechanism that empowered the banks. Rural reform was changed to technical assistance plans for peasants who already had land.

From the 1970s, economic analyses focused on short-term equilibria and promoted a pragmatic and technical approach to economic policy design

(Flórez, 2000, 2009). Inflation, unemployment, and high oil prices stopped financial aid from industrialized to developing countries, and many Latin American countries defaulted on their debts. The orthodox neoliberal paradigm took over (Toye & Toye, 2004).

It was a critical moment in the economic policy debate in Colombia. Ocampo[11] and Lora (1988) identified two opposite positions. Orthodox economists in the government considered not defaulting as key for the country to keep a good standing in the international financial market and access new credits (Ocampo & Lora, 1988, p. 101). Heterodox economists saw the debt crisis as an opportunity to renegotiate the growing external debt to use the resources liberated to promote economic growth (Ocampo & Lora, 1988). In the end, three new credits were contracted (Garay, 1991),[12] with drastic economic adjustments to overcome macroeconomic imbalances (Junguito, 206, p. 366). Heterodox critics saw the negotiations as conditioning domestic economic policy to the dictates of the IMF. It was a matter of economic principles and conditions and "of national convenience" (Ocampo & Lora, 1988, p. 138). No traces of *cepalino* ideas were left. Economic agents and economists in Colombia agreed to the world's financial authority's supervision over domestic public finances.

In 1994, a group of heterodox economists published an evaluation of development policies implemented between 1950 and 1900 (Misas, 1995). The evaluation found an oligopolistic and concentrated manufacturing industry with high-profit margins that favored larger economic groups with greater financial power. State action favored the generation of economic income and reduced implicit subsidies for the middle class with consequences for consumption and aggregate demand (Misas, 1995). According to this evaluation, the economic situation in 1990 was favorable to free-market reforms with a business sector that, given its conglomerate structure, could access the new profit opportunities from international trade. The neoliberal model still prevails with the support of orthodox free-market thinking.

9.3 The neoliberal phase

In this text, we identify neoliberalism with development policies that privilege pro-market measures. Among such policies, we can find that education, health, and housing are transformed from rights to market services; supply subsidies are dismantled; fiscal, commercial, and balance-of-payments stability become a priority; and strict monetary control is implemented to minimize inflation. Market competitiveness, where the rich and the poor are supposed to compete on an equal footing, is the epitome of the neoliberal paradigm. Although it might not always be achieved, neoliberals hold fast to this ideal scenario.

During the 1980s, neoliberal economists came to positions of power worldwide. Capitalist globalization required specialized professionals to handle market operations, investments, transnational loans, and economic crises. These professional economists handled, for better or worse, the 1983 Latin American external debt crisis, the 1999 world crisis, and the 2008 recession in industrialized countries. In Chile, the effect of the Chicago School's presence on its economy during the dictatorship is well known (Ffrench-Davis, 2005; Montecinos, 2009), and it was a response to the *cepalino* government project from 1970 to 1973 (Fajardo, 2022). Mexico changed its policies toward greater liberalization after the debt crisis, even if this country was recognized as a champion of nationalism in Latin America. The new conceptions of economists conducted this change, and they formed the body of advisers to governments during the decades after the 1980s (Babb, 2003). This action of the new economists worldwide has been criticized. Economist Joseph Stiglitz (2002, 2012), a former chief economist of the World Bank and economic adviser to Bill Clinton, argued that the mismanagement of the 1998 crisis was the responsibility of the WB and the IMF, a criticism that he would later reaffirm in 2010 in the face of the 2008 crisis. In Colombia, the liberalization process began in the 1980s and was consolidated in 1991.

Orthodox economists, trained in what was portrayed as the hardest of the social sciences, have risen to the highest positions in politics as monetary advisers to local or multilateral credit organizations (BM, IMF). Some have even been elected as presidents in Latin America. Their rise to power results from how the region was inserted into the world economy, in the sphere of influence of the United States, or the Americanization of the economy (Drake, 2005; Montecinos & Markoff, 2009). During the last 30 years, in Colombia and elsewhere, a new cultural pattern that values this knowledge displaced lawyers, who had traditionally played the role of politicians or advisers to politicians in the 20th century.

Economists, unlike other intellectuals, have claimed to be the engineers of power through planning, budgeting, and designing fiscal and macroeconomic policies. A case in point is Currie, who advised presidents Laureano Gómez, Alberto Lleras, and Misael Pastrana. As heirs of Bourbon landowners in the 17th century or engineers and law officers in the first half of the 20th century, contemporary economists believe they possess specialized and legitimized knowledge, indispensable both to politicians and groups of economic power and to draft laws in Congress. This expert knowledge has also placed economists beyond political responsibility (Bejarano, 1999; Palacios, 2005).

The close connection between economics and political power is widespread in Latin America. Shared interests and perspectives between local and international actors explain the support for specific economic policies (Stallings, 1992; Babb, 2003). Consumption patterns and lifestyles have brought together business people, technocrats, and middle- and upper-class sectors that share international networks. High-level technocrats are trained within specific paradigms accepted in industrialized countries, which connects professors, graduate students, public officers, and think tanks (Montecinos & Markoff, 2009). Flórez (2000, 2009) identifies a technocratic consensus in Colombia stemming from the power-sharing scheme between Liberals and Conservatives during the *Frente Nacional* (1958–1974).

There has been a close link between economists with orthodox neoclassical training and neoliberal economic policies between 1974 and 2021.[13] These economists, primarily trained at Los Andes University, with graduate studies in the United States, have occupied influential positions in policy-making, including the management of the Foundation for Education and Development (Fedesarrollo), one of the most renowned economic think tanks in the country. They have also been ministers of finance, mining, and agriculture, members of the board of directors of the Central Bank, and international officers in the World Bank, the IMF, and the International Bank for Development (see Table 9.1). Fedesarrollo, in particular, became "the academic alter ego of governments" (González, 1995, p. 143). The consensus left no space for alternative economic paradigms.

The technocratic turn goes hand in hand with the constant search in the Western world to rationalize the activity of states. Public administration techniques have become increasingly specialized, and economic policy-making lies beyond the scope of the law, accounting, or business administration. In developing countries, economic training came rapidly to par with the industrialized world. Technical economic knowledge evolved from a practical need to manage multilateral external debt packages into a form of action by the elites in power. As an instrument of power, technical expertise limits the access of the middle and popular classes to public debate; it restricts discussions on planning, economic policy, and development to a small select group of specialists.

As in the rest of Latin America after the 1970s, the Colombian network of orthodox economists in government positions, Fedesarrollo, and Los Andes University favor market-oriented economic reforms that reduce state intervention. Cárdenas Santamaría,[14] a central figure in this network, highlights its positive consequences: "The relationship between Fedesarrollo and the Ministry of Finance and Public Credit (MHCP) is part of the institutional framework that has empowered the technocracy and has allowed a responsible management of the Colombian economy" (Cárdenas, 2020, p. 140). José Antonio Ocampo[15] is an exception to this rule, serving in high offices at a national and international level. Ocampo is a leading figure in Latin American structuralism and has held *cepalino* views in Colombia. During his time as chair of Fedesarrollo, Ocampo brought new perspectives, including economic history and social policy.[16] However, Ocampo and *cepalino* views remained marginalized in Colombia during this period, as had been the case before.

The consolidation of the new paradigm came with the market liberalization reforms of César Gaviria's administration (1990–1994).[17] The labor, financial, international, agricultural, and industrial markets were deregulated to implement the Washington Consensus. Fedesarrollo, local businesses, and the IMF backed the reforms (Junguito, 2016, p. 398). The development plan did not include any specific action for agriculture because, according to the neoliberal view, tariff reduction and price regulation would be enough (Cuevas, 1995, p. 85; Ocampo & Perry, 1995, p. 49). This view proved wrong as the plan did

Table 9.1 Economists who have held main positions in the Colombian government 1980–2021[1]

Name	Treasury	Board of Directors Banco de la República[3]	Ministries (X: directors of other public agencies)	Directors of Fedesarrollo / (Members only X)	International Official — IMF	WB	IDB	ECLAC	Dean and Professor Uni. Andes	Undergraduate Studies — University of Los Andes	Postgraduate studies — United States	Europe	PhD — United States	Europe
01. Rodrigo Botero Montoya	(1974–1976)			(1970–1974)										
02. Eduardo Wiesner	(1980–1982)	X	X		X	X	X		X	X	X			
03. Roberto Junguito	(1983–1984); (2002–2003)	X	Minister of Agriculture	(1974–1978)	X					X	X		X	
04. César Gaviria	(1986–1987)	X	Minister of Government							X				
05. Luis Fernando Alarcon	(1987–1990)	X					X			X	X			
06. Rudolph Hommes[4]	(1990–1994)	X	X			X			X	X	X		X	
07. Guillermo Perry	(1994–1996)	X	Minister of Mines (1988–1989)			X	X			X	X		X	
08. José Antonio Ocampo	(1996–1997)	X	Minister of Agriculture	(1984–1988)				X	X		X		X	
09. Juan Camilo Restrepo	(1998–2000)	X	Minister of Agriculture							X	X		
10. Juan Manuel Santos	(2001–2002)	X								x	X		
11. Alberto Carrasquilla	(2003–2007 / 2018–2021)	X	X	X			X		X	X	X		X	
12. Oscar Iván Zuluaga	(2007–2010)	X	X											
13. Juan Carlos Echeverri	(2010–2012)	X	X				X			X	X			

		M/ of Mines, M/ of Transport, M/ of Development[5]												
14. Mauricio Cárdenas Santa María	(2012–2018)		(1996–1998; 2003–2008)							X	X	X		X
15. Carlos Caballero Argaez	X		X					X	X	X			X	
16. Leonardo Villar	X	X	(2012–2018)	X					X		X		X	X
17. Juan José Echavarría	X	X	(1998–2003)					X		X				X
18. Miguel Urrutia Montoya	X	Minister of Mines	(1978–1982; 1989–1991)		X		X	X		X		X		
19. Carlos Caballero Argaez		Minister of Mines	(1982–1984)					X		X				
20. Eduardo Lora			(1991–1995)		X									
21. Roberto Steiner	X		(2009–2012)	X	X	X		X	X	X		X		
22. Sergio Clavijo	X	X		X			X	X	X			X		
23. Fernando Tenjo	X	X					X	X	X		X			
24. Antonio Hernández[2]	X													
25. Luis Bernardo Flórez[2]	X	X												
26. Salomón Kalmanovitz	X								X					

Source: Resumes of each economist on the website of each institution.

[1] This table shows the economists who have held an important public office, their undergraduate and postgraduate studies by region of the world and their participation in international organizations

[2] Undergraduate National University

[3] The Ministers of Finance are in their own right members of the Board of Directors of Banco de la República

[4] Industrial Administrator from California State University

[5] Minister of Mines, Transport and Economic Development

not consider international market price distortions, agricultural subsidies in industrialized countries, or the almost nonexistent local and regional markets. The result was a severe crisis in the agricultural sector.[18]

Ocampo was appointed Agriculture Minister in 1993. New policies were implemented to overcome the crisis; it was understood that "[...] today no one doubts that agriculture requires special consideration in any process of trade liberalization, nor does anyone believe that the mere implementation of a strategy of open markets makes agricultural production flourish, as if by miracle" (Ocampo & Perry, 1995, p. xiii). The new policy issued an agrarian reform law (Law 160 to 1994). Among its main measures it granted "the initiative to peasants interested in acquiring a plot" (Ocampo & Lora, 1988, p. 147), and defined peasant reserve zones and norms prohibiting the accumulation of wastelands. Ocampo's policy countered neoliberal plans, but it would have a short life.

The 1999 financial crisis marked another turn in Colombia's confrontation between neoliberal and heterodox paradigms. Roberto Junguito, who had already negotiated terms in 1983 with the IMF, and Murilo Portugal, a member of the IMF executive board, as the country's representatives, reached an Extended Facility Agreement with the IMF in December 1999. The agreement included, again, "semi-annual reviews with the Fund in each of the three years" (IMF et al., 1999, p. 3) of macroeconomic policies and a package of structural reforms that had begun in 1990.[19] The government made the macroeconomic adjustment, and in the new government that began in 2002, Junguito was appointed Minister of Finance to give continuity to the established policy.[20] The policy of conditionality was reimposed.

By this time, Ocampo had been appointed Executive Secretary of ECLAC. In his *Un Futuro económico para Colombia* (2001), Ocampo anticipated that Latin America would have low growth and high inequality by the end of the century. The pro-market reforms implemented in Colombia in 1991 transformed the economic model from a mixed protected economy with export promotion to a more open economy for international trade (Ocampo, 2001, p. 19). However, after ten years, "the destruction generated by the greater external competition did not have its counterpart in the creation of export capacities" (Ocampo, 2001, p. 21). As Minister of Agriculture, he had put in place controls to avoid the destruction of the agricultural sector. From ECLAC, he diagnosed that the liberalization of markets in Colombia was an "inward opening" (Ocampo, 2001, p. 21).

Market liberalization, according to Ocampo, brought about unemployment and economic exclusion of less productive population groups. To counter this, "the state is the mechanism par excellence that modern societies have developed to find an adequate balance between market and society, between private interest and collective interest" (Ocampo, 2001, p. 35). However, possible state failure made promoting social organizations to channel collective interest and foster social cohesion necessary. Both the state and the market respond to society. Ocampo also stated that macroeconomic stability should be complemented by active, productive development policies to support small and medium businesses because, contrary to the neoliberal view, individual entrepreneurs could not make the economy competitive by themselves.

Un Futuro económico para Colombia found few echoes. The country was already deep in neoliberal policies. The government renewed its close collaboration with the IMF, which led to a Flexible Credit Line in 2009, later renewed nine times until 2020. This Flexible Credit Line was the third time the IMF's conditionality policy remained in force.[21] According to orthodox economists, both in government and in Fedesarrollo, economic liberalization and this conditioned financial policy resulted in responsible management of the Colombian economy.

In 2003, Ocampo, Enrique Cárdenas (Mexico) and Rosemary Thorp (England) published *Industrialización y Estado en la América Latina. La leyenda Negra de la postguerra* (2003), an edited volume of studies on Latin America, which began in 1996 in England and 1997 in Colombia. The volume presents an assessment of the industrialization by import substitution model (Cárdenas et al., 2003, p. 10). The authors conclude that the model had to be changed, but the neoliberal model was not a good substitute, as the Colombian agriculture case had shown. Four years later, Ocampo co-authored with Ángela Parra *The continuing relevance of terms of trade and industrialization debates* (2007). The book contains 24 case studies on the deterioration of terms of trade in Latin America between 1985 and 2002, confirming Prebisch and Singer's results.[22] In 2010 Ocampo published with Luis Bertola *El desarrollo económico de América Latina desde la Independencia* (2010). The authors analyzed the region's economic performance in the last 200 years and criticized the "messianic tone" (Ocampo & Bertola, 2010, p. 233) with which neoliberal reforms began when another lost half-decade was beginning. Ocampo and Bertola present neo-structuralism as the alternative to neoliberalism. Neo-structuralism had four axes:

a) active countercyclical macroeconomic policies to avoid the imbalances in the upswing of external financing cycles and to expand the space for countercyclical policies during the downswing; b) the combination of external openness with open regionalism; c) active productive and technological policies that promote innovation, now designed for open economies; and d) placing equity at the center of development.
(Ocampo & Bertola, 2010, p. 231)

Over time, these elements became priorities for multilateral institutions such as the WB and the IMF after the 2008–2009 crisis. "The diversity and influence of some alternative visions were evident both in macroeconomic management models and in the scope and speed of some of the structural reforms" (Ocampo & Bertola, 2010, p. 231). These alternative visions were patent in cases of political opposition to the privatization of public companies. For example, Chile's copper and oil companies, its development bank, and a first-tier state bank remained public. Only Argentina, Bolivia, and Peru privatized their financial sectors. "As a result of these trends, and despite the privatization of many companies, the share of public companies in non-agricultural GDP was practically not reduced in the region in the 1990s" (Ocampo & Bertola, 2010, p. 231).

Neo-structuralism has had a small impact in Colombia. 11.5% of the shares of the largest state-owned company, the oil company Ecopetrol, were sold, public telecommunications enterprises were privatized, and the labor market was deregulated. Perhaps most troubling is the increase in the trade deficit and the public debt in the hands of national and foreign capitalists. This almost nonexistent influence of neo-structuralism in Colombia, or the presence of other alternative economic approaches to policy, can also be seen in the rest of the region, especially in the training of economists.

> With a few exceptions, the intellectual traditions of *cepalino* thought have been disappearing from the curriculum and programs of development economics courses in Latin American universities [...] their contributions are practically unknown or deliberately ignored [...].
> (Moreno & Matallana, 2016, p. 548)

The vast majority of economists in Colombia have been trained in a single neoliberal paradigm that prioritizes growth and macroeconomic stability. They have delivered some elements of their promise and have even included balanced budget goals as part of the constitution. At Fedesarrollo's 50th anniversary, Cárdenas described how the think tank, with the support of the IDB, was instrumental in including fiscal sustainability in the constitution. Fedesarrollo produced a report on the economic effects of the 1991 Constitution, which was the basis of raising fiscal sustainability to constitutional status,[23] meaning that the high courts must consider the fiscal impact of their sentences when preparing their rulings. According to the former minister, the study: "identified how fiscal sustainability was more difficult to achieve in an environment characterized by a greater number of actors with decision-making capacity" (Cárdenas, 2020, p. 144). That other actor was the Constitutional Court which on several occasions decided to favor the demands for protection of thousands of citizens claiming their rights to health and education. Once the constitution was modified, a fiscal rule was established (Cárdenas, 2020, p. 144). An autonomous committee of seven members was created to ensure effective compliance with the fiscal rule. Five of them are "experts of recognized professional or academic prestige in the field of public finance" (Law 1473/2011, art. 14).[24] The committee started with three representatives of Los Andes University, an independent consultant, and the director of Fedesarrollo. The chairman of the committee is also a former director of Fedesarrollo.

The economic results of the neoliberal era have not been the best compared to those of previous periods. From 1906 to 1930, the era of economist lawyers, average GDP growth was 5.5%; during the era of industrialization by import substitution, from 1931 to 1989, average GDP growth was 4.7%; finally, in the era of professional economists, average growth has been 3.3%. There have been three economic crises (1983, 1999, 2020) during the neoliberal period, which, although related to global cycles, have been faced by accepting the conditionality of the IMF in the management of domestic economic policy. This situation has made the Colombian economy vulnerable, as shown in its national debt: between 1925 and 1994, the average public debt (internal and external) was 13.6% of GDP, with peaks in 1935 (26% of GDP) and 1986 (21% of GDP); in the following neoliberal years, indebtedness has grown significantly, from 15.9% of GDP in 1995 to 64.8% of GDP in 2020.[25] As Ocampo and Bertola (2010) point out, for Latin America as a whole, GDP growth was lower between 1990 and 2008 with market reforms (3.4% on average) than in the period of state-led industrialization from 1950 to 1980 (5.5% on average).

9.4 Conclusion

During the first half of the 20th century, the most outstanding economists sought to understand the country's economy. They outlined some preliminary ideas on dualism, defense economics, and Latin American economic cooperation. International missions arrived in the 1950s to assess the Colombian economy. The following two decades witnessed a short debate between Lauchlin Currie and *cepalino* ideas. Currie, neither an orthodox nor a Keynesian economist, prevailed, and the ideas of the center and the periphery or dualism were rejected.

The debt crisis opened the way to neoliberalism and an economic technocracy that prioritized macroeconomic stability through a balanced balance of payments, public budget, inflation control, exchange rate devaluation, and free markets. During the neoliberal period, Ocampo implemented structuralist policies to contain the agricultural crisis of the 1990s. However, the reforms were short-lived, and an economic model that favors open markets in line with financial interests prevails. *Cepalino* ideas have stood alone and marginalized.

Statistical sources

DANE
Banco de la República
Contraloría General de la República
International Monetary Fund

Notes

1 We use the word paradigm to denote an epistemic community of economists and politicians that adhere to a body of thought of economic ideas and share the identification of similar problems and modes of solution (Haas, 1992).
2 For a *cepalino* perspective, see Ocampo and Bertola (2010); for a neoclassical perspective, see Bulmer-Thomas (2008). Babb (2003) and Romero (2019) analyze the Mexican case and Ffrench-Davis (2005) the Chilean experience.

3 See the works by Alejandro López, *El Trabajo* (1928), *Problemas Colombianos* (1927), *Idearium Liberal* (1931), *The end of laissez-faire* and *El desarme de la usura, La depresión económica, sus causas y sus posibles remedios* (1933); Antonio García, *Bases de economía contemporánea* (1948); Luis Nieto, La cooperación económica interamericana. *El Trimestre Económico., XIV*(4), 516–533 (1948). Luis Nieto Arteta is the other main figure, alongside Luis Ospina Vásquez, quoted in Meisel's chapter in this volume on the beginnings of Colombian economic historiography. López, Nieto Arteta, and García agreed on their dual view of the world economy divided between industrialized and creditor nations and commodity-producing and debtor nations, which called for economic cooperation strategies between Latin American countries.

4 For specific details about the labor market in these studies, see Álvarez, Villaveces, Meléndez, and Peña in this volume.

5 The recommendation followed the UN's support for international aid programs similar to the Marshall Plan (Fajardo, 2022).

6 Currie's was not an isolated criticism. Many American economists had been critical of *cepalino* ideas upon the publication of the ECLAC Manifesto in 1948. Jacob Viner, a Chicago School of Economics member and Keynes critic, asserted that Prebisch's manifesto was "a set of evil fantasies, a distorted historical conjecture and simplistic hypotheses" (Dosman, 2001, p. 102).

7 Currie developed his ideas during the New Deal and postwar period as a high-ranking US Federal Administration economic officer. He has been portrayed as having embraced Keynes's *General Theory* (Sweezy, 1993), but Currie wrote that "[…] although I had long considered myself a Keynesian, I felt (and still feel) that we had little to learn from the *General Theory* in policy matters" (Currie, 1963, p. 124).

8 Fajardo (2022) reconstructs the internal discussions at ECLAC about foreign aid and credit from the center to the periphery. Those against it considered these measures increased periphery–center dependence, whereas those in favor believed that countries could manage their debt levels without compromising their macroeconomic policy.

9 Other reforms included the administrative reorganization of the state, following the advice of the Ford mission led by Harvard University.

10 Guillermo Perry (Perry & López, 2019, pp. 58–59) offers an account of how President Pastrana "purged" the economic policy-makers' team of the previous Lleras Restrepo administration, including Perry himself.

11 In his work, Ocampo (1979, 1984) presented Colombia as a second periphery country in the world economy.

12 The contract amounts were Jumbo, US$1 billion in May 1985; Concorde, $1 billion in July 1987; Challenger, US$1,648 million in December 1988 (Ocampo, 1988).

13 Many of these economists attended Los Andes University. Economists from the United States have been involved with its Economics Department since 1963, and alumni have pursued graduate studies in the United States. This close connection led to a similar curriculum at Los Andes University with an anti-*cepalino*, monetarist, and orthodox influence (Mayor and Zambrano, 2016, p. 332). Palacios (2005) describes the situation in the late 20th century.

14 Mauricio Cárdenas Santamaría served twice as director of Fedesarrollo (1996–1998 and 2003–2008) and four times as minister: Finance (2012–2018), Mining (2011–2012), Transportation (1998–1999), Economic Development (1994). He was also director of the National Planning Department (1999–2000).

15 Ocampo served as General Secretary of ECLAC (1998–2003), Deputy Secretary of the United Nations (2003–2007) and Minister of Agriculture and Finance and Public Credit.

16 Ocampo edited the book *Historia económica de Colombia* in 1987 and was in charge of the journal *Coyuntura Social*.

17 Gaviria had served as Finance Minister for one year in the previous administration.
18 The sector grew minus 2% of GDP in 1992 (Ocampo & Perry, 1995, p. 221).
19 Tax and labor reform, the creation of private pension funds, and the improvement of the foreign investment regime, among others. See International Monetary Fund, Ministry of Finance, and Bank of the Republic (1999), *Colombia's extended agreement with the International Monetary Fund.*
20 A politician, economist, former senator, and grandson of a former president of Colombia referred to Roberto Junguito as follows:

> His national and international prestige was so high that his arrival in office immediately generated the confidence that made the most painful adjustment programs possible. Not even Congress people dared to oppose his measures. He managed to straighten out the key variables in a short time [...].
>
> (Gomez, 2019)

21 IMF, Press releases on the Flexible Credit Line, 2010, 2011, 2013, 2015, 2017, 2018, 2020, and 2022. See https://www.imf.org/es/News/Articles/2021/04/29/imf-executive-board-concludes-review-of-colombia-flexible-credit-line-arrangement; for 1999, Ministry of Finance, Bank of the Republic, IMF (1999). Colombia's Extended Agreement with the International Monetary Fund, Bogotá, DC.
22 There may be a few hypotheses in economics that have stood the test of both time and new statistical techniques so well. [...] We can also say something similar about the basic idea of classical development economics: that industrialization is an essential ingredient of development. It also seems to have stood the test of time very well. (Ocampo & Parra, 2007, p. 157)
23 Legislative Act 3 of 2011, amending articles 334, 339, and 346 of the Political Constitution. Law 1473 of 2011 was issued, which defined the criteria for the fiscal rule that would guarantee fiscal sustainability.
24 See Ministry of Finance and Public Credit (2013). *Advisory Committee on Tax Rule*, Minutes No. 1
25 DANE; Banco de la República.

Bibliography

Babb, S. (2003). *Proyecto: México. Los economistas del nacionalismo al neoliberalismo.* México, D.F: Fondo de Cultura Económica.
Bulmer-Thomas, V. (2008). *The Economic History of Latin America Since Independence* (2nd ed.). Cambridge University Press.
Cárdenas, E., Ocampo, J. A., & Thorp, R. (2003). *Industrialización y Estado en la América Latina. La leyenda negra de la postguerra* (Vol. 94). Fondo de Cultura Económica.
Cárdenas, M. (2020). Fedesarrollo y el Ministerio de Hacienda: 50 años de simbiosis deliberante. In X. Cadena (Ed.) *Fedesarrollo: 50 años de influencia en la política pública, 1970–2020* (pp. 139–172). Fedesarrollo.
Cuevas, H. (1995). La gestión estatal en el sector agropecuario (1986–1993). In L. B. Florez (Ed.), *Colombia. Gestión económica estatal de los 80's. Del ajuste al cambio institucional* (Vol. II, pp. 67–103). CID-Universidad Nacional de Colombia; CIID-Canadá.
Currie, L. (1963). *Ensayos sobre planeación.* Tercer Mundo Editores.
Dosman, E. (2001). Los mercados y el Estado en la evolución del manifiesto de Prebisch. *Revista de la CEPAL, 75*, 89–105.

Drake, P. W. (2005). The hegemony of US economic doctrines in Latin America. In V. FitzGerald & R. Thorp (Eds), *Economic doctrines in Latin America. Origins, embedding and evolution* (pp. 72–96). Palgrave Macmillan.

ECLAC. (1957). Análisis y proyecciones del desarrollo económico. El desarrollo económico de Colombia (Vol. III). Naciones Unidas. Departamento de Asuntos Económicos y Sociales. (E/CN.12/365/Rev.1).

Fajardo, M. (2022). *The world that Latin America created. The United Nations Economic Commission for Latin America in the development era.* Harvard University Press.

Ffrench-Davis, R. (2005). *Entre el neoliberalismo y el crecimiento con equidad.* LOM Ediciones.

Flórez, L. B. (2000). Apuntes sobre el pensamiento económico colombiano en la segunda mitad del siglo XX. In F. Leal & G. Rey (Eds), *Discurso y razón. Una historia de las ciencias sociales en Colombia* (pp. 83–126). Tercer Mundo Editores – Ediciones Uniandes – Fundación Social.

Flórez, L. B. (2009). Colombia: Economics, economic policy and economists. In V. Montecinos & J. Markoff (Eds), *Economists in the Americas* (pp. 195–226). Edward Elgar Publishing Limited.

Garay, L. J. (1991). *Colombia y la crisis de la deuda.* CINEP, Universidad Nacional de Colombia – Facultad de Ciencias Económicas.

Gómez, M. (2019). Roberto Junguito Bonnet, *Portafolio.* https://www.portafolio.co/opinion/miguel-gomez-martinez/roberto-junguito-bonnet-columnista-548006

González, J. I. (1995). Fedesarrollo y la economía positiva. In H. Gómez (Ed.), *Economía y opinión. 25 años de Fedesarrollo* (pp. 131–148). Tercer Mundo.

Haas, P. (1992). Introduction: Epistemic communities and international policy coordination. *International Organization Foundation, 46*(1), 1–35.

International Monetary Fund (IMF), Ministerio de Hacienda, & Banco de la República. (1999). *Acuerdo extendido de Colombia con el Fondo Monetario Internacional.* Banco de la República.

Junguito, R. (2016). *Historia económica de Colomba en el siglo XX.* Universidad Sergio Arboleda.

Lebret, L. J. (1958). *Estudio sobre las condiciones del desarrollo de Colombia.* AEDITA, Editores Ltda. CROMOS.

Love, J. (1980). Raúl Prebisch and the origins of the doctrine of unequal exchange. *Latin American Research Review, 15*(3), 45–72. http://www.jstor.org/stable/2502991

Mayor, A. and Zambrano, C. (2016). *Economistas antiguos y modernos, gigantes y enanos y su enseñanza en Colombia. Entre la formalización matemática y la pérdida teórica: el manual de economía en las primeras facultades universitarias, 1945–1980.* Universidad Autónoma de Colombia.

Misas Arango, G. (1995). De la industrialización sustitutiva a la apertura: el caso colombiano. In L. B. Florez (Ed.), *Colombia. Gestión económica estatal de los 80's. Del ajuste al cambio institucional* (Vol. II, pp. 3–68). CID-Universidad Nacional de Colombia; CIID-Canada.

Montecinos, V. (2009). Economics: The Chilean story. In V. Montecinos & J. Markoff (Eds), *Economists in the Americas* (pp. 142–194). Edward Elgar Publishing, Inc.

Montecinos, V., & Markoff, J. (2009). *Economists in the Americas.* Edward Elgar Publishing, Inc.

Moreno, Á. & Matallana, H. (2016). Reseña: *Neoestructuralismo y corrientes heterodoxas en América Latina y el Caribe a inicios del siglo XXI,* Alicia Barcena and A. Prado (eds) (2015), CEPAL. *Cuadernos de Economía, 35*(68), 547–554.

Ocampo, J. A. (1979). Desarrollo exportador y desarrollo capitalista colombiano en el siglo XIX (una hipótesis). *Desarrollo y sociedad, 1*, 135–144.

Ocampo, J. A. (1988). Cuatro décadas de endeudamiento externo colombiano. In J. A. Ocampo & E. Lora (Eds), *Colombia y la deuda externa* (pp. 11–84). Tercer Mundo, Fedesarrollo.

Ocampo, J. A. (2001). *Un futuro económico para Colombia*. Alfaomega editores.

Ocampo, J. A. (2013). América Latina frente a la turbulencia económica Mundial. Conferencia dictada en el Seminario sobre Neoestructuralismo y Economía Heterodoxa. *Prebisch y los desafíos del desarrollo del siglo XXI* (1 ed., pp. 26:33 minutos). CEPAL.

Ocampo, J. A., & Bertola, L. (2010). *El desarrollo económico de América Latina desde la independencia*. Fondo de Cultura Económica.

Ocampo, J. A., & Lora, E. (Eds.) (1988). *Colombia y la deuda externa*. Tercer Mundo; Fedesarrollo.

Ocampo, J. A. & Parra, M. A. (2007). The continuing relevance of terms of trade and industrialization debates. In E. Pérez Caldentey & M. Vernengo (Eds), *Ideas, policies and economic development in the Americas* (pp. 157–183). Routledge Taylor & Francis Group.

Ocampo, J. A., & Perry, S. (1995). *El giro de la política agropecuaria*. Tercer Mundo Editores; Fonade-DNP.

Palacios, M. (2005). Knowledge is power: The case of Colombian economists. In V. FitzGerald & R. Thorp (Eds), *Economic doctrines in Latin America. Origins, embedding and evolution* (pp. 182–216). Palgrave McMillan - St Antony's College.

Perry, G. & López, I. (2019). *Decidí contarlo. Conversaciones sobre cincuenta años de economía política en Colombia*. Penguin Random House.

Romero M. E. (2019). *Los orígenes del neoliberalismo en México: la escuela austriaca*. Fondo de Cultura Económica.

Sandilands, R. (1990). *Vida y política económica de Lauchlin Currie*. Fondo Editorial Legis.

Stallings, B. (1992). La influencia internacional en las políticas económicas: Deuda, estabilización y reforma estructural. In S. Haggard & R. R. Kaufman (Eds), *La política de ajuste económico. Las restricciones internacionales, los conflictos distributivos y el Estado* (pp. 59–117). CEREC.

Stiglitz, J. E. (2002). *El malestar en la globalización*. Editora Aguilar.

Stiglitz, J. E. (2012). *Caída libre. El libre mercado y el hundimiento de la economía mundial*. Editora Aguilar.

Sweezy, A. (1993). La revolución keynesiana y sus pioneros: los keynesianos y la política del gobierno 1933–1939. *Cuadernos de Economía* (pp. 18–19, 101–118). Translation by Mario García of the paper originally published in *American Economic Review* Proceedings 62, May 1972, pp. 139–41. Original work published in 1972).

Toye, J. & Toye, R. (2004). *The UN and Global Political Economy. Trade, Finance, and Development*. Indiana University Press.

Villamizar, J. C. (2013). *Pensamiento económico en Colombia. Construcción de un saber, 1948–1970* (1st ed.). Editorial Universidad del Rosario.

10 Between the Hedgehog and the Fox

The Birth of Colombian Economic Historiography, 1942–1955[*]

Adolfo Meisel

10.1 Introduction

In the short time between 1942 and 1955, three academic publications created a profound break in the historiography of Colombia, which until then had been dominated by political history. For the first time, three authors explored the economic history of Colombia over a long period. Although from different backgrounds, academic training, and intellectual approaches, they all contributed to creating a solid tradition in the economic history of Colombia. These authors were Luis Eduardo Nieto Arteta, a Marxist; Luis Ospina Vasquez, a member of the Conservative party and the political elite; and James J. Parsons, a geographer from the University of California, Berkeley.

A researcher in any field needs to familiarize themselves with the intellectual contributions of those who came before to understand how knowledge is constructed gradually and collectively. This is especially important in a country like Colombia, where many of the leading academics are trained abroad, so there is the risk that they may dismiss or ignore it due to a lack of familiarity with the local intellectual tradition. Every generation writes its own history. However, there is also the need to reread the classics in the light of contemporary concerns, both to view their limitations and to explore insights and interpretations that had been overlooked because, for some reason, they were not of interest in previous generations due to the topics highlighted by the paradigm from which they worked, or because of changes in societies' problems and concerns.

10.2 Luis Eduardo Nieto Arteta: The Introduction of Historical Materialism

Luis Eduardo Nieto Arteta published his book *Economía y cultura en la historia de Colombia* (*ECHC*) in 1942.[1] It represented a break with the past in many aspects of the historiography of Colombia. Until that date, the study of the

* The author benefitted from comments on a previous version by Salomon Kalmanovitz, Andrés Álvarez, and Haroldo Calvo.

DOI: 10.4324/9781003289241-12

country's past had been dominated by traditional political narratives involving the actions of members of the criollo elite. In the first place, Nieto concentrated on economic institutions and their reform or continuity. His interpretations of the independence process, the reforms of the mid-19th century, the period known as that of radical liberalism (1863 to early 1880s), as well as the political regime of the final years of the century, the Regeneration, were evaluated differently to what had been the prevailing opinions.

At least two main characteristics of *ECHC* made it stand out as having a new and attractive perspective on the country's economic history from colonial times to the end of the 19th century: it was the first time historical materialism had been applied to an analysis extending over a long period in Colombia, and the author used two sources that had not been systematically applied in writing the national history at the time. These sources were the writings of several 19th-century politicians (Salvador Camacho, Miguel Samper, Jose Maria Samper Agudelo, Anibal Galindo, Antonio Nariño, Rafael Nuñez, among others), and the memoirs written by the finance ministers at the end of their terms in office.

Most comments on *ECHC* when it appeared in 1942 were favorable. However, a young historian who a few years later would direct the first history department in a Colombian university and who is considered to be the founder of what in the 1960s came to be known as *la Nueva Historia de Colombia*, Jaime Jaramillo Uribe, was critical of the dualism that, according to Nieto, characterized the national economy. He was referring to the contrast between the manufacturing Oriental region without *latifundia*, and the central part, where *encomiendas* and *resguardos* had been essential and *latifundia* were present. This simplification left out, for example, the dynamic mining and commercial Antioqueño region, and the Caribbean coast, where slavery was present (Jaramillo Uribe, 1942).

However, even for the second edition, in 1962, well-informed history scholars praised the advance that Nieto's book represented. For example, in the opinion of Robert C. Beyer:

> When this work appeared in its first edition in 1942, it represented a striking departure in Colombian historical writings ... Turning his back on the customary concerns of Colombian historians for either attacking or defending or glorifying protagonists in history, the author wrote a balanced, thoughtful, and lucid account of the economic evolution of Colombian society.
>
> (Beyer, 1966, pp. 115–116)

Beyer's argument is very clear: Nieto inaugurated a new way of seeing the Colombian past in which economic processes, institutions, and labor relations were substituted for the actions of political and military men from the elite. That was the basis for its favorable reception and its main strength.

From the perspective of the present, we can now analyze the main limitations of Nieto's book, not without taking into consideration that in more than 80 years, the advances in the country's economic historiography have been Significant, so we have at our disposal a vast literature which was not available when Nieto wrote *ECHC*.

When writing his book, Nieto Arteta had clear his main goal: he wanted to apply historical materialism to studying the country's economic history. He had considered himself a Marxist since the early years of his law studies at the Universidad Nacional in Bogotá. By 1932, at 19 years old, Nieto Arteta was publishing small essays defending Marxism as a scientific worldview (Cataño, 2013). In 1933, he joined a Marxist group of intellectuals, Grupo Marxista, who were critical of what they perceived as the very dogmatic variant of Marxism followed by the local Communist Party. His political participation was mainly ideological.

His interpretation of Colombia's history from colonial times to the end of the 19th century is often mechanical and simplistic. On occasions, it even seems to go against all the evidence, such as when he praises the achievements of the Regeneration period (1886–1899) and argues that it was, in fact, a revolution. We will dwell on this point further.

Nieto Arteta divided the economy of the colonial period into two regions where the labor relations and characteristics of rural property were significantly different. In the East, where the departments of Norte de Santander and Santander are now located:

> [...] as a result of the fortunate annihilation of the indigenous population – *guanes*, *citareros*, etc. – an economy that was not strictly colonial was created. In the villages, there are no *encomiendas* or slavery. Small property is present. This is true colonization [...]. Small village property and the economy of workshops in the cities are the economic facts of the Colombian region.[2]
>
> (Nieto Arteta, 1996, p. 14)

In contrast to the Santanderes, Nieto presents the colonial economy of central Colombia, the current departments of Cundinamarca, Boyaca, and parts of Huila and Tolima, as a region where:

> [...] the continued existence of the indigenous people after the occupation of the territory of the Chibcha Empire by the Conquistadors [...] produced the formation of a typical colonial economy: encomienda, immense latifundia that were not cultivated, and land concessions by the Crown.
>
> (Nieto Arteta, 1996, p. 15)

Nietos's two-region model of the Colombian economy in the colonial period has several problems. First, he exaggerates the degree of the differences between the Eastern and central areas. Both regions permanently excluded a non-negligible indigenous population from equal education and land access. Furthermore, both regions had local artisan production and manufacturing.

Another shortcoming of Nieto's two-region contrast is that he left out the former Cauca province, Antioquia, and the Caribbean region. This meant he left out about half of the total population and most of the enslaved population, mainly located in these areas. Slavery on the Caribbean coast was concentrated in the large urban centers; in Cauca and Antioquia, it was concentrated in mining sites, making the picture more complex for the colonial economy. Among many other reasons, we can see that the economy and the population were growing for at least the last 50 years before independence. So as Nieto suggested, it was not static.

In his analysis, Nieto attributes almost all the shortcomings of the colonial economy to the fiscal regime established by Spain: "[...] the economic and fiscal institutions it created in America eradicated all prosperity" (Nieto Arteta, 1996, p. 18). The reason for this overdetermination of the fiscal regime in Nieto's discussion of the colonial regime is that he closely followed the criticisms of the colonial institutions by the leaders of Colombia's independence and the liberal politicians and ideologues who, in the 1850s, reformed some of the colonial institutions that still existed. Their views were focused on the fiscal system, so they paid no attention to the inclusiveness of society or the concentration of land among a small group. As is well known, land ownership was the primary form of wealth and a source of inequality at the time.

Other limitations to economic prosperity, perhaps even more important than the fiscal regime, are ignored in his analysis, for example, land distribution and social and economic opportunities in access to education for the indigenous and enslaved population.

The central part of *ECHC* is dedicated to the social and economic reforms of the 1850s. Eight chapters are dedicated to that topic, the colonial economy and independence are discussed in seven, and the final part of the 19th century in five. In a sense, it may be considered that this is the book's main strength, although I will argue that the arguments presented are not supported by empirical evidence. In his view, the Independence War basically left intact the colonial fiscal system and much of the legislation related to land and other matters. Thus, he argued that the colonial period had extended until 1850. How did he arrive at this conclusion? The evidence he supplies comes from long quotes from liberal thinkers of the 19th century, many of whom had participated in implementing some of the reforms of the mid-century. Hence, they tended to exaggerate by saying that nothing had changed with independence and the following decades and that reforms from the 1850s were an unprecedented revolution. However, suppose one looks at the empirical evidence. In that case, the lack of change before 1850 seems exaggerated, and the changes at mid-century do not seem so exceptional, nor do they seem to have had the revolutionary effects Nieto mentions.

Nieto is clearly wrong about the lack of changes in the colonial tax system after independence. By 1836, 15 colonial taxes, such as the tribute on Indians, had been abolished. They represented 25.4% of the tax revenues of 1801, so this was a significant change (Jaramillo et al., 1997; Bordo & Cortés-Conde, 2001). The colonial tax system depended on many taxes, some of which were costly to collect, so their net income was relatively small. However, after independence, the fiscal authorities of the republic reduced or eliminated those costly taxes and moved towards cheap collecting taxes: tariffs on imports. While in 1808–1809 custom taxes were 9.3% of total revenues, by 1842–1843 they represented 38.2% (Jaramillo et al., 1997).

The rapid review of the evolution of the tax system exposed above shows that many of Nieto's arguments were not based on empirical evidence. The problem with Nieto's treatment of the topics analyzed is that all his evidence came either from the memoirs of the ministers of finance, which on many issues had a biased perception of the economic problems and the economic policies, or from the opinions of many of the liberal ideologues of the 19th century, who could also have opinions which were not solidly based on the facts. Rather than presenting evidence, in part because there was almost no economic historiography that he could have used, Nieto opted for very long quotes from the two sources we have mentioned. As Gonzalo Cataño has shown, 51% of the book comprises quotes from different texts. In Chapter 14 on the tax system, 79% of the text comes from direct quotations (Cataño, 2013, p. 217). This excessive level of quotations was in part a result of the absence of a tradition of solid monographic studies on the economic history of the country, which would have implied that the author needed to advance his knowledge of these topics by going to the archives and other primary sources such as the press. However, Nieto was a brilliant young man who started researching this topic when he was only 22 years old and wanted to make a quick impact. Although he worked very hard, he lacked the necessary erudition to write a book as complex as he intended. Indeed, rather than being a perfectionist, he was avid for intellectual recognition, which he achieved significantly.

In the last chapter, Nieto separates himself from the Colombian left, which had been very critical of the regime known as the Regeneration (1886–1899). This movement established a new constitution in 1886, eliminating the 1863 Constitution, which was very liberal, decentralized, separated the powers of the church and state, and guaranteed freedom of expression. For Nieto, the Regeneration was a democratic movement, and the Constitution of 1886 was a liberal one. His evidence for those claims was, once again, lengthy quotes from the writings of Rafael Nuñez, one of the leading architects of the Regeneration. Nieto ignored the objective of the separation of church and state, authoritarian tendencies in the constitution, and the mechanisms of control of free speech that it included. The regime ended in the War of the Thousand Days (1899–1902) between the ruling coalition of conservatives and liberals against the liberals who were out of power. This is perhaps the most controversial chapter, since he overlooks all the authoritarian characteristics of the

Regeneration to interpret it as a democratic revolution, even though most liberal and leftist historians see it as a reactionary counter-revolution.

From an economic history point of view, I find that the best chapters of *ECHC* are the three related to foreign trade. In Chapter 17, the author analyzes the behavior of tobacco exports from 1834–1835 to 1891, reflecting the boom from 1854–1855 to 1874–1875. Nieto presents the values exported every year, weights, and main destinations. He constructed this series from the memoirs of finance ministers, which contemporary Colombian economic historians use today.[3] In Chapter 18, the data on exports of cinchona and indigo are analyzed. Finally, in Chapter 20, the series for total exports are presented. Since the data are in nominal terms, Colombian pesos, and there was inflation in the country in the second half of the 19th century, the interpretation of the data is problematic.

One of the limitations of *ECHC* is that it is narrowly focused on the Colombian experience and makes no effort to present the evolution of the national economy in relation to other economies, especially those of other Latin American countries. This has been a shortcoming in most of Colombia's economic historiography and continues even now.

10.3 James Parsons: The Protagonism of Geography

In the summer of 1946, James J. Parsons, a young PhD geography student from Berkeley University, arrived in Medellín. The dissertation he prepared over the following years was published in 1949: *Antioqueño Colonization in Western Colombia*. It was published in Spanish in Medellín in 1950 and rapidly became Colombia's most influential study of regional economic growth.[4] In the years that followed, there was a proliferation of studies about the Antioqueño experience: colonization, mining, entrepreneurial history, coffee production and exports, industrialization, and transportation, among others.[5]

Antioquia and the departments colonized by the Antioqueños – Caldas, Risaralda, Quindio, and parts of Tolima and north of Valle del Cauca – were the most economically dynamic regions of Colombia by the 1940s, and their populations had achieved the highest standard of living in the country. What explained this Antioqueño exceptionality? This is precisely the question that James J. Parsons asked in his dissertation.

Parson's book is divided into 12 chapters. The first six relate to the region's geography and the colonial period. In Chapter six, he refers to Antioqueño colonization. The narrative centerpiece of the book, is the core of the new interpretation of the history of the region offered by Parsons. Most references to his contribution to understanding the uniqueness of Antioquia's development are mentioned in this chapter. In the following six chapters, the author refers to population growth and specific sectors of the economy. However, he could have ended with Chapter six, and the publication would have been just as influential, at least in Colombia. To assemble these chapters, Parsons did extensive fieldwork and conducted ample research in primary sources such as government reports and periodical publications. In the initial chapters, Parsons commented that up to the end of the 19th century, most travelers were shocked by the lack of education, backwardness, and overall poverty of the Antioqueños (Parsons, 1997). However, 200 years later, Antioquia and the departments of the Antioqueño colonization had the highest standard of living in Colombia. What changed in Antioquia between the late 18th century and the middle of the 20th century? His answer is not formulated explicitly but through a narrative about the colonization process of the south and west of Antioquia by peasants and artisans without land, which created a new and more egalitarian social structure. This occurred through a prolonged confrontation with the *latifundium* owners, who often had titles of property of colonial origins. These titles to extensive areas were owned by elite families such as the Aranzazu, who claimed all the lands east of the Cauca River between Chinchiná and the Arma creek (Parsons, 1997, p. 119). These peasant–*latifundium* struggles are often referred to as a battle between hardworking peasants and absentee owners of enormous extensions of unexploited land, the *latifundios*, a dispute between axes and legal papers.

Two of the final chapters refer to the new sources of wealth in Antioquia during the 20th century: coffee and industry. In Chapter 10, Parsons describes the expansion of coffee production in Antioquia and its areas of colonization, a phenomenon of the late 19th century and the early 20th century. Initially, coffee was produced in Colombia in Norte de Santander and, towards the end of the 19th century, in Cundinamarca. However, the land between 1,000 and 2,000 meters above sea level in Antioquia, Caldas, Risaralda, Tolima, Quindio, and north of Valle del Cauca, turned out to be ideal for coffee production. Thus, by 1913–1914, 46% of all coffee was produced in this area, and by 1956–1959, the participation had increased to 76% (Parsons, 1997, p. 213).

The prosperity generated by coffee exports in the 20th century led to a significant expansion of GDP per capita in Antioquia and the departments of the Antioqueño colonization. This expanded the market for essential goods and, therefore, the demand for domestic industrial goods: textiles and processed foods. Thus, Medellín, Antioquia's capital, became the main industrial center of Colombia. In 1964 there were 25,300 workers in the textile sector, 37% of all industrial workers in Antioquia (Parsons, 1997, p. 265).

James J. Parsons' book provided a solid academic explanation for Antioquia's economic success in the first decades of the 20th century. Well researched and amply documented, it rapidly became a very influential contribution to the historiography of Colombia. However, research published in the following years, paradoxically by North American scholars, has shown that Parsons' view of colonization exaggerated its egalitarian nature. We will discuss some research that questioned Parsons' claims and calls to moderate Parsons' conclusions later.

Historian Keith H. Christie (1978) argues that the supposedly egalitarian nature of Antioqueño colonization is largely a myth. Through a very detailed analysis of the colonizers, he illustrates the strength of families from the oligarchy in the movement toward the south:

> Poor and modest families clearly could survive on the frontier, and some even prospered despite the heavy hand of the better families. Although there was some room to move, the opportunity was circumscribed, often to a great extent. The best families dominated the social and political life of the frontier.
>
> (Christie, 1978, p. 267)

On balance, we can say that Antioquia's exceptionality was not the product of racial, ethnic, or cultural factors but of the prevailing conditions that, since the late 18th century, had created a climate that favored capital accumulation through mining and commerce. This, in turn, led to the consolidation of a dynamic business elite that was the most economically solid in the country by the mid-19th century (Twinam, 1985, p. 241).

Later, a group of small farmers and peasants began colonizing sparsely populated areas south of the Antioquia department, boosting the regional economy. However, with the accelerated growth of coffee exports since the first years of the 20th century, Antioquia and its colonized zones presented the growth rates that made them the most prosperous region of Colombia. The expansion of regional markets, thanks to the income from coffee exports, led to a strong local demand for basic industrial goods. As a result, Medellín's rise as Colombia's leading industrial city was facilitated. As historian Jaime Jaramillo Uribe put it:

> [...] after the success of industrialization it seemed logical to say that "we are different"; it was a success because we have certain peculiarities, such features, and the myth or stereotype was reinforced by North American historians who found some individuals who 'are like us gringos' somewhere in Latin America, and that is why initially the search for an ultimate cause was so strong.
>
> (in Melo, 1982, pp: 31–32)

Part of the success of Parsons' book, in addition to its academic quality, was that it gave academic respectability to the imagined uniqueness of the Antioqueños.

10.4 Luis Ospina Vasquez: Economic History from the Bottom Up

In 1955, Luis Ospina Vasquez published *Industria y protección en Colombia, 1810–1930*. This book and the two discussed in the previous sections constitute the foundational bibliography of Colombian economic historiography.

Luis Ospina Vasquez was trained as a lawyer at the Universidad Nacional in Bogotá and studied economics in England and the USA. He was a member of the Colombian elite: grandson of Mariano Ospina Rodriguez, son of Pedro Nel Ospina, and cousin of Mariano Ospina Pérez, all Colombian presidents. Additionally, he was married to the daughter of President Carlos Lleras Restrepo. His family was wealthy and owned coffee and cattle haciendas. He was elected to the Colombian Senate and the Department Assembly of Antioquia (Safford, 1978).

Only in the late 1960s did *Industria y protección* begin to be amply recognized in the Colombian academy, thanks to the advent of the so-called *Nueva Historia de Colombia*, whose mentor was Jaime Jaramillo Uribe and to which a group of young and talented historians belonged, German Colmenares, Jorge Orlando Melo and Margarita Gonzalez, among others. This influence increased after the second edition was published in 1974.[6]

I consider that the main strength of *Industria y protección en Colombia, 1810–1930*, is that its author was generally very rigorous in documenting the facts and arguments that he presented. He read widely in the secondary literature available at the time and in various primary sources and archives. Another evident strength is that he discussed Colombia's principal economic regions and was familiar with the geography, main economic activities, and even the milieu in which business enterprises were conducted.

Ospina Vasquez was, like Nieto Arteta, an avid reader; however, his knowledge of the country resulted also from his familiarity with the country's political and economic elite, of which he was a distinguished member, being the son of a President and from a wealthy and well-connected family. It was also due to his professional activities, such as being a senator in the Colombian Congress, a member of the Departmental Assembly of Antioquia, the owner of a large cattle ranch in the Sinu área of the Colombian Caribbean, and a coffee farm in Bolombolo, Antioquia.

Since the mid-1970s, a myth has been created around Ospina Vasquez's book among Colombian economists and historians. They consider this author so rigorous that none of his arguments have been found to be mistaken. However, we can document that, in many cases, the research published since the publication of *Industria y protección* has shown that Ospina was wrong or held views that are highly questionable from an empirical perspective. For example, in the obituary of Luis Ospina Vasquez, F. Safford, discussing the contributions of scholars of the generations that followed him, says that: "…none, so far, has implied any substantial reconsideration of Ospina's work" (Safford, 1978, p. 467).

I will mention a few instances where it has been shown that the evidence refutes Ospina's analysis:

1 He states, "The colonial period did not leave us a clear and systematic record of the public accounts"(Ospina, 1974, p. 62). Completely wrong. The Spanish Empire probably had the most organized system of fiscal accounts in the world. There are extensive records in the Archivo General de Indias in Seville, Spain, and in the Archivo General de la Nación in Bogotá,

Colombia. Herbert Klein holds that "[...] the Spanish American treasuries have left an enormous historical record"(Klein, 1998, p. 3). New Granada was no exception. Hermes Tovar has reconstructed the accounts of the main treasuries of the 16th century (Tovar, 1999). For the 18th century, 1761–1800, I obtained from the Archivo General de Indias the year-by-year and account-by-account income data for the treasuries of New Granada. I published the results in 2015 (Meisel, 2015).

2   Ospina considered that the effects of the elimination of mortmain in Colombia in the 1860s were minimal: "[...] it had secondary importance because of economic and social aspects [...]" (Ospina, 1974, p. 289). However, at the time, the economic aspects of the disamortization of church property by the liberals in the 1860s had not been analyzed. Ospina did not read the memoirs of the Minister of the Treasury, as can be corroborated by checking his bibliography. Although he did study the memoirs of the Ministers of Finance, information on disamortization was not discussed in those memoirs because the office charged with that process belonged to the Ministry of the Treasury. Had he studied the memoirs of the Treasury Minister, Ospina would have been aware of the importance of that reform. He merely followed the dismissal of disamortization that most Conservative party members made at the time, primarily for ideological reasons, which had become an accepted fact. However, when the information on all the expropriated properties and loans is summed up, it can be said that hardly any other reform of the 19th-century republican governments was as significant as this one. The expropriated property represented a value that was at least 16% of the Colombian GDP of 1860 (Jaramillo & Meisel, 2010, p. 312).

3   Ospina attributes part of the rapid increase in coffee exports from 1880 to 1898 to the nominal devaluation of the peso in relation to the pound and the US dollar (Ospina, 1974, p. 346). However, when the fact that there was higher inflation in Colombia compared to the US and England is taken into account, and the real exchange is calculated, the result is that there was no devaluation of the peso at the time.[7] Again, he repeated what some Conservative party members had said during the Regeneration without rigorous analysis (Caro, 1958, pp. 23–24).

From the current Colombian economic historiography perspective, it is possible to find additional areas in which the ideas or facts presented by Ospina Vasquez have evident shortcomings.

I will first refer to his controversial view on the colonial period. He stated, "The colonial period has been our great excuse [...] the insistence of those who want to see in our economic policies only the prolongation of the colony, specifically the Spanish colony [...]" (Ospina, 1974, p. 522). He continues criticizing the Liberal Party, which expressed in a national declaration in 1935 its intention of: "[...] demolishing the colonial economy established by the Spaniards [...]" (Ospina, 1974, p. 522).[8] Ospina minimizes the colonial legacy in land distribution, access to opportunities for education, and a race-relations regime that discriminated against indigenous, black, and mixed-race people, which has shown tremendous persistence. To a large extent, that legacy explains why Colombia is one of the countries with the highest levels of income concentration and regional inequalities in the world.

An explicit limitation of Ospina's analysis is that his export and import data were nominal.[9] Since during the second half of the 19th century, especially after 1886, there were significant changes in the price level, the nominal series for exports are inadequate for long-term economic analysis. Furthermore, once adjusted for the changes in the average price level, it is necessary to divide by the population to obtain the data in real terms per capita since there was sustained growth in the size of the Colombian population. The estimates of per-capita exports for Colombia in the 19th century were only available when William P. McGreevey and Jose Antonio Ocampo calculated them in the 1970s and 1980s using different methodologies.[10]

William P. McGreevey estimated the exports and imports of Colombia from the imports and exports from/to Colombia by some of the leading trading partners: the US, Great Britain, France, and the ports of Hamburg and Bremen (McGreevey, 1971). Alberto Umaña criticized those estimates, arguing that there had been a large re-export trade via Panama, which biased the exports and imports data to Colombia (Umaña, 1979). Jose Antonio Ocampo also discards the use of the trade statistics of Colombia's main trading partners in the 19th century because there are problems in addition to the one pointed out by Umaña. Among those shortcomings, he mentions that the trade date of the US with Colombia before 1838/9 and Great Britain before 1846 included trade with Ecuador and Venezuela (Ocampo, 2013, p. 60).

The export and import series for Colombia that McGreevey used in his book is the one he constructed using the data of the country's main trading partners. They are presented in per-capita terms, an advance in relation to Nieto Arteta and Ospina, but in current dollars. This is somewhat surprising since, in a footnote, McGreevey (2015, p. 137) comments that when the data is deflated, there is a smaller variation in the data.

An economic historian who uses the Colombian exports series is Jose Antonio Ocampo. However, he presents the annual data in per-capita terms and deflates the result by using a Paasche and a Laspeyres price index, using the prices of the main export products (tobacco, coffee, and cinchona), all in gold prices. Real exports are reported as a biannual index with 1802 – 1804 = 100 (Ocampo, 2013, p. 65).

A final reference to Ospina's book's shortcomings that I would like to discuss is the lack of an international comparative perspective allowing the author to contrast local economic growth in the long run with other relevant cases. Thus, it would be possible to analyze whether, for example, growth was hindered for some reason or was very successful. For this purpose, I will contrast *Industria y protección* with what is, for me, the best economic history of a Latin American country published in the 1950s: Celso Furtado's *Formaçao economica do Brasil* (1959).

I will mention only one of the strengths of Furtado's economic history of Brazil. He systematically compared the economic development of Brazil and the US in the 19th century in a chapter dedicated to that topic.[11] Based on that comparison, he concluded that "The main cause of the relative backwardness of the Brazilian economy in the first half of the 19th century was, therefore, the damming up of its exports" (Furtado, 1971, pp. 116, 153–171). Brazilian exports in that period grew in pounds sterling by 0.8% annually while the population increased by 1.3% per year (Furtado, 1971, p. 116).

10.5 Conclusion

Before 1942, there was a complete absence of books on the economic history of Colombia. The political history of a traditional narrative style of great men and significant events dominated national historiography. This changed after 1942, when a young lawyer, Luis Eduardo Nieto Arteta, published *Economía y cultura en la historia de Colombia*. There he presented an unorthodox Marxist interpretation of the country's economic history in the 19th century.

In what was in many ways a response to Nieto Arteta's book, in 1955, Luis Ospina Vasquez published an economic history of Colombia from independence to 1930. This last work was generally well documented, inductive in its reasoning, and usually very careful in its claims. It was written from a moderate conservative point of view.

Thus, we can say that from its very beginning Colombian economic historiography has advanced between the waters of a deductive, paradigmatically oriented approach and a more inductive, empirically driven history without an explicitly formulated theoretical background. As we have seen in many ways, both authors differed in their social and regional origins, intellectual styles, and personalities.

A third book I consider part of the foundational literature on Colombian economic history is the study published in 1949 by the North American geographer James J. Parsons on Antioqueño colonization. Because of its rugged topography – the Andes divides into three mountain ranges when it enters Colombia – this has been a country where regions and regionalism have played an enormous role in the economy, politics, and culture. Throughout the 19th century, but especially in the first half of the 20th century, Antioquia and the areas its people colonized were the most successful economically among all the regions of Colombia. Thus, it is necessary to analyze the Antioqueño phenomena to understand Colombian economic history.

Finally, I refer to what I perceive as the main limitation of Colombia's historiography from its beginning in the 1942–1955 period: the absence of an international comparative perspective. We can observe this in Nieto Arteta and Ospina Vasquez, who are so different in many other respects. This is a very persistent characteristic, and I think the younger generations of economic historians need to be fully aware of it to overcome it.

Appendix

Table 10.A1   Characteristics of the three authors discussed

Characteristic	Luis Eduardo Nieto Arteta	James J Parsons	Luis Ospina Vasquez
Intellectual style	Hedgehog	Fox	Fox
Major work published at age	28	34	50
Profession	Lawyer	Geographer	Lawyer
Main Activity	Government positions	Professor	Lived a life of leisure most of the time
Family background	Modest	Middle-class	Son and grandson of presidents of Colombia
Long-run impact of main work	Considered a pioneering effort but mostly evaluated	Considered a classic	Considered a classic
General political orientation	Heterodox Marxism	Not known	Conservative
Interested in geography	No	Yes	Partially
Interested in the study of regions	Yes	Yes	Yes
Use of international comparisons to further understand the Colombian experience	No	No	No

Notes

1   Luis Eduardo Nieto Arteta was born in Barranquilla in 1913. He studied there in a Jesuit school where he was an outstanding student. While still in high school, he declared himself an atheist, which almost got him expelled. He studied law at the Universidad Nacional in Bogotá, where he was considered a brilliant student. His undergraduate thesis introduced the ideas of the positivist philosopher of law Hans Kelsen in Colombia. In the early 1950s, a rightist Conservative government expelled him from the foreign services – he was a diplomat in the Colombia embassy in Buenos Aires. This led to economic difficulties and the separation from his wife and children since he accepted a judicial job in Barranquilla, and they remained in Bogotá. He committed suicide in 1956 in that city. See Meisel (1992).

2   His reference to annihilating the native population as "fortunate" is outrageous and inaccurate. It is an unfortunate word choice, even by the standard of the time he wrote it. However, the absence of a large indigenous population has since facilitated the establishment of small properties in rural areas of the Orient region. These more inclusive institutions led to a more prosperous and equal society in the colonial period. However, there was always a presence of indigenous people and an extensive *mestizaje* process between Spaniards and indigenous women. Recent genetic studies reveal the extent of this *mestizaje*. For example, a study by Humberto Ossa et al. (2016) shows that the current population of the Santanders has a 35% participation of indigenous lineages, 58% European, and 7% African. Thus, there was no annihilation of the indigenous population.

3 For example, Jose Antonio Ocampo (2013, p. 62) used similar data for the trade statistics of the 19th century. The difference is that Nieto presented the data in nominal terms, and Ocampo constructed a series of per-capita exports in real terms.
4 The Spanish edition has been re-edited three times.
5 Among these, some of the most influential contributions are Lopez Toro (1970), Hagen (1963), Safford (1965), Christie (1978), and Twinam (1985).
6 At the time, I was a student in the third semester of economics at the Universidad de los Andes. I was aware that the book was being published and was expecting it with great enthusiasm because of the comments I heard about it from some of my professors. As soon as it arrived at the bookstores, I bought the copy I still use; it still has the date of the day I acquired it in Cartagena: July 25, 1974. In 2019, the Economics Department of the Universidad de los Andes published a third edition. It contains notes by the author, which he was taking for a future revised edition he never wrote, probably because, in his final years, he was almost blind.
7 For an estimate of the real exchange rate in that period and the discussion around the apparent stimulus to coffee exports from the nominal devaluation of the peso, see Meisel & López (1990).
8 Much of the current Colombian economic historiography gives great weight to the negative effect of the colonial legacy on long-run development via the institutions that were left behind. In this recent literature, the influence of the work of Douglass North, James Robinson, and Daron Acemoglu is evident. See for example Acemoglu et al. (2012) and Fergusson, Molina, Robinson & Vargas (2017).
9 Ospina used the 19th-century trade statistics that Nieto Arteta published in his book, which he obtained from the memoirs of the Finance Ministers. Nieto Arteta also has the shortcoming of not adjusting his data for inflation.
10 In the book he published initially in English in 1971, William P. McGreevey constructed a series of Colombian exports and imports from 1845 to 1909 using as the source the foreign trade statistics reported by Colombia's main trading partners (McGreevey, 1971). The reason for that was that, apparently, the quality of the Colombian data was not very good because of the presence of contraband, among other things.
11 For a discussion of the economic ideas of Celso Furtado, see Love (1996).

Bibliography

Acemoglu, D., García-Jimeno, C., & Robinson, J.A. (2012). Finding Eldorado: Slavery and Long-Run Development in Colombia. *Journal of Comparative Economics*, 40(4), 534–564.
Beyer, R. C. (1966). "Book Review of *Economía y cultura en la historia de Colombia*. 2d. ed. By Nieto Arteta, Luis Eduardo Ediciones Tercer Mundo", *The Hispanic American Historical Review*, 46(1), 115–116.
Bordo, M. D., & Cortés-Conde, R. (2001). *Transferring Wealth and Power from the Old to the New World: Monetary and Fiscal Institutions in the 17th through the 19th Centuries*. Cambridge University Press.
Caro, M.A. (1958). *Escritos Sobre Cuestiones Económicas*. Impr. del Banco de la República.
Cataño, G. (2013). *La introducción del pensamiento moderno en Colombia, El caso de Luis E. Nietow Arteta*, Universidad Externado de Colombia.
Christie, K. H. (1978). Antioqueño Colonization in Western Colombia: A Reappraisal. *Hispanic American Historical Review*, 5(2), 260–283.
Fergusson, L., Molina, C., Robinson, J., & Vargas, J.F. (2017). The Long Shadow of the Past: Political Economy of Regional Inequality in Colombia. *Documento CEDE* 2017-22, Universidad de los Andes, Facultad de Economía, CEDE.

Furtado, C. (1971). *The Economic Growth of Brazil: A Survey from Colonial to Modern Times*. The University of California.

Hagen, E. (1963). *El cambio social en Colombia: el factor humano en el gesarrollo económico* (vol. 1). Ediciones Tercer Mundo.

Instituto de Estudios Colombianos. (1979). *Historia economica de Colombia, Un debate en marcha*. Banco Popular.

Jaramillo, J., Meisel-Roca, A., & Urrutia-Montoya, M. (1997). Continuities and Discontinuities in the Fiscal and Monetary Institutions of New Granada 1783–1850. *Borradores de Economía*, 74, pp. 283–330.

Jaramillo, R. L., & Meisel, A. (2010). Mas álla de la retorica de la reacción, analisis económico de la desamortización en Colombia, 1861–1888. In: A. Meisel & M. T. Ramírez (eds), *Economia colombiana del Siglo XIX*. FCE-Banco de la República.

Jaramillo Uribe, J. (1942). Reseña de economia y cultura en la historia de Colombia. *Educación*, 4: 450.

Klein, H.S. (1998). *The American Finances of the Spanish Empire: Royal Income and Expenditures*. The University of New Mexico.

López Toro, A. (1970). *Migración y cambio social en Antioquia durante El siglo diez y nueve*. CEDE: Universidad de los Andes.

Love, J.L. (1996). *Crafting the Third World: Theorizing Underdevelopment in Romania and Brazil*. Stanford University Press.

McGreevey, W. P. (1971). *An Economic History of Colombia 1845–1930*. Cambridge University Press Cambridge.

McGreevey, W. P. (2015). *Historia económica de Colombia, 1845–1930*. Ediciones Uniandes-Universidad de los Andes.

Meisel, A. (1992). Luis Eduardo Nieto Arteta: la soledad de la inteligencia. *Huellas*, 34, 5–12.

Meisel, A. (2015). Reformas borbónicas y presión fiscal, 1761–1800. In: Meisel, A. & Ramírez, M.T. (eds), *La economía colonial de la Nueva Granada*. FCE-Banco de la Republica.

Meisel, A., & López, A. (1990). Papel moneda, tasas de interés y revaluación durante la Regeneración. In: A. Meisel-Roca, F. J. Ortega-Acosta, J. E. Ibáñez-Nájar, A. López, H. J. Gómez Restrepo, & M. Lombo-Vanegas (eds), *El Banco de la República: antecedentes, evolución y estructura*. Banco de la República.

Melo, J. O. (1982). Comentarios. In: Simposio Los Estudios Regionales en Colombia, el CAso de Antioquia & FAES (Foundation: Antioquia Colombia). *Memoria del Simposio Los Estudios Regionales en Colombia, el Caso de Antioquia: realizado en Medellin del 6 a 11 de agosto de 1979*. Fondo Rotatorio de Publicaciones FAES.

Nieto Arteta, L.E. (1996). *Economia y cultura en la historia de Colombia* (8th ed). Banco de la República, El Ancora.

Ocampo, J.A. (2013). *Colombia y la economía mundial 1830–1910*. Ediciones Uniandes-Universidad de los Andes.

Ospina, L. (1974). *Industria y protección en Colombia 1810–1930*. Editorial Oveja Negra.

Ospina Vásquez, L. (2019). *Industria y protección en Colombia, 1810–1930*. Ediciones Uniandes-Universidad de los Andes.

Ossa, H., Aquino, J., Pereira, R., Ibarra, A., Ossa, R. H., Pérez, L. A., Granda, J. D., Lattig, M. C., Groot, H., Fagundes de Carvalho, E., & Gusmão, L. (2016). Outlining the Ancestry Landscape of Colombian Admixed Populations. *PloS one, 11*(10), e0164414. https://doi.org/10.1371/journal.pone.0164414

Parsons, J. J. (1997). *La Colonización Antioqueña en el Occidente de Colombia.* Banco de la República.

Safford, F. (1965). Significación de los antioqueños en el desarrollo económico colombiano: Un exámen crítico de las tesis de Everett Hagen. *Anuario colombiano de historia social y de la cultura*, 3, pp. 49–69.

Safford, F. (1978). Obituary. Luis Ospina Vasquez. *Hispanic American Historical Review*, *58*(3), pp. 466–467.

Tovar Pinzón, H. (1999). *El Imperio y sus colonias, las Cajas Reales de la Nueva Granada en el Siglo XVI.* Archivo General de la Nación.

Twinam, A. (1985). *Mineros, comerciantes y labradores: las raíces del espíritu empresarial en Antioquia: 1763–1810* (vol. 6). Fondo Rotatorio de Publicaciones FAES.

Umaña, A. (1979). Problemas estadísticos en el análisis del periodo Liberal, 1845–1885. In: Instituto de Estudios Colombianos (ed.), *Historia económica de Colombia, un debate en marcha.* Banco Popular.

11 Towards the Professionalization of Economics in Colombia 1934–1990

A Crossroads of Different Paradigms

Salomón Kalmanovitz

11.1 Introduction

Economics is a diverse discipline. According to Khun's classification, it is not a "mature science" precisely because several conflicting paradigms orient it. This coexistence of orientations (Katouzian, 1980) presents a heterogeneous scenario that is expressed similarly when the discipline develops within different countries. In the case of Colombia, the development of academic production in economics is late compared to the corpus that constitutes economics in Anglo-Saxon countries. However, the distance is relatively smaller in relation to Europe. The modernization the country underwent during the 1930s allowed an important advance in literary and journalistic language, in the consolidation of engineering and the dissemination of the natural sciences. However, the social sciences – which had been developing for over one hundred years in the West – would not start flourishing until the 1960s in Colombia. Nevertheless, some individual works produced in the early period served as the basis for the attempts to institutionalize economics in universities and the public sector. In this chapter, I seek to explore the consolidation of the professionalization of academic production in economics in Colombia, beginning with an analysis of pioneering and solitary authors up to the formation of the main academic centers.

Attempts to institutionalize the teaching of economics began in the country, in both the private and public universities, after 1945. In both cases, there were difficulties in achieving an academically prepared faculty and in establishing a curriculum that would develop good professionals and researchers. The latter was only achieved, in part, in the last four decades of the 20th century.

The difficulties of institutionalizing economics in Colombia should not come as a surprise. The profession is conceived as a remedy for underdevelopment or as a way of moving from the disorder of informality and clientelism to the planning of all variables; it also confuses the very nature of the task with that of the business administrator and the accountant. The existence of a very precarious prior tradition in the practice of analysis, limited economic literature, and the fact that those involved in its institutionalization were not able to

DOI: 10.4324/9781003289241-13

continue or deepen it led to a system that hybridized the three professions. However, it did not develop the skills of socioeconomic analysis in students because it did not train them in social sciences or humanities (Currie, 1968). This initial orientation would be corrected in the 1970s and more rapidly in private universities than in public ones; it only spread to the entire university system – which followed the guidelines of the leading universities – in the 1990s.

The same political path that the country went through from 1945 onwards – especially the conflict known as *La Violencia* – explains why the discipline was developed based on the most immediate interests of businesspeople, without recognizing that the required personnel should be cultivated and have the liberal philosophical bases to become a researcher or an analyst. The truth is that economics taught in universities during the 1950s lacked theory and applied studies. The latter was developed outside the academy, in government agencies and in some guilds.

Institutionalization was driven, in turn, by what has been defined as "social demand". This demand pushed initially for the practical exercise of the profession, and later required that its conceptual bases also be developed within the country (Vasco, 1983). In the case of economics, pressure on the education system came from international credit agencies that required good analyses of macroeconomic variables that the national government should know and negotiate. This 1960s development led many Colombian students to enroll in graduate programs in the United States and England. Upon their return, they reorganized economics studies within the most important universities in the country. Before that, there were focused demands from the National Bank, the General Comptroller of the Republic, and the Banking Superintendence, but they were supplied by law school graduates trained in daily practice.

The early forms of academic analysis of economic problems in Colombia show an important influence of heterodox currents and a close relationship with developments in other social sciences. This chapter will show how Marxism and *Cepalino* structuralism were influential during the years before the establishment of academic institutions formally dedicated to economic analysis. It further explains how academic production in economics in Colombia had an exploratory beginning contrary to developments elsewhere in the world and a late but accelerated convergence towards the dominant paradigms from the 1970s. However, this convergence did not occur through a theoretical intellectual production but rather through the adoption of empirical methods and analytical approaches typical of the discipline's mainstream.

In addition to this introduction, the essay consists of the following sections: *La Revolución en Marcha* (The Revolution in Motion) (1934–1942) and Economics; The Beginnings of the Institutionalization of Economics (1945–1953); The Consolidation of Applied Economics and Macroeconomic Policy (1950–1970); The Development of Economics in the 1970s and 1980s; and a Conclusion or Synthesis.

11.2 *La Revolución en Marcha* (The Revolution in Motion) and Economics: 1934–1942

The reforms undertaken by the López Pumarejo administration between 1934 and 1936 profoundly shaped the country's life in all areas of activity, including social thought and education. The great demands on the progressive intelligentsia of that time imposed by the transformations attempted in the agricultural and social fields contributed to the formation of prominent figures in economics. Carlos Lleras Restrepo, Antonio García, Luis Eduardo Nieto Arteta, Antonio José Restrepo, and Antonio Montaña Cuellar all faced the intellectual challenges of these intense years, gaining their legacy from predecessors such as Esteban Jaramillo, Guillermo Torres García, and Alejandro López.

A crucial institutional precedent is found in the foundation of the Escuela Normal Superior in 1936, which was the incubator not only of social sciences and ethnology but also of a scientific attitude that profoundly influenced the development of a liberal pedagogy in the country and especially of the first quests for an interpretation of the reality of Colombia. Here Antonio García began teaching, and Rudolf Hommes – brought from the Karl Marx Institute in Berlin – taught political economy perhaps for the first time in the country's history. Its graduates include Darío Mesa (promoter of sociology), Jaime Jaramillo Uribe (father of the so-called "new history"), and Virginia Gutiérrez (promoter of anthropology). Among the teachers, Antonio García was in charge in 1945 of founding the Institute of Economic Sciences, associated with the Faculty of Law of the National University of Colombia, where he would rely on several Spanish emigrants to train economists in Colombia (Ospina, 1984).

Gerardo Molina recreates the academic and intellectual atmosphere of the time in his prologue to the second edition of Torres García's book (in Torres García, 1980, p: ii):

It must remain to our credit that the very few works and essays published on the Colombian reality were greeted by us with joy and quickly assimilated, which was the best demonstration of our appetite. I still remember the impact produced on us by two books by Alejandro López *Problemas colombianos* [Colombian issues] and another on *El trabajo* [Labor], which appeared during that period. Alfonso López Pumarejo's speeches, conferences, and messages had the same sense of fruitful discovery, which was a kind of journey into the interior of our collective existence, with the elucidation of the economic issues that affected it as a compass.

This was so because, at the public level, basic questions about the economic and constitutional future of the Republic, which until then had been taken for granted, were being elucidated. The free play of the market was opposed to the intervention of the State in exchange rate control and in declaring the default of a large part of the debts contracted before the Great Depression, facts that had to be constitutionally justified.

La Revolución en Marcha (The Revolution in Motion) of President López Pumarejo stirred up ideas and promoted individual work as well as substantial institutional change. At that time, according to Antonio García, "it became necessary to carry out the first social-scientific diagnoses of Colombian society and to literally create a new instrument of analysis and a modern and structured institutional apparatus for research, measurement, and recording of economic and social phenomena" (García, 1987, p: vii).

11.3 The Beginnings of the Institutionalization of Economic Practice

At that time, the Comptroller's Office oversaw this mission under the direction of Carlos Lleras Restrepo, who would initiate census studies in 1938 and household consumption studies based on contemporary techniques. An industry census was also done in 1945. According to the information gathered, key steps were taken to develop a modern statistical system.

Luis Vidales emphasizes the importance of the organizational decisions taken during this phase in his book *History of Statistics in Colombia*:

> The measures taken at that time gave this branch the central guidelines it has today, and this includes the centralization of the systematization work in the Comptroller's Office, the installation of collecting stations in all the country's departments and municipalities, the obligation to report the figures requested to citizens and businesses, and the principle of "statistical reserve" that protects that information from being used by the treasury, customs or the police.
>
> (Vidales, 1978, p. 129)

The Comptroller's Office regularly published the *Anuario General de Estadística* and the magazine *Anales de Economía y Estadística*, which changed its name to *Economía y Estadística* and later became the *Boletín Mensual de Estadística* with the creation of the DANE (National Administrative Department of Statistics) in 1951. In 1938, Carlos Lleras Restrepo's book *National Statistics: its Organization, its Problems* established the new organizational norms given to the systematization of Colombia's economic and social statistics and their importance for understanding the limits of the state's economic policy.

Although the National Bank had taken office in 1923, its statistical bureau was only organized in 1928 on the advice of a German technician. It began to publish its monthly journal a little earlier. Monetary, financial, foreign trade and exchange rate statistics were concisely presented, and there was little analysis of them. It was not until 1945 that the bureau was elevated in status and renamed Economic Research. Ten years later, it began to publish *Cuentas Nacionales*, an instrument without which it is difficult to obtain an integrated macroeconomic vision of the country's productive and commercial activities.

11.4 The Pioneering Paths of Heterodoxies: The Influence of Structuralism, Marxism, and German Historicism

In the 1940s, Colombia had the minimal bases of the different schools of economics into which the universal panorama was divided. Followers of the classical and neoclassical schools expanded their principles. However, the critical tendencies of the German historical school (List, Schmoller) – which had already been spread as early as 1919 by José Antonio Restrepo in *Modern Imperalism* – and those of Marxism – in the work of Luis Eduardo Nieto Arteta and the intellectuals of the Communist Party – developed more intensely.

The influence of the German historical school was important in all regions of late capitalist development, as it constituted an ideological basis for adopting strategies of forced and conscious economic development. Indeed, Gustav Schmoller, Adolf Wagner, and Friedrich List developed theoretical frameworks as a critique of the foundations of classical liberal theory and its applications to international trade. According to them, the state had to practice a policy of industrialization, making credit and taxation policies conducive to the consolidation of industrial and financial monopolies that would better defend themselves in international competition.

The historical school had a significant influence on the Meiji restoration in Japan (Ito, 1980, p. 13). However, while the rising empire imposed itself from 1882 onwards, orienting the industrializing policy and corporativism, it would emerge only weakly in the 1920s in a country like Colombia. The school became halfway institutionalized with Antonio García's efforts in 1945 and influenced Jorge Eliecer Gaitán's political program. García was dismissed from the National University in 1949, but the historical school found a late follower in Rojas Pinilla when his fall had already been announced.

11.4.1 García Nossa and the Structuralist Perspective

Antonio Garcia was the founder in 1945 of the Institute of Economic Sciences, which was attached to the Faculty of Law of the National University. The Institute served as the basis for the Faculty of Economics, organized by a conservative administration in 1951. García was commissioned by the Comptroller's Office in 1936 to prepare the *Geografía económica de Caldas*, published the following year. This book constituted a rupture with the dominant intellectual milieu in Colombia since it was based on fieldwork, using all available statistics. Until then, there was a very limited pragmatic tradition in the country of explaining social problems beyond factors of a supposedly humanistic (López de Mesa), racial (Laureano Gómez), or constitutional nature. García vindicated the work of the colonizing mass that left Antioquia; he ventured into the fields of demography, history, production, productivity, the freedom of producers, and the distribution of land and income, for which he resorted to the concept of class.

In 1938 García published in Quito his *Outline of the Colombian Economy*, where he states that pre-capitalism institutions constitute obstacles to development, pointing out, in particular, the indigenous and agrarian issues. At the Escuela Normal, he developed his lecture notes, which he expanded at the Institute of Economic Sciences to give birth to his book *Basis of Contemporary Economics* in 1948.

The founding of the Institute went through many difficulties, including the reluctance of President Alfonso López Pumarejo, who, being a banker, asked García if there were not enough financiers in the country trained in the school of life to make it unnecessary to produce economists. Once the Institute was up and running, it was attacked by the conservative press, and even the liberal press was unsympathetic to what the Institute was working on. *Semana* magazine commented in 1951, when García was in exile, that the new school

> ... was initiated under the Marxist influence that then dominated the National University. Its directors, more politicians than men of science, initiated the students in the "superstructure and infrastructure" of *Das Kapital* with almost absolute disregard for the economic theory of the classic founders of the science.
>
> (Vallejo, 1984)

However, García did not rely so much on Marxism but on the organicism of the German historical school, which was critical of classical economics. Marx, on the contrary, considered himself within the Anglo-Saxon tradition and mocked List in the *Critical History of Surplus Value*. It is perhaps one of García's weaknesses that, in relying on these nationalist theories, he abandoned the abstract and universal conceptual apparatus of classical theory and the "toolbox" of neoclassical microeconomics. There is haste in the analysis to derive protection policies, the strengthening of public intervention, and the corporate apparatuses of workers and small producers (cooperatives) to counteract the corporations and guilds of capitalists and bankers.

The organic conception underlying García's work concerns the harmony that capitalism develops within the economic body it invades. Thus, in his analysis of Colombia, García defines it as

> a "sub-capitalist country" because it does not have a "homogeneous capitalist culture" [...]. In a culturally sub-capitalist country, if the economy is an archipelago of isolated economic forms, can the State be a unitary enterprise with the capacity to give the nation an organicity and a system?
>
> (García, 1948, p. 487)

Hence, García is also one of the founders of the Latin American theory of dependency that would later be radically developed in the works of André Gunder Frank, Theotonio Dos Santos, and Mario Anubla. The difference between the theory's origins, which García deduces from German organicism and the dependency paradigm, can be found in the resort to Keynesianism applied to Latin America by Prebisch and ECLAC. They later radicalized and combined Marxist and Leninist elements in the dependency theory. García studies Keynes with interest in the development of the conception of state intervention and war economy but rejects his theoretical method of partial equilibrium and macroeconomic relations. "Keynes is the orthodox economist of monopoly capitalism, whose fundamental problem is that of full employment" (García, 1948, p. 479).

For García, war economy and planning are central concerns, as they are pathways to overcome economic backwardness and political autocracy. His experience with civil populism such as that of Gaitán, for whose platform he elaborated fundamental points presented at the infamous 1945 Colón Theater speech, led him to understand the difficulties of successful movements that do not have access to weapons. The experience of Perón in Argentina, Rojas Pinilla in Colombia, and military populism, in general, made him try to ensure that his conceptions were put into practice by this type of movement.

11.4.2 *Marxism and economic history*

In 1942, Luis Eduardo Nieto Arteta published the work *Economy and Culture in Colombian History*, which had a notable influence in opening a new perspective for the development of the social sciences in the country. Nieto continued the work of Alejandro López, published at the end of the 1920s, which had already made a critical assessment of the pre-capitalist forms bequeathed by Spanish colonization and how they constituted a burden for the economic and political progress of the Colombian nation. Unlike those who made an argument for national history and claimed that national unity was the legacy of independence and Santanderism (i.e., that there were public liberties and equality among Colombian men from that moment on), these authors pointed out the marked differences in the regional development of the country as a result of the symbiosis between Spanish settlers and indigenous people, and also how capitalist development was more elusive in some regions than in others (Jaramillo Agudelo, 1976). They affirmed that national unity is yet to be achieved. This process depended on obtaining the rights of peasants, indigenous peoples, workers, and artisans and on agrarian and political reforms that fulfill the promise capitalism carries within its structure: equality of men before the law.

11.5 Consolidation of Economics in Higher Education

With the founding of the Institute of Economic Sciences, the economist career in public universities began. It had a full-time faculty that included several Spanish emigrants, who established a vital dynamic of discussing the economic problems that beset the country. The Institute published a journal, *Cuadernos de Economía Colombiana*, which died out when the Institute was purged by the conservative administration and became the Faculty of Economics of the National University in 1951.

From that moment on, the basic orientation of the curriculum changed: pure economics was no longer studied, and finance, accounting, and business administration appeared as subjects specific to the training of economists. In addition, a considerable part of the program was devoted to the study of law, probably because the teachers were primarily lawyers and exercised their academic functions on a part-time basis. The research effort that García had led was lost and for many years there were no economists but rather professional hybrids: administrator, accountant, lawyer-economist.

In 1944 a School of Economic Sciences was created at Antioquia University, and began to operate the following year, also attached to the Law School. Economics managed to establish itself independently in 1946, and José Eduardo Cárdenas Nanetti, who had had valuable experience at the Institute of Economic Sciences of the National University and is considered to be the leading mentor in Antioquia, was appointed as Director in 1947. The curriculum had 31 subjects taught annually, of which only 29% were dedicated to economics, 16% to mathematics and statistics, 16% to law, 13% to administration, 13% to accounting, and the remaining 13% to English (Posada, 1984). In 1954 the school began publishing its *Revista de Ciencias Económicas*, which lasted until 1965. It mainly published graduate theses and lectures from renowned economists invited to the faculty, such as Wilbur T. Meek, from the Louisiana Polytechnic Institute, and Luis Ospina Vásquez, who lectured on planning and management in 1958.

On the private university side, the first faculty of economics was founded in 1948 at Los Andes University. It was a response to the attempts of the Gimnasio Moderno school to set up studies in industrial economics, a combination of engineering and business administration, far from teaching and developing a theoretical science. However, it served as the basis for a curriculum with a sufficient load of applied mathematics and statistics to facilitate the take-off of economics as such.

It can be deduced from these first attempts at institutionalization that there was little understanding of the training needs of economists and researchers. The discipline was not conceived as a social science that requires the support of humanistic subjects and the development of a capacity to theorize; rather, it was understood as derived from law but with a somewhat more technical character provided by administration and accounting. It was also thought that research abilities are achieved through a graduate thesis after four or five years of studies, during which this aptitude has been minimally developed. In addition, the faculty was part-time and did not have a pool of research or the time and resources to carry it out.

11.6 The Consolidation of an Applied Economy and the Development of Macroeconomic Policies

During the 1950s, the social demand for economics had a considerable dragging effect on the development of applied analysis. Three major projects organized from outside the country were vital for the institutionalization of economics from the macroeconomic analysis point of view: the IBRD or World Bank mission, led by Lauchlin Currie in 1949, which made an assessment of the country's creditworthiness and analyzed several major investment projects (IBRD, 1951); the mission headed by Father Lebret, which obtained fewer results but made substantial demographic and regional balances (Lebret, 1958); and, finally, an ECLAC mission that came to set up the national accounts and, for this purpose, made an estimate of the macroeconomic variables of the national produce from 1923 to 1950, and established the statistics of continuous collection that still make up the national accounting system today (ECLAC, 1957).

The significance of the Currie mission goes beyond his comprehensive diagnosis of the development state of the nation. The Canadian advisor settled in the country, proposed the creation of the National Planning Department – which was finally organized in 1959 – and made important studies on agriculture and railroad transportation. Currie also proposed an ambitious employment plan, the so-called *Operación Colombia* (Operation Colombia), which aroused much controversy in the 1960s, and a balance of the teaching of economics and social sciences in the country. As director of the Economics Department of the National University in 1968, he gained the opportunity to reform the way these sciences were taught. He attracted foreign professors and sent many graduates to postgraduate studies abroad (Currie, 1985).

11.6.1 Macroeconomic Stabilization Policies and the Keynesianism of the Synthesis

Currie's analysis of the Colombian economy in *Basis of a Development Program for Colombia* is a vision of Keynesian macroeconomics applied to development problems. Currie was a forerunner of Keynesianism when he was an advisor to President Roosevelt and justified significant public investments to emerge from the Great Depression. Currie found that in Colombia, there were obstacles to capital accumulation that could not be removed without the careful intervention of state action. In this first attempt at planning, goals were only set for constructing a transportation system, and the statistical basis for planning was improved. In Currie's words, the instruments available to him on his arrival in 1949 were minimal: "There was no series on the cost of living or on the means of payment, no demographic figures since 1938, almost nothing on production, and it was almost impossible to understand fiscal and monetary policies" (Currie, 1963).

Currie would insist in his *Operación Colombia*[1] that the problem of Colombian development was based on insufficient demand "… to allow the industry to achieve the economies of large-scale production. …" (Currie, 1963, p. 47).

The Lleras Camargo administration did not approve Currie's program because the country was committed to the slightly more ambitious Keynesian reformism promulgated by the Kennedy administration in its Alliance for

Progress, for which ECLAC acted as a continental advisor, and also because of the agrarian reform proposed as a response to the Cuban revolution in the continent. A new conservative administration in 1970 gave a new impetus to Currie's construction plans, which had a remarkable result in the financing of housing in Colombia.

Another economist who emigrated to Colombia during the 1950s was Albert Hirschman, who also left his mark on the public policy developed by the *Frente Nacional* (National Front) governments. Hirschman understood that agrarian reform was necessary to unleash economic progress in the country (Hirschman, 1973). Liberating the land market and turning the impoverished peasants working on eroded hillsides into productive farmers on better land in order to make them a middle class that would defend a democratic political system was fundamental to this reform. The strategy seemed viable because it divided the landowning class between those who had already devoted their property to commercial agriculture and dairy farming and those who kept their unproductive estates as a store of value. Hirschman criticized Currie's land tax proposal because it would unite the landowning class against him to thwart it. In his book *The Strategy of Economic Development*, Hirschman reconstructed the country's agrarian issue history.

11.6.2 Developmental Keynesianism: the ECLAC

From a methodological point of view, the differences between ECLAC's and Currie's Keynesian interpretation lie in the concept of equilibrium. While for the former, the underdeveloped economic system rested on a chronic point of structural disequilibrium, for Currie, the laws of general equilibrium operated, provided that the repressed forces of the markets, particularly the financial market, were allowed to be unleashed. In ECLAC's opinion, reforms to such structures were necessary and required increased state intervention in the agricultural, industrial, foreign trade, and fiscal fields. For Currie, on the other hand, it was enough to organize capital markets more adequately (raising the real interest rate to attract more resources) and expand private credit to obtain more far-reaching results.

However, according to ECLAC, there is a permanent imbalance in Latin American foreign trade, which is reflected in unfavorable exchange prices that show excess supply that is rarely eliminated. This leads, in Prebisch's version, to the fact that the productivity gains of the system end up being appropriated by the center while the periphery stagnates irremediably (Prebisch, 1969). Another structural imbalance prominent in ECLAC's theory resides in the agricultural sector, where backward social relations prevent productivity gains. This leads to permanent inflationary pressures that can only be overcome with comprehensive agrarian reforms. Then, inflation is not a monetary problem or a problem of financing with primary emission but of a backward agrarian structure, which would later be explained by the "redistributive struggle".

In 1960, the new National Planning Department was closely advised by ECLAC technicians, who, along with Jorge Méndez and Edgar Gutiérrez, prepared the first four-year plan. The plan was transformed into a ten-year plan due to pressure from the Kennedy administration to grant financing to the country. This plan established annual product growth targets of 5.6% so that per-capita growth remained at 2.6%, and by clearing the macroeconomic equation, they derived the required investment coefficients and added goals on import substitution. The analysis became sectoral later, but its degree of disaggregation was insufficient and did not establish the mechanisms that lead private entrepreneurs to undertake the magnitude of investments designed in a general and abstract way.

11.6.3 A Marginal Attempt at Dependency Theory Colombian Style

The development of the dependency theory in the country was outside the institutional framework. A group of intellectuals left the Communist Party in 1962 and started an occasional publication called *Estrategia*, the first three issues of which published Mario Arrubla's "Studies on Colombian underdevelopment". The group was composed of Estanislao Zuleta – who would produce an extensive work on history, psychoanalysis, and literary criticism – Marco Palacios, Alvaro Tirado, and Jorge Orlando Melo – who would later stand out as a professional historian. As small as the group was, it achieved a remarkable renewal of culture and social sciences in the following decades.

Arrubla has the merit of preceding the dependency theorists with theoretical arguments of greater depth, although his thoughts were only widely disseminated with the publication of his book in 1969. Before Gunder Frank and Dos Santos made international headlines, Arrubla had managed to raise the same problems of a stagnant economy that engulfed the continent's entire intellectual community during the 1960s. With the same basis as ECLAC, which was engaged in a conciliation with the Kennedy administration, dependency theory radicalized its conclusions and proposed that the cure for underdevelopment was not bourgeois reformism but a socialist revolution.

Arrubla's argument has the merit of having been developed in Colombia. He used Marx's reproduction schemes as a conceptual apparatus and found that the peripheral system is condemned to simple reproduction. He also found an internal market insufficient to absorb industrial production, which condemned the country to long-term stagnation (Arrubla, 1974). Arrubla's argument was well received among intellectuals who relied on this thinking to organize their vision of the country's economic and social development, and became a guiding paradigm for much social science research developed during the 1970s. However, the dependency paradigm quickly ran out of steam in the face of the new expansive directions the Colombian economy was taking during the same years and was questioned at national and Latin American levels. It was only superseded in the 1990s.

11.6.4 The Institutionalization of Economic Research

There was almost no progress in the institutionalization of economics during the 1950s, with the notable exception of the establishment of the DANE in 1951, which began to carry out samples of agricultural production in 1953 (Vidales, 1978, p. 43) and was responsible for the first Agricultural Census in 1960. Public and private universities had programs that could train business-people and middle managers, but they were far from producing technicians and researchers. Research was not developed to any great extent. Notable in-depth works appeared not because of organized work in teaching or research centers but rather for reasons like international training and personal work.

This situation changed substantially in the following decade as the National Planning Department (DNP) required qualified personnel to carry out a wide range of applied studies, and the Center for Economic Development Studies (CEDE) was organized at Los Andes University. The CEDE undertook analyses of unemployment for the first time in the country, using an extensive survey (CEDE, 1968), and developed demographic studies that analyzed the population censuses of 1938, 1951, and 1964. The work of Álvaro López Toro – an ingenious application of the Ricardian theory of land rent to the history of the colonization of Antioquia, which was made public in 1973 – also stands out (López Toro, 1973).

At Antioquia University, the Center for Economic Research (CIE) was organized in 1962, but its proliferation of research and publications would become more evident in the 1970s. The university's accounting program was created in 1963, reflecting more differentiation in the market and specialization in the economics curriculum (Posada, 1984).

In 1966 and 1967, Currie was engaged in making a diagnosis of higher education in social sciences and economics. At that time, he operated the Faculty of Sociology at the National University and greatly impacted opinion with his publications on violence in Colombia. His conclusion is bleak and reflects the conservative triumph in the civil war of 1946–1956 and then the accommodation of liberalism to the two-party regime established in 1957. The Faculty of Economics was a fiefdom of one of the factions of conservatism, but the modernizing administration of Félix Patiño in the National University attached it to the Faculty of Human Sciences so that Currie could carry out his reform. The Development Research Center (CID) was founded in 1968. With visiting professors like Albert Berry and Miguel Urrutia – who taught in the Anglo-Saxon tradition in the now Department of Economics – the CID undertook a research series on urbanism, history, and economics. A good number of graduates were sent abroad for postgraduate studies, and it was they who, in the following decade, vigorously promoted research at the DNP, DANE, and in the National University itself. They also supported the curricular reforms at Valle University and the Pedagogical University of Tunja.

The Foundation for Higher Education and Development (Fedesarrollo), a private foundation whose board of directors includes representatives of the business and financial world, was established at the end of the 1960s. This foundation gave a considerable turn to economic research in Colombia, and gave a neoclassical orientation to the study and teaching of economics. Its researchers were engineers who had graduated from Los Andes University and undertaken postgraduate studies in economics at North American universities. Fedesarrollo considerably modified the economic science situation in the country during the following decade.

11.7 The Development of Economics in the 1970s and 1980s

The economic literature in Colombia has seen significant development since the 1970s. Regarding currents, critical literature on dependency and Marxism developed rapidly at the beginning of the decade. There was research on the agrarian issue, published from 1974 onwards, derived from the political interest awakened within academia by the great peasant mobilizations of 1971 and 1972. There was also a debate on the coherence of dependency, with a current emerging that criticized it and tried consolidating Marxist fundamentalism. Large-scale research production began which by the end of the decade had consolidated the hegemonic position of the CEDE and Fedesarrollo in economic studies.

From 1975, a monetary sub-current also emerged strongly, generating copious literature through the Banking Association and its annual symposiums on the capital market in Colombia. Other orientations emerged, such as Kaleckian macroeconomics, neo-Keynesianism, Keynesian fundamentalism, and neo-Ricardianism, but these were developments of the 1980s. Dependency theory faded away, and critical currents were generally extinguished.

11.7.1 Academic Marxism and Economics at its Frontiers

At the beginning of the 1970s, the country underwent intense political processes manifested in the peasant struggles, the student movement, and the development of independent currents within the trade union movement. Periodical publications multiplied, and political problems were discussed based on Marxism inherited from the past (the work of Nieto Arteta and Hernández Rodríguez began to circulate again). However, it was also nourished by new French influences – particularly the works of Althusser and Poulantzas – and Anglo-Saxon influence –with the school of Paul Sweezy, Paul Barán, and André Gunder Frank. Maoist currents were expressed through the publishing house La Pulga and the magazines *Ruptura* and *Uno en dos*, Trotskyist currents with the publishing houses La Oveja Negra and La Carreta and the magazines *Ideología y Sociedad* and *Teoría y Práctica*, and less radical points of view in *Cuadernos Colombianos*. The Communist Party revived its *Estudios Marxistas* but had nothing new to offer.

Anteo Quimbaya's book, *The Land Issue in Colombia* (Quimbaya, 1967), appeared in 1967, but it was no more than a description of the 1960 Agricultural Census. It offered a reduced perspective compared to the theoretical and applied discussions of the agrarian problem based on the sophisticated elaboration of Marx's rent theory carried on by the other political groups. It also seemed reduced compared to more flexible analyses of agricultural statistics.

Orlando Fals Borda organized an "action research" group called La Rosca, mainly dedicated to studying the agrarian issue on the Atlantic coast. It tried to recover the history of the peasants while contributing to their organization. This exercise produced *The History of the Agrarian Issue in Colombia* and Fals Borda's tetralogy *Dual History of the Coast*, which the author finished in 1986 (Fals-Borda, 1980, 1981, 1984 and 1986).

A seminar on Colombian studies, Seprocol, was organized at the DANE in 1970. Essential studies on industrialization and industrial structure (Misas & Corchuelo, 1973, 1980), rural development and agrarian structure (Kalmanovitz, 1974), and documentary and petroleum history (Villegas, 1975) emerged.

Dependency theory was widely disseminated. Arrubla's work was republished 14 times between 1969 and 1975 and had followers at the CIE, from the Antioquia University (CIE, 1973) and the National University – although after 1975, since in 1972 many of the professors who participated in the political debates were dismissed and were reinstated only after 1975. However, there were no substantial contributions from those who defended the dependency position; they were only nourished by the international currents that had developed similar positions in Latin America, the United States, and Europe (Bejarano, 1974).

In 1971, "A propósito de Arrubla" (Kalmanovitz, 1974) appeared in mimeograph. There, the theoretical premises of dependency theory were questioned, and an empirical demonstration that capitalism had developed rapidly in the country was made. The simple reproduction schemes used by Arrubla were replaced by reproduction on an expanded scale, and the conditions under which capital accumulation was slowed down or accelerated were specified more clearly by criticizing the starting point that assumed a simple type of reproduction. The text also included a theory of the transition from feudalism to capitalism and an interpretation of the Colombian transformation. Finally, emphasis was laid on the need to analyze the internal dynamics of societies and their productive and social conformation before assuming a priori that imperialism was overdetermining their movement.

These are the beginnings of more extensive works that were published in the 1980s: *The Late Development of Capitalism* (1983) and *Economy and Nation: A Brief History of Colombia* (1985). During this period, other criticisms of the dependency position were added (Lima, 1974; Bejarano, 1974b) and its role as a guiding paradigm for studies was fleeting. In truth, this position never had a foundation differentiated from other currents of thought, which allowed some to combine an Arrublian position with another that explicitly relied on Lauchlin Currie (Bejarano, 1974a). In this phase, a newly cultured reading public was avidly receiving economics and politics publications, even the significant proportion that showed no rigor. However, the public began to demand better quality, and classified authors according to their conceptual rigor, whether they worked based on primary sources and whether they displayed originality in their approaches. In the following decade, the previous political mobilization declined, and magazines and publishing houses were disappearing. A good many of the intellectuals who militated or sympathized with the radical political movements joined different sectors of the liberal party or took refuge in academic cloisters.

11.7.2 From Synthesis Keynesianism to Monetarist Orthodoxy

The country's neoclassical literature base is Fedesarrollo, since it not only published its quarterly journal of analysis of the economic situation but also produced research of the most varied types: studies on the capital market, planning and income distribution, international trade, project evaluation, quantitative history, natural resources, ecology, employment, and applied macroeconomics. Its connections with the North American academic world have been substantial. Through those connections, Albert Berry, Robert Slighton, Richard Nelson, T. Paul Schultz, Richard Slitor, David Morawetz, Lance Taylor, and Carlos Díaz Alejandro worked in the country.

Two of Fedesarrollo's directors, Rodrigo Botero and Roberto Junguito, served in the Ministry of Finance, and a third, Miguel Urrutia, was head of National Planning and Minister of Mines. The circulation of its magazine *Coyuntura Económica* was restricted. However, it was read by the country's highest public and private power echelons, and its editorials were reproduced in the press whenever they appeared. Several of its publications attempted to reach university audiences, such as *Readings on Colombian Economic Development* (1978), *Essays on Colombian Economic History* (1980), and a series of books on Colombian macroeconomics – collections that disseminated econometric methodologies and quantitative history. Its influence on economic policy has been substantial, even though the institution has changed its team on more than one occasion, and its orientation has been transformed, especially from 1982 onwards.

From the beginning, Fedesarrollo criticized the policies of protection and low interest rates that had been recommended and justified by ECLAC to force industrialization. Fedesarrollo stated that Colombian industrial development had been inefficient and that the lack of competitiveness of national production in international markets was due to a deficient allocation of foreign currency and credit, both granted by administrative mechanisms of political rather than market selection. The effective protection received by the industry was analyzed, and an attempt was made to establish which branches had special advantages in foreign trade, which mechanisms hindered exports, and how much industrial installed capacity was used. Fedesarrollo's researchers wondered if the whole system would not work better with a complete re-establishment of the capital market.

Monetarism, as the extreme wing of the neoclassical school, played a fundamental role in the new orientations. For this purpose, Edward Shaw and Ronald McKinnon were invited to the country in 1970 and 1974, respectively. Both defended the idea of deepening financial intermediation to allocate credit more efficiently to leverage investments, which should increase the economy's savings rate. The combination of financial freedom and external liberation should lead the country to emulate the success of the Asian countries known in Anglo-Saxon jargon as NICs (newly industrialized countries): South Korea, Taiwan, Hong Kong, and Singapore. This goal was not possible because of the enormous differences between their institutions and those of Colombia.

The national impulse towards monetarism came from the Banking Association. From 1970 onwards, it organized frequent seminars on the capital market in Colombia, filling several volumes on the national financial intermediation system and proposing to radically liberalize it (National Bank & Banking Association of Colombia, 1971–1974; Cabrera, 1980).

11.7.3 Neo-Structuralist Resistance

The insistence on monetarism did not come so much from Fedesarrollo, because many of its technicians were convinced that the country could not do without a good dose of state intervention to monitor the distribution of income (Perry, 1978) or manipulate effective demand (Ocampo & Cabrera, 1980). Moreover, from 1982 onwards, Fedesarrollo was homogenized by what we could call "neo-structuralism", which – influenced by Professor Lance Taylor of MIT – took up some of ECLAC's positions on structural rigidities and demonstrated them by resorting to mathematical economics and econometrics. The works of José Antonio Ocampo, Juan Luis Londoño, José Leibovich, Juan José Echavarría, and Leonardo Villar (Londoño, 1985; Bourgignon & Leibovich, 1984; Echavarría and Perry, 1980) were part of this trend. The trend also includes the post-Keynesian contributions of the Cambridge school (England), derived from the seed of Michal Kalecki's work, which served as a basis for the most radical policies of the European labor parties on income redistribution through higher taxation, inflation of demand and low interest rates.

The work of José Antonio Ocampo in this field can be considered the most outstanding and influential in the economics community. His analysis of the origins of inflation in Colombia contradicted the monetarist thesis, according to which price increases are due exclusively to excessive expansions of the monetary mass. On the contrary, Ocampo pointed out that the rigidities present in the agricultural sector and in the country's foreign trade were the fundamental causes of price instability (Ocampo & Cabrera, 1980).

Ocampo reacted to the dependency crisis by searching for substitutes for the simple hypotheses of ECLAC (Ocampo, 1982) in Keynesian theory and contemporary developments in mathematical economics. However, Ocampo shared ECLAC's strange notion of disequilibrium, embellished with the stability derived from the general equilibrium models that would be the ultimate computation of his conception. Thus, his analysis does not foresee the often violent adjustments with which market forces "balance" the processes of capitalist accumulation through crises or inflationary booms.

Another front that received a great impulse from neo-structuralism is economic history, with the two impeccable and meticulous works by Ocampo (the second in collaboration with Santiago Montenegro), *Colombia and the World Economy, 1830–1910* (1985) and *World Crisis, Protection and Industrialization* (1984) (Ocampo, 1984; Ocampo & Montenegro, 1984), which filled many gaps in the existing historiography and opened the way for further research.

Another institution that influenced the development of the currents we analyzed was the CEDE of Los Andes University. At the beginning of the 1970s, many of the later members of Fedesarrollo joined the Center and made contributions in the field of economic history, project evaluation, and planning. Later, Ricardo Chica made a Kaleckian study of the manufacturing industry, including its productive structure, prices, and financing. Ulpiano Ayala devoted himself to revealing the dynamics of the informal sector (Chica, 1981, 1982, 1983, 1984, 1985). Samuel Jaramillo studied urban land rent, both theoretical and applied to Bogotá (Jaramillo, 1981). Some detailed econometric studies carried out at CEDE proved in the long run that formal minutiae do not add much if the issues under investigation are obvious.

Among the other university centers, it is worth noting the CIE of Antioquia University, the Economics Department of the National University, which finally recreated the CID in 1985, and whose professors maintained the high-quality production that fed its *Cuadernos de Economía*, and the CIDSE of the Valle University, which maintained a good research pace.

More applied studies were developed within National Planning, which began publishing its *Revista de Planeación y Desarrollo* in 1969. The Regional Population Center developed an econometric model for the country in 1974 and is credited with important demographic studies. The Economic Research Department of the National Bank was also strengthened, and from 1984, it published the biannual journal *Ensayos de Política Económica*. The Office of the Comptroller General of the Republic was also transformed, and its free publication, *Economía Colombiana*, reached the widest circulation in the field.

The radical literature of the journals of the 1970s was replaced in the 1980s by university journals, including *Desarrollo y Sociedad* from CEDE, *Cuadernos de Economía* from the National University, and *Lecturas de Economía* from Antioquia University. This also reflected the high levels of economic teaching in the country.

The Colombian Society of Economists, created in 1957, had a minimal role in building economic literature. Most of its energies were devoted to gaining political support within the bipartisan system to protect its professional interests. In 1984, the Academy of Economic Sciences was established, which tried to reconcile its structure of professional interests with the community of "scientists"; however, the latter's response was half-hearted because the criteria for admission to the academy were not very strict.

11.7.4 *Transformations in the Teaching of Economics*

During the 1970s, the training of professional economists was more clearly separated from business administrators or similar professions. Management, accounting, and law courses were refined, more social sciences and humanities were introduced, and economic theory was taught in depth in its three basic aspects of classical, neoclassical, and Keynesian economics, using contemporary sources and literature (Méndez, 1985).

At Antioquia University, the program was changed in 1975 to prepare professional economists in the strict sense of the term (Posada, 1984). In 1977, the National and Andes programs were adopted as models to be followed in university education in the country. However, they faced legal limitations to demanding better teaching quality within private universities, particularly concerning night programs (ICFES, 1977). These limitations were overcome by the accreditation processes led by the Ministry of Education from the 1990s onwards.

This made the panorama of economics teaching in most of the higher education system deficient until the end of the 20th century, to the extent that public universities were weakened in comparison with private universities, especially with the proliferation of night faculties that contributed to diminishing the quality of the system (Melo, 1985).

The most important event of this period was the creation of graduate programs and the interest in training research professors dedicated to academia. The first graduate programs were created at Los Andes University in 1963 and the National University in 1980. While the graduate program at Los Andes maintained its neoclassical Keynesian orientation, with hints of other schools, the National University's program was based on post-Keynesianism, neo-Keynesianism, and contemporary Marxism. In 1982, a program of specialization in economic policy was created at Antioquia University, which produced good analysts of the current situation. The graduate programs created in the remaining universities reproduced the same problems as most of the undergraduate education in the country: lack of full-time professors with research and publications to their names, part-time students who needed to work, and deficient libraries.

Thus, during the last years of the 20th century, a hierarchy formed with an elite level of programs that registered remarkable progress. While many traditional private and religious universities are the most expansive sector and have maintained average quality, small private universities offering evening courses have contributed to a reduction in quality and the tendency of the system to produce too many graduates.

11.8 Conclusion

What we have described above constitutes, in essence, a process of adaptation of the various international economic currents to local conditions, which has undoubtedly been rapid and successful. Until the 1950s, most of the advice to governments on orienting their expenditures, their external and internal financing, and the social accounting required to frame such policies, depended on foreign experts. This situation began to be overcome during the 1960s and was reversed in the 1980s. For example, the aid programs from North American universities that the CEDE of Los Andes University had received were suspended at the beginning of the 1970s because it was considered that the center had come of age.

To what extent can it be said that there is continuity between the country's early developments of economic thought, from Alejandro López to García and Nieto Arteta, to Arrubla, to the Cepaline thought, to neo-structuralism and Anglo-Saxon Marxism? There seems to be a fundamental methodological rupture between contemporary and previous thinking, based on the absorption, in Anglo-Saxon teaching centers, of the classical as well as neoclassical and Keynesian conceptual apparatus that had been rejected or rigidly adopted by previous generations. Continuity persists around the questions asked by the early researchers and which more contemporary ones are still trying to answer: Why is the country lagging developed capitalist countries? Where does the irrationality of the national production system come from? Where does its arbitrariness come from? Expensive or cheap money? Greater or lesser state intervention?

Consequently, the differences between institutions in method and concepts slowly disappeared among the majority of economists (López 1984). Marginalist economic theory, general equilibrium models, matrix algebra, input-output tables, slightly more refined statistics, and econometrics have been adopted by mainstream economists, but also by neo-structuralists and post-Keynesians. However, some post-Keynesians and Marxists have developed ideas about systems finding equilibrium through unstable and often violent adjustments. The professionalization and the internationalization of economics was a rupture with the conceptual apparatus of those who introduced the German historical school into the country, and whose approaches lacked those concepts and working tools. Economics became a toolbox for policy and private decision making, a technical tool embraced by a large majority of scholars, think tanks and consulting firms.

Note

1 A detailed analysis of the influence of both Currie and the foreign expert missions in Colombia can be found in Chapter 8, this volume.

Bibliography

Arrubla, M. (1974). *Ensayos sobre el subdesarrollo colombiano* (8th ed.). Editorial La Carreta.

Bejarano, J. A. (1974a). Currie: Diagnóstico y estrategia. *Cuadernos Colombianos*, 1(3), pp. 407–434.

Bejarano, J. A. (1974b). Desarrollo clásico y desarrollo dependiente: la cuestión del mercado interno. *Cuadernos Colombianos*, 1.

Bourgignon, F. & Leibovich, J. (1984). Factores de oferta y demanda en el desarrollo. Un modelo agregado al desequilibrio aplicado a Colombia. *Cuadernos de Economía.*

Cabrera, M. (Ed.) (1980). *Inflación y política económica.* Asociación Bancaria de Colombia

CEDE. (1968). *Empleo y desempleo en Colombia.* Italgraf.

Chica, R. (1981). El empleo en las grandes ciudades colombianas. Working paper. *Documentos CEDE*, 65.

Chica, R. (1982). Una descripción de la evolución de la estructura industrial colombiana, 1958–1980. Working paper. *Documentos CEDE*, 70.

Chica, R. (1983). Una aproximación kaleckiana a la acumulación de capital. *Desarrollo y Sociedad*, 10, pp. 37–70.

Chica, R. (1984). El desarrollo industrial colombiano, 1958–1980. *Desarrollo y Sociedad*, 12, pp. 21–24.

Chica, R. (1985). La financiación de la inversión en la industria manufacturera colombiana, 1970–1980. *Desarrollo y Sociedad*, 15 & 16, pp. 193–285.

CIE (1973). *Contribución al estudio del desempleo en Colombia.* Universidad de Antioquia

Currie, L. (1963). *Ensayos sobre planeación.* Editorial Tercer Mundo.

Currie, L. (1968). *Desarrollo económico acelerado: la necesidad y los medios.* Fondo de Cultura Economica.

Currie, L. (1985). *Evaluación de la asesoría internacional en los países en desarrollo.* CEREC.

Echavarría, J. J. & Perry, G. (1980). Aranceles y subsidios a las exportaciones: análisis de su estructura sectorial y de su impacto sobre la apertura de la industria colombiana. *Coyuntura Económica 11*(2), 191–228.

ECLAC. (1957). El desarrollo económico de Colombia. http://hdl.handle.net/11362/9008

Fals Borda, O. (1980). *Mompox y Loba. Historia doble de la Costa (Tomo I).* Carlos Valencia Editor.

Fals Borda, O. (1981). *El presidente Nieto. Historia doble de la Costa* (Tomo II). Carlos Valencia Editor.

Fals Borda, O. (1984). *Resistencia en El San Jorge. Historia doble de la Costa* (Tomo III). Carlos Valencia Editor.

Fals Borda, O. (1986). *Retorno a la tierra. Historia doble de la Costa* (Tomo IV). Carlos Valencia Editor.

García, A. (1948). *Bases de la economía contemporánea.* Plaza y Janés.

García, A. (1987). *Geografía Económica de Caldas*, Banco de la República, Bogotá.

Hirschman, A. (1973). *La estrategia del desarrollo económico.* Fondo de Cultura Económica.

IBRD. (1951). *Bases de un programa de fomento para Colombia.* Banco de la República.

ICFES. (1977). *La enseñanza de la economía en Colombia.* Bogotá: ICFES.

Ito, M. (1980). *Value and Crisis.* NYU Press.

Jaramillo Agudelo, D. (1976). *La nueva historia de Colombia.* Colcultura.

Jaramillo, S. (1981). *Producción de vivienda y capitalismo dependiente: el caso de Bogotá.* CEDE.

Kalmanovitz, S. (1974). Crítica de una teoría de la dependencia: a propósito de Arrubla. *Ideología y Sociedad*, 10, pp. 50–90.

Katouzian, H. (1980). *Ideology and Method in Economics.* NYU Press.

Lebret, L. J. (1958). *Estudio sobre las condiciones de desarrollo de Colombia, Misión Economía y Humanismo.* Presidencia de la República.

Lima, E. (1974). El fetiche del sector I: crítica a la cuestión del mercado interno. *Ideología y Sociedad*, 10.

Londoño, J. L. (1985). *Ahorro y gasto en una economía heterogénea: el rol macroeconómico del mercado de alimentos*. Coyuntura Económica.

López, H. (1984). ¿Por qué la superproducción de administradores y economistas en Colombia? *Lecturas de Economía*, 15, pp. 77–102.

López Toro, A. (1973). *Análisis demográfico de los censos colombianos 1951–1964*. CEDE.

Melo, J. O. (1985). Crecimiento y expansión de la educación superior en Colombia: una feria de ilusiones. *Lecturas de Economíam*, 16, pp. 253–271.

Méndez, R. (1985). El Icfes y la formación de los economistas: una aproximación académica. *Lecturas de Economía*, 18.

Misas, G., & Corchuelo, A. (1973). Contribución al estudio del grado de concentración en la industria colombiana. *Boletín Mensual de Estadística*, 266, pp. 83–117.

Misas, G., & Corchuelo, A. (1980). Internacionalización del capital y ampliación del mercado interno colombiano. 1958–1974. *Lecturas de Economía*, 2, pp. 83–117.

Montenegro, S. (1984). El surgimiento de la industria textil en Colombia, 1900–1945. In J.A. Ocampo & S. Montenegro (Eds), *Crisis mundial, proteccionismo e industrialización: ensayos de historia económica, Bogotá*. CEREC, pp: 141–232.

National Bank & Banking Association of Colombia. (1971–1974). *El mercado de capitales en Colombia*, 4 volumes. Bogota.

Ocampo, J. A. (1982). De Keynes al análisis post-keynesiano. *Desarrollo y Sociedad*, 9, pp. 21–53.

Ocampo, J. A. (1984). *Colombia y el mercado mundial, 1830–1910*. Siglo Veintiuno Editores.

Ocampo, J. A., & Cabrera, M. (1980). Precios internacionales, tipo de cambio e inflación. In M. Cabrera (Ed.), *Inflación y política económica*. Asociación Bancaria de Colombia.

Ocampo, J. A. & Montenegro, S. (1984). *Crisis mundial, proteccionismo e industrialización: ensayos de historia económica, Bogotá*. CEREC.

Ospina, J. M. (1984). La Escuela Normal Superior: círculo que se cierra. *Boletín Cultural y Bibliográfico*, XXI(2), pp. 3–16.

Perry, G. (1978). Introducción al estudio de los planes de desarrollo en Colombia. In H. Gómez, & E. Wiesner Durán (Eds), *Desarrollo económico colombiano*. Fedesarrollo.

Posada, C. E. (1984). Los cuarenta años de la Facultad de Ciencias Económicas de la Universidad de Antioquia: apuntes sobre su primera época. *Lecturas de Economía*, 13, pp. 143–156.

Prebisch, R. (1969). Problemas teóricos y prácticos del crecimiento económico. In A. Bianchi (Ed.), *América Latina, ensayos de interpretación económica*. Editorial Universitaria.

Quimbaya, A. (1967). *El problema de la tierra en Colombia*. Ediciones Suramérica.

Torres García, G. (1980). *Historia de la moneda en Colombia*. FAES.

Vallejo, J. (1984). *Sobre la enseñanza de la economía*. Universidad del Valle.

Vasco, C. E. (1983). Historia social de las ciencias en América Latina, aportes conceptuales y metodológicos. *Ciencia, Tecnología y Desarrollo*, 7(3). pp. 303–313. Colciencias.

Vidales, L. (1978). *Historia de la estadística en Colombia*. Banco de la República, DANE.

Villegas, J. (1975). *Petróleo, oligarquía e imperio*. Tercer Mundo Editores.

12 100 Years of Economics on the Board of the Banco de la República

*Ricardo José Salas-Díaz**

12.1 Introduction

The Banco de la República began its operations on the morning of July 23, 1923. It was six months earlier than planned to avoid the contagion effect of a bank run. The early opening of the bank acting as a lender of last resort was not a unanimous decision. While Edwin Kemmerer saw benefits to this decision, Félix Salazar was reluctant (Meisel Roca, 1990a). In general, decisions in uncertain times do not follow consensus and are, to some degree, affected by the experiences of those who have taken them. There is evidence that personal traits, such as gender, the university in which a person studied, and previous experiences, such as exposure to high inflation or unemployment in youth, affect monetary policy decisions (Bordo & Istrefi, 2018; Masciandaro et al., 2018; Malmendier et al., 2021).

This chapter contributes to the analysis of economic ideas in Colombia by narrating the life histories of the board members of the Banco de la República. Understanding the trajectories of the individuals within a group will contribute to analyzing the evolution of this group's ideas. In addition, personal trajectories are a dynamic component that helps to understand the development of an institution (Sáenz Rovner, 1992; Adolph, 2013). The biographical dataset for this study uses data from the board members' public CVs, press and other secondary sources, minutes of the board meetings from 1923 to 1991, and extracts from the *Revista del Banco de la República*, an institutional journal that has circulated monthly without interruption since 1927.

Since 1923, the Banco de la República has maintained its functions of issuing the country's bank notes and being the bank of the government and

* PhD candidate, Department of Economics, UMass Amherst. This research would not have been possible without the funds of the Fulbright-Colciencias scholarship, UMass Amherst Graduate School Fieldwork Grant, and PERI Research Assistantship with Gerald Epstein. Special thanks to the board office secretariat of the Banco de la República for their assistance with information; Ted Zuur and Marta García for commenting on a preliminary version; Adolfo Meisel, Jimena Hurtado, Carlos Brando and Juanita Villaveces for their comments; the presentation assistants at the 7th ALAHPE conference, in particular Samuel Demeulemeester; and Edwin López, Juan Sayago, and Juan C. Acosta for the comments received on related works.

DOI: 10.4324/9781003289241-14

commercial banks. This stability does not mean that its ownership, objectives, and governance have remained unchanged. Several reforms to the bank's governance affected the traits of board members. Ideas, private experience, and academic preparation favored the participation of different social groups in different periods. This chapter uses the reforms that affected the governance of the Banco de la República as reference points to anchor people's trajectories to a determined institutional framework and a development stage of the country.

After two failed attempts to create a central bank, the design for the Banco de la República empowered private banks to appoint most of the members of the initial board (Ibañez Najar, 1990; Hernández Gamarra, 2001). The economic environment of the Great Depression made it necessary to revisit the economic institutions. In 1931, the first reform to the bank board included business associations on the board. It empowered coffee growers to appoint one member and farmers and tradespeople to appoint another. The appointees of the Coffee Growers Federation (*Federación Nacional de Cafeteros* – FNC) became long-serving board members. Two years later, a new reform halved the bankers' participation.

In 1951, the third reform empowered the National Industrialist Association (*Asociación Nacional de Industriales* – ANDI) and cattle ranchers to nominate board members. This enlargement of business associations was against the recommendations of several international advisors.

A reform in 1963 transferred the monetary, exchange, and credit authorities from the private Board of Directors to an entire government-appointed board, the *Junta Monetaria*. This new authority required the assistance of two economic advisors who led discussions but did not have voting power. These technical figures had usually studied postgraduate programs in US institutions and were associated with the Department of Economics and the Center of Development Economics Studies (*Centro de Estudios Sobre Desarrollo Económico* - CEDE) of Los Andes University.

In the 1980s, a proposal for more independence from the government arose from the technical units of the Banco de la República. The 1991 Constitution adhered to this proposal, removed most of the development functions of the bank, and reformed the board. Each president appointed two board members per term. Most subsequent presidents followed an informal rule by which graduate titles and professional experience in economics became decisive traits of the appointees.

12.2   1880–1923: The Long Road for the Banco de la República Foundation

Colombia experienced two unsuccessful attempts to create a national issuing bank. In 1880, the Banco Nacional was created in Colombia. It was a public-private bank that served as the government's bank and had the power to issue currency. It became a public bank due to the reluctance of private banks to support the new institution and closed in 1896 after failing to pay its debts due to clandestine bail-outs of the government's deficit (Meisel, 2001; Cardenas, 2013). In 1905, the government founded Banco Central to stabilize the amount of circulating money and the exchange rate and unify the country's banknotes (Junguito & Rincón, 2007; Avella Gómez, 2009). The Banco Central was empowered with the right of issue for 30 years, committed to unifying the legal currency, acting as the government's bank, and maintaining a stable exchange rate (Junguito & Rincón, 2007; Meisel Roca, 2016). Four years later, Banco Central requested additional time to unify the legal currency. Political detractors leveraged this to attack the bank, and shortly after, Congress removed the bank's authority to issue banknotes and transformed it into a private bank (Hernández Gamarra, 2001; Meisel Roca, 2016).

Between 1909 and 1922, Congress discussed 31 projects regulating banking activity (Gómez Arrubla, 1983). In 1913, during the government of Carlos E. Restrepo, two of these proposals aimed to create a central bank named Banco de la República (Hernández Gamarra, 2001; Meisel Roca, 2016). The name was related to the Republican coalition, the political union between moderate conservatives and liberals which had elected Restrepo as president (Melo, 2017; Sastoque Ramírez, 2018).

In 1914, delegates from the United States and Colombia signed the Urrutia–Thompson Treaty to re-establish the trade relationships that had been tarnished because of the involvement of the United States in the secession of Panama (Drekonja-Kornat, 1983; Drake, 1989). The agreement stagnated in the United States Congress because the Colombian government wanted, in addition to reparations, official recognition of the role of the United States in the secession of Panama (Torres del Río, 2015; Caballero, 2016). The Colombian tax system was highly dependent on import duties. A budget deficit crisis broke out in 1917 due to the war in Europe (Drake, 1989; Junguito & Rincón, 2007). The stagnation of foreign investment and potential access to credit markets amid the economic crisis pushed the conservative Colombian governments to re-establish commercial relationships with the United States (Drake, 1989; Ardila, 2010; Meisel Roca, 2016). In 1921, the United States Congress ratified the Urrutia–Thompson Treaty. It included US $25 million in reparations but did not acknowledge the role of the United States in the secession (Ardila, 2010; Caballero, 2016; Melo, 2017).

Between 1921 and 1922, Congress discussed two central bank proposals. The discussion speeches expressed distrust in the government and aimed for monetary orthodoxy (Ibañez Najar, 1990). Despite opposition, the conciliation resulted in Law 30 of 1922, which empowered the government to promote and fund a bank of issue, transfer, deposit, and discount named Banco de la República.[1] On October 23, Congress approved Law 60. It directed the government to hire five experts to reorganize government services, taxes, and other revenues, delaying the bank's foundation. The recently inaugurated president Pedro Nel Ospina empowered Enrique Olaya to find and hire those experts

(Santos Molano, 2005). At the suggestion of the US Department of State, Olaya invited Edwin Kemmerer to become the head advisor (Seidel, 1972; Drake, 1989). What came to be known as the Kemmerer Mission arrived in Colombia in 1923, charged with a general study of the economic situation, and organized the existing laws to create the basic legal and organizational principles of the Banco de la República. Political parties and the press supported the orientations of the mission. With few voices against it, the mission passed eight laws from the ten bills it sent to Congress (Drake, 1989; Hernández Gamarra, 2001).[2]

12.3 1923–1931: The Age of Bankers and Businessmen

Distrust in the government led to a central bank in which the government contributed half of the capital but had no power of decision (Avella Gómez, 2009; Hernández Gamarra, 2013; Sastoque Ramírez, 2018). The new central bank law, Law 25, empowered the government to nominate and appoint up to three members of the bank's board with a voice but no vote for three-year periods. Although the law did not require it, the finance minister was usually appointed.[3] Domestic banks were allowed to nominate up to four members, two of whom had to be bankers, while the other two had to be businesspeople, farmers, or professionals. Foreign banks could nominate up to two members, one of whom had to be a banker while the other had to be a businessman, farmer, or professional. The mission's members proposed the inclusion of foreign bank delegates under the assumption that they would be less prone to government pressures (Ibañez Najar, 1990). Table 12.1 shows the evolution of the constitution of the Monetary Authority Board (*Junta Moneteria*).

From 1923 to 1931, forty men served on the board of the Banco de la República. It was possible to establish a place of birth for 28 of them. Ten were born in Bogotá, followed by eight from Antioquia and Caldas, and six abroad; two in Boyacá and Santander, and one in each of the departments of Bolívar, Huila, Tolima, and now Valle del Cauca. Among the board members, the second governor, Julio Caro, was the longest-serving with 20 years. Private stockholders' representative Vicente Vargas spent five years on the board. On average, board members appointed in this period served for 25 months. Government appointees were supposed to be on the board for three years, but they served a shorter time, finance ministers 13 months, and other government representatives two years. Bankers' appointees served an average of 40 months, while business representatives served an average of 16.

During the period, ten board members were reappointed. José J. Pérez and Félix Salazar were both governors and directors. Private shareholders, domestic banks, and government representatives appointed Esteban Jaramillo and Jesús M. Marulanda for different periods. Domestic and foreign banks appointed Sam Koppel, Luis Williamson, and Manuel Escobar. Government and foreign banks appointed Simón Araujo. Manuel V. Ortíz was appointed by the government and the domestic banks, and Otto Gerding twice by the foreign banks.

Table 12.1 Evolution of the Monetary Authority Board

Appointed by	1923–1931	1934–1951	1951–1963	1963–1991 (MB)	1991 to date
Government	Delegate	Min. Finance	Min. Finance	Ministers of Finance,	Min. Finance
	Delegate	Delegate	Delegate	Development,	Director
	Delegate	Delegate	Delegate	and Agriculture	Director
				Director of the	Director
				Planning	Director
				Department	Director
Domestic banks	Banker	Banker	Banks delegate		
	Banker	Banker			
	Business people/ Farmers		Banks delegate		
	Business people/ Farmers				
Foreign banks	Banker	Banker	Bank delegate		
	Business people/ Farmer				
Business associations		Coffee growers	Coffee growers		
		Farmers and trade business associations	Farmers and cattle ranchers		
			Trade business associations and industrialists		
Board	Governor	Governor	Governor	Governor	Governor

Sources: Law 25 of 1923, Law 82 of 1931, Law 46 of 1933, Decree 2057 of 1951, Law 21 of 1963, Decree 2206 of 1963, Political Constitution of 1991. Created by the author.

Notes: In the late 1920s, other bank stockholders nominated a member. From 1931 to 1933 the Bankers were still empowered to nominate business/farmer representatives. In the late 1960s, three other members were incorporated into the *Junta Monetaria* with no voting power.

Government appointees had previous experience of public office, but having an association with the banking business was the most common trait. Of board members, 55% were former officers or stockholders of a private bank.[4] Foreign banks appointed nine men: three nationals and six foreigners. Five of these foreigners served as bank representatives, while Kemmerer's advisor and North American banker, Walter Van Dusen, served as businessman.

The banking business was highly concentrated and hierarchical at the time of the foundation of the Banco de la República (Sastoque Ramírez, 2018). In 1925, three of the 28 banks in the country held roughly 40% of the deposits. These were the Banco de Bogotá and the Banco de Colombia, founded in Bogotá in 1871 and 1875, respectively, and the third, the Banco Alemán Antioqueño, which was founded in Bremen in 1912 (Meisel Roca, 1990c)—one explanation of why most domestic bankers' representatives had a relationship with one of these banks.

In addition to bankers and public servants, both government and banks appointed a few pioneering industrialists to the board. The government appointed to the interim board the treasury minister Gabriel Posada Villa and Lucas Caballero. Domestics banks appointed Manuel Escobar and Nicolás Camargo. Foreign banks appointed Jose Manuel Rodríguez.[5]

The three governors of the bank were from the Conservative Party. However, despite the conservative pre-eminence, there was some balance on the first board. Félix Salazar and Lucas Caballero served in opposing armies during the *Guerra de los Mil Días*, the last partisanship civil war. However, both were appointed to the interim board during the government of Pedro Nel Ospina. President Miguel Abadía appointed as minister the Liberal Party member Eduardo Vallejo.

After the Banco de la República managed the bank run, it had to administer a period of prosperity and fall known as the "dance of the millions." Between 1922 and 1928, government spending on infrastructure and public goods multiplied by ten, relying on the good international coffee market conditions, low interest rates, and abundant international loans instead of new taxes (Bejarano, 1989; Kalmanovitz & López, 2006; Junguito & Rincón, 2007). The booming economy boosted inflation and created a scarcity of agricultural goods, harming the newly consolidated waged working class (Bejarano, 2007; Torres del Río, 2015). The Great Depression closed the credit markets, hit coffee prices, and hurt the Colombian import-dependent tax system (Junguito & Rincón, 2007; Sánchez & Bedoya, 2016).

12.4   1931–1951: Business Associations on the Rise

The first liberal president in the 20th century, Enrique Olaya Herrera, was elected amid a crisis. In 1930, Olaya hired Kemmerer for the second time to reformulate the institutions and deal with the constraints on foreign loans and the fall in coffee prices (Ibañez Najar & Meisel Roca, 1990; Caballero, 2016). The recommendations of the new mission included a better-balanced board (between bankers, businesses, and the government), more tools to enable an expansive monetary policy, such as lower reserve rates, open market operations, and expanding the limits on loans to the government (Ibañez Najar & Meisel Roca, 1990).

Law 73 of 1930 expanded the Banco de la República's loans to their stockholders, while Law 82 of 1931 granted the bank exchange rate policy and management of the gold reserves. Law 82 empowered the FNC to select one member, and farmers and trade business associations to nominate another member.[6] Law 46 of 1933 reduced banks appointment power to three.

From 1931 to 1951, sixty-eight people served on the board, including two governors, Julio Caro (1927–1947) and Luis Ángel Arango (1947–1957).[7] In contrast to the previous period, just three members were reappointed: Arango, Esteban Jaramillo, and Gonzalo Córdoba. In this period, private stockholders appointed five people, the FNC another five, and the chambers of commerce and farmers' associations together another five. Foreign banks appointed 11 people, national banks 14, and the government 29.

There were 15 finance ministers during these 20 years, six of whom were liberals and seven conservatives. Liberal presidents tended to govern with bipartisan cabinets, attributing part of the success of their economic policies to the work of conservatives (Lleras Restrepo, 1987; Tirado Mejía, 2018). President Olaya only appointed conservatives ministers,[8] while López and Santos appointed liberals and conservatives. However, no liberals were appointed to the board when the conservatives regained the presidency in 1946.

Reduced private banks power over appointments did not decrease the importance of bankers on the board or the relevance of the Banco de Colombia and the Banco de Bogotá,[9] which each have one former officer as governor. From 1930 to 1951, 14 directors were related to domestic banks and 11 were foreign bank representatives, eight of whom were foreign born. During the 1930s, the average time spent on the board by a foreign bank appointee was one year. Giovanni Serventi (1931, 1932, and 1938) and Arthur Thompson (1931, 1939) served for longer. In the 1940s, the three directors appointed by the foreign banks were Colombian born.[10]

12.4.1 The Increasing Power of the Coffee Growers

The Society of Coffee Producers, founded in 1904, rapidly evolved into the Colombian Agricultural Society. In the mid-1920s, the government reduced food tariffs in the face of inflation. Coffee growers—whose activities were labor-intensive and required waged jobs for harvesting, de-pulping, and drying—favored liberalization, while the rest of the agricultural producers were against it because they paid in kind (Caballero, 2016; Melo, 2017). This division led to the creation of the FNC during the second coffee congress in 1927. Facing a fall in the price of coffee, the FNC promoted and rapidly achieved the passage of a tax to "protect and defend coffee." Later, in 1929, they created a barter system based on coffee stored in the FNC warehouses (Caballero, 2016). In 1930, the coffee growers gained preferential credit through the Banco de la República (Drake, 1989), and in 1931, the FNC obtained the right to appoint one member to its board.

Coffee growers guided the Banco de la República's orientation while using their influence on the government to maintain favorable exchange and trade policies for coffee exports (Caballero, 2016). For 60 years, the FNC appointed a member to the board of the monetary authority. Their appointees were the most stable figures on the board, surpassing even the governors. During that time, seven FNC appointees—of whom four were current or former FNC directors— served, whereas there were eight bank governors and 27 finance ministers. The FNC appointed five people to the board in these 20 years. Nevertheless, ten board members were FNC directors or belonged to the National Committee of Coffee Growers.[11]

12.4.2 Industrialists' Quest for Power

During the 1920s, the growth of the coffee economy, together with its shift to waged labor, increased the demand for manufactured products. This also required transportation improvements, ranging from roads and railroads to ports and cable cars (Caballero, 2016; Melo, 2017). Government investments enhanced conditions for the industry and created a national market. In the first half of the 20th century, the government invested much of its budget in railroads, roads, and electricity generation and transmission (Bejarano, 1989; Caballero, 2016; Jaramillo-Echeverri et al., 2016). In the 1930s, industrial growth was encouraged by protectionist policies. Its growth would later skyrocket under the import-substitution drive required by World War II (Ocampo, 1984; Jaramillo-Echeverri et al., 2016).

In 1935, the government of López Pumarejo negotiated a trade agreement with the United States. The agreement granted a quota for Colombian coffee exports in exchange for reductions in textile tariffs and US cigarette taxes. The industrialists considered this unfavorable, but the conservative coffee growers in the FNC also declared against it. They were promoters of free trade policies, but they were reluctant to sign the agreement under a liberal presidency. The agreement was finally signed following the resignation of the conservative director of the FNC, Mariano Ospina (Caballero, 2016).

World War II reduced imports and the availability of international transportation for Colombian exports, and restricted government funds because of the tariffs' relevance. This boosted the local production of goods and increased the power of the industrialists (Ocampo, 1984). The ANDI was created in 1944 in Medellín at the suggestion of López Pumarejo and by some of the industrialists affected by the trade agreement with the United States.[12] In five years, the ANDI succeeded in ending the agreement and becoming a powerful institution (Caballero, 2016).

Another success was the transformation of public speech. Politicians from both parties used to disagree with protectionist measures due to a possible rise in consumer prices. Nevertheless, the ANDI used the press to create the rhetoric that industrialists' interests corresponded to national interests (Sáenz Rovner, 1992; Caballero, 2016). The ANDI did not acquire its power to nominate to the board of the Banco de la República until 1951; however, between 1946 and 1951, five board members of the ANDI were appointed.[13] The participation of industrialists in the government was not merely due to associative interest but also because of a personal quest of the industrialists who saw success in public administration as a critical step in their careers (Restrepo Santamaría, 2016).

12.4.3 Tragedy and Reconstruction

Kemmerer's defense of the gold standard met with Keynesian ideas, allowing the bank to incorporate developing policies (Meisel Roca & Jaramillo-Echeverri, 2017). During the 1940s, a political discussion occurred regarding the role of the Central Bank and monetary and credit policy effects on development. Some promoters of reform wanted the Banco de la República to play a fundamental role in development by subsidizing long-term lending and unifying monetary and credit policies under its authority (Ochoa Díaz & Martínez Montealegre, 2005; Meisel & Barón, 2010; Jaramillo-Echeverri et al., 2016). Conservative president Mariano Ospina Pérez, who had been a strong defender of free trade policies when he was the FNC director, drove some of these changes along with his finance minister, the industrialist José M. Bernal (Restrepo Santamaría, 2016; Bushnell, 2021).

A tragedy led to changes in economic institutions. On April 9, 1948, Jorge E. Gaitán, a liberal leader supported by unions and workers, was assassinated. An infuriated crowd ransacked surrounding stores, burnt trams, and destroyed government offices. The president called the army into the city in an action that resulted in the death of many citizens.[14] The Colombian government applied for a US $78 million loan from the International Bank for Reconstruction and Development (IBRD) for reconstruction of the city (Banco de la República, 1948). The president of the IBRD, John McCloy, hesitated to grant the loan due to the amount and distrust of its usage (Sáenz Rovner, 2001). The IBRD accepted but sent a mission led by Lauchlin Currie to assess the country's needs and create allocation recommendations (Sandilands, 2015).

The Banco de la República hosted the Currie Mission, which resulted in a comprehensive study with recommendations on diverse sectors of the economy (Currie, 1950). Money and banking sections, directed by Richard Musgrave, looked to broaden the control mechanisms of the Banco de la República. The document recommended increasing the number of technical experts to advise the board and monitor economic indicators, allowing the bank to do open market operations and adjust rediscount rates and reserves ratios (Currie, 1950). In 1950, the Colombian government created the bipartisan Committee of Economic Development to implement the Mission's recommendations and hired Currie as an advisor (Sáenz Rovner, 2001; Álvarez et al., 2019). In 1952, the IBRD sent Albert Hirschman as economic policy advisor (Sandilands, 2015; Álvarez et al., 2019).

12.5 1951–1963: Credit Policy and a Corporatist Board

The Banco de la República's term as a bank of issue was about to expire. The government invited an international commission from the Federal Reserve of New York, directed by Daniel Grove, to organize adjustments to the banking structure and credit policies (Caballero, 2016; Gómez Pineda, 2017). Based on their report, the bank created the Commission of Banking Reforms to analyze the feasibility of extending the bank's lifespan and reforming its structure and objectives (Meisel Roca, 1990a). The country then had several proposals for reforms whose implementation involved academic debates among foreign advisors[15] (Banco de la República, 1950; Sandilands, 2015; Álvarez et al., 2019).

In 1951, multiple decrees and laws reformed the Banco de la República. These empowered the bank with the exchange policy and increased the development of credit tools (Kalmanovitz & López, 2006). The bank was allowed to subsidize interest rates, modify interest discount rates and reserves, and grant the government larger loans (Meisel Roca, 1990b; Ochoa Díaz & Martínez Montealegre, 2005; Hernández & Jaramillo-Echeverri, 2017). Decree 756 of 1951 redefined the bank's objectives, expressing that "The Banco de la República will make a monetary, credit and exchange policy to stimulate the proper conditions for the development of the Colombian economy."

Decree 2057 of 1951 extended the bank's right of issue for an additional 20 years. It also changed the board's composition, empowering the government to appoint three members, domestic and foreign banks to appoint three, and the FNC one. It also allowed the associations of agriculture producers (*Sociedad de Agricultores de Colombia* - SAC) and cattle ranchers (*Federación de Ganaderos* - FEDEGAN) to nominate people for one appointment, and the trade chambers associations (*Cámaras de Comercio*) and the ANDI another. One of the government appointments had to be the finance minister. The decree diminished the appointment power of commercial banks, nominally increasing the voting power of the government, which was the one in charge of appointing the two members among the nominees of the trade associations.

Empowering trade business associations followed the idea of the corporatism state of Laureano Gómez, president from 1950–1954 (Sáenz Rovner, 1992). These changes to the board were against the missions' recommendations (Hernández & Jaramillo-Echeverri, 2017). While the Banking Committee believed that the board should have a detailed understanding of economic sectors, it recommended against giving business associations the power to nominate members (Meisel Roca, 1990b). The Banking Reform Commission went so far as to advise that banks should not be allowed to appoint board members, since these institutions were the most affected by the board's decisions (Ochoa Díaz & Martínez Montealegre, 2005).

In June 1953, General Rojas Pinilla obtained power through a coup d'état. After his resignation in 1957, an interim military faction ruled the country for a year (Melo, 2017). The power of the business associations did not decline, however.[16] During these years, there were 34 men on the board, six appointed twice by different actors. The FNC representatives were their directors Manuel Mejía and Arturo Gómez, but three other directors were previously members of the national coffee committees. There were also two representatives of chambers of trade and industrialist associations: Bernardo Restrepo, an industrialist, and Aurelio Ramos, whom the general had previously appointed to manage a regional chamber. In addition, three other men had previously been members of the board of the ANDI. The SAC and the cattle ranchers' association had four representatives.

During this period, the bank encouraged the creation of public development banks. In 1953, the government sold its shares in the central bank. These resources served to buy shares in the Caja de Crédito Agrario, Industrial y Minero, a development-public bank for projects in agriculture, industry, and mining (Banco de la República, 1954; Meisel Roca, 1990b). In 1953, the Banco de la República promoted the creation of the Coffee Bank (*Banco Cafetero*), which started operations in 1954 under the management of a former board member. In 1956 the government created the Cattle Bank (*Banco Ganadero*). The board of the Banco de la República discussed granting loans to the new institution. Law 26 of 1959 obligated the banking institutions to focus at least 15% of their deposits on agricultural development investments. The policy was successful, at least in numbers. From 1950 to 1962, a third of the overall loans in the country were for agricultural activities (Kalmanovitz & López, 2006).

12.6 1963–1991: A Tale of Two Boards… and the Technical Politicians

Following the experiences of Paraguay, Guatemala, and Ecuador, the government decided to remove the monetary authority from the bank in 1963. The idea of aligning exchange and monetary policies with fiscal expenditure promoted the creation of the *Junta Monetaria*. Before 1963, the board of the Banco de la República had a majority of members related to the banks and the private sector (Hommes, 2021).

Expressing the conflict of interest that business associations held over the monetary policy permitted minister of finance Carlos Sanz de Santamaría to successfully transfer the board powers to the *Junta Monetaria*. Sanz's successor Diego Calle Restrepo also defended this position (Hernández & Jaramillo-Echeverri, 2017). The reputation of the ministers probably provided confidence to the private sector and the banks.[17] Law 21 of 1963 created the *Junta Monetaria* with the main objective of promoting growth. The *Junta Monetaria* had tight control of the banking sector, a loose inflationary policy, and a strong focus on exchange policy (Caballero, 2016). The bank board became an administrative entity that followed the decisions taken in the *Junta Monetaria*, and this governance structure would remain unaltered until the new Constitution of 1991.[18]

All members with voting power in the *Junta Monetaria* were appointed directly by the president, except for the Banco de la República's governor.[19] The members were the finance, development, and agriculture ministers and the chief of the Planning Department. The Banking Superintendent and the director of the Colombian Institute of Foreign Trade (*Instituto Colombiano de Comercio Exterior* – Incomex) became members without voting power in 1968 and the Economic Secretary of the Presidency in 1969.

12.6.1 *Dawn of the Technocrats*

Undergraduate economics programs expanded rapidly, from three economics programs that started before 1946 to 16 in 1966.[20] According to the comptroller's office, the enrollment growth rate in economics-related programs doubled the growth of the entire university enrollment. The demand for economics professionals from the business associations and the Kemmerer institutions increased with the creation of new government institutions and research centers in Bogotá. During the 1950s, the creation of the National Statistics and the Planning Department (*Departamento Nacional de Planeación* – DNP) encouraged the hiring of a technical bureaucracy. In 1958, the Rockefeller Foundation supported the creation of the CEDE at Los Andes University (Álvarez et al., 2019).[21] In 1962, Currie founded the Center of Research for Development (CID) at Universidad Nacional (Rivera, 2002a).

In the following years, there was a demand for these technical politicians in the state administration, especially during the Lleras Restrepo presidency (1966–1970). These were professors at Colombian universities—most of them had studied economics and had postgraduate degrees from foreign universities (Caballero, 2016; Hommes, 2021). In 1970, Manuel Carvajal, an industrialist, and Rodrigo Botero, the former Economic Secretary of Lleras R., founded the research institute Fedesarrollo (Sáenz Rovner, 1992; Perry, 1995). It became home to technical politicians and played a role in the transition from the elites of Antioquia and Caldas to a more centralized promotion of ideas (Restrepo Santamaría, 2016; Cadena, 2020).

The Banco de la República played a twofold role in the rise of technical politicians. The advisors of the Junta Monetaria were the top technical positions for economists in the government, and the bank created a program to sponsor postgraduate studies in foreign universities in 1980 (Gamboa et al., 2016). Table 12.2 is a complete list of members of the Board of Advisors between 1963 and 1991.

The Junta Monetaria had two technical advisors, one in foreign trade and the other in monetary and sectoral policies (Hernández & Jaramillo-Echeverri, 2017). Decree 2206 stated that the two experts should have the "best qualifications possible" and enough credentials. They were all males between 29 and 45 years and had graduated studies in the United States when appointed. The higher share of their undergraduate studies was economics, but there were several engineers, a few lawyers, and one philosopher. Half of them were born in Bogotá, and a slightly larger share studied in Bogotá during their undergraduate studies. In their trajectories, 45% were professors at the Universidad de los Andes, and four were directors of the CEDE before being advisors to the board. The same proportion of advisors (23%) worked before in the DNP, the Banco de la República, or the Ministry of Finance. After their term of office as advisors, these individuals played a more significant role in the public sector. Several of them became members of the Junta Monetaria as finance ministers (Restrepo, Hommes), directors of the DNP, or other ministers (Gómez O., Ruíz, and Montenegro). They took part in the new board created in 1991 as directors (Caballero, Jaramillo, and Gómez R.) or governors of the Banco de la República (Ortega and Urrutia).

Table 12.2 Board Advisors, 1963–1991

Name	Period		After		Before			CEDE	ANDES	Higher Studies
			Board members	Cabinet Positions	DNP	Banco de la República	Ministry of Treasury			
Hernándo Gómez Otálora	1964	1968	JM	x			x			PhD
Álvaro López Toro	1964	1965								MA
Jorge Ruíz Lara	1965	1970	JM	x				x	x	PhD
Miguel Urrutia Montoya	1968	1970	JDBR	x			x	x	x	PhD
Leonel Torres	1970	1974								-
Francisco J. Ortega Acosta	1970	1975	JDBR			x		x	x	MA
Eduardo Sarmiento Palacio	1974	1978			x				x	PhD
Haroldo Calvo	1977	1978						x	x	PhD (c)
Juan Camilo Restrepo	1975	1981	JM	x						PhD
Luis Eduardo Rosas	1978	1982		x	x					PhD (c)
Jorge García García	1981	1982		x	x	x			x	PhD
Juan Carlos Jaramillo	1982	1984				x				PhD
Fernando Montes N	1982	1984				x	x			PhD
Manuel Ramírez G	1984	1985							x	PhD
Carlos E. Caballero Argáez	1984	1986	JDBR	x						MA
Gilberto Gómez A	1985	1987								PhD
Armando Montenegro	1986	1989	JM	x		x				PhD
Rudolf Hommes Rodríguez	1987	1988	JDBR	x						PhD
Javier Fernández Riva	1988	1990			x		x		x	PhD
Jaime Jaramillo Vallejo	1989	1991	JDBR							PhD
Ulpiano Ayala	1991	1991			x		x		x	PhD
Hernándo J. Gómez R.	1990	1991	JDBR	x						PhD

Sources: Cárdenas & Partow (1998), Hernández & Jaramillo-Echeverri (2017), Academia Colombiana de Ciencias Económicas, Archivo del Banco de la República. Created by the author.

12.6.2 Dusk of the Junta Monetaria

The most common trait among the 58 members of the Junta Monetaria was previous public service: 19 had served as congressmen and 12 as secretaries or governors in a department. However, there was a large group with executive positions in technical jobs: 15 worked in the finance ministry, ten in the Banco de la República, ten in the DNP, and eight worked for the government development banks. They also held high judicial offices: six were either on the State Council or in the Supreme Court. The technical path was non-negligible: six members of the Junta Monetaria had worked previously at the IDB, six at Fedesarrollo, three at the CEDE, and two at the CID. They had teaching experience: seven were professors at Universidad de los Andes, four at Pontificia Universidad Javeriana, four at Universidad Nacional, and one from each of the EAFIT, Antioquia, and Externado universities. Finally, there was a reduced group of trade business representatives: four from the Agricultural Association, two from the FNC, two from the ANDI, and one in each from the cotton, cattle, and insurance associations.

In the 1980s, an orthodox critique of the relationship between the Junta Monetaria and the government started to emerge among economists and within the Banco de la República. The arguments for independence and inflation control only echoed in the late 1980s, when some economists confronted the government for using recurrent devaluations as fiscal resources (Avella Gómez, 2014; Alesina et al., 2000). The call for the a new constitution allowed these economists to introduce substantive changes to the bank (Alesina et al., 2000). They aimed to increase their independence from the president by eliminating the Junta Monetaria and the direct funding of development activities. The government proposal was more radical: to isolate the Banco de la República from its scope. The constitution removed the development credit and functions (Hommes & Melo, 2017).

12.7 1991–2023: Technical Directors in an Independent Inflation-Oriented Central Bank

The 1991 Constitution transformed the objectives and governance of the bank. The Constitution and Law 31 of 1992 established the Banco de la República as an independent public central bank whose main objective is price stability. This legislation dissolved the Junta Monetaria and returned its functions and authorities to the board of the Banco de la República. The Constitution and Law 82 of 1992 resolved that the Board of Directors of the Banco de la República would be composed of seven members: the governor, the finance minister, as president of the board, and five co-directors appointed in groups of two by each president in the middle of their presidential term, to avoid the control of the board by one government (Avella Gómez, 2014).

Presidents have usually appointed board members with a professional and academic record. Eight of the 35 board members were previously ministers,[22] 12 deputy ministers,[23] and 11 worked at DNP.[24] Like the advisors of the Junta

Monetaria, 88% of board members studied abroad, and most of them had postgraduate degrees. Nevertheless, they are a homogeneous group. Since 1991, just four women have been on the board.[25] Economics is the most common program for undergraduate studies (83%), and the Universidad de los Andes is the most common alma mater (63%). Three governors were previously board members and directors of Fedesarrollo, and at least ten board members worked previously at this institution.[26]

12.8 Discussion: A Redefinition of the Board in the 21st Century

The board of the Banco de la República has had several reforms to its structure. Each one permitted the participation of particular societal interests. Early board structures promoted bankers' appointees, then later stimulated the business associations. Both groups obtained larger *de facto* representations through government appointments. However, as stated by international advisors and former ministers, the direct participation of banks and business associations created a conflict of interest. In 1963, the transfer of the private board powers to the Junta Monetaria encouraged the participation of technical advisors in the bank. Since then, there has been an increase in economists from the capital who have completed postgraduate studies abroad as board members.

The current governance model looks for appointments on merit, not representation. Nevertheless, the shortlist of people with academic and professional records has created a closed group that reinforces the participation of similar people on the board. After being confirmed on the board, most board members have demonstrated some degree of independence. However, recent events have raised questions about the board's independence from the government may encourage debate about the representation that a powerful institution like the central bank's board must have within a democracy and its implications for economic policy.

Notes

1 Rather than an apolitical denomination, the name expressed the commitment of a group of liberal and conservative politicians and business leaders. That across-the-aisle cooperation supported the bank's continued existence during the conservative hegemony (until 1930) and later during the liberal republic (from 1930 to 1946).

2 The approved laws were a tax on business documents (Law 20), the reorganization of the ministries (Law 31), the creation of the Banco de la República (Law 25), the organization of the national budget (Law 34), the organization of the tax administration (Law 36), the creation of the comptroller department (Law 42) and the banking supervisor office (Law 45), and the requisites for bills of exchange. Congress did not approve an income tax modification and a ticket tax.

3 Only two finance ministers did not serve as board members: Juan Antonio Gómez, appointed for four months in 1926, and Carlos Echeverri Uribe, appointed for six days in 1934. The appointment of the finance minister was considered a good tradition. In 1929, board members expressed satisfaction when minister Pérez replaced Nicolás Pineda (Banco de la República, 1929).

4 Félix Salazar and Guillermo Gonzalez were former directors of Banco Central. The first governor, José J. Pérez, was a stockholder of the Banco de Bogotá, and the third governor, Julio Caro, had several positions at the Banco de Colombia (Sastoque Ramírez, 2018): Seven other board members were related to the Banco de Bogotá, Banco de Colombia, and Banco Alemán Antioqueño.

5 Gabriel Posada was an Antioquian chemist and one of the founders of Postobón, the largest soft drinks company; Lucas Caballero owned textile, liquor, and chocolate industries; Manuel M. Escobar was one of the founders of the Banco Alemán Antioqueño and the Siderúrgica de Medellín (a steel company), the owner of a retail sales business, a leather company, the largest movie theater chain in the country, and a stockholder of Cervecería Antioqueña (a beer company); Jose Manuel Rodríguez and Nicolás Camargo were shareholders and managers of food industries and construction companies (Otero Muñoz, 1948; Meisel & Viloria, 1998; Dávila, 2003; Campuzano Hoyos, 2013).

6 Kemmerer did not suggest the presence of unions on the board as he did in Chile (Drake, 1989).

7 The board granted Caro the honorary title of President of the Bank at his retirement (Banco de la República, 1947).

8 Olaya Herrera's finance ministers were Francisco de Paula Pérez, Jesús María Marulanda, and Esteban Jaramillo. He also appointed the future conservative president Roberto Urdaneta as a government representative.

9 Banco Alemán Antioqueño: Manuel Escobar (1929–1932); Banco de Bogotá: Luis Soto (1928–1933), José J. Pérez (1931–1933), Liberio López (1934–1946), Martín del Corral (1949–1951), and Gov. Luis A. Arango (1947–1957); Banco de Colombia: Gov. Julio Caro (1927–1947), and Roberto Michelsen (1925–1945). Banco Central: Guillermo Gonzáles (1933–1934). Banco Hipotecario: Jorge Obando (1945). Two directors appointed by the FNC, Manuel Mejía and Camilo Sáenz, were also bankers. The banking association was created in 1936. Julio Caro was among its founders; Luis Ángel Arango and Ignacio Copete were both presidents of the Banking Association and later elected governors of the Banco de la República (Urrutia, 1983).

10 World War II could have made it difficult to appoint foreigners, especially Italians and Germans, and encouraged the selection of people with political and economic expertise. Jorge Arturo Andrade (1940) helped the first Kemmerer mission. Felix García (1941–1942) and Gonzalo Córdoba (1943–1951) were previously banking superintendents. Andrade and Córdoba also served previously on the board.

11 Directors: Camilo Sáenz, Alejandro López, Manuel Mejía; National Coffee Committee Members: Manuel Valdivieso, Jorge Obando Lombana, Esteban Jaramillo, Álvaro Díaz, Francisco de Paula Pérez, Carlos Lleras Restrepo, Antonio Álvarez Restrepo.

12 The ANDI comprises the directors of the Colombian Tobacco Company, the two largest textile producers in the country, Fabricato and Coltejer, and the beer company Cervecería Unión (Sáenz Rovner, 1992).

13 Government-appointed finance ministers Carlos Sáenz (1945) and Jose María Bernal (1947–1949), and Bernando Restrepo (1949–1951). Domestic banks appointed José M. Tamayo (1946–1948) and Martín del Corral (1949–1951). Luis Soto (1928–1933) served on the bank's board before the ANDI.

14 The Banco de la República board rapidly aligned with the president. The editorial note of the Revista del Banco de la República condemned the assassination of Gaitán and praised the "energy, calm, and bravery" of the president, the newly bipartisan cabinet, and the army (Banco de la República, 1948).

15 Currie and Hirschman were also economic advisors to the government. The country hosted several missions during the 1950s, including an IMF mission on exchange controls, the Mission of Economics and Humanism (Lebret), and the ECLAC created a report. Chapter 8 in this volume discusses several labor missions.

16 Initially, the ANDI supported Rojas Pinilla's government, looking for stability (Restrepo Santamaría, 2016). The *Revista del Banco de la República* described it as a separation of powers (Banco de la República, 1953).
17 As seen above, minister Carlos Sanz was a board member of the ANDI. Diego Calle was a successful businessman with high credibility in the private sector (Sáenz Rovner, 1992; Restrepo Santamaría, 2016).
18 Ten years later, through Law 7 and Decree 2617, the government nationalized the Banco de la República. However, the two boards remained (Hommes & Melo, 2017).
19 The governor was still elected by the bank's board.
20 Bogotá: School of Industrial and Commercial Administration (1943), Gimnasio Moderno. School of Economics and Statistics (1949), Universidad de los Andes. Institute of Economics Sciences (1945) and School of Economic Sciences (1952), Universidad Nacional de Colombia. Economics School (1950), Pontificia Universidad Javeriana. Medellín: Department of Economic Sciences (1944), Universidad de Antioquia. In the 1960s, the Universities Rosario and Externado in Bogotá, and Autónoma and Nacional in Medellín (Sáenz Rovner, 1992; Rivera, 2002b; Tirado Mejía, 2014; Álvarez et al., 2019). See Chapter 9, this volume, for a detailed discussion of economics education.
21 See Chapter 7, this volume, for an extensive discussion of the Ford and Rockefeller scholarships.
22 Agriculture: Antonio Hernández, Carlos Cano, and José Ocampo; Development: María Cuellar; Finance: Roberto Junguito and José Ocampo, both twice, Alberto Carrasquilla; Mining: Miguel Urrutia, Carlos Caballero
23 Deputy finance ministers: Carolina Soto, Ana Maiguashca, Leonardo Villar, Sergio Clavijo, Juan Zárate, Juan Laserna, María Cuellar, Luis Flórez, Francisco Vallejo; Industry and trade: Juan Echavarría, Labor: Gerardo Hernández; Agriculture: Carlos Ossa.
24 Directors: José Ocampo, María Cuellar, Luis Flórez, Francisco Vallejo, Miguel Urrutia; deputy directors: Hernándo J. Gómez, Fernando Tenjo; chief programming unit: José D. Uribe; director of investment and public finance: Carolina Soto; director's assistant: Juan M. Laserna.
25 Just six women from 1923 to 2022. Chapter 13 in this volume presents an extensive discussion of women's participation in economic policy in the 20th century.
26 Directors of Fedesarrollo: Leonardo Villar, Roberto Steiner, Mauricio Cárdenas, Juan Echavarría, Miguel Urrutia, Guillermo Perry, José Ocampo; Carlos Caballero, Roberto Junguito. Researcher: María M. Cuellar.

Bibliography

Adolph, C. (2013). *Bankers, bureaucrats, and central banks politics: The myth of neutrality*. Cambridge University Press.
Alesina, A., Carrasquilla, A., & Steiner, R. (2000). *The central bank in Colombia*. Fedesarrollo.
Álvarez, A., Guiot-Isaac, A., & Hurtado, J. (2019). La formación de una tecnocracia pragmática: Los inicios de la formación profesional de economistas colombianos. *Desarrollo y sociedad*, *82*: 41–71.
Ardila, J. P. (2010). *Antiimperialismo e imperialismo por invitación - la opinión pública colombiana frente al Tratado Urrutia-Thomson*. [Monografía de grado]. Universidad de los Andes.
Avella Gómez, M. (2009). *Pensamiento y política monetaria en Colombia 1886–1945*. Banco de la República.
Avella Gómez, M. (2014). La independencia de la banca central en Colombia desde 1923. Aspectos institucionales. *Revista de Economía Institucional*, *16*(30), 171–214.

Banco de la República. (1929). NOTAS EDITORIALES. *Revista del Banco de la República, 2*(17), 77.

Banco de la República. (1947). Don Julio Caro. *Revista del Banco de la República, 20*(235), 343–344.

Banco de la República. (1948). LOS SUCESOS DEL NUEVE DE ABRIL. *Revista del Banco de la República, 21*(246), 403–404.

Banco de la República. (1950). Técnicos Bancarios. *Revista del Banco de la República 23*(271), 495.

Banco de la República. (1953). NOTAS EDITORIALES. *Revista del Banco de la República, 26*(308), 599–604.

Banco de la República. (1954). CUARTA REUNIÓN DE TÉCNICOS DE LA BANCA CENTRAL DEL CONTINENTE AMERICANO. *Revista del Banco de la República*, 786–789.

Bejarano, J. A. (1989). La Economía Colombiana entre 1922 y 1929. In G. Zea (Ed.), *Nueva Historia de Colombia: Economía, Café, Industria.* Vol. 5, Planeta.

Bejarano, J. A. (2007). El despegue Cafetero. In J. A. Ocampo (Ed.), *Historia Económica de Colombia* (pp. 195–232). Planeta/Fedesarrollo.

Bordo, M., & Istrefi, K. (2018). Perceived FOMC: The making of hawks, doves, and swingers. *NBER Working Papers, 24650.*

Bushnell, D. (2021). *Colombia Una nación a pesar de sí misma.* Planeta.

Caballero, C. (2016). *La economía colombiana del siglo XX.* Penguin Random House.

Cadena, X. (2020). *Fedesarrollo: 50 años de influencia en Política Pública.* Fedesarrollo.

Campuzano Hoyos, J. (2013). *Fuentes documentales para la Historia Empresarial La industria en Antioquia 1900–1920.* EAFIT.

Cardenas, J. (2013). Evolución histórica del Banco de la República en Colombia: una aproximación. *Finanzas y Política Económica, 5*(2), 71–87.

Cárdenas, M., & Partow, Z. (1998). Does independence matter? the case of the Colombian Central Bank. *Documentos de trabajo Fedesarrollo 9205.*

Currie, L. (1950). *Basis of a development program for Colombia.* World Bank.

Dávila, C. (2003). *Empresas y empresarios en la historia de Colombia Siglos XIX–XX: una colección de estudios recientes.* Norma.

Drake, P. (1989). *The money doctor in the Andes.* Duke University Press.

Drekonja-Kornat, G. (1983). Colombia: Learning the foreign policy process. *Journal of Interamerican Studies and World Affairs, 25*(2), 229–250.

Gamboa, J., Gomez-Gonzalez, J., Hirs-Garzon, J., Meisel-Roca, A., & Ojeda-Joya, J. (2016). El programa de apoyos para estudios en el exterior del Banco de la República y la formación del capital humano en el área económica en Colombia. *Borradores de Economía, No.973.*

Gómez Arrubla, F. (1983). Creación y organización del Banco de la República. In F. Gómez-Arrubla (Ed.), *Historia del Banco de la República 60 años* (pp. 43–68). Banco de la República.

Gómez Pineda, J. (2017). El Banco de la República durante 1951–1963: La Estabilidad Macroeconómica en la Balanza. In J. D. Uribe (Ed.), *Historia del banco de la República, 1923–2015* (pp. 121–184). Banco de la República.

Hernández, A., & Jaramillo-Echeverri, J. (2017). La Junta Monetaria y el Banco de la República. In J. D. Uribe (Ed.), *Historia del Banco de la República 1923–2015* (pp. 185–273). Banco de la República.

Hernández Gamarra, A. (2001). La banca central en Colombia: Banco Nacional (1880), Banco Central (1905), Banco de la República (1923). *Credencial Historia 135. La Banca en Colombia.*

Hernández Gamarra, A. (2013). Office of the Comptroller General of the Republic: A debate that is ninety years old. In C. G. República (Ed.), *Contraloría General de la República Ninety Years. A transparent vision.* (pp. 183–223). Contraloría General de la República.

Hommes, R. (2021). *Así lo recuerdo.* Penguin Random House.

Hommes, R., & Melo, J. E. (2017). El debate sobre la Banca Central en la Constituyente de 1991. In J. D. Uribe (Ed.), *Historia del Banco de la República 1923–2015* (pp. 353–384). Banco de la República.

Ibañez Najar, J. E. (1990). Antecedentes legales de la creación del Banco de la República. In A. Meisel Roca (Ed.), *El Banco de la República: antecedentes evolución y estructura* (pp. 194–237). Banco de la República.

Ibánez Najar, J. E., & Meisel Roca, A. (1990). La segunda misión Kemmerer. In A. Meisel Roca (Ed), *El Banco de la República: antecedentes, evolución y estructura* (pp. 342–364). Banco de la República.

Jaramillo-Echeverri, J., Meisel-Roca, A., & Ramírez-Giraldo, M. T. (2016). La Gran Depresión en Colombia: Un estímulo a la industrialización, 1930–1953. *Cuadernos de Historia Económica y Empresarial* 39: 1–49.

Junguito, R., & Rincón, H. (2007). La política fiscal en el siglo XX en Colombia. In J. Robinson, & M. Urrutia (Eds), *Economía Colombiana del siglo XX: Un análisis cuantitativo* (pp. 239–313). Banco de la República/Fondo de Cultura Económica.

Kalmanovitz, S., & López, E. (2006). *La Agricultura Colombiana en el siglo XX.* FCE/ Banco de la República.

Lleras Restrepo, C. (1987). La obra económica y fiscal del liberalismo. In P. Mendoza Neira, & A. Camacho Angarita (Eds), *El liberalismo en el Gobierno, 1930–1946.* Minerva.

Malmendier, U., Nagel, S., & Yan, Z. (2021). The making of hawks and doves. *Journal of Monetary Economics, 117,* 19–42.

Masciandaro, D., Profeta, P., & Romelli, D. (2018). Do Women Matter in Monetary Policymaking? *Bocconi Working Paper, 88.*

Meisel, A. (2001). Orígenes de la banca comercial en Colombia: la banca libre, 1870–1886. *Credencial Historial 135.* https://www.banrepcultural.org/biblioteca-virtual/credencial-historia/numero-135/origenes-de-la-banca-comercial-en-colombia

Meisel, A., & Barón, J. (2010). A historical analysis of central bank independence in Latin America: the Colombian experience, 1923–2008. *Revista de Historia Economica-Journal of Iberian and Latin American Economic History, 28*(1), 83–102.

Meisel, A., & Viloria, J. (1998). Los alemanes en el Caribe colombiano: El caso de Adolfo Held. *Boletín Cultural y Bibliográfico N.35,* 49–100.

Meisel Roca, A. (1990a). El Banco de la República 1946, 1954 y la reforma de 1951. In A. Meisel Roca (Ed.), *El Banco de la República: Antecedentes, evolución y estructura* (pp. 434–481). Banco de la República.

Meisel Roca, A. (1990b). La creación del Banco de la República y sus primeras reformas. In A. Meisel Roca (Ed.), *El Banco de la República: antecedentes, evolución y estructura.* (pp. 278–341). Banco de la República.

Meisel Roca, A. (1990c). Los bancos comerciales en la era de la banca libre 1871–1923. In A. Meisel Roca (Ed.), *El Banco de la República: antecedentes, evolución y estructura* (pp. 166–193). Banco de la República.

Meisel Roca, A. (2016). Antecedentes del Banco de la República, 1904–1922. *Revista del Banco de la República 89*(1060), 25–40.

Meisel Roca, A., & Jaramillo-Echeverri, J. (2017). Las políticas del Banco de la República durante un auge entre dos crisis, 1930–1951. In J. D. Uribe (Ed.), *Historia del Banco de la República 1923–2015* (pp. 1923–2015). Banco de la República.

Melo, J. O. (2017). *Historia mínima de Colombia*. El Colegio de México.

Ocampo, J. A. (1984). Economía Colombiana en la década del treinta. In J. A. Ocampo, & M. Santiago (Eds), *Crisis mundial, protección e industrialización* (pp. 19–56). Norma.

Ochoa Díaz, H., & Martínez Montealegre, Á. (2005). El comportamiento de la inflación en Colombia durante el período 1955–2004. *Estudios Gerenciales, 95*, 75–94.

Otero Muñoz, G. (1948). *El Banco de la República, 1923–1948*. Banco de la República.

Perry, G. (1995). 25 años de Fedesarrollo. Una visión retrospectiva. *Coyuntura Económica: Investigación Económica y social, 49*(1–2), 171–175.

Restrepo Santamaría, N. (2016). *Empresariado antioqueño y sociedad 1940–2004*. Penguin Random House.

Rivera, M. (2002a). Departamentos en la Facultad de Ciencias Humanas: Integración para el desarrollo, 1966–1978. In G. Hernández, & B. Herrera (Eds), *Búsquedas y logros desde la academia 50 años Facultad de Ciencias Económicas* (pp. 82–120). Universidad Nacional de Colombia.

Rivera, M. (2002b). Institucionalización de los Estudios Económicos en la Universidad Nacional de Colombia 1945–1952. In Antonio Hernández y Herrera Beethoven (Eds), *Búsquedas y logros desde la academia* (pp. 29–50). Universidad Nacional de Colombia.

Sáenz Rovner, E. (1992). *La ofensiva empresarial: industriales, políticos y violencia en los años 40 en Colombia*. Universidad de los Andes.

Sáenz Rovner, E. (2001). La misión del banco mundial en Colombia, el gobierno de Laureano Gómez (1950–1951) y la Asociación Nacional de Industriales. *Cuadernos de Economía 20*(35), 245–265.

Sánchez, F., & Bedoya, J. G. (2016). La danza de los millones y la gran depresión en Colombia, 1923–1931. *Documento CEDE 1107*.

Sandilands, R. (2015). La Misión del Banco Mundial a Colombia de 1949, y las visiones opuestas de Lanclin Currie y Albert Hirschman. *Revista de Economía Institucional, 17*(32), 213–232.

Santos Molano, E. (2005). La misión Kemmerer. *Credencial Historia, 184*. https://www.banrepcultural.org/biblioteca-virtual/credencial-historia/numero-184/la-mision-kemmerer

Sastoque Ramírez, E. C. (2018). *El papel de los banqueros en la construcción del Estado y la soberanía monetaria en Colombia (1980–1931)*. Universidad Externado de Colombia.

Seidel, R. (1972). American reformers abroad: The Kemmerer missions in South America, 1923–1931. *The Journal of Economic History, 32*(2), 520–545.

Tirado Mejía, A. (2014). *Los años sesenta: una revolución en la cultura*. Penguin Random House.

Tirado Mejía, A. (2018). *Aspectos políticos del primer gobierno de Alfonso López Pumarejo 1934–1938*. Universidad Nacional de Colombia.

Torres del Río, C. M. (2015). *Colombia Siglo XX: Desde la Guerra de los mil días hasta la elección de Alvaro Uribe*. Pontificia Universidad Javeriana.

Urrutia, M. (1983). *Gremios, política económica y democracia*. Fondo Cultural Cafetero.

13 A Mere Guest?

The Slow Process of Women's Participation in Top Decision-Making Positions (1950–2000)*

Marta Juanita Villaveces-Niño, Ricardo José Salas-Díaz and Pilar Torres-Alvarado

13.1 Introduction

During the 20th century, economic decision-making positions were mostly occupied by men. Colombia was no exception. Although women are still a minority in the economics profession, women's representation in public sector decision-making positions has increased slowly since 1950, women having acquired the right to study for a university degree (1934), the right to be elected to representative roles (1954), and the right to participate (vote) in politics (1954).

In this chapter, we trace how women in Colombia reached decision-making positions. Following Goldins's (2006) analysis of women's participation in the labor market as an evolutionary response and as a revolution in terms of women's genuine decisions and choices, we look at how women's participation in the economics profession evolved. Changes began in 1934 with the possibility of pursuing university degrees and in 1943 with the creation of formal economics undergraduate programs. After attending university, these women worked their way toward senior economic positions in the private and public sectors. Concrete and visible legislation and inclusive actions marked the evolutionary path. In contrast, the revolutionary path imprinted on women's particular experiences about their perceptions of the moment, when their decisions followed their own choices rather than those of others. The revolutionary path implied women's gradual empowerment and the construction of their identities through their interest in particular economic policy matters and the creation of a differentiated language among economists.

The evolutionary path shows how women dealt with the constraints and opportunities they faced in their professional careers in economics while complying with their culturally assigned roles and still being able to arrive at senior positions. Their revolutionary path shows how the unique research and policy topics these women pursued helped forge their specific identity in economics.

* For research assistance we are grateful to Jenny Moreno and Sara Caicedo, both women studying economics at the National University of Colombia.

DOI: 10.4324/9781003289241-15

With this chapter, we aim to fill the gap in the literature explaining the documented low participation of women in academia and public economic policy. The past can give us clues to the historical causes of these differences; we use a qualitative and institutional approach to describe the timing of women's enrolment in and graduation from economics courses and their initial participation in senior positions. The political scenario also played a significant role in opening up possibilities for public participation for women economists. The military dictatorship, the transition to democracy, and the competitive democratic game changed views and attitudes in policy-making and political parties on women in decision-making positions. With the 1991 Constitution, women's participation in the political process became a priority.

The individual and personal dimensions that mark the revolutionary aspect of the process are harder to pin down. However, women's academic production and participation in the written press present subtle changes in their positions that hint at a probably revolutionary identity construction process.

This chapter divides the second half of the 20th century into three stages of women's inclusion in decision-making positions that coincide with the rise of economists in power. From 1950 to 1974, women achieved some political equality. However, this period was a "slow awakening" due to political factors and the lack of female access to higher education. From 1974 to 1989, women participated in the top decision-making positions "at the rulers' initiative." The economic slowdown, partisan stability, and the rise of guerrilla violence permitted women's access to these spheres, backed up by their previous political participation and access to higher education programs. From 1989 onwards, the participation of women in the cabinet is constant, showing that it was no longer a fortuitous decision of the president in office but a constant commitment to have women in ministerial positions or the cabinet. The 1991 Constitution established conditions of equality. The constitution does not translate into rapidly closing the gender gaps in the following decade, as shown by labor market indicators. A gap in elite public jobs and academia remains despite new legislation. Even if a larger share of women enrolled in economics at the undergraduate level, glass ceilings hindered them from reaching top decision-making jobs, graduate studies, and research positions.

This chapter contributes to the literature in three ways: first, we describe how women came to participate in top decision-making positions in the economy in Colombia; second, we address the entry mechanisms to decision-making positions; finally, we account for these women's academic production and the topics they brought to the public and academic debate. To our knowledge, this is the first analysis that integrates these three elements for the Colombian case.

13.2 Toward Female Participation in Top Economic Positions

The long-run gender bias in economics has also been observed in women's representation in leadership positions (Stainback et al., 2016), both in the private and public sectors. The steep road to reaching top positions shows the interaction of three issues: formal norms and legal restraints that have to evolve to accept women's participation in top-level positions; informal rules or social norms that historically assume women are less capable of making decisions (Niederle, 2015); and the strong masculine voice, representation, and participation in economics that explains the perception of women's inferior role in the discipline.

Women's participation in top positions and political representation has not gone hand in hand with economic development and greater participation in the labor force (Jaquette, 1997, p.26). Excluding women from technocratic appointments in the 1970s and 1980s was justified with presumed objective arguments related to gender differences in education (Burris, 1989), thus reproducing non-gender neutral practices and advantages (Acker, 1990; Stainback et al., 2016).

The economic and social tensions of the 1980s due to market-oriented reforms and austerity programs led to a wave of female mobilization around care, health, and public services (Jaquette, 1997). Women's increasing participation in the political arena attests to their specific political attitudes, which are more concerned with "soft issues" than military spending or war (May et al., 2014). In the 1990s, with the third wave of feminism, women fought against social norms rather than for rights, as they had done before (Heywood & Drake, 1997; Henry, 2004). Attempting to build their life projects outside gender stereotypes, women aimed at being able to make genuine personal and individual choices. Women's participation in any sphere or activity should be their own decision rather than the result of a man's *good intentions*. Implementing this goal required legislation and quota laws to increase women's political participation and appointment to high-ranking positions.

Until the 1930s, the law in Colombia did not allow women to enroll in universities and restricted their political participation. Gender biases also led to informal exclusion confining women to middle and lower positions in the labor market, particularly as domestic workers, secretaries, and nurses (Iregui-Bohórquez et al., 2021). The slow road to participation began in the 1930s when women were allowed to pursue university studies; in the 1940s, women became citizens, and in 1954, they won the right to vote.

Access to higher education and political representation were fundamental in appointing women to presidential cabinets (Sotomayor & Huertas-Hernández, 2021). The first women to enter higher education in Colombia triggered the political discussion in Congress during the Liberal Republic.[1] In 1932, women acquired the right of ownership and disposal of their wealth and goods. The same year Congress passed a bill that allowed women to access higher education. In 1933 women obtained the right to receive a high-school degree, opening the possibility of entering higher education programs. In 1934 the creation of the Ministry of Education promoted the discussion about women's access. Some universities opened specific sections for women the following year, and 57 women joined their programs (Uribe, n.d.). [2]

Gender biases persisted during the emergence of public technocratic organizations in the late 1960s. The appointment of women to decision-making positions in Colombia combines internal and external factors in a similar fashion, as Jacquette (1997) and Goldins (2006) describe. The country's economic performance, access to universities, increasing political rights, and the agenda and decisions of presidents in office came into play with what Goldin calls the "quiet revolution," that is, women's own dynamic decisions about their professional careers. Other common economic and social privilege factors were also present (Wills, 2007). Inclusion was not for all women, and those from advantaged backgrounds had access to top positions, sometimes inherited from a close male relative (Wills, 2007).

We follow Iregui-Bohórquez et al.'s (2021) periodization and Jaquette's (1997) analysis of the link between economic development and women's representation and participation to propose three periods to retrace how women's participation in decision-making positions in Colombia evolved from a role in the shadow of men to an active position with their own agenda: first, the "slow awakening" from 1950 to 1974, then "participation at the ruler's initiative" from 1974 to 1989; and finally from 1989 to 2000, "gaps remain with new legislation."

These three periods include four explanatory variables: economic growth, women's participation in the labor market, education, and the political scenario. From 1950 to 2000, the interaction between these variables explains the transition between the three periods we identify with increasing participation of women – even if they represent less than 30% of the legislative and executive branches today.

Figure 13.1(a) shows the three periods and the evolution of the growth rate during those periods. It is widely accepted in the literature that women's participation in the labor market positively correlates with higher levels of economic growth. Between 1950 and 1980, Colombia experienced significant growth rates, close to 6% per year. This growth was sustained mainly by industrial activity, which generated changes in the participation of women in the labor market and brought about social changes associated with the urbanization process. As shown in Figure 13.1(b), women's participation in the labor market increased from 17% in 1950 to about 37% in 1980, although it was still low, and especially unskilled labor showed visible growth.

External and internal crises slowed growth in the 1980s. Women were invited to join the cabinet and participate in issues that were sensitive for the country (Jaquette, 1997). There is no clear connection between women's participation and economic activity during the next decade. Nevertheless, women's participation in the labor market rose from about 37% in 1980 to almost 60% in 2000, in unskilled and skilled activities, and in different economic sectors.

During the first period, women had low access to university education, which explains why they were appointed to any position requiring expert knowledge. In the 1960s and 1970s, women increasingly enrolled in higher education programs, giving them the knowledge and expertise needed to occupy decision-making positions.

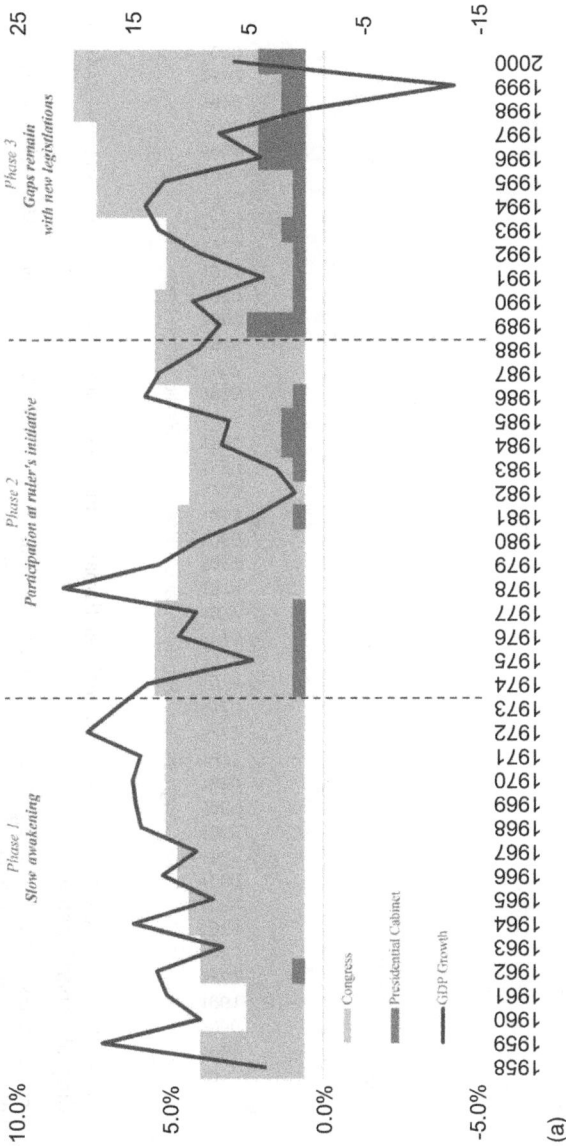

Figure 13.1 (a) Stages of women's participation in top decision-making positions (1950–2000), including GDP growth.

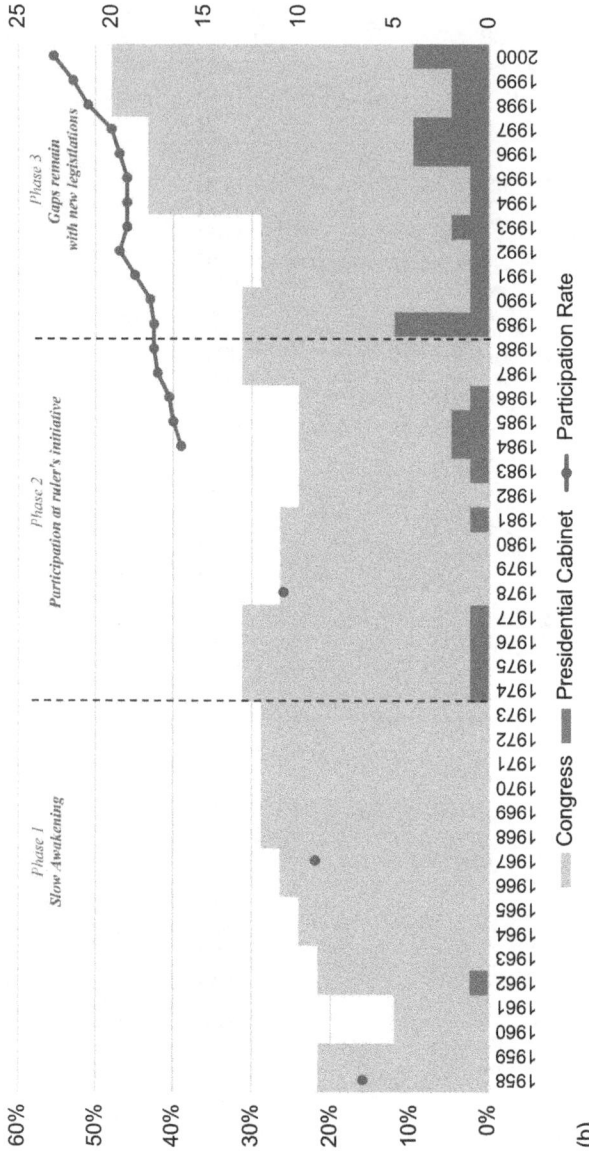

Figure 13.1 (Continued) (b) Stages of women's participation in top decision-making positions (1950–2000), including labor participation.

Source: Congress – Inter-Parliamentary Union: women in parliament, 2022; Presidential cabinet – Martínez Garnica, 2018; GDP – Greco. 2002, Iregui-Bohórquez et al., 2021. Own calculations.

Notes: GDP growth is represented by the blue line and the left axis. Women in both Congress and presidential cabinets are in numbers. Women in presidential cabinets reflects women in the cabinet on 7 August of that year.

   The first period in this story takes place under a dictatorship (1953–1957), followed by a transition to democracy marked by a political agreement between the traditional parties called the National Front, where any change to the dominant male political status quo was out of the question. Electoral competition, economic crisis, political violence, and more educated women were the key elements in the second stage. A new political constitution consecrating equality of rights but a persistent low economic capacity were the characteristic features of the third phase in the participation of women in top decision-making positions.

   The first two periods show an increase in women's participation in economic decision-making positions, whereas there is a slight stagnation between the second and third periods.

   We reviewed the participation in the main public entities that directly and indirectly make economic decisions. We considered the following as direct decision-making institutions: Banco de la República (central bank), the National Planning Department, the Ministry of the Treasury, the Tax and Customs Department, the National Statistics Department, and the Banking Superintendence. We included all the other ministries as part of indirect economic decision-making institutions. We also included the participation of women in academia as professors affiliated to the main economics departments in the country (Table 13.1). Some of the women we identified move from one

Table 13.1 Women in top economic positions, 1950–2000

	1950–1974	1974–1988	1989–2000	Total
National Planning Department	—	1	1	2
Monetary authority*	—	1	2	3
Deputy Finance Minister	—	1	—	1
Banking Superintendent	—	—	2	2
Tax and Customs Department	—	—	1	1
Statistical Department	—	—	1	1
Ministers	2	7	10	19
Deputy Minister (other Ministers)	—	10	3	13
Academia		6	9	15
Total	**2**	**26**	**29****	**57**

Source: Martínez Garnica, 2018; Wills, 2007, Appointment decrees, press, web sources. Own calculations.

* Monetary Board from 1964 to 1991, and Board of directors of the Banco de la República 1950–1964 and from 1991

** Underestimated; we do not have information for DM (other Ministers) 1989–2000

Table 13.2 Women's participation in the legislature, 1950–2000

Legislature	1950–1974	1974–1989	1989–2000	Total
Lower Chamber (*Cámara de Representantes*)	30	29	29	88
Upper Chamber (*Senado de la República*)	4	4	22	30
Total	34	33	51	118

Source: Inter-Parliamentary Union: women in parliament, 2022, Estadísticas electorales Registraduría Nacional (1968, 1970, 1974, 1978, 1982, 1986, 1990). Own calculations.

Note: row and column totals may not sum up because the same women could be elected in more than one period.

institution to another, and not all are economists; some have law degrees or graduated from other social sciences programs.

In Colombia, to date no woman has been appointed as minister of the Treasury, nor has there been a female governor of the central bank, the two top economic decision-making positions in the country. However, since the 1970s, there has been a slight rise in female economists in the presidential cabinets and other relevant economic positions.

Table 13.2 presents the number of women in Congress. Women's participation in the legislative branch gives them visibility and may be a way for them to access other spheres of power. The increasing number of women suggests a greater gender representation and gender visibility.

13.3 1950 to 1974: "The Slow Awakening"

The slow awakening describes how women gained some rights with no real participation because their participation required social movements demanding social changes (Wills, 2007). The National Front (1958–1974) guaranteed an arranged transition to democracy that locked political power between the two traditional political parties, making any change impossible without their approval. In this context, women were rarely appointed to top positions, and only when the leaders of the political parties decided to give them some participation. During Rojas Pinilla's dictatorship, Josefina Valencia was appointed Education Minister and remained in office from September 1956 until May 1957. Esmeralda Arboleda, former secretary of the Liberal Party, became the first female Communication Minister in 1961, under the Lleras Camargo administration, and she was the first woman to be elected to the Senate (1958–1960). Arboleda was a well-known figure in the country because she had been active in the referendum for women's vote and had been an outspoken opponent of the dictatorship. Following in Arboleda's footsteps, women's political participation in Congress increased slowly. During the 1960s, an average of 9.2 women were elected to Congress. In the late 1960s and the beginning of the 1970s, this number was 12.

The student-led social protests worldwide and access to the contraceptive pill fostered the second wave of demands from women in the 1960s after their mobilization to gain the right to vote. Their roles as wives and mothers in the private sphere were denounced as cultural barriers to personal, educational, and professional achievement. These barriers hindered women from entering higher education and obtaining professional degrees, slowing down their arrival at decision-making positions (Ochoa Nuñez, 1977; Pontificia Universidad Javeriana, 2011).

In 1950, María Elvira Santos was the first female economist to graduate from the Gimnasio Moderno, an elite private school that had created an Economics Department in 1943. The number of women graduating from economics programs increased between 1950 and 1974, reaching almost 10% of the total of people graduating with a BA in economics (according to the data from the *Statistical Yearbooks* of the Comptroller's Office). The gender gap in economics was larger than in the rest of the higher education system. By the end of the period, women represented 25% of total graduates (Ochoa, 1977). Between 1946 and 1966, the first two decades of formal economic programs in universities, only 90 women completed their degrees compared to 1190 men.

This first period, "slow awakening," did not see many women in decision-making spaces. However, their gradual participation in higher education and politics was the starting point for material changes in the years to come.

13.4 1974 to 1989: Participation at the Initiative of Men in Power

The first competitive elections since 1952 took place at the end of the National Front in 1974. With them came hope for greater political participation and representation for minority and traditionally excluded groups, including women. Political parties saw an electoral opportunity in the "female" discourse, included campaign slogans specifically addressed to women, and organized rallies with women.

Liberal candidates, like Alfonso López Michelsen, included women's issues in their campaign discourses, advocating for legal and social equality, civil marriage, and civil divorce. Using the phrase "we must talk to women, 'man to man,' we must talk to women on equal terms,"[3] López Michelsen made a strong stand for equality. Once in office, López Michelsen promulgated the Statute on the Equal Rights of Men and Women (Decree 2820 of 1974), which eliminated all legal dispositions of parental authority over adult women. López Michelsen appointed a well-known public figure from Antioquia as Labor Minister. María Elena Jiménez had a long civil service career as a councillor, departmental deputy, Chamber representative, and senator. After Jiménez left office, Sara Ordoñez was appointed as Minister of Communications; Ordoñez would later become Banking Supervisor and Health Minister.

An economic slowdown marked the 1980s. The slowdown, from 5% to 3% annual GDP growth, came with unemployment, lower incomes, higher poverty and informality, the absence of social security, and the war between the government and guerrillas. Ten women were appointed deputy ministers during the Betancur administration (1982–1986), following Maristella Sanín, Minister of Labor and Social Security, during the previous Turbay administration. Betancur's bold appointments proved challenging to execute. His cabinet members, all men, could not or would not find suitable candidates; they needed to go beyond their own biases and traditional views (López, 2018). Finally, ten young women with the required skills and education were appointed. However, no woman was appointed to Betancur's first cabinet. In 1983, Noemí Sanín assumed the post of Communication Minister until 1986. Three women, Doris Eder de Zambrano, Liliam Suárez, and Marina Uribe de Eusse, successively occupied the post at the head of the Education Ministry (see Table 13.3).

Table 13.3 Women in top decision-making positions, 1974–1989

Name	Institution	Position	Year
María Elena Jiménez de Crovo	Ministry of Labour	Minister	1974
Sara Ordoñez de Londoño	Ministry of Communication	Minister	1976
Maristella Sanín de Aldana	Ministry of Labour	Minister	1981
Noemí Sanín Posada	Ministry of Communication	Minister	1983
Doris Eder de Zambrano	Ministry of Education	Minister	1984
Liliam Suárez Melo	Ministry of Education	Minister	1985
Marina Uribe de Eusse	Ministry of Education	Minister	1986
María Mercedes Cuellar	Deputy Public Works Minister	Deputy Minister	1982
Margarita Durán	Deputy Transport Minister	Deputy Minister	1982
Flor Ángela Gómez	Deputy Housing Minister	Deputy Minister	1982
Beatriz de la Vega	Deputy Health Minister	Deputy Minister	1982
Laura Ochoa de Ardila	Deputy Foreign Affairs Minister	Deputy Minister	1982
Clara Victoria Colbert	Deputy Education Minister	Deputy Minister	1982
María Elena Paez de Tavera	Deputy Labor Minister	Deputy Minister	1982
Margarita Mena Quevedo	Deputy Mining and Energy Minister	Deputy Minister	1982
María Cristina Mejía	Deputy Communication Minister	Deputy Minister	1982
Cecilia López Montaño	Deputy Agriculture Minister	Deputy Minister	1982
María Mercedes Cuellar	Deputy Finance Minister	Deputy Minister	1984
María Mercedes Cuellar	National Planning Department	Director	1986
María Mercedes Cuellar	Monetary Board	Director	1986
Carmen Elisa Flórez	Universidad de los Andes	Professor	1983
Astrid Martínez	Fedesarrollo	Researcher	1981^
Elssy Bonilla	Universidad de los Andes	Professor	1979^
Nohra Rey de Marulanda	Universidad de los Andes	Professor	1977^
Fanny Kertzman	Fedesarrollo	Researcher	1986^
Olga Lucía Acosta	Banco de la República	Researcher	1985^
María Luisa Chiappe	ANIF	Director Research	1981

Source: Wills, 2007; Martínez Garnica, 2018; Press, web sources, own calculations.

^Approximate date.

More women also arrived in academia.[4] In the 1980s, two women with PhDs in economics, Nohra Rey and Carmen Elisa Flórez, became directors of the Center of Studies in Development Economics (CEDE for its Spanish acronym) at Los Andes University. Rey received her doctorate from the University of Sussex and Flórez from Princeton University. They became pioneers in the study of labor economics and demography, but their successful academic careers remained exceptional in Colombia. Women were less likely to receive financial support to pursue graduate studies from local funding institutions. The central bank created a scholarship program for Colombian students to attend prestigious international universities, especially in the United States, so they could come back to the civil service after completing their PhD. During the program's first decade, less than 16% of the awardees were women. In the years to come, one in four scholarships were awarded to women.

13.5 1989 to 2000: The Gap Remains Despite New Legislation

1989 marks the beginning of the third stage, when women constantly appear in top decision-making positions and not as the result of an executive decision by the president in office. This constant presence is backed by the 1991 Political Constitution that gave equal rights to men and women and banned discrimination against women.

These institutional changes allowed the women who had previously occupied decision-making roles to strengthen their position and network, and to consolidate the good standing they had built among their male peers.[5] Other women were appointed to these positions, mainly due to their graduate studies and previous contact with technocrats and policymakers (men and women). Examples include Astrid Martínez, who worked in the oil, energy, and transport sector; Nohora Rey and Carmen Flórez, the first and second female directors of the Center for Studies on Economic Development at Los Andes University; Consuelo Corredor, the first woman to become Dean of the Economics School of the National University; and María Teresa Ramírez, Martha Misas, and Ligia Melo, economic researchers at the central bank.

However, Figure 13.2 and Table 13.4 show that a glass ceiling prevented women from reaching top decision-making positions in traditionally male ministries like finance (Iregui-Bohórquez et al., 2021; Archila, 2013; Wills, 2007).

Despite constitutional and legislative changes, gender stereotypes remained in the public imagination, presenting women as less capable of making complex decisions, exercising authority, or occupying top positions. More was needed, and several women's organizations began lobbying for quota laws in 1998. The movement proved successful with the approbation of Law 581 of 2000 (Wills, 2007). The debate was complex and found opposition in male and female economists, who considered any quota contrary to the meritocracy that should be the primary selection criterion to access top decision-making positions. By the end of the 20th century, women's increasing participation in the labor market was considered a sign of greater gender equality, and many

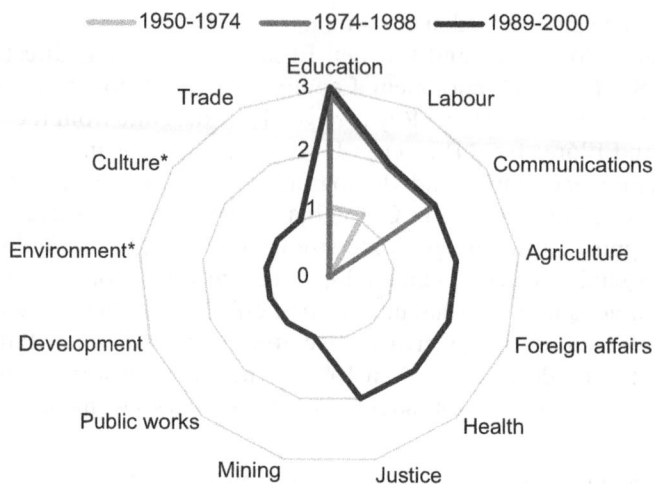

Figure 13.2 The number of female ministers (1950–2000).

Source: Martínez Garnica, 2018, web sources. Own calculations.

Notes: The Ministries of Environment and Culture were created in the 1990s.

Table 13.4 Women in top decision-making positions 1989–2000

Name	Institution	Position	Year
María Teresa Forero de Saade	Ministry of Labour	Minister	1989
Luz Priscila Ceballos Ordoñez	Ministry of Infrastructure	Minister	1989
Mónica de Greiff Lindo	Ministry of Justice	Minister	1989
Margarita Mena de Quevedo	Ministry of Energy	Minister	1989
María Mercedes Cuellar	Ministry of Development	Minister	1989
María del Rosario Sintes Ullóa	Ministry of Agriculture	Minister	1990
María Mercedes Cuellar	Banco de la República	Co-Director	1991
Noemí Sanín Posada	Ministry of External Affairs	Minister	1991
Maruja Pachón de Villamizar	Ministry of Education	Minister	1993
María Luisa Chiappe de Villa	National Statistic Department	Director	1994
Cecilia López Montaño	Ministry of Environment	Minister	1994
María Sol Navia Velasco	Ministry of Labor	Minister	1994
María Emma Mejía	Ministry of Education	Minister	1995
Cecilia López Montaño	Ministry of Agriculture	Minister	1996
María Luisa Chiappe de Villa	Banking Superintendency	Superintendent	1996
María Teresa Forero de Saade	Ministry of Health	Minister	1996
María Emma Mejía	Ministry of External Affairs	Minister	1996

(Continued)

Table 13.4 (Continued)

Name	Institution	Position	Year
Olga Duque de Ospina	Ministry of Education	Minister	1996
Cecilia López Montaño	National Planning Department	Director	1996
Alma Beatriz Rengifo	Ministry of Justice	Minister	1997
Martha Lucía Ramírez	Ministry of Commerce	Minister	1998
Sara Ordoñez Noriega	Banking Superintendency	Superintendent	1998
Fanny Kertzman	Tax and Customs Department	Director	1998
Claudia de Francisco	Ministry of Communication	Minister	1998
Gina Magnolia Riaño	Ministry of Labour	Minister	1998
Luz Amparo Fonseca	Ministry of Agriculture	Deputy Minister	1998
Clemencia Forero	Ministry of External Affairs	Deputy Minister	1989
Catalina Crane	Ministry of Finance	Deputy Minister	2000
Astrid Martínez	Universidad Nacional de Colombia	Professor	1989^
Carmen Elisa Flórez	Universidad de los Andes	Professor	
Elssy Bonilla	Universidad de los Andes	Professor	
Martha Misas	Banco de la República	Researcher	
Nohra Rey de Marulanda	Universidad de los Andes	Director	
Consuelo Corredor	Universidad Nacional de Colombia	Dean	1998
Ligia Melo	Banco de la República	Researcher	1988^
María Teresa Ramírez	Banco de la República	Researcher	1989^
Olga Lucía Acosta	CONFIS	Advisor	

Source: Wills, 2007; Martínez Garnica, 2018; Press, web sources, own calculations.

^Approximate date.

prophesied that the gender gap would disappear as women would be more educated, gain more experience and "merit" their appointment to top decision-making positions in the public sphere.

13.6 Women in Top Decision-making Positions: Education and Academic Production

Most of the women in this study attended private universities (61%) in Bogotá (77%), with a high representation of graduates from Los Andes University, recognized as the epicenter of technocracy in the country (Álvarez et al., 2019; Vitoria de la Hoz, 2019; Dargent, 2011). These women followed the (strongly male) Colombian technocracy trends in their careers. Moreover, their training in private universities also attests to their most likely wealthy family backgrounds, given the high tuition fees and the lack of scholarships to attend these schools.

In line with Villaveces-Niño and Caballero-Argáez (2020), we find women who reach top decision-making positions, like their male counterparts in technocracy in the 20th century, are mainly economists and lawyers; 39.5% of these women are economists, 24% lawyers and 36% have other professional training (Table 13.A1).

The publication pattern we find using the information on the internet associated with these women also shows the difference between the periods we have identified (see Figure 13.3). We find no publications between 1950 and 1974, which can be explained by women's late entry into economics programs and the challenge they faced in gaining visibility and consolidating their place in the economics community.

Between 1974 and 1989, women economists start publishing academic papers (Figure 13.3). We found 58 publications. However, these publications mainly belong to three women: Astrid Martínez authored 44.6% of the publications, followed by Carmen Elisa Flórez with 26.8%, and finally, Cecilia López with 7.1%. Other authors did not account for more than 3.6% of the publications.

Academic production almost doubled between the second and third periods, reaching 109 publications between 1989 and 2000. During these 11 years, Carmen Elisa Flórez authored 42.6% of the publications, while Martha Misas and Astrid Martínez authored 8.51%. The concentration evidenced in the second period persists between 1989 and 2000. The sample we find using the internet also shows the persistence of these publications, giving a sense of the possible influence and visibility of these women in the economics community.

There was a noticeable increase in publications after 1986 (Figure 13.4). Before 1986 the average number of publications was 2.7; after 1986, the average increased to 10.2, indicating a more stable and noticeable participation of women economists in the public debate.

Figure 13.5 shows the topics on which women economists published, as reported by Krapf et al., 2016 and Dolado et al., 2012 for the United States. In

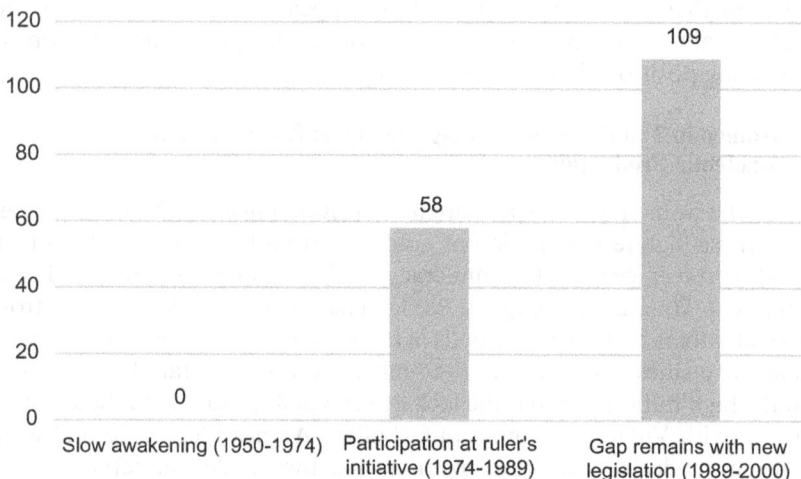

Figure 13.3 Number of publications per period.

Source: Resumes (CVs) of 38 women in top economic positions. Own calculations.

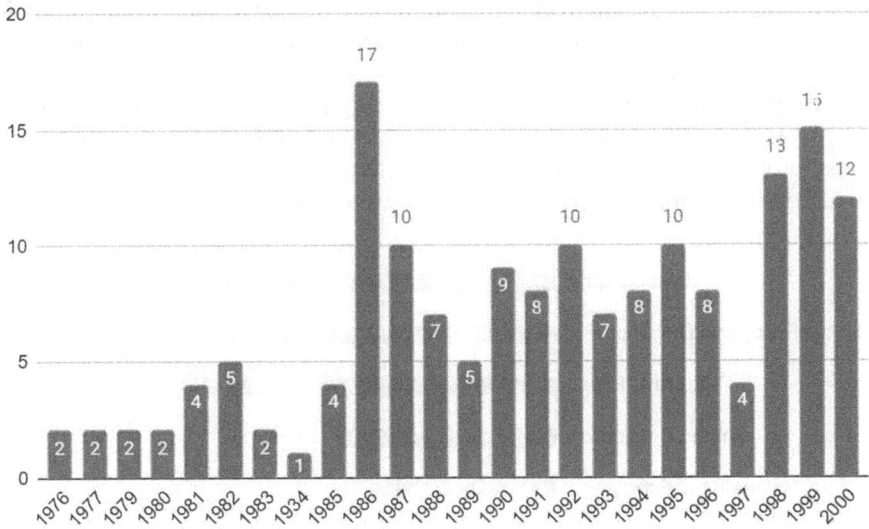

Figure 13.4 Number of publications per year.

Source: Resumes (CVs) of 38 women in top economic positions. Own calculations.

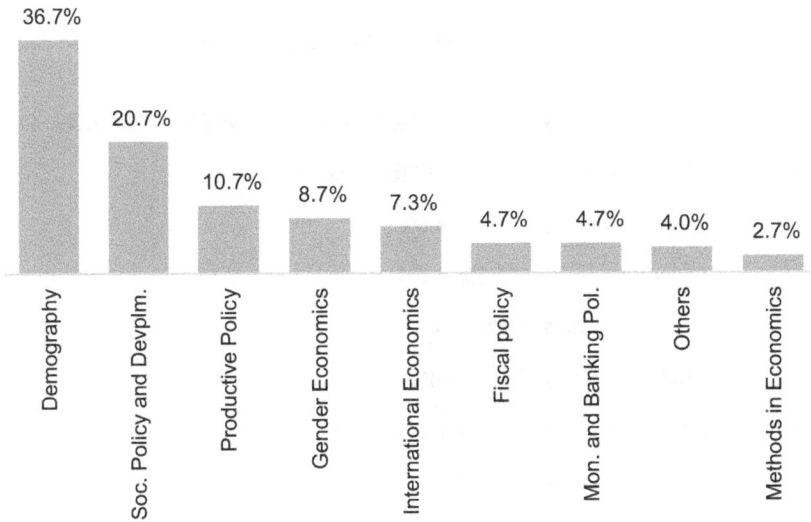

Figure 13.5 Women's participation in research topics (1974–2000).

Source: Resumes (CVs) of 38 women in top economic positions. Own calculations.

Colombia, the largest share of publications is in demography. This might indicate that women concentrate on family and household issues, considered mainly female spaces.

Comparing the topics between periods (Figure 13.6), it is possible to see that women publish primarily on topics related to their positions and those most prominent in the local economic debate. For instance, issues such as industrialization or the agricultural sector are visible in the second period and

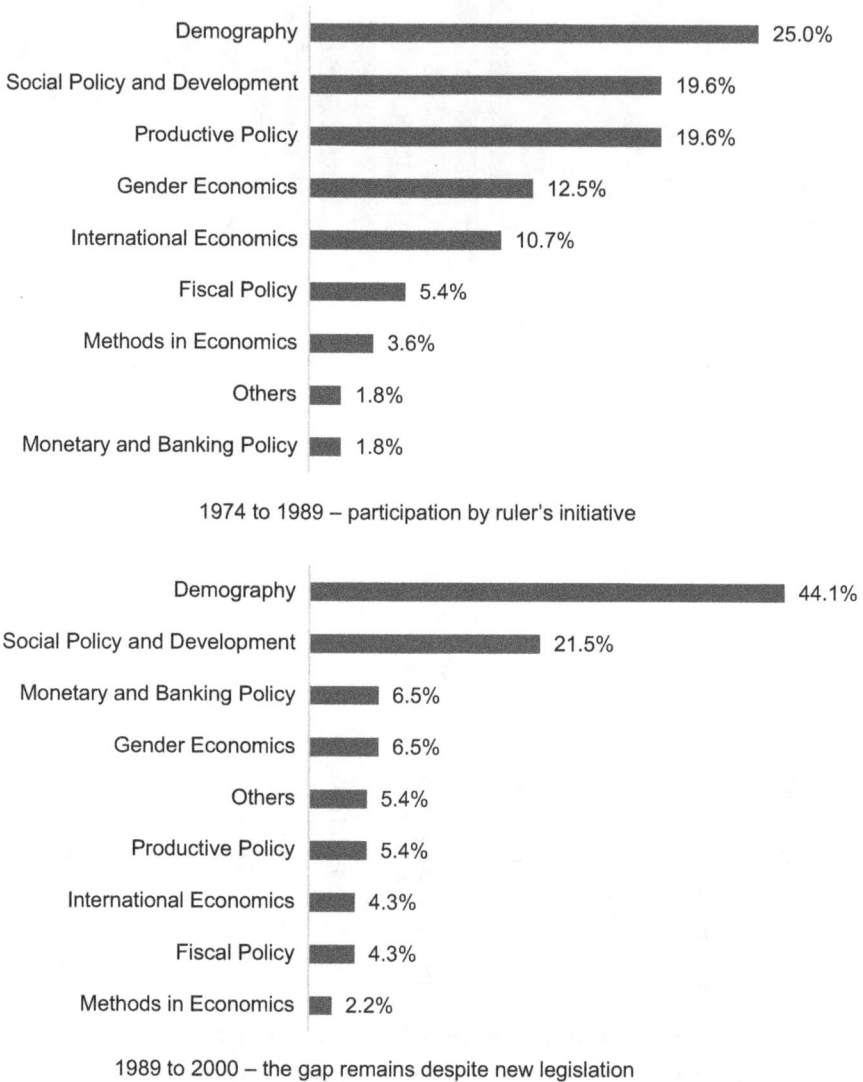

Demography	25.0%
Social Policy and Development	19.6%
Productive Policy	19.6%
Gender Economics	12.5%
International Economics	10.7%
Fiscal Policy	5.4%
Methods in Economics	3.6%
Others	1.8%
Monetary and Banking Policy	1.8%

1974 to 1989 – participation by ruler's initiative

Demography	44.1%
Social Policy and Development	21.5%
Monetary and Banking Policy	6.5%
Gender Economics	6.5%
Others	5.4%
Productive Policy	5.4%
International Economics	4.3%
Fiscal Policy	4.3%
Methods in Economics	2.2%

1989 to 2000 – the gap remains despite new legislation

Figure 13.6 Percentage of topics of academic publications, by period.

Source: Resumes (CVs) of 38 women in top economic positions. Own calculations

lose relevance in the third, in line with the change in the economic growth model, based on industrialization until the 1980s and on globalization in the 1990s. Moreover, these women introduced and pioneered research in gender issues in the 1970s (Puyana, 2007), in line with the advances in women's rights that women's movements had put on the public agenda early in the 20th century.

Elssy Bonilla, Nohra Rey de Marulanda, and Cecilia López were crucial figures in these publications dealing with the role of women in the household, their participation in the labor market, the ensuing tension between care and labor, and how the media participated in defining and perpetuating gender roles in society. A close connection between these publications and causes women championed led to changes in public policy advancing gender equality. As a senator, Cecilia López passed Law 1413 of 2010, which included the care economy in the national accounts. However, these women also participated in other policy debates associated with productivity or monetary policy, showing how they kept current on topical disciplinary and policy issues.

13.7 Conclusion

Education, persistence, and privilege are key elements explaining the increase in women in top-level decision-making positions in the Colombian economy. Legal and institutional changes that advanced women's rights to access higher education in the 1930s or participate in political elections in the 1950s, along with the political decisions by some men in the higher spheres of the national government, opened the way for women to become professional economists and reach top-level positions.

Women's participation increased steadily as more women were formally trained in higher education institutions. They also published more and led the way to new research topics. From a context of rigid political rules during the National Front to more democratic and competitive rules between 1974 and 1989, women entered the high ranks of government officials due to decisions by presidents such as López Michelsen and Betancur who were committed to including women in top decision-making positions. Professional women from privileged backgrounds were among the first to be appointed to these positions.

In the last phase of the 20th century (1989–2000), we find two important facts: on the one hand, the participation of women in the presidential cabinet becomes constant, showing the commitment always to keep a woman in a ministerial position and, on the other, the change in the rules of the game with the 1991 Constitution that gave equal rights to men and women and established non-discrimination. However, as we have said throughout this chapter, rights alone do not generate changes, and affirmative or explicit actions are necessary to materialize them. Throughout this period, there was no significant change in women's participation in decision-making positions or their publications, which indicates resistance to change. Thus, in 1998, a quota law was discussed to encourage greater participation of women; this law was enacted in 2000, and its full consequences are yet to appear.

Despite the changes and advances in women's participation in top decision-making positions, a closed and masculine culture reinforced gender stereotypes that led to questioning women's skills and abilities to occupy these positions. These women persevered, and even if there is still an important gender gap in top decision-making positions, they have left their imprint, especially in academic contributions. The small participation in decision-making positions was ultimately a step towards an important contribution to academic production.

Appendix

Table 13.A1 Women in top decision-making positions, economists and others

Name	Undergraduate	Degree
María Mercedes Cuellar	Andes	Economics
María Luisa Chiappe de Villa	Javeriana	Economics
Marina Uribe de Eusse	de Antioquia	Economics
Cecilia López de Montaño	Andes	Economics
Fanny Kertzman	Andes	Economics
María del Rosario Sintes Ullóa	Andes	Economics
Claudia de Francisco Zambrano	Andes	Economics
Cecilia Maria Velez	Jorge Tadeo Lozano	Economics
Carmen Elisa Flórez	Andes	Economics
Astrid Martínez	Nacional	Economics
Elssy Bonilla	Nacional	Sociology
Martha Misas	Nacional	Matg
Nohra Rey de Marulanda	Andes	Economics
Consuelo Corredor	Externado	Economics
Ligia Melo	Pedagogica	Economics
María Teresa Ramírez	Andes	Economics
Olga Lucía Acosta	Nacional	Economics
Sara Ordoñez de Londoño	Javeriana	Law
Maria Elena Jiménez de Crovo	No information	No information
María Emma Wills	Andes	Political Science
Esmeralda Arboleda de Uriba	del Cauca	Lay
Maristella Sanín de Aldana	No information	No information
Noemí Sanín de Posada	Javeriana	Law
Doris Eder de Zambrano	del Valle	History
Liliam Suárez Melo	Rosario	Law
María Teresa Forero de Saade	Javeriana	Medicine
Luz Priscila Ceballos Ordoñez	del Cauca	Engineering
Mónica de Greiff Lindo	Rosario	Law
Margarita Mena de Quevedo	de Medellin	Law
Maruja Pachón Villamizar	No information	No information

(Continued)

Table 13.A1 (Continued)

Name	Undergraduate	Degree
María Sol Navia VElasco	San Buenaventura	Law
María Emma Mejía Velez	del Valle	Journalism
Olga Duque de Ospina	Santo Tomas	Law
Alma Beatriz Rengifo Lopez	Javeriana	Law
Martha Lucía Ramírez	Javeriana	Law
Gina Magnolia Riaño	Externado	Law
Maria Cristina Serje de la Ossa	Andes	Anthropology
Josefina Valencia de Hubach	No information	No information

Notes

1 The Liberal Republic, between 1930 and 1946, corresponds to the period during which the Liberal Party won the presidential elections for four consecutive terms.
2 The ambiguity of the law allowed for different responses. Some universities, like the Antioquia Univeristy and the Pontificia Universidad Javeriana, created a Women's School. In contrast, some local governments, like Antioquia's, created women's colleges, the *colegios mayores* with different programs from those offered in the universities for men.
3 "*a la mujer hay que hablarle 'de hombre a hombre'; hay que hablarle en pie de igualdad.*"
4 The underrepresentation of women in academia was an international concern. It was clear that traditional economic explanations of discrimination based on preferences underestimated the lack of women in economics. In the 1970s, the American Economic Association created the Committee on the Status of Women in the Economics Profession (CSWP), giving visibility to this situation (Lundberg & Stearns, 2019). Fifteen years later, the Royal Economic Society created a Committee on Women in Economics (Booth & Bennett, 2002). Despite these initiatives, women remained a minority in PhD programs and research positions by the end of the 20th century.
5 For example, Noemí Sanín, former Communication Minister during the Betancur administration, was Foreign Affairs Minister under President Gaviria, María del Rosario Sintes was Minister of Agriculture in the same administration and later became Communication Minister with President Pastrana, and Maruja Pachón's family connections made her close to President Gaviria.

Bibliography

Acker, J. (1990). Hierarchies, jobs, bodies: A theory of gendered organizations. *Gender and Society*, *4*(2), 139–158.

Álvarez, A., Guiot-Isaac, A. M., & Hurtado, J. (2019). La formación de una tecnocracia pragmática: los inicios de la formación profesional de economistas colombianos. *Desarrollo y Sociedad*, *82*, 41–71.

Archila, M. (2013). Aspectos sociales y políticos de las mujeres en Colombia, siglos XX y XXI. In Memorias del XVIII Congreso de la Asociación de Colombianistas. Asociación Colombiana de Historiadores.

Booth, C. & Bennett, C. (2002). Gender mainstreaming in the European Union: Towards a new conception and practice of equal opportunities? *The European Journal of Women's Studies*, *9*(4), 430–446.

Burris, B. (1989). Technocracy and gender in the workplace. *Social Problems, 36*(2), 165–180.

Dargent, E. (2011). *Technocracy and Democracy in Latin America. The Experts Running Government.* Cambridge University Press.

Dolado, J. J., Felgueroso, F., & Almunia, M. (2012). Are men and women economists evenly distributed across research fields? Some new empirical evidence. *SERIEs, 3*(3), 367–393.

Goldins, C. (2006). The quiet revolution that transformed women's employment, education, and family. *American Economic Review, 96*(2), 1–21.

Henry, A. (2004). *Not my mother's sister: Generational conflict and third-wave feminism.* Indiana University Press.

Heywood, L., & Drake, J. (Eds). (1997). *Third wave agenda: Being feminist, doing feminism.* University of Minnesota Press.

Iregui-Bohórquez, A. M., Melo-Becerra, L. A., Ramírez-Giraldo, M. T., & Tribín-Uribe, A. M. (2021). *El camino hacia la igualdad de género en Colombia: todavía hay mucho por hacer.* Banco de la República.

Jaquette, J. (1997). Women in power: From tokenism to critical mass. *Foreign Policy, 108*, 23–37

Krapf, S., Kreyenfeld, M., & Wolf, K. (2016). Gendered authorship and demographic research: An analysis of 50 years of demography. *Demography, 53*(4), 1169–1184. https://doi.org/10.1007/s13524-016-0482-x

López, C. (2018, December 28). Belisario Betancur, un presidente feminista. *El Tiempo.* https://www.eltiempo.com/cultura/gente/belisario-betancur-fue-un-presidente-feminista-segun-cecilia-lopez-309784

Lundberg, S., & Stearns, J. (2019). Women in economics: Stalled progress. *Journal of Economic Perspectives, 33*(1), 3–22.

Martínez Garnica, A. (2018). *Memorias de las administraciones del Poder Ejecutivo Nacional. 1819-2018. Gabinetes ministeriales, memorias anuales de los ministros, biografías de gobernantes.* Departamento Bogotá, D.C.: Administrativo de la Función Pública

May, A.M., McGarvey, M.G. & Whaples, R. (2014). Are disagreements among male and female economists marginal at best? A survey of AEA members and their views on economics and economic policy. *Contemporary Economic Policy* 32(1): 111–132.

Niederle, M. (2015). Gender. In J. H. Kagel & A. E. Roth (Eds), *The handbook of experimental economics* (vol. 2, pp. 481–716). Princeton University Press.

Ochoa, H. (1977). La mujer en el sistema educativo. In Asociación Colombiana para el Estudio de la Población, *La mujer y el desarrollo en Colombia.* Asociación Colombiana para el Estudio de la Población.

Pontificia Universidad Javeriana. (2011). *Universidad Javeriana femenina: primero años.* Pontificia Universidad Javeriana.

Puyana, Y. (2007). Los estudios de mujer y género en la Universidad Nacional de Colombia. In M. León, T. Valdés, J. Anderson, M. Sagot, G. Herrera, Y. Puyana Villamizar, G. Castellanos, M. Viveros Vigoya, J. Barreto Gama, D. Meertens, J. Serrano & A. Cabezas (Eds), *Género, mujeres y saberes en América Latina.* Universidad Nacional de Colombia.

Sotomayor, P. and Huertas-Hernández, P. (2021). El camino hacia los gabinetes ministeriales: un estudio de los factores que influyen en la designación de mujeres ministras en Ecuador y Colombia, 1978–2018. *Colombia Internacional* 1(105):29–55.

Stainback, K., Kleiner, S., & Skaggs, S. (2016). Woman in power: Undoing or redoing the gendered organization? *Gender and Society*, *30*(1), 109–135.

Uribe, M. T. (n.d.). Llegan las mujeres. Memoria. Universidad de Antioquia: Protagonista y testigo. Documento multimedia: http://200.24.17.24:10039/wps/portal/udea/web/inicio/campanas/memoria

Villaveces-Niño, M. J., & Caballero-Argáez, C. (2020). Technocracy, decision making and economic policy in Colombia. In P. Sanabria-Pulido, N. Rubaii (eds) *Policy Analysis in Colombia*, Bristol University Press, 203–222.

Viloria de la Hoz, J. (2019). Reflexiones sobre la formación de los economistas y la investigación económica en Colombia. *Economía & Región*, *1*(1), 54–63.

Wills, M. E. (2007). *Inclusión sin representación: la irrupción política de las mujeres en Colombia (1970–2000)*. Norma.

Index

Pages in *italics* refer to figures and pages in **bold** refer to tables.